EUROPE
SINCE 1945

an introduction

Peter Lane

Batsford Academic and Educational
London

© Peter Lane 1985
First published 1985

All rights reserved. No part of this publication
may be reproduced, in any form or by any means,
without permission from the Publisher

Typeset by Deltatype, Ellesmere Port
and printed in Great Britain by
Billings Ltd, Worcester

Published by Batsford Academic and Educational
an Imprint of B. T. Batsford Ltd
4 Fitzhardinge Street, London W1H 0AH

British Library Cataloguing in Publication Data

Lane, Peter, *1925*–
    Europe since 1945 : an introduction.
    1. Europe——History——1945–
I. Title
    940.55   D1051

    ISBN 0–7134–4739–7
    ISBN 0–7134–4740– Pbk

EUROPE
SINCE 1945

For my mother, who saw it all, and in memory of my father who only saw some of it.

Contents

Preface

What is Europe?

The vigorously Roman Catholic (and biased) historian, Hilaire Belloc (1870–1953), claimed that 'Europe is the Faith'. He must have welcomed the publication in 1949 of the Preamble to the Statute of the Council of Europe, which drew attention to 'the spiritual and moral values which are the common heritage of their peoples and the true source of individual freedom, political liberty and the rule of law, principles which form the basis for all genuine democracy'. But the Council of Europe was concerned, in 1949, only with non-communist countries. Like the equally ambitiously titled European Economic Community, the Council of Europe seemed to define Europe as those countries to the west of the 'iron curtain'.

It is true that these countries share a common heritage – a mix of Greek philosophy, Roman legal ideas and Judaeo-Christian religious insights which, taken together, have moulded western Europe for two thousand years. But the cultural, social and political traditions of eastern Europe, of those countries behind Churchill's 'iron curtain', have been very different. If one accepts the Council of Europe's terms of reference, these countries, it seems, do not form part of 'Europe'.

General de Gaulle thought otherwise. He spoke of a Europe which extended 'from the Atlantic to the Urals'. This 'Europe' would have included the countries of eastern Europe but would have excluded the vast region of Siberia and the rest of the Soviet Union; it would also have excluded Turkey – although she has joined all the 'European' organisations formed since 1945 and is an important member of the European defence system based on NATO.

As long ago as April 1888, Lord Salisbury claimed for the British, 'We are part of the community of Europe and we must do our duty as such.' But in 1963 de Gaulle used his political power to block Britain's application to join the EEC. In common with many people in Britain itself, de Gaulle claimed that Britain, although geographically a part of Europe, was, even in 1963, still more concerned with the wider world than with Europe as such.

There is, then, wide disagreement as to what 'Europe' consists of; in this book, however, it is taken to include the Soviet Union, Turkey and Britain, as well as the countries of Continental western and eastern Europe on both sides of the iron curtain.

The scope of the book

Since 1945 the individual nation-states of Europe (other than the Soviet Union) have not enjoyed the sort of influence which they exercised up until 1939. Indeed, 'Europe' as a whole has almost ceased to be a force in world affairs; the countries to the west of the iron curtain form part of a US-dominated 'system' while the countries to the east of it are, to a greater or lesser degree, controlled by the Soviet Union. 'Europe' has become the subject of superpower condominium. One of the main themes running through the book is the examination of how, why and when 'Europe' declined in importance as the superpowers gained increasing power.

The various nation-states of western Europe have undergone major economic, political and social development, in what might be termed a transnational fashion. Similarly, the countries of eastern Europe have had their own common experiences. These 'transnational experiences' are examined in what is a second theme running through the book. However, the internal development of some of the nation-states deserves examination, both to help facilitate the study of their comparative development and to point up some of the features of that development.

Considerations of space have led to the exclusion or brief treatment of some topics and countries. There is, for example, no examination of the smaller states of Scandinavia and the Low Countries, save where they have a bearing on wider themes. On the other hand, there is a separate study of the histories of Britain and France (the 'victors' in 1945) and of Germany and Italy (the 'vanquished'); these are the more important nation-states and they have influenced the affairs of their smaller neighbours.

There is a chapter on Portugal, Spain, Greece, Turkey and Cyprus because events in these countries have either had their own significance (e.g. the growth of democracy in the Iberian region) or contributed in a major way to developments in Europe as a whole.

The decline in the importance of the nation-states has been one of the forces making for integration. The move towards political, economic and military unity forms another of the major themes running through the book.

The aim of the book

The book is intended to be, as its title suggests, an introduction to post-war European history, providing a basic knowledge of developments in post-1945 Europe and an understanding of the context in which those developments took place. It does not claim to offer novel perceptions or original scholarship; it is not as interpretative nor as analytical a work as would be needed by a third-year undergraduate. It will, I hope, point students to more detailed and specialised studies which they will understand better for having read this wide ranging but introductory guide.

Acknowledgements

For permission to quote passages of some length, the author and publishers would like to thank the following:

Harvester Press, *A New History of England, 410–1975*, L. C. B. Seaman
Thames and Hudson, *From Sarajevo to Potsdam*, A. J. P. Taylor
Penguin Books, *Europe since Hitler*, W. Laqueur
Oxford University Press, *English History, 1914–45*, A. J. P. Taylor
Duckworth, *A Hundred Years of International Relations*, F. S. Northedge and M. J. Grieve
Macmillan, *Inside the Third Reich*, A. Speer
Collins, *The Way the Wind Blows*, Lord Home; *De Gaulle*, A Crawley
Browne and Nolan, *This is my Story*, Louis Budenz
Hodder and Stoughton, *Nuremberg*, A. Neave; *The Best of Cameron*, James Cameron
Collins, *The Siege of Berlin*, M. Arnold-Forster
Alcove Press, *Out of the Ruins*, W. Laqueur
Longman, *Contemporary England, 1914–64*, W. N. Medlicott
Heinemann, *A Prime Minister Remembers*, F. Williams
Heinemann, *Ernest Bevin: Foreign Secretary*, A. Bullock; *Moscow Mission*, W. Beddel Smith
Hollis and Carter, *East Wind over Prague*, J. Stransky
Elek Books, *The Agony of Czechoslovakia*, K. Weiskopf
Sidgwick and Jackson, *We Will Bury You*, J. Sejna
Weidenfeld and Nicolson, *Memoirs, 1945–54*, K. Adenauer
Brown and Co., *Memoirs*, G. R. Kennan

1
Europe at the end of the Second World War

For many centuries European states dominated world affairs. Since 1945 they have been overshadowed by the Soviet Union and the United States. There may be disagreement as to when, precisely, the two super-powers 'took over' from Europe. By 1914, the USA was the world's leading industrial power; but it was the decision of European statesmen which saved the world from war in September 1938 and which plunged the world into war a year later. For reasons of space, it is possible, here to offer only a summary of the evidence to show: 1. Europe's legacy to the world; 2. the emergence of the USA as a world power; 3. the destructive effects of the Second World War; 4. the European demand for a new social and political order; 5. the wartime growth of internationalism.

During the European Renaissance, men first learnt to be 'self-regarding' rather than 'God-regarding'. In most places today, people have followed this European example. There is no longer a theocratic control of man's affairs; Europeans, with their 'man-centred' ideas have shown the world a different way of looking at things. During the eighteenth century, the philosophers of the 'Enlightenment' inspired the leaders of the American and French Revolutions: from their writings and from the experiences of those Revolutions there emerged the modern concept of Human Rights. The fact that these rights are ignored in many countries should not be allowed to mask the truth that one of Europe's legacies to the modern world has been the notion that men have a variety of civil, political, economic and social rights (Document 1.1, p. 17).

Eighteenth century 'Enlightenment' had been preceded by the scientific revolution of the seventeenth century, forming the background to the Industrial Revolution which allowed Europeans to enjoy a standard of living that was the envy of the rest of the world. The USA was the first non-European country to follow the European pattern; Japan was the first Asiatic country to adopt European methods of production. Today, almost every country is industrialising.

Industrialisation provided European states with the means of conquering and controlling vast areas of the non-European world. The 'scramble for Africa', the control of a large part of Asia and the domination of the economies of countries elsewhere were both cause and effect of the industrialisation. But that very control ensured the further spread of European ideas by colonial teachers and administrators and among colonial peoples eager to rid themselves of European control but not of European ideas and example.

By 1914, the USA had emerged as the world's leading industrial power. But even as late as 1939 the USA followed a policy of 'isolationism'. It was the Second World War which forced the USA, unwillingly, to accept the role for which her industrial power fitted her. In 1946, Secretary of State Byrnes admitted, 'We have learned, whether we like it or not, that we live in one world, from which we cannot isolate ourselves. We have learned that peace and well-being cannot be purchased at the price of peace or the well-being of any other country.' It was Roosevelt who inspired the issuing of the Atlantic Charter in 1941 with its concepts of human rights and freedom; it was the USA which became the arsenal of democracy and one of the two major contributors to the defeat of the Axis Powers. In later chapters we shall see how, why and when the two 'contributors', the USA and the Soviet

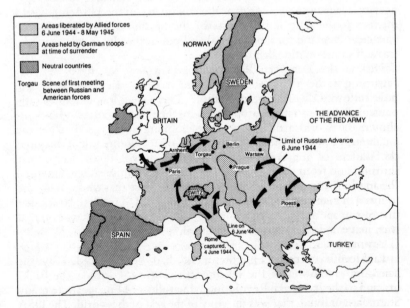

1.1 The liberation of Europe and the defeat of Germany, 1944–5

Union, engaged in the Cold War as each struggled to impose its philosophy on as much of the world as was possible.

Writing in 1947, Winston Churchill remarked, 'What is Europe? A rubbish heap, a charnel house, a breeding ground of pestilence and hate.' Certainly the Second World War had seen death and destruction on a hitherto unprecedented scale (Figure 1.1). Thirty million Europeans died as a result of a war which left much of Europe resembling 'lunar landscapes . . . dotted with heaps of rubble and bomb craters, deserted and stinking ruins that had once been business centres and residential areas.'[1] (Document 1.2, p. 19)

After the First World War, the world had lapsed into a period in which nations waged economic warfare on one another; nations increased tariff barriers, adopted policies aiming at autarky and ignored the fact that one country's imports are another's exports. Instead of solving their nations' problems, the pre-Keynesian politicians exported unemployment from one country to another. There was every reason to suppose that, following the more destructive war of 1939-45, the economic depression would be more severe. (Document 1.3, p. 19)

But during that war, there emerged a new concept of internationalism. Led by the USA and Britain, the nations of the world founded the International Monetary Fund and signed the General Agreement on Tariffs and Trade. Both of these aimed at the expansion of trade in the post-war world. Linked with these international agencies and agreements was the United Nations Organisation and its many specialist agencies. It was hoped that these would lead to the development of trade, the extension of human rights to people who had been previously denied them, and to the creation of 'one world.' And in devastated Europe, too, there was the emergence of a demand for a new social and political order. In France and Italy, leaders of resistance movements produced charters in which they outlined their hopes for a more just and equitable economic and social framework. In Britain, the Churchill-led Coalition government produced a sheaf of White Papers and Reports on Full Employment, a better distribution of industry, an attack on slum housing and the creation of a Welfare State. In his best-selling *Report*, Sir William Beveridge noted that '. . . the purpose of victory is to live in a better world than the old world. . . .' Europeans regarded that *Report* as 'the blue print for the future.' Out of the devastation of war, it seemed, a new world would emerge. (Figures 1.2 and 1.3)

Beveridge and the authors of the resistance charters were, in a sense, inward looking. Keynes and the founders of the IMF were, on the other hand, internationalists. Both were aiming at the creation of a new order. So, too, were others. 'By 1945, the Soviet Union and the United States had been transformed by war into developed, independent powers capable of over-shadowing all others. And in the continents of Asia and Africa, the emergence of Japan, and the dissemination far and

1.2 'The Last Enemy': the artist, Vicky, expresses popular hope for the post-war world

"MAKE WAY!"

1.3 The artist Low's view of the widespread determination to create a new world after 1945

wide of those major European exports, Anglo-Saxon ideas of liberty and Marxist critiques of capitalism and imperialism, were not less pregnant with change. England and western Europe had invented modern power-politics and modern concepts of liberty and social justice; but now, from all parts of the world their inventions were about to be turned against them. The brief period during which the talented, thrusting peoples of the small peninsula of the Eurasian land-mass and its British off-shore island had dominated the rest of the world was coming to an end.'[2]

Documentary evidence

Document 1.1

Since 1945 there have been many international agreements on the issue of Human Rights. Some have originated in the United Nations Organisation: the first article of the Charter of the UN lays down that 'The Purposes of the United Nations are: To achieve international agreement . . . in promoting and encouraging respect for human rights and for fundamental freedoms for all. . . .' In 1948 the General Assembly of the UN approved the Universal

Declaration on Human Rights. The following extract from that Declaration shows how the concept of these Rights has been deepened and widened to include a number of socio-economic rights.

There is little evidence that this, and similar international agreements, have made much difference to the lives of the majority of the world's population. However, such earlier agreements may have served as a basis for the more recent growth of concern for Human Rights as expressed by the US government under President Carter and by the majority of countries which signed the Helsinki Agreement in 1975 (Document 13.1, p. 285). The different interpretations of 'Human Rights' by the US and western powers on the one hand and by the Soviet bloc on the other have led to increased tensions between the two sides (Documents 13.3, p. 286 and 13.4, p. 287).

The Universal Declaration of Human Rights

'Article 23

1. Everyone has the right to work, to free choice of employment, to just and favourable conditions of work and to protection against unemployment.

2. Everyone, without any discrimination, has the right to equal pay for equal work.

3. Everyone who works has the right to just and favourable remuneration ensuring for himself and his family an existence worthy of human dignity, and supplemented, if necessary, by other means of social protection.

4. Everyone has the right to form and to join trade unions for the protection of his interests.

Article 24

1. Everyone has the right to rest and leisure, including reasonable limitation of working hours and periodic holidays with pay.

Article 25

1. Everyone has the right to a standard of living adequate for the health and wellbeing of himself and his family, including food, clothing, housing and medical care and necessary social services, and the right to security in the event of unemployment, sickness, disability, widowhood, old age or other lack of livelihood in circumstances beyond his control. . . .

Article 26

1. Everyone has the right to education. Education shall be free, at least in the elementary and fundamental stages. Elementary education shall be compulsory. . . . Higher education shall be equally accessible to all on the basis of merit.

2. Education shall be directed to the full development of the human personality and to the strengthening of respect for human rights and fundamental freedoms. It shall promote understanding, tolerance and friendship among all nations, racial or religious groups, and shall further activities of the United Nations for the maintenance of peace.

3. Parents have a prior right to choose the kind of education that shall be given to their children.'

(Approved by the General Assembly of the UNO, 1948)

Document 1.2

Konrad Adenauer (1876–1976) had been Chief Burgomaster of Cologne (1917–33) and President of the Prussian State Council (1920–33) until he was dismissed from both offices by the Nazis, who imprisoned him in 1934 and again in 1944. He was reinstated as Burgomaster of Cologne in 1945 until sacked by the British military administration for alleged inefficiency. He played a major role in West Germany's recovery (see pp. 27–30, 64–8, 71–6 and 189ff).

Germany in defeat, 1945

'I was deeply shaken by the sight of Cologne. The city's population before the war had been roughly 760,000. Now there were about 32,000 inhabitants in the districts on the left bank of the Rhine. The right bank was still occupied by German troops. The fiercest fighting had ceased, but shots were still being exchanged. . . . The task confronting me in a war-ravaged Cologne was a huge and extraordinarily difficult one. The extent of the damage suffered by the city in air raids and from the other effects of war was enormous. More than half of the houses and public buildings were totally destroyed, nearly all the others had suffered partial damage. Only 300 houses had escaped unscathed.

The damage done to the city by the destruction of streets, tram rails, sewers, water pipes, gas pipes, electrical installations and other public utilities, was no less widespread. It is hard to realise the threat this constituted to the health of the people. There was no gas, no water, no electric current, and no means of transport. The bridges across the Rhine had been destroyed. There were mountains of rubble in the streets. . . . Cologne was a ghost city. People were living as best they could in the cellars of bombed houses. They did their cooking on primitive brick fireplaces, using lignite briquettes. They fetched water in pails and tin bowls from the few pumps that had remained intact. . . .

Every day thousands of citizens streamed back into Cologne, on foot or by whatever transport was later available in goods trains. I can still see those open freight cars, jammed with people who wanted to get home again, no matter what hardships were involved. Pale, tired, haggard, they carried the few belongings they still had, and usually found nothing but their destroyed homes. . . .'

(Konrad Adenauer, *Memoirs 1945–53*, pp. 20–22)

Document 1.3

In 1945 many people assumed that Churchill, the war-leader, would take the Conservative Party to victory in the General Election. The Labour Party's victory in July 1945 was, in part, an electoral reaction to the depression of the 1930s (for which the Conservatives were, unfairly, held to blame) and, in part, a reflection of the European-wide shift to the left (see pp. 136ff). The government led by Clement Attlee had to grapple with the economic effects of the war (pp. 138–9 and 164ff) while also introducing major social reforms, many of which had their origins in the Beveridge Report of 1942 (pp. 15 and 137).

Export or die

'A lot of people envisaged the Labour government's victory as going to build a new world at long term. A lot of other people envisaged it as an opportunity to get back on the results of a great deal of Tory rule. But the most pressing item on the agenda was to reconstruct the war industry of this country; to redeploy the labour force to enable us to earn our keep in the quite ludicrous situation which arose from the sudden cut-off of American aid. We had sold most of our foreign investment. We had no export products nor export markets to replace these overseas earnings, and suddenly, almost overnight, by Congressional decision, all this aid, which had been enabling us to live while we were fighting for the allied cause and while we were taking a disproportionate share of the war burden, was cut off. We were in a most extraordinary position then, but theoretically we were one of the most powerful countries on earth.

As time went on it became clear that whatever grandiose ideas people might have, it was the bread and butter jobs of getting those demobbed people into industry earning our keep in exports, export or die, all this productivity campaign, this bread and butter stuff, that was more, much more, important. In the early part of the Attlee administration, there were problems of just taking to bits various war time controls, of finding out what controls, what rationing, for instance, would have to continue, so as to enable us to make a transition to peace time. It was a dominant issue just to live day by day in order to come out of it in a position where Britain could have the rewards which everyone felt that, having won the war, they were entitled to.'

(Max Nicholson in Alan Thompson, *The Day Before Yesterday*, Granada, 1971)

FURTHER READING

ADENAUER, K., *Memoirs, 1945–54*, Weidenfeld and Nicolson, 1966–8

ARNOLD-FORSTER, M., *The Siege of Berlin*, Collins, 1979

BALOGH, T., *The Dollar Crisis*, Blackwell, Oxford, 1949

BULLOCK, A., *Ernest Bevin: Foreign Secretary*, Heinemann, 1983

LAQUEUR, W. AND RUBIN, B., *The Human Rights Reader*, New American Library, 1979

LUARD, E., ed. *The International Protection of Human Rights*, Thames and Hudson, 1967

NICHOLAS, H. G., *The United Nations as a Political Institution*, OUP, 1967

POSTAN, M. M., *An Economic History of Western Europe, 1945–64*, Methuen, 1967

PRICE, H. B., *The Marshall Plan and its Meaning*, OUP, 1955

ROBERTSON, A. H., *Human Rights in Europe*, 2nd ed., Manchester UP, 1977

2

The post-war settlement, 1945–55

Wartime agreements

'Perhaps you think that because we are allies of the English we have forgotten who they are and who Churchill is. They find nothing sweeter than to trick their allies. And Churchill? Churchill is the kind who, if you don't watch him, will slip a kopek out of your pocket. And Roosevelt? Roosevelt is not like that. He dips his hand in only for bigger coins.'
  Stalin talking to Djilas, the Yugoslav Communist. See also pp. 48, 101–2, 132.

In December 1941, the British Foreign Secretary, Anthony Eden, went to Moscow to negotiate the terms of the Anglo-Soviet Treaty, which was signed in May 1942 (Document 2.2, p. 37). Churchill and Eden wanted that Treaty to incorporate Russia's territorial claims in eastern Europe. They thought that it would be better to have such claims negotiated while Russia was still dependent on western aid than to leave the negotiations until the end of the war, by which time Russia might well be in a stronger negotiating position. Roosevelt would not allow such recognition of territorial claims. In the Atlantic Charter (p. 14), endorsed by Stalin in January 1942, the three leaders had agreed that there would not be any territorial adjustments without the 'freely expressed wishes of the peoples concerned'. So Article 5 of the Anglo-Soviet Treaty read: 'The High Contracting Parties agree to act according to the principles of not seeking territorial aggrandisement for themselves, and of non-interference in the internal affairs of other States.'

At the Casablanca Conference (January 1943), Roosevelt announced the terms for the ending of the war: 'Unconditional surrender'. Churchill was later to claim that the announcement of this statement at a press conference had taken him by surprise. In fact, Roosevelt had warned Churchill of what he was going to say; the matter had been discussed in the British War Cabinet which had rejected Churchill's plea that Italy should be excluded from this demand.[1] Roosevelt wanted to assure Stalin that the western allies would not make a compromise peace with Germany. He and his advisers also wished to ensure that no post-war German government would be able to haggle over peace terms.

By August 1944 it was clear that the Allies would win the war; Russian forces had driven the Germans from Russian soil and were driving their way westwards (Fig. 1.1, p. 14); in the west, the Allied forces had finally taken Monte Cassino, so that their drive to take Italy would be the speedier, while in France the invading forces were well established under the protective covering of the Allied air command.

While Stalin and Churchill were making plans for the future of post-war Europe, Roosevelt and his advisers were emphasising that it was US policy to get out of Europe as quickly as possible as soon as the war ended. It may have been this knowledge of declared US policy which caused Churchill to try to arrange a bi-lateral agreement with Stalin. Churchill suggested, in May 1944, that Rumania should form part of Russia's 'sphere of influence' if, on his part, Stalin would agree that Greece would fall under British control. Roosevelt refused to be party to such an 'imperialist' agreement. In October 1944, Churchill suggested to Stalin that they should make their own agreement, with Russia having 90 per cent of the control of Rumania, Britain having 90 per cent of control of Greece, while they shared control in Yugoslavia on a 50–50 basis. Churchill extended his proposal so that Bulgaria would be 'shared' between Russia and Britain on a 75–25 basis, while in Hungary they would share control on a 50–50 basis. Churchill, perhaps fearful of the future historian's examination of such an agreement, said, 'Might it not be thought rather cynical if it seemed we had disposed of these issues, so fateful to millions of people, in such an offhand manner? Let us burn the paper.' Stalin, who had gained the influence he needed and who had little fear of future historians, replied: 'No, you keep it.'[2]

This bi-lateral disposition of the fate of millions of people in four or five countries was hardly in accord with the terms of the Atlantic Charter or of the Anglo-Soviet Treaty of 1942. Russian and Allied behaviour at the Yalta Conference (February 1945) merely confirmed the nature of the world of *realpolitik* in which Stalin and, to a lesser extent, Churchill moved and had their being. It has sometimes been claimed that the meeting of the three Allied leaders at the Crimean resort in February 1945 marked 'the high tide of allied co-operation and understanding'. In fact, Stalin distrusted both Churchill and Roosevelt, while Churchill, as we have seen, feared a lack of US support in post-war Europe and was constantly being thwarted by Roosevelt who distrusted his 'imperialist adventurism'. There was more appearance than substance to the often-lauded co-operation.

At Yalta, the Allied leaders re-affirmed the principles of the Atlantic Charter – Churchill and Stalin forgetting, obviously, the agreements reached in October 1944. Russia promised to join the war against Japan 'within a month of the defeat of Germany'. In return, Russia was to receive half of the island of Sakhalin. Roosevelt promised that he would be responsible for persuading the Chinese leader, Chiang Kai-shek, to allow this handover of what was traditionally seen as Chinese territory. Roosevelt had made his choice; Stalin and Russia were more important than Chiang and China.

But the discussions at Yalta had more substantial issues to decide. The Allied leaders agreed on the treatment of Germany (Fig. 2.1), the frontiers of post-war Poland (Fig. 2.1) and the Russian take-over of the Baltic States of Estonia, Latvia and Lithuania. They also issued a 'Declaration on Liberated Europe.' This promised:

1. The right of peoples to choose the form of government under which they wished to live.

2. The restoration of sovereign rights and self-government to the re-conquered peoples.

3. Free elections as soon as possible.

There was immediate criticism of the agreement (Document 2.2, p. 37). The western leaders seemed to have ignored the fact that eastern Europe would be liberated by the Red Army, so that the Russian government would have the decisive say in what was to happen in those countries (Fig. 2.1). If the western leaders were, in fact, conscious of this reality, then they appear to have been ignorant of the ideological divisions between Russia and the democratic west; they appeared to have no knowledge of Soviet concepts of 'sovereign rights', 'self-government', democracy, the will of the people, human rights and the claims of the 'democratic centralists' (p. 105) who insist on enforcing 'the true faith' on everyone within their orbit.[3]

Stalin appeared to be satisfied with the Yalta agreement. He could afford to look forward to the final defeat of Germany. Hitler's suicide on 30 April 1945 effectively brought the German resistance to an end. Various German leaders disagreed as to the best way to arrange a surrender; Speer, Himmler, Doenitz and Goering all vied, but vainly, to see if they could make some deal with the western Allies.[4] On May 4, there was an armistice in north west Germany; on May 7, there was unconditional surrender in all theatres of war. On May 8, Keitel and three representatives of the Wehrmacht solemnly sealed that capitulation at the Soviet Headquarters at Karlshorst, near Berlin.

The Allied leaders met again at Potsdam in July and August 1945. When they assembled, Harry Truman had replaced Roosevelt, who had died in April 1945. Before the Conference ended, Attlee had replaced Churchill as leader of the British delegation, following Labour's victory at the General Election, the results of which were declared on July 26. During their discussions, the various leaders reached agreement on the new boundary between Germany and Poland and the holding of a Foreign Ministers' Conference to work out a peace treaty with Germany. They also agreed on the way in which defeated Germany would be governed until that treaty had been signed.

2.1 The Russian control of Eastern Europe, 1944–7 when Yugoslavia was still behind the 'Iron Curtain', Stalin tried to gain control of the Dardanelles and Greece, and the USA was being drawn into European affairs, almost against its will.

The Polish question

'I know of no government which stands to its obligations even in its own despite more solidly than the Russian Soviet government. I decline absolutely to embark here on a discussion of Russia's good faith.'
Churchill in the House of Commons during a debate on the Yalta Agreement,
27 February 1945.

At Yalta the Allied leaders had reached what was described as a 'temporary arrangement' concerning the frontiers of post-war Poland. The Russian claim to a large portion of eastern Poland was agreed; Russia was to shift her frontier westwards to, roughly, the boundary which had been proposed by Lloyd George in July 1920 in an attempt to

settle Russo-Polish relations. The following negotiations were handled
by the British Foreign Secretary, Lord Curzon, who thus gave his name
to the line of demarcation proposed as the Russo-Polish frontier. The
line, from Grodno through Brest-Litovsk and Przemysl to the
Carpathians, would have excluded from Poland lands predominantly
inhabited by Ukrainians, Lithuanians and Russians. The Poles
rejected the proposal, continued their war with the Bolshevik government and subsequently secured twice as much territory as Lloyd
George had suggested. In September 1939 the Curzon Line (with some
minor adjustments) became the boundary between the German and
Russian regions of occupied Poland. In 1945 it was accepted as a
definitive frontier by the Polish and Soviet governments. The area
taken from Poland was about half of its pre-war territory, containing
about one-third of its pre-war population. In the debate in the
Commons on 27 February 1945 Churchill argued that 'the Russian
claim is just and right . . .' although he went on to suggest that the
Yalta Agreement was merely to be a guide and not a rule.[5] Some of his
critics wondered whether, in fact, Russia would ever disgorge what she
now claimed and, more pertinently, whether Russia would honour the
other terms of the Agreement (Documents 2.1, p. 36 and 2.2, p. 37).

In compensation for the losses in the east, Poland was to gain former
German territory in the west, where the frontier would be the Oder-
Neisse Rivers. This deprived Germany of about one-fifth of her pre-
war territory; Poland gained rich agricultural land as well as the
resources of the industrialised regions of Silesia. Nine million Germans
were forcibly expelled, or fled from the danger they might face as four
and a half million Poles moved westwards to occupy the 'new Poland'
(Document 2.3, p. 38). It is, perhaps, understandable that after six years
of German occupation of Poland, the 'invading' Poles sought their
revenge on the Silesian Germans. 'As soon as the Poles took over they
began to terrorise the population. The Polish militia behaved in an
atrocious manner. The sight of the Polish militia approaching one's
house was enough to set one trembling with fear. Indeed, they were
feared more than the Russians.'[6]

The acceptance of these changes by the western leaders – in February
1945 – persuaded Stalin that they would accept other Russian violations
of the principles of the Atlantic Charter (p. 14) and of the Anglo-Soviet
Treaty of 1942 (p. 21). If the west was prepared to accept this treatment
of 'free and sovereign peoples', if they were prepared to ignore these
denials of 'human rights', then they would hardly lift a finger should
Stalin decide to impose his will on eastern Europe after the war
(Chapter 3 and Fig. 2.1).

Having gained approval for the territorial changes that he wanted,
Stalin then turned to the question of the government of post-war
Poland. Most of Poland's pre-war leaders had gone into exile to form a
Free Polish government-in-exile in London. Thousands of their

supporters had followed them, to fight for the Allies. Thousands of Poles, who had stayed behind, joined a resistance movement called the Home Army. After Hitler had attacked Russia in 1941, Stalin sent aid to this resistance movement. At the same time, he sent in Moscow-trained Poles to organise a separate resistance movement. The leader of this Stalinist group was a Pole named Bierut, who had been appointed head of the Polish section of the NKVD in 1936. Bierut was helped by another Pole, Gomulka, to build up the People's Workers' Party, controlled by Polish communists with their loyalties to Moscow.

In April 1943, the Germans found a mass grave in the Katyn Forest which contained the bodies of some 4,000 Polish army officers, captured when the Russians invaded eastern Poland in 1939. These representatives of the landowning class, and thousands of other leading Poles who were also 'missing', had been murdered by the Russians anxious to weaken the social and political fabric of Poland. Stalin, not surprisingly, denied the charge, and broke off relations with the London-based government-in-exile. Instead, he formally recognised the National Council of the Homeland set up by Bierut in January 1944. When the Russians crossed the pre-war Polish frontier and began to push towards Warsaw, Bierut set up the National Committee of Liberation to govern Poland after the war.

As the Russians approached Warsaw, the Home Army rose up against the German occupation forces. They assumed that, with aid which could be dropped by Russian airplanes, they would help the Russian advances. Stalin refused to send in aid; indeed, he ordered a halt to the Russian advance; his forces, already on the outskirts of Warsaw, watched the destruction of the Home Army – and the removal of another group which might have resisted a Russian take-over.

On 31 December 1944, Bierut's National Council announced that its chairman would be the President of the new Poland while the National Committee would form the new government. These decisions, made before the Yalta Conference, were in direct contravention of the principles of the Atlantic Charter and the yet-to-be signed Declaration on Liberated Europe (p. 23). In March 1945, to ensure the complete success of his anti-Polish moves, Stalin, via Marshal Zhukov, invited 16 surviving leaders of the Home Army to discuss how they might help in the war against Germany. On their arrival, they were arrested, imprisoned in the Lubianka prison in Moscow, brought to a 'show trial' and sentenced to lengthy prison sentences for alleged sabotage.

In July 1945, the Russian-controlled government was formally installed in power. By the time the government-in-exile returned from London, the communists had taken control. When the Allied leaders met at their Potsdam Conference, the western leaders were fully aware of the way in which, in Poland, Stalin had disregarded promises and treaties. Communists throughout the world were not surprised by the cynical behaviour of 'their' leader. The Comintern, through which

Stalin had once controlled the policies of Communist parties every-where, had been abolished in 1943 as a token gesture towards western susceptibilities. But through the well-established network created by the Comintern, Communists everywhere were constantly reminded of the party line. In April 1945, Jacques Duclos, the leader of the French Communist Party, distributed a letter to all Communist Parties. This formed the basis of an article in the *World Telegraph* and was the subject of wide discussion in, among others, American Communist party groups. It showed that there would always be 'a state of war' until such time as 'the Soviet régime governs the earth . . .' To that end, 'the Soviet Union will have to undermine and destroy the chief example of capitalism, American imperialism, and do a thorough job of it.' The editor of the American *Daily Worker* asked the Secretary of the US Communist Party, 'Does that mean we are going back to the old so-called "sectarian" days?' 'There will be truces, no doubt, in this war . . . but the objective must be made clear, that this American imperialism must be destroyed.'[7] This discussion took place shortly after the three Allied leaders had met at Yalta and after Churchill had confirmed his belief in Russia's 'good faith', a pre-requisite for the peaceful settlement of post-war Europe.

The German 'settlement'

'To the victors belong the spoils of the enemy.'
                                                    The Life of Jackson (1860)
'In war, resolution; in defeat, defiance; in victory, magnanimity; in peace, goodwill.'
Used by Churchill as the 'Moral of the Work' in each volume of *The Second World War*.

The Allied leaders, meeting at Yalta, had agreed on the treatment that was to be meted out to Germany after her 'unconditional surrender'. The agreement covered the following subjects:

1. *The punishment of war criminals.* This had been the subject of much inter-Allied discussion. A plan made by the US Secretary of the Treasury, Henry Morgenthau Jr., proposed that major war criminals should be identified and shot as the Allies advanced into Germany. Churchill, Eden, Lord Simon, the Lord Chancellor and some members of the Foreign Office, believed that the Allies should simply execute some fifty to a hundred Nazi leaders. The Cabinet rejected their scheme – which might well, if implemented, have made 'martyrs' out of the executed. Stalin, for his part, rejected the Morgenthau plan, fearing that the Allied leaders would be accused of having executed the leaders out of mere revenge.[8] Instead, it was decided to organise a series of war trials (p. 33).

2. *The need to ensure that Germany did not 'rise' again.* In view of the German invasions in 1914 and 1941, the losses suffered and the damage

sustained by Russia during the two World Wars, it is not surprising that
Russia should have demanded 'never again'. De Gaulle, too, on behalf
of France, demanded that Germany should be so treated as to ensure
that she should never again provide a threat to French security. France,
after all, had suffered in 1870, 1914 and 1940. De Gaulle wanted the
dismemberment of Germany; there must be no fourth Reich. Instead
there should be a loose federation of old pre-Bismarckian German
states, an autonomous republic west of the Rhine and international
control of the Ruhr.[9]

This French demand was in line with a scheme proposed by Henry
Morgenthau Jr. He proposed the internationalisation of the Ruhr and
the Kiel Canal area, the setting up of a North German state, including
much of old Prussia, Saxony and Thuringia, and the creation of a South
German state comprising Bavaria, Wurtemberg, Baden and some
smaller areas. He proposed that the Ruhr 'should not only be stripped of
all presently existing industries but so weakened and controlled that it
can not in the foreseeable future become an industrial area.' Although
this scheme for the 'pastoralisation' of Germany was approved by
Roosevelt and Churchill at the Quebec Conference in September 1944,
it never became official policy.[10] Allied treatment of Germany took a
different course (see below).

3. *The demilitarisation of Germany.*

4. *The need to seek out and somehow deal with members of the Nazi Party.*
This task proved more difficult than had been supposed when the Allied
leaders and their advisers first ventured into the field of 'de-
nazification'. There had been, after all, some eight million or so
members of the Party. Were the conquering Allies intended to root out
all these? There were many professional men (such as judges) whose
career had depended on joining the Party as, in modern Britain, many
people are forced by closed-shop agreements to join trade unions. Were
all these to be debarred?

The difficulty was, perhaps, best revealed by the initial work on the
proceedings which led to the opening of the Nuremberg trials (p. 33). It
was determined that each defendant would have the right to be
defended by a German lawyer. However, it quickly became clear that
almost all German lawyers had been members of the Nazi Party. So,
ironically, while de-nazification was going on at one level and while
troops were forbidden 'fraternisation' with the conquered, the Allied
lawyers, judges and other officials were being forced to employ ex-
Nazi lawyers. The Allies faced the same problems when efforts were
made to create local governments throughout conquered Germany.
The majority of councillors and council officials had been members of
the Party; it would have been impossible to help Germany rise from the
rubble without their co-operation.

Why had people joined the Nazi Party? A young man who had not
joined explained the problem that had faced his contemporaries:

'National Socialism offered all that a young man would desire – activity, responsibility for his fellows, and work with equally enthusiastic comrades for a greater and stronger fatherland. It held out official recognition, and careers that had been unthinkable before; while on the other side there were only difficulties and dangers, an empty future and heartrending doubts.'[11] In the 1920s, Keynes and others had convinced·many in Britain that Germany had been harshly treated at Versailles. Hitler promised the Germans that he would tear up that harsh Treaty. It is not surprising that he won massive support, nor that millions should have supported the politician who promised to cure Germany's economic problems, worsened by the effects of the worldwide depression in 1931–2. Many Catholics saw Hitler as a bulwark against atheistic Communism; many industrialists financed the Party in the hope that Hitler would regenerate Germany industry.

So, while some leading Party members were tried at Nuremberg and other lesser mortals tried elsewhere, and while de-nazification and trials have gone on since 1945, it was not possible to punish, in any way, the majority of those who had been willing to join and fight for the Nazi Party.[12]

5. *German reparations*[13]. At Yalta, it was agreed that those countries 'which have borne the main burden of the war, have suffered the heaviest losses' were entitled to compensation from post-war Germany. Reparations were to be taken from Germany's 'national wealth' – equipment, machine-tools, ships, railway stock – and from 'annual deliveries of goods from current production' as well as from 'the use of German labour'.

At Potsdam, it was agreed that Russia and Poland were entitled to take their reparations from the Soviet zone of Germany and from German investments abroad. The western Allies and other nations in the west would take their compensation from the western zone of Germany and from German foreign investments. Additionally, the Conference agreed that the Russians had the right, in exchange for raw materials and food, to the remaining steel, chemicals and machine making plant in the western zones.

6. *The future government of Germany*. At Potsdam the Allies had declared that 'it is not the intention of the Allies to destroy or enslave the German people. The Allies want to give the German people the chance to prepare itself to rebuild its life on a democratic and peaceful basis.' It had already been agreed, at Yalta, that Germany would be divided into zones of occupation; Stalin insisted that, if the western Allies wanted France to have such a zone of occupation, then it had to be carved out of the regions already designated for occupation by Britain and the USA. It had also been agreed that Berlin should be divided into allied zones of occupation – although it was 176 km deep inside the Russian zone of occupied Germany.

The four occupying Powers agreed to pursue common policies,

supervised by the Allied Control Commission, made up of the four Commanders-in-Chief. There was to be no central German government, but democratic institutions were to be restored and developed at local level. Common economic policies would ensure 'the equitable distribution of essential commodities . . . to produce a balanced economy throughout Germany and reduce the need for imports. . . .'

This, it was agreed, was to be a 'temporary arrangement', until the Allies had had time to set up a central democratic German government with which they would make a peace treaty. Such optimism was the result of a refusal to recognise the deep divisions between East and West which we will examine in Chapters 3 and 4. These divisions were made the more manifest at the Foreign Ministers' Conference which met in Paris in 1946 to settle peace treaties with Germany's defeated satellites.

The German problem was set aside as being too difficult for mere Foreign Ministers to cope with; but even on the minor matters of the subordinate Treaties (below) there proved to be plenty for the delegates to argue about. Molotov and Vishinsky, the Soviet delegates, contested every issue, dismissing Anglo-American arguments as perversions of the truth. The western Allies reacted by becoming equally unyielding. It is ironic that Britain's representative at this Conference was the former trade union leader, Ernie Bevin, now Foreign Minister in the Labour government. He, like other Labour leaders, had argued, during the election campaign of 1945, that Labour would be the better able to deal with Russia than the Conservatives, since 'Left will talk with Left'. Bevin's bitterness at Russian intransigence led him to become the architect of the anti-Soviet alliances in western Europe.

In November–December 1947 the Foreign Ministers met in London. Here they quarrelled over the level of reparations due to the Russians, who refused to accept the western request for the export of food from the eastern (and agricultural) zone of Germany to the hungry western zones. The western Allies insisted that there could be no constitutional progress made until there had been an economic agreement. They also wanted to ensure that the future government of Germany would be a federal one. Since neither side wanted to risk the loss of its own German area to the other side, the notion of a united Germany had to be abandoned; inevitably there was a move towards the consolidation into separate east and west German states (Chapter 4). By the end of 1947 (as we shall see in Chapters 3 and 4) the Russians had consolidated their hold of eastern Europe as a whole. The Cold War had already begun.

Treaties with other countries

The failure to find the basis for the formation of a German government, with which a treaty might be negotiated, helped ensure that the conflict between East and West, which was to be at the centre of European history for the next thirty years, would most involve the 'German question'.

The USA, Britain, Russia, China and France drew up the terms of the treaties with other defeated countries, which were submitted in the summer of 1946 to a conference of twenty-one other nations which had fought against Germany and her allies. The treaties were signed on the 1 February 1947.

1. *Italy* The Russian government insisted that the treaty had to be imposed on Italy (because of the 'unconditional surrender' statement) rather than negotiated with the new Italian government. Italy lost her former African colonies, the Greek-inhabited Dodecanese islands, gained from Turkey in 1912 and now ceded to Greece, and the province of Venezia-Giulia (gained by Yugoslavia). Trieste and its hinterland was declared a Free Territory, to be administered by the UN. In 1954 Russia and Yugoslavia agreed that the city of Trieste should return to Italian rule – the hinterland having already been seized by the Yugoslavs. Italy's armed forces were reduced to 300,000 men and most of its ships divided among the Allied powers. Like Germany, Italy had to pay reparations; in her case, these went to Russia, Greece, Yugoslavia, Czechoslovakia, Albania and Ethiopia.

2. *Hungary, Bulgaria and Rumania* In a series of difficult negotiations, the western allies got Russia to accept the inclusion of guarantees of civil rights in the treaties with these countries. The Russians forced the Allies to agree to the stationing of Russian troops in Rumania and Hungary, one step along Russia's road to imposing her will on eastern Europe (Fig. 2.1).

3. *Finland* The Treaty with Finland confirmed Russian annexation of the Karelian Peninsula and of the ice-free port of Petsamo, gained as a result of the Russo-Finnish war which had started in November 1939.

4. *Austria*, part of that Greater Germany created by Hitler's invasion of March 1938, was treated differently from other conquered territories – but differently also from Germany. The country was divided into four zones of occupation, but was allowed to form a national government in 1945 after free elections had led to an anti-Communist majority in Parliament. The Allies retained occupying forces, as Stalin tried to link the future of Austria with that of Germany. In 1955 the USA, Russia, Britain and France signed the Austrian State Treaty which provided for the withdrawal of occupying forces and the restoration of Austria's independence within the boundaries of 1937. The Treaty reaffirmed the ban, first imposed after the First World War, on any *Anschluss* linking Germany and Austria. It also forbade the restoration of the Habsburg monarchy and required the Austrian Parliament to pass a law pledging Austria to permanent neutrality. Some western optimists claimed this marked a major shift in Russian policy. In fact, Russia welcomed the appearance of neutralist Austria which provided a long wedge between the northern and southern members of NATO. To try to further counteract the US-dominated western alliance, Russia signed the

Warsaw Pact with her eastern European satellites on the day after the signing of the Austrian State Treaty. It is argued that the Soviet government intended to use this Pact as a bargaining counter in negotiations with the USA. If so, it has failed.

A shift in US policy towards Europe

'Only an inexcusable tragedy of errors could cause serious conflict between us . . .' 'But', he continued, 'We will not and we cannot stand aloof if force or the threat of force is used contrary to the purposes and principles of the UN Charter. . . . If we are to be a great power we must act as a great power, not only in order to ensure our own security but in order to preserve the peace of the world.'
Secretary of State Byrnes, February 1946, quoted in *Dept. of State Bulletin XIV*, 10 March 1946

Talking with Bidault in Paris at the beginning of May, Byrnes acknowledged that he had been criticised for yielding too much to the Russians and added: 'This period had passed and American opinion was no longer disposed to make concessions on important questions.'
Bullock, *Ernest Bevin: Foreign Secretary*, p. 239

Europe has grown accustomed to the American presence in Europe and has had cause to be grateful for US generosity towards Europe. It was however far from clear, in the months immediately following the end of the war, that the US would want to involve herself in Europe's affairs.

Churchill had become aware, during the war, of the American insistence that US troops would 'come home' once the fighting was over. This helps to explain his support for General de Gaulle once he was in power in liberated France. Churchill felt that Britain would need French aid to police Europe, guard against a German resurgence and confront Russia in post-war Europe.[14]

Attitudes did not change with the death of Roosevelt in April 1945. Truman inherited Roosevelt's notion of Britain as an expansive, imperialist power, even when Attlee replaced Churchill as Prime Minister. Indeed, the accession to power of a socialist government raised the hackles of American conservatives, thus ensuring even greater US suspicion[15]

In March 1946, Churchill made his famous 'Iron Curtain' speech in Fulton, Missouri. This speech angered President Truman, who saw it as the utterance of a warmonger, out of office and unaware of Truman's ability to handle the leader whom he affectionately referred to as 'Uncle Joe'. Truman's advisers, such as Marshall, Bedell Smith and Cordell Hull, favoured a moderate policy towards Russia; the few such as Forrestal, who called for a tougher line, were isolated.

The change in policy came slowly and over many months. Bedell Smith spoke for the disillusioned when he said, early in 1947, 'One cannot reach agreement with the Russians without Germany'. Marshall, another convert to reality, declared that the Russians were 'coldly determined to exploit the present state of Europe to propagate communism.' The changed opinions of Truman's advisers were reflected in his own change of policy, as illustrated by the Truman Doctrine which we will examine in Chapter 4.

The Nuremberg trials, 1945–6

The Fuhrer once more expressed his determination to clean up the Jews in Europe pitilessly. There must be no more squeamish sentimentalism about it. Their destruction will go hand in hand with the destruction of our enemies.

The Goebbels Diaries, 1942

At Potsdam, the Allied leaders confirmed that the surviving leaders of the Third Reich would be put on trial. It was necessary, said the Potsdam communiqué, to make clear to the Germans 'the terrible crimes committed under the leadership of those whom, in the hour of their success, they openly approved and obeyed.'

By then the German surrender had taken place; Allied forces had entered the death camps, freed the skeleton-like survivors and discovered both the means by which so many millions had been murdered and the mass graves of some of these victims. The crimes committed by the Nazis were unprecedented – and the criminals had to be punished in the name of common humanity.

If it was necessary to show the German people the nature of the regime which they had supported, it was also necessary to show younger Germans and future generations how far an uncontrolled system might go. The trials played their part in an educative process which has gone on into the 1980s as books, films, memoirs, other and later trials, have kept the memory of the savagery of the Third Reich alive.

The trials also served to educate a wider world. The evidence used to condemn the criminals was provided by the system, by the criminals themselves. It was they who had compiled the documents and kept the careful records. Without this self-supplied evidence the world might never have known the full truth of the Jewish extermination plan and the slave labour programme of Albert Speer.[16]

The Tribunal which conducted the trials was the by-product of a UN commission set up in 1943. The Tribunal and the trial gave the new UNO a credibility and helped to prove the determination of the new organisation to act vigorously in pursuit of peace and international justice.

The trials opened on 20 November 1945 and lasted until 1 October 1946. It was significant that the trial was held in Nuremberg, the nursery of that Nazism which had been born at Munich. Here, each September from 1933 to 1938, Nazi Party rallies had been held. These were carefully staged propaganda exercises: competitive games, torch-light processions and oratorical displays, and a major policy speech each year from Hitler. It was at one of these rallies (September 1935) that Hitler announced legislation reducing all Jews in Germany to second class citizens. These 'Nuremberg Laws' defined Jews, closed professions to Jews and denied them the right of marriage with non-Jews. Hitler, Hess, Gurtner (Minister of Justice) and Frick (Minister of the Interior) signed them. From this it was a short step to the pogrom of 1938 and to the 'Final Solution' and the programme of extermination.[17]

Airey Neave, one of the British War Crimes Executive team, served the Allied indictment on the 21 top Nazis awaiting trial. He wrote:

> At the entrance to the Palace of Justice, a tram stopped beside us as we showed our passes. A row of hostile faces watched me. I stared back in anger. I was not yet ready to forgive or forget. The clothes of the passengers had the same drab colour as if they had risen from the tomb. Their expressions were fixed in misery and hate.
>
> The women especially looked at me with real bitterness. There was nothing to buy in the shops of Nuremberg. One could not buy a new hat, a new kettle, a yard of ribbon, a baby's napkin. They wore no make-up and their shoes let in the autumn rain. They bought the barest rations in the shops and took them to their wretched bombed-out homes where there was neither warmth or light. But I could feel no pity at this time as I confronted them.
>
> 'It was Hitler who did this to you!' I shouted at them in German. They turned their faces from me.[18]

The 21 top Nazis on trial had been selected by the Allies to represent the three groups who were thought to be the most guilty. These were (i) the German General Staff; (ii) the German government and (iii) other leaders and officials. Not all the most guilty were on trial. Some, such as Hitler himself and Goebbels, had committed suicide. Some, such as Martin Bormann, had escaped – some with Allied help, as has become clear in the trial of 'the Butcher of Lyons', Klaus Barbie. Many of those who escaped were recaptured, often by Israeli teams, and, like Eichmann, put on trial. Many others, who were not thought to be 'top' Nazis, were put on trial later on – sometimes by Allied courts, sometimes by German courts.

The Nuremberg criminals were arraigned on four counts. First, it was claimed they had entered into a conspiracy with Hitler to commit the crimes which made up the rest of the indictment. These were (i) crimes against peace, (ii) crimes against humanity and (iii) war crimes. There was no difficulty in proving their guilt, because they had kept the most meticulous records.

Some of the criminals showed signs of repentance as the trial went on. Hans Frank, former Governor General of Poland, said that 'a thousand years shall pass and this guilt of Germany will not be erased.'[19] Goering escaped the executioner by committing suicide in his cell. Neither repentance nor suicide, however, saved them from the sentence passed on them by the Tribunal. They and eight others were condemned to death, three were acquitted, and the remaining six were condemned to long terms of imprisonment.

There was then, and has been since, a good deal of criticism of the Trials. The accused had been accused of having violated international law – which by definition can be applied only to states and not to individuals. The Court was not, in spite of claims made for it, 'international'; the prosecuting countries also acted as judges. Nor were other 'criminal countries' put on trial; the Italians, for example, were not tried for their aggression against Ethiopia, Albania, Greece and Egypt; nor were the Russians tried for their invasion of Finland. Indeed, when the Tribunal was considering German aggression against Poland in 1939, the lawyers were not allowed to mention the secret agreement under which Poland was divided between two aggressors – Germany and Russia.

But, as even critics acknowledged, what else could have been done? The crimes had been unprecedented and the criminals had, somehow, to be punished. Airey Neave wrote,

> Frank was hanged in the gymnasium of the prison on October 15, 1946. I have never doubted the justice of this sentence and it was fitting that the body of this arch-racist, like that of Streicher and the others who were executed, should be cremated in the ovens of Dachau, re-lit for the occasion. Frank had not been squeamish about murdering 7½ million innocent people. Why should the world be squeamish about his end?[20]

In subsequent chapters we will examine the 'miracle' which transformed the economies of Germany and Italy. We will also examine the ways by which Germany re-entered the Concert of Europe, which led to the signing of a Treaty of Friendship between France and Germany. In view of the hatred so evident in 1945–6, this change of heart – on all sides – may be seen as an even greater 'miracle'.

Documentary evidence

Lord Dunglass (Document 2.2) had been Parliamentary Private Secretary to Prime Minister Neville Chamberlain (1937–9). A Conservative MP, he resigned his seat when he succeeded his father as Earl of Home in 1951. In 1963 he disclaimed his title when he became Prime Minister, and was henceforward known as Sir Alec Douglas Home.

In 1945 he criticised Churchill's too ready acceptance of Stalin's 'sincere' (Document 2.1) promises as regards the future of Poland. Post-war history has justified this criticism. Indeed, Churchill himself had had a change of mind by the time he made his 'Iron Curtain' speech in 1946 (Document 4.1, p. 77).

In his memoirs (Document 2.3), Churchill tried to justify the Allied acceptance of the situation facing them in July 1945. He also drew attention to the problems which had faced pre-war statesmen, following other boundary changes. In 1871, Bismarckian Germany had taken Alsace and Lorraine from defeated France which had, thereafter, sought a war of revenge. The re-incorporation of these two regions in France in 1919 was one cause of the tension between France and Germany in the inter-war period. The victorious Allies had further antagonised German national feeling in 1919 by giving one of Versailles' new creations, Poland, a slice of Eastern Prussia so that Poland might have a pathway to the sea at Danzig. This so-called Danzig Corridor (referred to in Document 2.3) was a major cause of German-Polish enmity and may be seen as the most immediate cause of the outbreak of the Second World War in September 1939.

Document 2.1

Churchill reports to the Cabinet after the Yalta Conference, February 19, 1945
So far as Premier Stalin was concerned he (Churchill) was quite sure that he (Stalin) meant well to the world and to Poland. He (Churchill) did not himself think that there would be any resentment on the part of Russia about the arrangements that had been made for free and fair elections in that country. On arrival in the Crimea he (Churchill) found that the situation had undergone an extraordinary change. In three weeks the Russian army had fought its way from the Vistula to the Oder; almost the whole of Poland had been liberated; in many parts of the country so reconquered the Russians had been warmly welcomed and great cities had changed hands very nearly intact. In his discussions at the Crimea Conference he had been at pains at all times to press the policy that had been approved by the War Cabinet viz. a free and independent Poland, sovereign in her own territories; with a government more broadly composed than it had been, and with the principles of free and fair elections maintained. Whatever criticisms there might be of the arrangements that had been reached he felt no doubt that they were on any broad and statesmanlike view the best practicable and that they were truly in the interest of Poland. Premier Stalin, at the beginning of their conversations on the Polish question, had said that Russia had committed many sins against Poland, and that she had in the past joined in the partitions of Poland and in cruel oppressions of her. It was not the intention of the Soviet Government to repeat that policy in the future. He (Churchill) felt no doubt whatever that in saying that Premier Stalin had been sincere.

He (Churchill) had a very great feeling that the Russians were anxious to work harmoniously with the two English-speaking democracies. Premier Stalin was a person of great power in whom he (Churchill) had every confidence.'

             (quoted in M. Arnold-Forster, *The World at War*, Collins, 1974)

Document 2.2

A British criticism of the Yalta Agreement. Lord Dunglass in the House of Commons, February 27, 1945
A first British desire is to provide over the widest area possible a setting in which the individual may live out his life in liberty and under justice. This is a British concept but we believe it to be a world interest. It would be comfortable to believe that relationships between different communities of men were always governed by reason, but the reality of history reveals that the governing principle is power.

    Power has not been destroyed in this war – it has been redistributed. It is still used. Any settlement at the time must take account of it.

The world can never pass from the old order to the new – from the old order of the rule of a force to the new order of the rule of law – except by way of a period during which the Great Powers are themselves willing, and are seen to be willing, to exercise restraint in the use of power. The position in post-war Europe will be one of great power and great weakness side by side, and that does not lead to stability.

One reason why there is world concern over the differences between Russia and Poland is because it is the first case – a test case – in the relationship between a Great Power wielding great military might, and her smaller, weaker neighbour.

Does the (Yalta) Treaty conform to that section of the Atlantic Charter which reads "The High Contracting Parties desire to see no territorial changes that do not conform to the wishes of the people concerned"?

I believe if you try to force what is an act of power within the framework of the Atlantic Charter you will not whitewash the act, but you will break the Charter.

The Prime Minister says that he accepts this as an act of justice. We have in our history accepted this kind of arrangement as a fact of power, but I cannot be asked to underwrite it as an act of justice. This is not a quibble of words. I believe most profoundly that it is an essential British interest that we should be seen to preserve our moral standards in international behaviour.

I turn therefore to the second instrument which regulates our relations with Russia – the Anglo-Russian Treaty of 1942. If I might interpret the word "treaty" to the Prime Minister it would be that a treaty is "a rule and not a guide". Perhaps the House will allow me to read Article 5.

"The High Contracting Parties agree to act according to the principles of not seeking territorial aggrandisement for themselves and of non- interference in the internal affairs of other States."

Did Russia adhere to the clauses of the Treaty signed with us in 1942? and would she make her actions correspond to her pledged word?

Did Russia hold approximately the same ideas and conceptions of the structure of Europe as we did? On the answer to these three questions very much depends. Unless you have sanctity of treaties, unless nations are going to keep their pledged word there is not even the minimum condition present for the coherence of international society.

(Lord Home, *The Way the Wind Blows*, Collins, 1976, pp. 93–4)

Document 2.3

The new boundaries of Russia, Poland and Germany, 1945
'We had agreed at Yalta that Russia should advance her western frontier into Poland as far as the Curzon Line. We had always recognised that Poland in her turn should receive substantial accessions of German territory. The question was how much? How far into Germany should she go? There had been much disagreement. Stalin had wanted to extend the western frontier of Poland along the river Oder to where it joined the Western Neisse; Roosevelt, Eden and I had insisted it should stop at the Eastern Neisse. All three heads of Governments had publicly bound themselves at Yalta to consult the Polish Government, and to leave it to the Peace Conference for final settlement. This was the best we had

been able to do. But in July 1945 we faced a new situation. Russia had advanced her frontier to the Curzon Line. This meant, as Roosevelt and I realised, that the three or four million Poles who lived on the wrong side of the line would have to be moved to the west. Now we were confronted with something much worse. The Soviet- dominated Government of Poland had also pressed forward, not to the Eastern Neisse, but to the Western. Much of this territory was inhabited by Germans, and although several millions had fled many had stayed behind. What was to be done with them? Moving three or four million Poles was bad enough. Were we to move more than eight million Germans as well? Even if such a transfer could be contemplated, there was not enough food for them in what was left of Germany. Much of Germany's grain came from the very land which the Poles had seized, and if this was denied us, the Western Allies would be left with wrecked industrial zones and a starved and swollen population. For the future peace of Europe here was a wrong beside which Alsace-Lorraine and the Danzig Corridor were trifles. One day the Germans would want their territory back, and the Poles would not be able to stop them.'
(Winston Churchill, *The Second World War and an Epilogue on the years 1945–57,*
Cassell, 1959, pp. 943–4)

FURTHER READING

ADENAUER, K., *Memoirs, 1945–54,* Weidenfeld and Nicolson, 1966–8

BUCHAN, A., *The End of the Post War Era,* Weidenfeld and Nicolson, 1974

CALVOCORESSI, P., *World Politics since 1945,* Longman, 1968

CHILDS, D., *Germany since 1918,* Batsford, 1980

CONOT, R. E., *Justice at Nuremberg,* Weidenfeld and Nicolson, 1984

DESCHNER, G., *Warsaw Uprising,* Pan Books, 1972

FEIS, H., *Churchill, Roosevelt, Stalin,* OUP, 1957

FEIS, H., *Between War and Peace: The Potsdam Conference,* OUP, 1960

FEIS, H., *From Trust to Terror: The Onset of the Cold War, 1945–50,* OUP, 1970

JACKSON, J. HAMPDEN, *The Post War Decade,* Gollancz, 1961

LAQUEUR, W., *Out of the Ruins of Europe,* Alcove Press, 1972

MEE, C. L., *Meeting at Potsdam,* Deutsch, 1975

NEAVE, A, *Nuremberg,* Hodder and Stoughton, 1978

SPEER, A., *Inside the Third Reich,* Weidenfeld and Nicolson, 1971

TOLSTOY, N., *Victims of Yalta,* Hodder and Stoughton, 1977

TRUMAN, HARRY S., *Years of Trial and Hope, 1946–1953,* Signet Books, 1956

TUSA, A. J., *The Nuremberg Trials,* Macmillan, 1984

WILMOT, CHESTER, *The Struggle for Europe,* Collins, 1951

3

The Soviet domination of Eastern Europe, 1945–53

The seeds of mutual hostility

'I do not believe that Soviet Russia desires war. What they desire is the fruits of war and the indefinite expansion of their power and doctrines.'
Churchill at Fulton, Missouri, March 1946

The Russian policy of gaining control of the countries of eastern Europe was both a cause and an effect of the Cold War (Chapter 4). Stalin wanted a *cordon sanitaire*, territory in eastern Europe under Russian control (Fig. 2.1, p. 24). His claim to such a buffer zone was accepted by the Allies in view of the results of the two German attacks on Russia in 1914 and 1941. While making this concession, the western Allies put their faith in the Declaration on Liberated Europe (p. 23) and in their hope that Stalin would honour this and other similar agreements. These hopes were dashed before the end of the war by Stalin's organisation of the communist take-over of Poland (pp. 23–7).

Russia's suspicion of the west was deep-seated. During the Russian Civil War (1918–21), Churchill had led the demands for an anti-Bolshevik crusade. Russians also remembered that, for many years, most western governments had refused recognition of the Communist government after 1917.

Again, the western Powers had signed a series of treaties at Locarno in 1925. These had been aimed, the Russians believed, at winning Germany away from the Treaty of Rapallo which she had signed with Russia in 1922, and bringing her into alliance with Britain, France and the other western Powers. The Locarno Treaties guaranteed the boundary arrangements made at Versailles only as regards the western boundaries of Germany. While such a guarantee satisfied France, Belgium and Holland, it increased Russian fear that, by having said nothing about Germany's eastern frontiers, the western powers were encouraging Germany to look to the east for *Lebensraum* and raw materials.

The Soviet government lived with this fear of a western invasion.

When Hitler came to power in January 1933, Stalin tried to co-operate with the western powers. Russia joined the League in 1934 (the year after Hitler had ordered the German delegation to leave). In 1935 he signed a formal alliance with France and with Czechoslovakia. But he saw how the western powers took no action when Hitler tore up the Treaty of Versailles. When Hitler announced German rearmament in 1935, Britain not only invited him to send delegates to London to discuss the question of rearmament but, later that year, negotiated the Anglo-German Naval Treaty which allowed the creation of that navy denied Germany by the Treaty of Versailles. Britain and France did not act when Hitler demilitarised the Rhineland in 1936 in defiance of both the Versailles and Locarno Treaties, nor when Mussolini attacked Abyssinia, nor when Germany and Italy helped Franco to power between 1936 and 1939. The western powers passively accepted the *Anschluss*, when Hitler brought Austria into the greater Reich in March 1938, although this was forbidden by the Treaties of Versailles and St Germain.

But Russian suspicion of the western powers was finally confirmed by the dismemberment of Czechoslovakia in 1938. Britain and France forced the Czechs to hand over the Sudetenland, so weakening Czechoslovakia both economically and militarily. This process was the product of three Conferences – to none of which was Russia invited, although she had a formal Treaty with the victim.

In March 1939, Hitler broke the promises made at Munich in 1938. He seized Bohemia, thus ending the existence of the state of Czechoslovakia. He also announced the end of the German-Polish Treaty of Friendship, thus signalling his future intentions towards his eastern neighbour. Britain and France then promised that, if Poland was attacked, they would come to her side. Just how they were to do this without the help of Russia, Poland's eastern neighbour, was not clear. Stalin did not believe that they were militarily capable of fighting; his agents led him to believe that powerful influences in both Britain and France would ensure that there would be no war against Germany.

His suspicions of the west and his fear of a German attack caused Stalin to undertake a *volte face* and to sign a non-aggression treaty with Hitler in August 1939. This left Hitler free, first to dismember Poland in September 1939, allowing Russia to take her share of that unhappy country, and then to turn his attention to the west again. Stalin may have hoped that there would now be a major conflict between Germany and the two major western powers which would serve to weaken these powers and Germany, and so provide additional breathing space for Russia's industrial and military development.

After Germany's attack on Russia in June 1941, Stalin constantly appealed for the opening of a second front in western Europe. Allied failure to open that second front, coupled with the high level of Russian losses in 1941, 1942 and 1943, confirmed Stalin in his belief that the western powers now wanted to watch the erstwhile allies bleed each other to death.

By 1945, the scientists of Britain and the USA had developed the atomic bomb. But the atomic secrets were kept from the Russians who, however, knew of them because of the work of Communist agents such as the scientists Klaus Fuchs and Nunn May. This secrecy between allies deepened Russian suspicions of the west.

The western powers, for their part, had every right to be equally suspicious of Soviet Russia (see also pp. 56–60 on the Cold War). Marxist-Leninism taught that war with the capitalists was inevitable. Lenin had declared that 'we cannot live in peace, one or the other will triumph.' During the 1920s and 1930s the Comintern had busily organised the activities of Communist parties throughout the world; there was, almost everywhere, a 'Russian' party. In addition there were, in the west, the many intellectuals who, although not committed Communists, saw Communism as 'the wave of the future'. For these, as for the 'Cold War warriors' of the west, the division between Russia and the west was not comparable to the old-fashioned division between, say, France and Germany. This was not a dynastic or nationalist division: it was one of ideologies. On their side, the Communists wished to promote a social, economic and political system which the west wished to defeat. For the west, too, has its ideology – of freedom. The division between the two sides is made deeper because of the different ways in which each side interprets the same words. For example, both sides of the ideological divide use the word 'democracy'. In the west, the word carries connotations of a multiplicity of political parties, freedom of elections and assembly and a wide dispersion of economic and political power. In the west, one finds centres of power separate from the Central Authority of the government of the day. There are, for example, a free press, independent local government, and powerful economic structures such as organisations of industrialists and workers. This diffusion of power provides a series of checks and balances against the power of the state. In the Soviet system, however, we find 'democratic centralism'; all power – political, social and economic – rests in the hands of the small number of people who run the state (p. 106). In Chapter 6 we will examine how and why Lenin imposed that system on Russia; we will also see that this has led to a system in which there is an absence of those freedoms which are taken for granted in the west, while there are a series of restrictions which the people of the west would find intolerable.

The mutual hostility which had existed before and during the war was deepened in the years following 1945. The Russians, for example, were suspicious of the western allies' attempts to re-build the economy of their zones in Germany from 1947 onwards (Chapter 4). On the other hand, western suspicions were increased by the way in which Russian-controlled parties took control in country after country in eastern Europe (Fig. 3.1). Everywhere, it seemed, the pattern was the same. First, the Communists co-operated with other political parties to form coalition governments; then, the coalitions were re-formed with the communists in the most important positions; later a one-party system was introduced.

SEE FOR YOURSELF. IS IT NOT OBVIOUS THAT THEY ARE "DEMOCRATIC GOVERNMENTS WHICH ENJOY THE CONFIDENCE OF THE OVERWHELMING MAJORITY OF THE PEOPLE OF THESE COUNTRIES"?

BEHIND THE CURTAIN

3.1 Molotov, of Russia, trying to persuade Bevin and Byrnes that Russia's treatment of the countries of eastern Europe was not contrary to the promises made in various wartime agreements and treaties. (Cartoon by permission of *The Standard*.)

Latter-day Russian hostility to the west may, finally, be seen as a manifestation of a deep-rooted division in Russian society. From the time of Peter the Great (1689–1725), many leading Russians have believed that Russia had a good deal to learn from the west; in the nineteenth century, Russian industrialisation owed a good deal to western capital, western industrialists and western technocrats; even in the 1930s, while Stalin was building his 'socialism in one country', he had to rely on a good deal of western expertise; Brezhnev's invitation to Fiat and other western firms to build factories in Russia in the 1970s was an essential part of his attempt to bring Russian industry up to western standards (p. 125). But these 'westernisers' have always found themselves at odds with the 'Slavophiles' who have thought, and still think, that Russia can only be contaminated by such contact with the west. If

Sergius de Witte (1849–1915) helped Russian industrialisation, he was opposed by Pobedonostev (1827–1907) and Plehve (1846–1904) who, finally, persuaded Nicholas II to dismiss the 'westerniser'. In pre-Communist days, the Slavophiles feared the contamination of 'Holy Russia'; in Communist days there has been and still is this same fear, now strengthened by the Communist party's ideological hostility to capitalism.

Until his death in 1948, Andrei Zhdanov was Stalin's lieutenant on all ideological issues. It was Zhdanov (under Stalin) who was responsible for the attacks on writers, composers, philosophers and painters for 'slavishly imitating western patterns'; 'cosmopolitanism' became a term of abuse to hurl at such 'westernisers'. Shostakovitch and Prokofiev were ordered to produce the sort of music that the Russian peasant could hum while at work; Lysenko was promoted because his views on genetics were at odds with traditional 'westernised' views; economists who dared to suggest that the western capitalist system might not break down were imprisoned. It is difficult to distinguish between the 'Communist' and the 'Slavophile' influences in such anti-western behaviour; the anti-western attitudes of Stalin and his advisers were all of a piece with the traditional 'Slavophile' tradition.

The initial take-over in eastern Europe

'. . . Russia . . . in foreign policy is . . . as imperialistic as . . . Peter the Great . . . is seeking to put around herself . . . whole groups of satellites . . . with the view of controlling every kind of place which is likely to come into contact with her.'[1]

Ernest Bevin, 1 January 1946

We have seen (pp. 23–7) how the Russians imposed a government of their choice on Poland once that country had been liberated by the Red Army (Document 3.1). That army also liberated the other countries of eastern Europe between the summer of 1944 and the spring of 1945 (Fig. 2.1, p. 24). The peoples of these countries had conceived a deep hatred for the Germans, who had tortured and murdered millions of innocent people. This hatred led them to give a fervent welcome to the liberators of the Red Army: 'columns of marching soldiers, dirty, tired, clad in ragged uniforms; columns of women and girls in military grey-green uniforms, high boots and tight blouses; the Agitprop Brigade . . . lorries belonging to the Political Commissariat and the NKVD.'[2]

Poland and Czechoslovakia, Bulgaria and Hungary, Rumania and East Germany were freed by the Red Army which, in its 'bag and baggage', brought the politicians and the secret police. There were, of course, 'home-grown' communists to lead the welcome to the liberators; Gomulka (in Poland), Rajk and Kadar (in Hungary), Tito (in Yugoslavia) were the representatives of a local breed of communists. But they were always suspect to Stalin, who preferred the 'Muscovites', those leaders who had been taken to Moscow and trained there. Such 'graduates' of the Comintern's school who returned with the Red Army were Dimitrov (of Bulgaria), Rakosi (of Hungary), Ulbricht (of Germany) and Gottwald (of Czechoslovakia). They had learned that national loyalties had no place in their lives; they had been taught absolute loyalty to the interests of the world-wide movement of which the Soviet Union was the standard bearer. They were quite prepared to be Stalin's puppets (Fig. 3.1).

Bulgaria, like Rumania and Hungary, was a backward, agricultural country in which a dictatorial government had ruled before 1939. The better-off peasants had formed a Peasants' Party to represent their interests but the Communist Party was banned. During the war there had been little resistance, and that mainly non-communist and nationalist. The country was liberated by the Red Army whose political advisers helped set up a Provisional Government. The local Communists were now free to campaign openly, but the people, having got rid of one tyranny, showed little inclination to support a new, Russian-inspired one. They wanted local democracy, national independence, social and agrarian reform.

The Russians realised that Bulgaria, like most of eastern Europe, depended in the immediate post-war days on aid from UNRRA (p. 60). They did not wish to antagonise the Americans who provided most of the aid distributed by that agency. So, following the line taken by Rakosi of Hungary, they 'sliced away' at the opposition. It was Rakosi who had explained how the various opposition groups could be got rid of, slowly and 'piece by piece' in what he called the 'salami technique'. The Russians made no effort to get rid of the Bulgarian King until September 1946. The Communists served in a government led by General Georgiou whom they had once attacked as the 'military fascist' who had fought against them in the 1920s and 1930s.

His government was a mixture of communists, socialists, representatives of peasants' parties and conservatives. The Red Army was, at first, popular and the local communists gained support in the shadow of that approval. However, before long, the behaviour of the Russians and the depredations of the Soviet advisers led to a lessening of that popularity and of support for the communists. However, they used their mass support to gain control of the Peasants' Party; hundreds of communists were sent to join that Party at a local level and to get themselves elected to various committees. This enabled them to demand the expulsion of over-conservative leaders from that Party, which they took over.

Georgi Dimitrov, who had won world-wide renown during his trial on the charge of having organised the Reichstag fire of 1933, had spent the period after that trial in Moscow. A hard-line Stalinist, he returned to Bulgaria in November 1945 and became Prime Minister a year later. He, like his counterparts in other east European states, ruled his country as if it were 'a suburb of Moscow'.

In *Hungary* the Communist Party had been banned, its leaders, such as Matyas Rakosi, serving terms of imprisonment before being sent to Russia in 1941 in return for Hungarian patriot flags which had been held in Moscow since the nationalist uprising of 1849. Another Hungarian communist, Laszlo Rajk, was appointed to rebuild the party organisation in liberated Hungary. In November 1945, there were free elections in which the Smallholders' Party gained four times as many votes as did the Communists. The Smallholders could have formed a government without communist assistance. But, in view of the temporary popularity of the Red Army, and in the hope of creating a government of national unity, they invited Rakosi to join the government. They made only one condition; that their Party Secretary, Bela Kovacs, should take the post of Minister of the Interior – which would have ensured Smallholders' control of the police, press, radio and cinema. Rakosi refused to accept this condition; he threatened that the Russians might well impose a government on the country. Having seen the largest political party succumb to such threats, Rakosi and Rajk then put their 'salami technique' into operation. First, they refused to serve with any party which did not promise full co-operation with their policies; then, having gained some power, they organised the dismissal of independent-minded ministers who might, later on, have led opposition. Some, such as Kovacs, were arrested, and even though his Party held the largest number of seats in Parliament, it was unable to get him released. Non-communist parties were taken over by a series of mergers, and, with Rajk as Minister of the Interior, the police were allowed to harass non-communist politicians; their meetings were broken up, their newspapers proscribed, and 'slice by slice' the opposition was whittled away. Rakosi then led a Stalin-type, hard-line government, whose secret police was so ruthless that it was one of the main causes of the Hungarian Revolution in 1956 (pp. 92–4).

Rumania, another backward peasant country, was liberated by the Red Army in 1944. In pre-war days, King Carol II had supported the activities of his semi-fascist government which had remained a member of the Axis group. When the Russians reached the Rumanian frontier in 1944, the new King, Michael, arrested the Prime Minister, Antonescu, made peace with the Russians and declared war on Germany. Rumania received lenient terms in the Paris Peace Treaties (p. 31). The liberating Red Army appointed a Provisional Government, retaining King Michael as Head of State – and awarding him the Order of Victory. However, he was forced to make concessions to the communist-dominated Democratic Front which was in power after March 1945. Gheorghiu-Dej, the General Secretary of the Rumanian Communist Party was Minister of National Economy in that coalition government. He was a 'local' communist, unlike the Moscow-trained Anna Pauker, the Foreign Minister from 1947 to 1952. In order to survive, he had to show himself even more loyal to Stalin than those Stalinists. In December 1947, King Michael was forced to abdicate and Rumania became a Peoples' Republic under a communist hard-line government.

On April 30, 1945, the day on which Hitler committed suicide in Berlin, a Russian airplane brought Walter Ulbricht to that occupied city to take charge of the *Russian Zone of Occupation of Germany*. Ulbricht had been a communist member of the Reichstag from 1928 to 1933 when the Party was expelled from the Reichstag by Hitler. Ulbricht then went to Russia, where he became a Soviet citizen and leader of the Free German Committee being prepared for the take-over when the war had been won. Back in Berlin in 1945, he gave his approval to the Oder-Neisse frontiers with Poland and allowed the Russians a free hand in the stripping of his zone of whatever might be useful to the Russian economy. This won the communists few friends and little influence. In October 1946, there were free elections in *East Berlin* at which the communists gained less than twenty per cent of the vote – much less than they had won before Hitler came to power. But, with the aid of the Russian army, Ulbricht imposed a Stalinist-type government on East Germany and East Berlin – as we shall see in Chapter 4.

There were to be no free elections in *Poland* where, as we have seen, the Russians had imposed a government in 1944 (pp. 23–7). Mikolajczyk, the leader of the pre-war Peasants Party, was then in London. By the time he returned, the communists had taken control. When the Peasant Party tried to resume its activities, the communist-controlled police disrupted its work, harassed and arrested some of its leaders, banned its meetings and manipulated local elections in such a way that Mikolajczyk, fearing for his life, fled to the west. The returning 'Muscovite' Bierut led the government, in which the secretary of the Polish Workers Party, Gomulka, was minister in charge of the territories annexed from Germany.

Yugoslavia's liberation owed little to the Red Army. Throughout the war, Josip Broz, better known as Tito, had led a resistance movement which had won international recognition. He had been trained in pre-war Moscow, but was much less of a 'Muscovite' than Ulbricht and other returning leaders in eastern Europe. Unlike them, Tito was not brought to power by the Red Army. He had managed to blend his brand of communism with anti-German nationalism in the struggle for liberation. This helps to explain, at least in part, the subsequent Tito-Stalin rift (pp. 49–50).

Yugoslavia was liberated in October 1944 and, during the next few months, Tito's supporters wiped out the small bands of opposition to communism. One result of this was that in the elections held in November 1945, Tito's National Front Party won ninety per cent of the votes. Tito proclaimed Yugoslavia a Republic and claimed that it was a 'People's Democracy', a title seized on by others in eastern Europe as a cloak-title for their Stalinist-type governments. In fact, Yugoslavia was governed by a quartet composed of Tito, Edward Kardelj, Aleksander Rankovia and Milovan Djilas (Doc. 6.1, p. 132).

Czechoslovakia had had a very different pre-war history to the other states in eastern Europe. Heavily industrialised, its people had enjoyed a 'western' standard of life. They also had a democratic system, in which even the Communist Party had been free to campaign. Under the leadership of such politicians as Tomas Masaryk and Eduard Benes, the country had prospered until 1938, when it had been dismembered by Germany and her satellites. During the war, a Czech resistance movement had been active inside the country, a Czech corps, under the leadership of General Svoboda, had fought alongside the Russians, and Benes had been actively at work trying to reconcile Russia with the USA and Britain.

The liberating Red Army installed a Provisional Government in power and elections were held in May 1946. At these, the Communist Party won 38 per cent of the vote – an electoral victory. Benes was elected President, the Communist Gottwald became Prime Minister and Jan Masaryk (son of Tomas) became Foreign Minister. Gottwald was another of the 'Muscovites'; he had been the representative of the Comintern in Czechoslovakia in the 1930. After the Munich Agreement of 1938 he went to Moscow where he took part in discussions with Benes in 1943. He returned, with Benes, to Czechoslovakia in 1945 intent on the Russification of his homeland – in due time.

The Stalinisation of the satellites, 1948–53

'Of course we shall join the Marshall Plan. We shall take their money and shall not accept their influence.'[3]

'The Soviet régime and the Popular Democratic régime are the two forms of one and the same system.'

Georgi Dimitrov of Bulgaria

In 1948 it appeared as if Russia had attained its major objective in eastern Europe. Everywhere there were governments which had either been imposed by the Russians or were Russian controlled.

The Truman Doctrine (p. 77) of March 1947 was a sign that the US had come to fear Russian expansion – particularly when Britain indicated her inability to maintain the role of guardian of Europe. The Marshall Plan (pp. 60–2) was the generous indication of US willingness to help Europe to recover. It was inspired, at least in part, by the fear that, if Europe were left to its own devices, it would not recover for many years; in the meantime, the Soviet system might appear that much more attractive to the people of the west if condemned to years of continued hardship.

In June 1947, the Americans offered their aid to the whole of Europe, including Russia. Stalin rejected the offer, fearing the growth of US influence in Russia. The coalition government in Czechoslovakia announced that it intended to take the aid. In February 1948 Stalin sent Zorin, one of his trusted diplomats, to warn Gottwald from such a course. Gottwald was already concerned at the decline in the vote for communist candidates in local elections. It might be that, at some time in the future, the communists would lose their control of the democratic government of the country. Zorin advised him that Russian troops were stationed on the Czech border, ready to invade if Marshall aid was accepted. Well-drilled communist demonstrators took to the streets, occupied factories and took control of the media. Slansky, the Communist Party general secretary, and Gottwald forced President Benes to appoint a new government containing a majority of communist ministers. Masaryk, who might have provided strong opposition to the imposition of a dictatorship, was summoned to a meeting and was found in the courtyard of the Foreign Ministry; he had, it was claimed, fallen from a window. Shortly afterwards, Benes resigned and Gottwald led a communist government. Czechoslovakia had been captured.

Within a few months, however, Stalin faced a new challenge. Tito, a graduate of the Moscow system, had not been brought to power by the Red Army. Stalin had considered, for some time, that Tito might prove less amenable than his well-trained puppets. He had organised a Yugoslav Communist Party in opposition to Tito and had tried, unsuccessfully, to organise a *putsch* to depose him and his colleagues and to instal new, more acceptable leaders.

In October 1947, Tito took part in the Warsaw Conference which led to the setting up of the Cominform which was meant to coordinate party activites throughout Europe (p. 62). Stalin intended that it should be the instrument through which he would dictate policy to his satellites in the Balkans. Tito rejected such Russian control. He claimed that every country had the right to choose its own 'road to socialism'. This was a heresy. Stalin ordered the Cominform to expel Yugoslavia from membership (ironically, at its first meeting in June 1948). The Cominform had to give up the plan to have its headquarters in Belgrade, while Tito was forced to look to the west for economic and military assistance. This led to a decline in external aid for the Greek Communists and so lessened the crisis in that country (pp. 57–60).

Tito claimed that the conflict between Yugoslavia and Russia arose from Russian 'attempts to enslave our country economically and politically, to liquidate its independence and make it into a colony'. Stalin feared that Tito's example might be followed by other leaders in his 'empire' and acted to squash any danger of there being others with ambitions of following 'local roads to socialism'. Dimitrov of Bulgaria, for example, although a ruthless Stalinist in internal affairs, had already shown signs of seeking an independent foreign policy. In August 1947, before the Tito-Stalin split, he had held conversations with Tito with a view to the creation of a dual republic of Yugoslavia-Bulgaria, and had signed an agreement for the close political, cultural and economic co-operation between the two states. Early in 1948, he had visited Rumania and spoken of an eventual socialist federation of all south-eastern Europe. Dimitrov was summoned to Moscow and forced to repudiate his policies. He was already suffering ill-health which may have excused him from playing a part in the orchestrated condemnation of Tito after June 1948. He was taken to Moscow for medical treatment and his convenient death was announced in Moscow in July 1949.

Gomulka of Poland (p. 44) was another who had claimed that Poland could find its own road to socialism, that it was not necessary to follow the Russian example. In the summer of 1948, following Tito's expulsion, he spoke publicly of the 'historic traditions of the Polish labour movement', which Stalin took as a sign that he supported Tito's nationalist stand. He was dismissed from his post in December 1948 and kept in prison from 1951 to 1955.

Georghiu-Dej of Rumania was a true hard-liner but he lacked the *imprimatur* of Moscow training. To prove his loyalty and to ensure that Stalin did not suspect him of Titoism, he organised a series of internal Party purges between 1950 and 1952, eliminating not only the many opportunists who had joined the party after the war, but even the Soviet trained 'Pauker group' (p. 46). The intensification of the reign of terror, which had begun in 1945, was continued until Dej became the undisputed master of Rumania – and a loyal Stalinist.

In *Hungary*, Laszlo Rajk had been entrusted by Stalin with the task of building the party organisation. He was Minister of the Interior from 1946 until August 1948, when he became Foreign Secretary. In May 1949, this 'non-Muscovite' was arrested and charged with having tried to forge links with Tito and with having been a secret police agent in the 1930s. At this show trial in September 1949 he confessed to all the crimes alleged against him and he was hanged a few days later. The evidence produced at his trial was admitted (in 1956) to have been falsified and he was rehabilitated in 1956 by Rakosi – the 'Muscovite' boss of the Hungarian party who had supervised the arrest, trial and execution.

Janos Kadar was another 'local' Communist Minister who fell foul of the 'Muscovite' Rakosi. Kadar had been active in the resistance during the German occupation. He had been a member of the Party's central committee since 1942 and from 1948 to April 1951 he was Minister of the Interior in Rakosi's Stalinist-type government. He had been responsible in the first instance for Rajk's arrest, trial and execution. In April 1951 he was arrested and tortured by his own creation – the secret police – and kept in prison until 1954.

Czechoslovakia had been the last of the 'satellites' to come within the Russian orbit. Gottwald, Clementis (who succeeded Masaryk as Foreign Minister) and Rudolf Slansky, the Vice Premier and Communist Party Secretary, ran a Stalinist-type government. But in

November 1951, Slansky, Clementis and twelve other leading Communist officials, most of them Jewish, were arrested, brought to a 'show trial' in November 1952 and accused of being 'Trotskyist, Titoite, Zionist, bourgeois, nationalist traitors' who were 'in the service of American imperialism'. Slansky, Clementis and nine others were found guilty and they were hanged on 2 December 1952. As in the case of Rajk in Hungary, the evidence against them was a total fabrication. In Czechoslovakia, as elsewhere, the show trials were the tip of a large iceberg. Jan Sejna was a student at the Commissars School in Velvety, about 65 km from Prague, in 1950. Later he wrote;

'This was the time of political upheaval, with the great purge trials of the old Party leaders, culminating in the execution of Rodulf Slansky, Secretary General of the Czechoslovak Party. Slansky himself began the blood-letting in 1948 and continued it in 1950 . . . the process caught up with him. I was to discover later that in these latest purges 2,000 Czechs and Slovaks lost their lives, and about 300,000 were imprisoned. Nobody could feel safe. Some of the staff vanished from the Commissars School and a grim pall of fear hung over us all.'[4]

Imposing the Communist system, 1945–53

'At the present moment . . . every nation must choose between alternative ways of life. The choice is too often not a free one. One way of life is based upon the will of the majority. . . . The second . . . is based upon the will of a minority forcibly imposed upon the majority.'[5]

Stalin may have wanted a subservient 'empire' for reasons of safety (p. 40). But once his 'chosen few' were in power, he forced them to run their countries in Russia's interests. Russia exploited eastern Europe to help restore its own economy. Hungary, Rumania and East Germany had to pay substantial reparations to Russia. The other countries were forced to sell much of their produce to Russia well under world market prices and to take Soviet goods at artificially high prices. Poland was forced to sell to Russia each year some 200,000 tonnes of sugar at half the world prices, uranium mines in Hungary and Rumania were sequestrated. In 1956 Khruschev admitted that Russia had robbed Poland of 500 million dollars' worth of goods during this period.[6] Hungary was robbed on the same scale while Rumania poured oil, wheat and raw materials into Russia, which also took 19 billion dollars worth of equipment from East Germany, about 40 per cent of the state's industrial capacity.

In each of the satellites, attempts were made to tackle long overdue social reform and economic reconstruction. By 1947 the pre-war level of industrial production had been reached. Most countries adopted short term plans, usually for a period of three years, to cope with their immediate economic problems. When partial recovery had been attained, longer-term Plans, for Five or Six years, were introduced. These centralised Plans aimed at developing heavy industries suited to the needs of the Soviet Union. The East Germans, for example, in their first Plan, aimed at raising production to 92 per cent above the 1950 level. In Hungary, Slovakia and Poland large uneconomic steelworks were developed, while in Bulgaria, new, heavy industry was started for which the raw materials were not readily available.

Firms previously owned by Germans were immediately taken over by the new governments, and in 1946 banks, insurance companies, iron and steel foundries, mines and some other industries were nationalised. 'Big' factories were taken over by the state; in Poland, for example, this was the fate of any factory employing more than 200 workers.

There were differences in the pace of land reform. In East Germany, Hungary and Poland, where the bulk of land had been owned by a small number of landowners, there was a mass re-distribution of land to the peasants. Subsequent governments of Poland have suffered because of the failure of the first post-war government to grasp the nettle of land collectivisation.

By 1949, eastern Europe was a region of land-owning peasants. But, for the communist faithful, re-distribution was merely one step along the road to collectivisation – as it had been in Russia in the 1920s. The communist governments pursued the aim of collectivisation slowly. Stalin had learnt that it was a mistake to rush the process; he had no wish to see a repeat of the famine from which Russia had suffered in the first years of his own attempt to collectivise Russian agriculture. He, and his representatives in eastern Europe, also knew that there was not enough machinery available in the immediate post-war years, machinery which was essential if the larger, collectivised farms were to be worked profitably.

By the end of 1948, industrial output had so improved that machinery was available. It had also become increasingly clear that a prosperous, independent, land-owning peasantry might be a major source of opposition to the communist governments imposed on the countries of eastern Europe. In 1949, collectivisation began, and over the next ten years or so was carried through with determined efficiency. By 1960, land had been almost totally collectivised, except in Poland and Yugoslavia.

The imposition of collectivisation was of a piece with the overall behaviour of the communist governments throughout eastern Europe. They were, as we have seen, and as Truman claimed in 1947 (p. 77), minority governments maintained in power by terror and force. The press was heavily censored when not directly state-owned; contacts with the west were forbidden, except through Berlin; intellectuals were particularly marked down for attack – in Hungary in 1950–2, 100,000 members of the middle class were sent, without trial, to forced labour camps. Everywhere, as in Czechoslovakia, the show trials were merely small indications of the extent of the terror. It was not only in Czechoslovakia that people went in fear; everywhere, the secret police permeated society and helped maintain coercive régimes.

The main resistance to the communist régimes in eastern Europe was provided by the churches – the Lutheran Church in East Germany and the Catholic Church in Hungary, Czechoslovakia and Poland. The communist governments attacked the churches in a variety of ways; in most countries the Church was deprived of its property, Church schools were taken over by the State and many priests imprisoned on trumped up charges so that, for example, by 1953 over a third of Lutheran Churches in East Germany had no pastor. But it was the Catholic Church which was the main object of attack, as the main centre of resistance to the tyranny of the would-be monolithic régimes.

The first leader to suffer was Archbishop Stepinac, the leader of the Church in Tito's Yugoslavia. During the war, the Croatian Stepinac welcomed the setting up of an independent Croatia by the Catholic-dominated resistance movement in that region. This brought him into conflict with the Croatian, Tito, who wanted a unitary State of Yugoslavia. In 1945–6 the two men held talks to try to arrive at some agreement on relations between Church and State. These failed, and Stepinac was arrested on the charge of having collaborated with the Germans during the war. In October 1946, he was sentenced to 16 years imprisonment. He was freed in 1951 and was created a cardinal by the Pope who wished to show support for the anti-communist leader. Stepinac refused to go to Rome to receive his cardinal's hat from the Pope, for he knew that Tito would not re-admit him to the country. He died of leukemia in 1960. His successor, Archbishop Seper, has been able to bring about easier relationships between the Church and the government in Belgrade.

The Hungarian government tried to undermine the power of the Prince-Primate, Mindszenty. He had been arrested and imprisoned by the Nazis in 1944–5 for publicising his anti-Nazi views. He clashed with the communist government in 1945–6 over its dissolution of the Catholic youth movement, but he was not arrested until December 1948. He had warned his followers that he might not be able to withstand the various pressures that could be imposed in the torture chambers used by the government. But at his trial in February 1949 he confessed only to anti-communist sympathies and was sentenced to life imprisonment. In July 1955 this was amended to house detention. In 1947 he had been created a cardinal as a sign of the Pope's support for this anti-communist leader. His arrest and imprisonment gained world-wide publicity and served to show the world the less acceptable face of communist rule.

In Czechoslovakia, the leader of the Church was Archbishop Beran, who was a prisoner in the Dachau concentration camps from 1941 to 1945. He was arrested in 1951, during the worst of the Czech purges, (pp. 50–1), and imprisoned. In 1964, his punishment was modified to house arrest and in 1965 he was allowed to leave Czechoslovakia to receive his cardinal's hat from the Pope.

In Poland, where some 90 per cent of the population is Catholic, the leader from 1948 was Archbishop Wyszynski, the Archbishop of Warsaw. He was named as a cardinal in 1953 but on the eve of his departure for Rome he was arrested and imprisoned. He was released during the Polish 'spring' of 1956 (pp. 87–8) and continued to lead the Church's opposition to the activities of the communist government.

Documentary evidence

Document 3.1

The Soviet forces liberated most of the countries in eastern Europe from German occupation. Along with the forces there came the Soviet political advisers and secret police (p. 44) who were to impose Moscow-oriented governments on each of the liberated countries.

The Red Army welcomed, 1944–5

'First come the tank divisions . . . composed of picked soldiers, the columns of guns and lorries, the parachute divisions, motor cyclists, technical units . . . But this . . . is only its vanguard. More than anything else the Red Army is a mass . . . columns of marching soldiers, dirty, tired, clad in ragged uniforms. Tens and hundreds of thousands of columns moving on the dusty roads of central and eastern Europe. They march slowly in close rank with a long even step. Sometimes a song bursts from the marching column, usually slow and poignantly sad. So they march, men young and old from Russian towns and villages, from the Ukraine and the Tartar Republics, the Ural Mountains and the Caucasus, the Baltic countries, Siberia and Mongolia. . . . And columns of women and girls in military grey-green uniforms, high boots and tight blouses, with long hair greased with goose fat. . . . And children, mainly small boys; the *bezprizorni* from burnt out villages and towns. Soldiers found them in the woods, exhausted and half mad with hunger and fright, without parents, without a home or a name. . . . Behind the spearheads drive the staff. . . . In German luxury cars . . . and lorries laden with furniture, beds . . . radios, frigidaires, wardrobes, couches . . . cases of china, kilometres of textiles, fur coats, carpets, silver . . . and lorries with tons of Russian delicacies, caviar, sturgeon, salami, hectolitres of vodka and Crimean wine. . . . Behind the staffs, more marching columns, without a beginning and without an end. And finally the rearguard; miles and miles of small light carts drawn by low Cossack horses. A grey old man sits in front of the cart. . . . In the back, under the canvas hood, there is a heap of straw and fodder, packages, tins of food and on top lies a sick soldier, a drunken woman, a pen containing a goose, a leg of smoked pork. . . . They drive today . . . as the Tartars used to drive centuries ago; in crowds and hosts, uncounted and uncountable, infinitely foreign and lost in all these western countries of which they have never heard and which they are utterly unable to understand; a flood from the steppes, spreading across Europe.'

(Stransky, J, *East Wind over Prague*, Hollis and Carter, 1950, pp. 22–3)

FURTHER READING

HERKZ, M. F., *The Beginnings of the Cold War*, Indiana UP, 1966
HUDSON, G. F., *The Hard and Bitter Peace*, Pall Mall, 1966
KENNAN, G. F., *On Dealing with the Communist World*, Harper and Row, 1964
LAQUEUR, W., *Out of the Ruins of Europe*, Alcove Press, 1972
TRUMAN, HARRY S., *Memoirs*, New English Library, 1958
WATSON, G. H. N. SETON, *The New Imperialism*, Bodley Head, 1961
WILMOT, CHESTER, *The Struggle for Europe*, Collins, 1951

4

The Cold War, 1945–55

Ancient and modern

Western suspicions of Russia long pre-dated the Bolshevik Revolution of 1917. At different times, different European states had been forced to take account of Russian expansionism (Document 12.3, p. 266). Britain, for example, had fought the Crimean War (1853–6) as part of her century-long policy of trying to keep Russia from gaining access to the Mediterranean. She had also feared Russian expansionism to the South East, and Britain's involvement in the tortured history of Afghanistan (Document 13.4, p. 287) was another prong of her anti-Russian policy. Austria and Germany, for their part, had feared Russian expansion into the Slav-occupied regions of south eastern Europe, an expansion which Russian diplomats summed up as Pan-Slavism. The Western powers had, at the end of the nineteenth century, come to fear Russian expansion into the Far East. It is worth noting that Britain's first permanent alliance since 1815 was the one signed with Japan (1902) which was seen as offering a Western-supported opposition to Russian ambitions in China.

We have seen that the United States had played little part in international affairs before 1917. Her diplomats and politicians had little, if any, concept of the continuity of Russian history (Document 13.3) or of Western opposition to Tsarist Russia. It is not surprising that the history-conscious de Gaulle should refer to Stalin as 'a latter-day Tsar'; de Gaulle understood the continuum in Russian history – internal as well as external. Few Americans could have appreciated that notion. This lack of what we may call 'background' helps to explain what some see as American naivety when considering American relations with Stalin at the wartime conferences. It also helps to explain why, when America became convinced that Russia had to be opposed, her politicians and diplomats tended to see the confrontation between East and West in ideological terms; they saw Communism as the enemy, an enemy which had come into being only with the Bolshevik Revolution of 1917. This view of post-war Russia is illustrated by Truman's message to Congress in which he outlined what has become known as the 'Truman Doctrine' (Document 4.2, p. 77).

More recently, some academic historians have re-examined the history of the relations between Russia and the West in the immediate post-war years, the period of the Cold War. In this re-examination, the 'revisionists' have drawn attention to the continuity in Russian policy (Document 12.3); they have challenged the view of the 'orthodox' historians who saw the Cold War in purely ideological terms; they have argued that the confrontation between East and West, between Russia and the United States, owed little, if anything to a clash of ideologies but was the latter-day manifestation of a long-standing hostility, with the United States playing the anti-Russian role which had once been played by Britain, France, Germany or Austria.

'Revisionists' and 'orthodox' alike have to consider the same historical events; they differ in their interpretations of some, if not all, of the evidence. There is no room in an introductory study such as this for a detailed consideration of the debate; the narrative will, it is hoped, provide the background against which the debate may be the better understood. The reading lists, and in particular those in Chapters 3–6, contain examples of work by historians of both schools for readers who wish to pursue a study of the debate.

Suspicion and reaction

'The imperialist camp having as its basic aim the establishment of the world domination of American imperialism and the smashing of democracy, and the anti-imperialist camp having as its basic aim the undermining of imperialism, the consolidation of democracy and the eradication of the remnants of fascism.'
From a statement issued by the newly-created Cominform, 23 September 1947

The mutual suspicion between the Soviet Union and the West was long-standing and deep rooted (Chapter 3); Stalin's policies in eastern Europe after 1945 served only to deepen western suspicions. The Soviet government asserted its control of the domestic affairs of every satellite country. Soviet diplomatic missions in these countries ensured a Soviet-orientated foreign policy. If any local politician stepped aside from the prescribed line, action was taken to bring him back to 'right thinking' or to get rid of him; Tito's rejection of Stalin's demands led to his subsequent dismissal from the Cominform (p. 49).

Bevin, who had hoped that 'Left will talk to Left', was angered by Russian intransigence during the Foreign Ministers' Conference in the winter of 1946–7. Truman and Byrnes, the US Secretary of State, did not share his concern at that time. Neither they nor Bevin welcomed Churchill's 'Iron Curtain' speech in March 1946 (Document 4.1, p. 77). In spite of the evidence, few Americans wanted to believe that Russia was not, still, that 'gallant ally' ruled by a smiling 'Uncle Joe'. They did not believe, yet, that the Russians were out for conquest of most of Europe at least (Fig. 4.1). Harry Hopkins was Roosevelt's most trusted adviser. It was Hopkins who had gone to Russia shortly after Hitler's forces had invaded that country. He had met Stalin and, on his return, had advised Roosevelt that the Lend-Lease aid should be extended to Russia. During the war, Hopkins had worked closely with Roosevelt, had met Stalin and his advisers on several occasions and had become convinced that, in the post-war world, Russia and the USA would be able to work closely together. 'We really believed in our hearts that this was the dawn of the new day. The Russians had proved that they could be reasonable and far-seeing and there wasn't any doubt in the minds of the President or any of us that we could live with them and get along with them peacefully for as far into the future as any of us could imagine.'[1] Hopkins died in January 1946 when it was still just possible to hold on to this 'impossible dream'.

It was not one single occurrence that caused the Americans to change attitudes and policies. Rather it was a series of events and non-events. Among the non-events, for example, was the failure of Allied discussions about the future of Germany (p. 64ff.). Among early events was Soviet policy in northern Iran where Soviet troops were temporarily stationed under the terms of the Anglo-Iranian-Soviet Treaty of 1942. In 1946 the Russians began to annex the Iranian province of Azerbaijan. The Iranian government appealed to the Security Council of the UN so that the issue received world-wide publicity. The Russians gave way, withdrew their troops and the UN had scored its first political success.

It was, perhaps, the Greek Civil War which provided the second and more important marker of the development of the Cold War. In August 1936, King George II of Greece had accepted the establishment of a right wing dictatorship under General Metaxas, which was in power when Greece was invaded by the Italians in October 1940. The Greeks threw the Italians back into Albania but were conquered by the Germans who invaded Greece in April 1941. Rival resistance groups maintained a guerrilla war against the occupying forces from 1942 until the British liberated Greece in October 1944. The communist-dominated National Liberation Front (EAM) with its guerrilla army, the National People's Army of Liberation (ELAS) wanted a communist revolution similar to Tito's in Yugoslavia; they opposed the return of the royalists, brought back by the British in 1944. There was civil strife between the two guerrilla forces in the winter of 1944–5, in spite of the efforts of Archbishop Damaskinos and the British ministers to arrange a peaceful settlement. On 12 February 1945 the royalists and ELAS signed the 'Truce of Varkiza' which left two-thirds of the country under the control of the communist-controlled EAM.

During this period Stalin had honoured the agreement he had made with Churchill (pp. 22–3) according to which Greece was part of the

British sphere of influence; the communists received no help from Russia. This Russian 'neutrality' ended when the second stage of the civil war broke out. In October 1946, the former leader of ELAS, Markos Vafiades, set up a Democratic Army of Greece and called on villagers for support. Aid poured in from Yugoslavia, Albania and Bulgaria while the Greek royalist army had the support of some 60,000 British troops.

In February 1947, Britain's economic weakness led to the decision to cut overseas involvements. In February 1947 she handed the responsibility for the Palestine Mandate to the UN; Britain could no longer afford to act as policeman in a country torn by civil war. In February 1947, too, Britain declared that she would have to withdraw her forces from Greece. It seemed as if the road was open to a communist take-over of yet another eastern European state.

At the same time there was the threat to Turkey. As early as March 1946 Stalin had made clear his intention to gain control, if possible, of the Dardanelles, the Straits over which Tsarist Russia had wanted to gain control and over which Britain had fought Russia in the nineteenth century (Fig. 2.1, p. 24). Stalin told Bedell Smith, the US Ambassador: 'Turkey is weak and the Soviet Union is very conscious of the danger of foreign control of the Straits which Turkey is not strong enough to protect. The Turkish government is unfriendly to us. That is why the Soviet government has demanded a base in the Dardanelles. It is a matter of our own security.'[2] Britain's withdrawal from Greece was an indication that she would be unable to maintain her traditional opposition to Russian ambitions to control the Dardanelles. Stalin would then be free to achieve Russia's 'historic mission' to control the Straits – and, in time, Turkey. In that event, Russia would have taken another step along the road to expansion and world domination.

Britain's withdrawal left a power vacuum in the eastern Mediterranean. Dean Acheson was Under-Secretary of State in 1947. He had advised Truman that the US had to play a more active role in world affairs. He was with Truman when he met the leaders of Congress in March 1947:

'When we convened the next morning in the White House to open the subject with our congressional masters, I knew we were met at Armageddon. This was my crisis. For a week I had nurtured it. These congressmen had no conception of what challenged them; it was my task to bring it home. Both my superiors, equally perturbed, gave me the floor. Never have I spoken under a more pressing sense that the issue was up to me alone. No time was left for measured appraisal. In the past eighteen months, I said, Soviet pressure on the Straits, on Iran and on northern Greece had brought the Balkans to a point where a highly possible Soviet breakthrough might open three continents to Soviet penetration. Like apples in a barrel infected by one rotten one, the corruption of Greece would infect Iran and all to the East. It would also carry infection to Africa through Asia Minor and Egypt, and to Europe through Italy and France. . . . The Soviet Union was playing one of the greatest gambles in history at minimal cost. We and we alone were in a position to break up the play.'[3]

On 12 March Truman sent a message which incorporated what became known as 'the Truman Doctrine': 'I believe it must be the policy of the United States to support free peoples who are resisting subjugation by armed minorities or by outside pressures. I believe that we must assist free peoples to work out their own destinies in their own ways.' (Document 4.2, p. 77).

Congress agreed to give economic and military aid to Greece and Turkey. This US decision to 'contain' communism marked the beginning of the handing over, by Britain, to the USA of the responsibility for keeping order in most parts of the world. Pax Britannica was to be replaced by Pax Americana. Since the Cominform was bent on expanding Russian influence, the two major powers could not avoid confrontation.

The division widens, 1947–8

'It would be neither fitting nor efficacious for this government to draw up unilaterally a program designed to place Europe on its feet economically. The roles of this country should consist of friendly aid in the drafting of a European program and of later support of such a program. The program should be a joint one, agreed by a number, if not all, of European nations.'

George C. Marshall, 1947[4]

The Soviet Union had welcomed the assistance provided to war-torn Europe by UNRRA (p. 45), financed largely by the USA which voted 3 billion dollars in aid as well as another 5 billion dollars by way of loans and economic aid to devastated areas. Russia viewed otherwise the military and economic aid to Turkey and Greece. Her suspicions were to be further increased by the Marshall Plan.

The money voted for UNRRA was running out in 1946–7 when it was clear that, in 1947, Europe had made only limited progress towards recovery. Indeed, the harsh winter of 1946–7 had served to illustrate the precarious nature of that recovery (p. 138). If there were to be no further aid, if Europe were to be left to its own devices, recovery would be a very long term affair. In the meantime, there would be the danger of social unrest by people unwilling to suffer continued deprivation; there would be, as it were, an economic and social vacuum in western Europe. Many American politicians and diplomats believed that the expansionist Russians might well decide to march westwards to fill the vacuum. George Kennan (see Document 4.6a, p. 80) was in a minority which did not accept the notion of Russian expansionism; the majority of influential Americans feared 'a spread of Soviet influence' (Document 4.6a) into a western Europe which would be in no position to defend itself.

In a speech to a graduating class at Harvard University on 5 June 1947, the US Secretary of State, George Marshall, drew US attention to Europe's condition and emphasised that the USA was willing to provide the aid that was needed to hasten European recovery. Marshall offered that aid to all the countries in Europe, provided that they could co-operate in the production of a plan for recovery. Bevin and the Foreign Ministers of Russia and France met in Paris where Molotov announced that Russia would play no part in such an operation. He claimed that the conditions on which the US offered the aid called for some form of all-European co-operation. This, he argued, offended against the principle of national sovereignty. And having refused Marshall Aid for herself, Russia refused to allow the states of eastern Europe to participate in the Plan (p. 48). This refusal, and the implementation of the Plan in western Europe, symbolised the divisions between east and west. Indeed, many historians regard this Soviet rejection of Marshall Aid as a crucial point in the evolution of the Cold War.

Bevin took the initiative following Marshall's speech. This is not surprising in view of the leading position occupied by Britain at this time and in the light of Britain's economic position (p. 164). Bevin's advisers appreciated that Britain's economic progress would be hindered by the shortage of dollars needed to buy the capital equipment, raw materials and food which were so badly needed. British exports would not be able to expand quickly enough or in sufficient volume to fill the so-called 'dollar gap'. Bevin saw Marshall's offer as a means of overcoming this shortage of dollars. He was also aware of the multilateral nature of British foreign trade; an improvement in the economic position of other countries in Europe (through the application of the help offered by Marshall) would further help Britain's economic recovery, since these other countries would provide better markets for British goods. Bevin's efforts in this regard were based on consideration for British interests. It must also be noted that the altruism of the Marshall Plan has been allowed, by some historians, to mask the fact that the economic development of Europe served American business interests. A run-down Europe, short of essential dollars and incapable of generating dollar-earning exports, would have provided a poor market for American goods. If American businessmen and industrialists failed to sell their goods in Europe, then the US economy would suffer, and the much-feared economic recession would take place, with large-scale unemployment on the pre-war scale becoming as much a feature of the US scene as of Europe's. The regeneration of the European economy played a part in ensuring the continued expansion of the US economy.

So, Bevin took the initiative following Marshall's speech. In July 1947 the representatives of 16 non-communist countries met in Paris. Spain was not invited to send a delegation; she was still considered to be 'fascist' (p. 80). Finland did not send a representative because she feared Russian anger. By September 1947 the Conference had provided details of Europe's much-needed imports. In April 1948 the US Congress allocated 5.3 billion dollars to implement the Plan. The 16

European countries set up the Organisation for European Economic Co-operation (OEEC) to ensure a 'sound European economy through the economic co-operation of its members'.

The Marshall Plan enabled Europe to import essential supplies paid for by each country in its own currency, which was then spent on reconstruction schemes planned by the OEEC or used to balance the internal budgets. Raw materials, fuel and badly-needed capital equipment arrived; there were developments in transport, agriculture and industry. When the Plan was wound up in 1951, some 13 billion dollars had been spent. For Britain, as for other countries, it ensured economic development and a standard of living that would have been unattainable without this US generosity (Document 4.3, p. 78).

The Russians saw it otherwise. In September 1947 Zhdanov, Stalin's henchman in the ideological struggle, announced that the Truman Doctrine and the Marshall Plan were 'twin forks' of US imperialist policy. Russia was implacably opposed to US ambitions. To that end she had mobilised the support of all the states of eastern Europe as well as the support of the 'freedom loving sections' of the peoples of Viet Nam, India, Egypt, Syria, Malaya, Indonesia and western Europe.

Cominform (the Communist Information Bureau) was founded in October 1947 after a conference at Warsaw of communist leaders from Russia, France, Italy, Bulgaria, Czechoslovakia, Hungary, Poland, Rumania and Yugoslavia. Its headquarters were to be in the Yugoslav capital, Belgrade (p. 49). Cominform was to co-ordinate party activities throughout Europe – under Zhdanov's leadership. In a major speech, he declared: 'A special task devolves on the fraternal Communist parties of France, Italy, Great Britain and other countries. If, in their struggle against the attempts to economically and politically enthrall their countries, they are able to take the lead of all the forces prepared to uphold the national honour and independence, no plans for the enslavement of Europe can possibly succeed.'[5] In November 1947 the French and Italian Communist Parties organised major strikes, aimed at bringing down the weak coalition governments in their respective countries. The strikes failed; political support for communism waned in both countries. On the other hand, the Greek communists were already in open revolt (p. 59) and in February 1948 the Czech communists overthrew the coalition government (p. 49). The language of the Cominform, the denunciations of capitalism and imperialism and the call to 'fraternal parties' to subordinate the interests of their countries to those of the world-wide movement, frightened western leaders such as Bevin, and, more significantly, Truman and Marshall (Document 4.4, p. 78).

At its first meeting the Cominform was called on to expel the 'heretic' Tito. But the construction of Russian-controlled organisations went on. In January 1949, Comecon (the Council for Mutual Economic Assistance) was set up in Moscow. Its aim was the improvement in trade between the Soviet Union and the other eastern European states. It was a Russian answer to the OEEC and the Marshall Plan. Its original members were Albania, Bulgaria, Czechoslovakia, Hungary, Poland, Rumania and Russia. East Germany joined in 1950, Mongolia in 1962 and Cuba in 1972.

Cominform and Comecon were fresh outward signs of the Russification of eastern Europe. American reaction to this Soviet expansionism was reflected in the Truman Doctrine and Marshall Plan. These major changes in US policy were voted through Congress because, there too, there had been a major change in attitudes and opinion. Before 1939, the Republican, Arthur Vandenberg, had been a leading member of the isolationist movement, and, in the Senate, an opponent of US involvement overseas. It was a sign of the times that, on 11 June 1948, he proposed in the US Senate a resolution which called for support of the UN, condemned Russia's excessive use of the veto in the Security Council and called on the US government to ensure the maintenance of peace 'by making clear its determination to exercise the right of individual and collective self-defence under Article 51 of the UN Charter should any armed attack occur affecting US national security.' Vandenberg and his fellow isolationists in Congress had been converted by Russian policies (Document 4.6b, p. 80). Their conversion was a reflection of a change in US public opinion, influenced by the activities of the Un-American Activities Committee which, under the guidance of hard-liners such as the young congressman, Richard Nixon, attacked anyone suspected of having communist sympathies. The first, well-publicised but inconclusive 'trial' of Alger Hiss before the Committee began in August 1948; after a second trial Hiss was sentenced in 1950 to five years' imprisonment for having perjured himself. In 1949, while the Hiss affair seemed to dominate the US political scene, the Soviet Union exploded its atomic bomb. The west no longer had a nuclear monopoly; a nuclear Soviet Union was, obviously, even more to be feared than one which was merely conventionally armed.

In February 1950 the junior senator from Wisconsin, Joseph McCarthy, took advantage of the near-hysteria which followed the second Hiss trial. He alleged that he had the names of 57 card carrying communists in the State Department and the names of another 205 people employed in that Department who were known communist sympathisers. McCarthy never produced any evidence to support his allegations; he changed the numbers from day to day; but by means of smears, half-truths and leading questions, he succeeded in discrediting prominent statesmen such as Marshall and Acheson and helped ensure a Republican victory in the 1952 elections. The Cold War had produced a hysteria in the USA in which McCarthyism flourished.

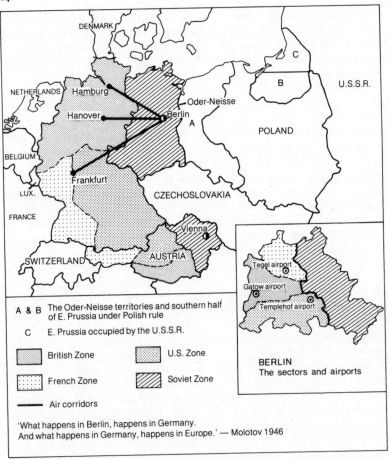

4.1 Divided Germany and divided Berlin. Molotov's quote indicates the importance which Russia, at least, attached to this region and provides a major reason for the Allied determination to maintain links with their zones in West Berlin.

The German problem, 1945–50 (Fig. 4.1)

'We shall do everything in our power to secure the maximum possible unification. Germany is a part of Europe, and recovery in Europe will be slow indeed if Germany with her great resources of coal and iron is turned into a poor house.'
Secretary of State James Byrnes at Stuttgart, 6 September 1946

Allied leaders had agreed at Yalta on the treatment of post-war Germany. But, in this as in much else, the Yalta agreement was not honoured. The conquerors could not agree on a common policy;

France and Russia adopted harsher measures in their zones of occupation than the British and Americans in theirs. And while the victors argued, the Germans suffered (Document 1.2, p. 19). By September 1946, when Byrnes was speaking at Stuttgart, some fourteen million penniless, ragged exiles had arrived in West Germany from communist-occupied Germany and from those areas of prewar Germany now occupied by the Polish resettlement. The British zone had been an industrialised and food-deficiency area before 1939. It had now to send part of its current output and capital equipment to France and Russia as reparations, but it received no reciprocal food imports from the agricultural area in the Russian zone.

One effect of this lack of common policy, of lack of Allied co-operation, was that in 1946 the British had to spend £80 million from their scarce dollar reserves on such food (p. 138). It was clear that the British could no more afford to act as 'occupiers' in Germany than they could in Greece and Palestine. It was also clear to the US commander, General Clay, that the Russians had no intention of co-operating to help govern Germany as one unit. In May 1946 he suspended reparations, deliveries from the US zone. A week later, in June 1946, the US suggested that the economies of the other zones should be integrated with that of the US zone. Russia and France rejected this proposal; only Britain agreed to accept the invitation and, after lengthy negotiations, a new economic unit known as 'Bizonia' came into being. This proved to be the starting point for the economic and political development of the future West Germany. The Council of States of the US zone was enlarged to take in the four States of the British zone. German joint executive committees were set up, each committee having one representative from each State and all these representatives being heads of State ministries.

In July 1946 the US authorities drew up a Plan for the economic reconstruction of Germany, hoping that an economically sound Germany would be self-sufficient and no longer a drain on the resources of the western Allies. Russia and France refused to discuss any such progressive plan. In the unusually harsh winter of 1946–7, conditions in Germany worsened as the inadequate transport system proved incapable of distributing the already scarce food and fuel. By the time Marshall announced US willingness to aid European recovery (5 June 1947) it had become clear that there could not be any European recovery without German participation in that process. All four Allies had been forced to accept the need to allow Germans to participate in the political life of occupied Germany (see below). The British and Americans argued that there had to be economic progress in parallel with this political development. Stalin, on the other hand, suspected that the Anglo-Americans wanted the re-emergence of German military power.

In the face of Russian refusal to co-operate, the British and Americans went ahead with their own plans. Marshall Aid would be siphoned into their zones of Germany when the Plan was finally adopted. But nothing could be done until there had been currency reform. Largely because the Soviet authorities allowed the indiscriminate printing of German banknotes, there was a raging inflation throughout all four zones of occupation. Few people were prepared to offer goods for sale in exchange for an increasingly worthless money. On 20 June 1948 the western Allies introduced the new Deutschmark into Bizonia. Ten old Reichmarks had to be handed over for one new Deutschmark. Each German adult was given first 40 and then, two weeks later, another 20 new marks. Cash suddenly became scarce; to try to get hold of some farmers and producers brought goods to market; within a few days shop windows were full.

The western powers had hoped that the Russians would allow a single currency (their Deutschmark) for the whole of Germany. On 22 June the Russians announced their own currency reform and declared that only the Russian-printed money would be acceptable in Berlin, including the three Allied zones. The western Allies announced that they would accept the East mark in the western zones, but only alongside their own Deutschmark. They insisted that the new Deutschmark had to be allowed inside their zones of occupied Berlin.

This, as we shall see, led to the blockade of Berlin between June 1948 and May 1949. But while Berlin endured that period of blockade, there was the start of an economic miracle in western Germany. By the end of July 1949 production rose by 25 per cent. Currency reform and Marshall Aid created the conditions in which the Germans could recover. Professor Erhard was appointed to direct the economic affairs of the three western zones in 1948. New industrial plants with the most modern machinery and methods were built. By 1950 production was back to the level of 1939; Germany was again the leading producer of steel, electrical goods and chemicals.

The Berlin blockade, June 1948–May 1949 (Fig. 4.1)

'We had made the Americans face up to the facts in the Eastern Mediterranean. As a result we got the Truman Doctrine. But it wasn't until the Berlin airlift that American public opinion really wakened up to the facts of life. Their own troops were involved in that. Before that, there'd been a lot of wishful thinking. I don't think they really appreciated communist tactics until Berlin.'[6]

Lord Attlee

Russian anger and suspicion of the intentions of the western powers had grown between 1946 and 1948. Zhdanov thought of the Truman Doctrine and the Marshall Plan as 'twin forks' of anti-Russian imperialism. While Bevin was organising the discussions which would lead to the formation of the OEEC, he was also playing a part in the London Conference of March 1948 which led to the western powers' decision to allow the West Germans to draft a constitution (p. 189). For the Russians, the currency reform was, at it were, the final straw.

On 1 April 1948, before the currency reform, the Russians had announced travel restrictions between their zone and West Germany. They saw a born-again West Germany as a capitalist threat to the east, West Berlin as 'a capitalist thorn in the communist body politic'. Through West Berlin a flood of refugees were flowing from east to west, enriching the one and impoverishing the other. The restriction on travel would, the Russians hoped, stem, if not halt, that flood.

Berlin is 175 km inside the Russian zone. The western Allies had access to the 2.4 million Berliners in their zones – by road, railway, canal and air. In reaction to the currency reform, the Russians announced an extension of restrictions. On 24 June 1949, Stalin published an order blockading all the land routes from the west to Berlin. He was sure that the western powers would have to leave their zones once the 2.4 million inhabitants ran short of food and coal. The Russians had their own bitter experience of blockaded cities; they had undergone the blockade of Leningrad when three million people had been cut off by German troops in the south and Finnish troops in the north. By the time that siege ended in 1944 over a million had died – 632,000 of them from starvation (p. 108). The Russians had also seen the Germans fail to relieve their beleaguered troops at Stalingrad, a failure marked by the death of 147,000 people and the capture of another 91,000 survivors. The Russians assumed, in 1948, that the western powers would be unable to supply their zones of Berlin and that they would be unwilling to force the Berliners to endure the sort of suffering inflicted on the people of Leningrad. They would cede their zones to the Russians.

General Clay's first reaction was to 'shoot his way' through the blockade. Fortunately, wiser counsels prevailed. Instead the western allies organised a massive airlift (Document 4.5, p. 79) which the Russians allowed to operate; they did not wish to risk a war either.

The scale of the airlift amazed everyone; the West Berliners needed a minimum of 4,000 tons of goods to be delivered every day, including huge quantities of coal for domestic heating and for the generation of electrical power. By the time the blockade ended in May 1949, 15,000 tons were being delivered daily. There had been, by then, 277,728 flights in which 2.3 million tons of goods were delivered, including 900,000 tons of coal. During this period of blockade, the people of West Berlin, only recently part of the 'German nation' which had supported Hitler, were portrayed as 'freedom fighters' on the side of the democratic west. The fact that there was no 'betrayal' of Berlin was important for the rest of Europe. If the Russians had succeeded in driving the western powers from Europe, they might then have been encouraged, Rakosi-wise, to adopt the 'salami technique' to gain control of sections of western Germany 'slice by slice'.

Stalin called off the blockade in May 1949. In the Four-Power New

York Agreement of 4 May 1949, the Russians agreed to lift the restrictions, while the western powers agreed to lift the restrictions they had imposed on communications between their zones and East Germany. This agreement was ratified at a Four-Power conference in Paris in June 1949. For the Russians, the blockade had been a failure. For the western powers, it had been a unifying period during which the bond between the western powers and the West Germans grew stronger. In the face of the threat to West Berlin, the western powers were forced to re-think their European strategy. As Attlee claimed, it was Berlin which most surely forced the US to come to terms with the reality of the Russian threat. One result of this re-thinking was the formation of NATO. Another was a realisation that West Germany had to be allowed to play a major role in the political, economic and military life of Western Europe.

NATO – cause and effect of the Cold War

'There is a valid long-term justification for a formalisation of the national defence relationship among the countries of the North Atlantic community (but) the conclusion of such a pact is not the main answer to the present Soviet effort to dominate the European continent and will not appreciably modify the nature or the danger of Soviet policies.'[7]

George Kennan, December 1948

The first post-war treaty of alliance was signed at Dunkirk on 4 March 1947. In the Dunkirk Treaty, Britain and France agreed to take joint action in the event of German aggression; Germany, and not Russia, was still seen as the major threat to European peace. That Treaty also pledged the two governments to hold constant consultation over economic matters of joint concern. That pledge was an acknowledgement of the need for closer economic co-operation than had been the norm before 1939.

On 1 January 1948, a new customs union became effective; Belgium, the Netherlands and Luxemburg ('Benelux') agreed on closer economic collaboration. On 17 March 1948, the Benelux countries and the Dunkirk Treaty partners signed the Treaty of Brussels, promising to give each other 'all military and other aid and assistance' if any of the five nations should suffer an attack in Europe. The Treaty also provided for quarterly conferences of the Foreign Ministers and set up a Permanent Committee and several economic and social sub-committees to promote the idea of a Western European Union. In Chapter 11 we will see that this Treaty marked a stage along the road to European integration. Here we should note that the Treaty and the formation of Benelux illustrate that there was, in post-war Europe, a realisation that military alliances ought to be linked to economic collaboration. The states of western Europe were as aware as Kennan was that the struggle for Europe, launched by the Soviet Union, would require more than mere military power and alliances.

British participation in such alliances marked a major shift in British foreign policy. Bevin's critics in Britain wanted him to put more trust in the UNO rather than in anti-Soviet blocs. Others, blinded less by idealism than by prejudice, argued that Russia was not a threat to Europe. However, the majority of people in Britain, of whatever political persuasion, supported Bevin's policy. So, too, did an increasing number of Americans, in the wake of the coup in Czechoslovakia and the Berlin blockade. The Vandenberg resolution which was passed by the UN Senate on 11 June 1948 called for the provision of aid in suitable cases to those countries which had entered into defence treaties (p. 63). The result was the signing of the North Atlantic Treaty on 4 April 1949, a month before Stalin called off the Berlin blockade (Document 4.6b, p. 80).

This Treaty was based on Article 51 of the UN Charter which permits the use of force in individual and collective self-defence against armed attack. The USA, Canada, Denmark, Iceland, Italy, Norway and Portugal joined the five countries of the Brussels Treaty in this new Treaty (Fig. 10.1, p. 217). It was, clearly, a military alliance – the members agreeing to regard an attack on any one of them in Europe or North America as an attack against all. In such an event the partners agreed to assist each other 'by taking forthwith such action as it deems necessary including the use of armed force, to restore and maintain the security of the North Atlantic area.' But NATO was meant to be something more than a merely defensive alliance. The members of the Organisation agreed 'to eliminate conflict in their international economic policies and to encourage economic collaboration', European-minded 'idealists' hoped that NATO would be the basis for a closely-integrated Atlantic Community. Their hopes were to be dashed; NATO remained, primarily, a military alliance.

NATO was at one level a sign of US determination to regard European defence as a matter of prime concern. At another level, it marked a major new militarisation of the Cold War confrontation. The now-dead Zhdanov might have seen it as a third prong to that 'fork' (p. 66). And although it did not become the basis for an Atlantic Community, it did have a close political structure and its members agreed that a large part of their national forces would serve in its international commands. National sovereignty, it seemed, was no longer as sacred a cow as in more isolationist days. By 1950, NATO had fourteen divisions and 1,000 aircraft as a 'shield' facing the 175 communist divisions and 20,000 communist aircraft, while behind the 'shield' was the 'sword' in the shape of the US-controlled atomic weapon. In subsequent chapters we will examine the shortcomings of the Organisation and the growth of suspicion, particularly in France, that the USA might not be willing to commit itself fully to the defence of Europe. We will also see how quarrels among the partners (such as Greece and Turkey over Cyprus) weakened the Alliance which, however, remains the main defence of western Europe.

Political development in the two Germanies, 1945–50

'We must have the courage to proceed with the government of West Germany quickly if the Council of Foreign Ministers fails to produce an answer for all Germany. I doubt very much if this action would imperil the quadripartite machinery. We cannot continue successfully unless we establish a governmental machinery for West Germany. The resentment of the Germans against colonial administration is increasing daily. Two and a half years without a government is much too long.'[8]

General Lucius Clay, US Commander in Chief, 3 November 1947

At Yalta, the Allied leaders had agreed that the various Commanders in Chief would form a Control Commission in a 'temporary arrangement' until a central, democratic government could be organised for the whole of Germany. The failure to achieve such a desirable objective has to be seen as one of the products of the Cold War, while the disputes over this question of German government and possible unification were among the factors which ensured that that War continued.

In accordance with their Yalta Agreement, the four occupying powers helped to develop political institutions at the local level. In the summer of 1945, almost before the dust of war had settled, the administration of Germany was built around the Länder. Some of these were based on old German states – Bavaria, Hamburg and Hesse in the west, Mecklenburg, Saxony and Thuringia in the east. In all, there were 11 Länder in the west and 5 in the smaller eastern zone.

The governments of the various Länder passed a number of reforms, reflecting in each case the political complexion of the occupying power. Thus, in the east, land was taken from the large landowners, the Junkers, and redistributed among the peasants, and private banks were confiscated and re-organised as Länder and provincial banks. On the other hand, in the western zones nationalisation schemes proposed by the Länder of Hesse, North-Rhine, Westphalia, Bavaria and Schleswig-Holstein were set aside by the western powers.

The activities of the Länder governments marked the return of Germany to political activity. Such activity required the emergence of political structures and the growth of organised political parties. It was the Russians who first allowed the formation of such parties in June and July 1945 and who permitted the formation of four parties. The *Christian Democratic Union* (CDU) was a widely based party, supported by Catholics and Protestants who favoured a religious basis to political action. It gained support from capitalists and liberals who believed in the free market economy as well as from trade unionists and others who wanted social reform and an extension of government activity. The *Liberal Democratic Party*, later to be re-named as the *Free Democratic Party* (FDP) was the successor to the pre-Hitler Liberal Party. Its members and supporters were suspicious of the influence of the churches in politics while they also favoured a more liberal economic policy than did the CDU. *The Social Democratic Party* (SPD) was the oldest of Germany's political parties, having been formed in Bismarck's time. It was Marxist in its philosophy, although it was essentially and for practical purposes unrevolutionary and 'gradualist' in its policies. In 1945 it called for an anti-fascist, democratic régime which would nationalise banks, insurance companies, mines and other industries. In many respects, this programme was similar to that put forward by the moderate British Labour Party during the election campaign of 1945. The *German Communist Party* (KPD) had been banned from Hitler's Germany. Many of its pre-leaders had fled to Russia and returned to Germany with the Red Army. Thirteen of the sixteen who signed the Party's manifesto in 1945 were 'Muscovites'.

Similar political parties were founded elsewhere in occupied Germany, but because of the absence of communications, there was little, if any, link between the scattered groups. Thus, in Bavaria, the Catholic-Protestant alliance became known as the *Christian Socialist Union* (CSU) while the anti-denominational Liberals were known as the *Free Democrats*. The first sign of zonal-wide politics took place in the British zone where, in February 1946, Dr Adenauer, a former Mayor of Cologne, was elected Chairman of the CDU in that zone.

Because of the communication problem, different groups of Social Democrats developed opposing attitudes towards the Communist Party. Under Grotewohl in Berlin, they called for close co-operation with the Communists; under Schumacher in the US zone at Hanover, they called for freedom of action and an independent party. The Communist Party in Berlin wanted to have an alliance with the Social Democrats until it had time to develop and grow as powerful as the SPD. The weak position of the Communists was revealed by the first post-war elections in Austria (November 1945), when they were badly beaten by the SPD. Under pressure from the Russians the Communists called for a *Socialist Unity Party* which would replace both existing working class parties.

Grotewohl and other leaders of the SPD advocated this fusion; Schumacher, with the help of the western allies, advocated a rejection of such a proposal. A referendum on the proposal was held in the western zones of Berlin when the majority voted against fusion but for close co-operation. Grotewohl then called a meeting to discuss the now-defeated proposal. Most of the delegates were drawn from the eastern zone of Berlin. This conference voted for fusion, and the Socialist Unity Party was formed in April 1946. It existed only in the eastern zone of Berlin and in the Soviet zone of Germany. Elsewhere in Germany, the SPD and KPD continued their separate existence.

In October 1946 there were elections for the Berlin City Council, held in all four zones of the city. The SPD gained 48.7 per cent of the vote against the Socialist Unity Party's 19.8 per cent, the CDU's 22.1

per cent and the Liberals' 9.4 per cent. By then, Schumacher had organised the first party conference of the West German Social Democrats, indicating that the working class were, politically, as divided as they had been in Germany in the 1920s.

Slowly, organs of government were established throughout occupied Germany. In May 1947, an Economic Council was created for the two zones making up Bizonia. Its members were elected by the regional parliaments. Its function was to propose and, if approved by the Anglo-American 'rulers', to implement regulations on economic matters. In 1948, the Anglo-Americans allowed the formation of a Council of States whose members were the Prime Ministers of the Länder together with their chief ministers. The Economic Council took on the role of a Lower House of a parliamentary system with the Council of State playing the role of an Upper House. In May 1947, the two allies allowed the formation of an Administrative Council – which was, in essence, the Cabinet of a parliamentary system. In February 1948, a German High Court was set up, so that, in the west, the Germans had all the organs thought essential to a democratic parliamentary system.

In the Soviet zone there were similar developments. In 1946, there were fifteen central administrative bodies which did the work usually done by the ministries in a modern state; by 1947, the Russians allowed these a good deal of independence. After the Anglo-Americans had formed Bizonia, the Russians set up a Permanent Economic Commission in their zone; two-thirds of its members were appointed by the Russian occupying authority, the rest were elected by trade unions and farmers' organisations. This Commission took over most of the work of the fifteen existing bodies.

In February 1948, Britain, France and the USA and the three nations of Benelux held a conference in London. The western powers were determined, in spite of Russian hostility – indeed, perhaps because of Russian unwillingness to co-operate – to create a new state from the three western zones. It was agreed that the West Germans should be allowed to draft a Constitution for this new state. The German Prime Ministers of the Länder were instructed to call a constituent assembly; they, in turn, asked the western powers to agree that the proposed new state would be only a temporary affair, pending the unification of the whole of Germany. They also proposed that the new state should not have, in the first instance, a Constitution but merely a Basic Law, until such time as Germany was re-united.

On 1 September 1948 the Parliamentary Council met. There were 27 members from the CDU-CSU, 27 from the SPD, 5 from the FDP and two each from the Centre Party, the Communists and the German Party. The FDP, which held the balance of power, wanted the Council to propose a strong centralised system of government. The SPD favoured such a system while the CDU-CSU favoured a de-centralised, federalised system, which was also supported by the influential American occupying power. As we shall see (pp. 189–90) the Constitution adopted was a federal one, approved by the Council on 8 May 1949. On 21 September 1949, West Germany came into being.

In the Soviet zone, a new constitution for a new state came into being at roughly the same time. Three German Peoples' Congresses were held between 1947 and 1949 to discuss a future German Constitution. By a variety of means the Communists gained control of these Congresses, until in May 1949 the people of East Germany were presented with a communist-approved list of candidates for elections for the third People's Congress. This Congress approved the Constitution of the state which came into being in October 1949 as the German Democratic Republic.

This division of Germany into two states was a result of the Cold War and of the mutual suspicions which prevented the creation of a united Germany. The hostility between the governments of the two Germanies after 1949 served to deepen the suspicions and increase tensions so that Germany became, for many, both the centre of and symbol of the Cold War. Other observers and politicians noted that, in spite of the deep hostility engendered by the division of Germany, this very division achieved a *de facto* balance while resolving the historic problem of an overwhelmingly powerful and populous Germany in central Europe.

West Germany – re-armament and re-unification

'I agreed with the Pentagon's strategic purpose . . . but thought their tactics murderous. Once we established the united command [of NATO] and had a planning center, the inevitable logic . . . would convince everyone that any plan without Germany was untenable. To insist on . . . the inclusion of Germany at the outset would delay and complicate the whole enterprise.'[9]

Dean Acheson, September 1950

Germany was not the only theatre in which the Cold War was played out. We have seen how Zhdanov urged the 'fraternal parties' of western Europe to help further the Russian cause (p. 62). Then there was the Russian-inspired attempt by the Greek Communists to overthrow the monarchist government (pp. 58–9), called off only in 1949 after the defection of Tito and the defeat of the Greek Communists in a major battle in August 1949.

But the Cominform was also responsible for organising action on the non-European front. There was a Communist-inspired rising in Indonesia in September 1948 (p. 62) and another similar rising in Burma which had recently gained its independence. Communist guerillas began their Malayan uprising in June 1948 which led to a war which officially did not end until 1960.

These Asian uprisings seemed, to many western observers, to follow a pattern. They took place against the background of the success of the

Chinese Communists under Mao Tse-tung whom many western observers saw, erroneously, as Stalin's puppet. The establishment of the Chinese People's Republic in 1949 increased western fears of communist expansionism – and so increased the demand for a stronger alliance, including, for example, the need for NATO to become more than a paper alliance.

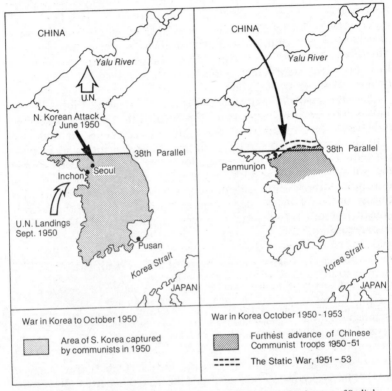

4.2 Sketch maps of the Korean War, 1950–3, which appeared to be part of Stalin's anti-western campaign, a cause of China's initial incursion into world affairs and an excuse for the anti-liberal hysteria which swept America.

The outbreak of the Korean War (Fig. 4.2) and the initial success of the North Korean army intensified the demand for the western powers to increase their military preparedness. This was what Bevin and others had been asking for since 1946; NATO was the outcome of western reaction to earlier Russian incursions (pp. 68–9). The USA had entered into its commitment to European defence before the Korean War. The success of Mao in China and the onset of the Korean War increased the commitment of the USA in the Far East. It is not surprising, then, that the USA began to take a fresh look at its NATO obligations in 1949 and 1950. At the same time, many western Europeans pointed to the comparable vulnerability (as they saw it) of West Germany to the Soviet bloc.

As West Germany recovered and became more prosperous, many American observers argued that she ought to be invited to make a contribution to the defence of the west, of which she was part. The US government argued that, in 1950, the Soviet Union enjoyed a superiority of conventional forces over the west. This imbalance might be corrected, at least in part, if West Germany was allowed to re-arm. The Truman government threatened to withdraw from NATO if Britain and France refused. Acheson, for the USA, and Bevin, for Britain, pointed out that France could hardly be expected to welcome the re-arming of Germany a mere five years after the end of the Second World War. Nor did the majority of Germans want to become part of a military complex; their memories, too, were bitter.

In October 1950, the French Prime Minister, René Pleven, proposed a scheme for a Western European Army in which officers and men of the various nationalities, including the Germans, would wear a European uniform, and serve under a European flag in a supra-national European Command (p. 227–8). Pleven hoped that this would ease French fears, create the extra strength demanded by the USA and incorporate the new West Germany more firmly into the democratic fold. In the summer of 1950 Churchill had suggested the creation of such a European army, in keeping with the spirit of the time which seemed to be leading the nations of western Europe towards various forms of integration (Chapter 11).

Churchill had become Prime Minister by the time that the Treaty establishing the European Defence Community was signed on 27 May 1952. France, West Germany, Italy, Belgium, the Netherlands and Luxemburg signed the Treaty. These were the countries which had already agreed to form the European Coal and Steel Community (April 1951) (pp. 225–6) and which were to form the European Economic Community in 1957 (pp. 228ff). It is noticeable that Britain did not sign the Treaty setting up the EDC; nor did she enter the ECSC or the EEC. In 1952, Eden, the British Foreign Minister, argued that Britain could not allow the incorporation of her forces into a European arrangement because of her worldwide commitments (pp. 227–8).

The refusal of the British to sign the Treaty led to its rejection by the French Parliament on 30 August 1954. The nationalist right-wing (with its historic fear of Germany) allied with the communist-led left-wing to kill off Pleven's proposed EDC. Dulles, Secretary of State in Eisenhower's government, threatened that the USA would have to make an 'agonising reappraisal' of its commitments to a Europe which seemed unwilling to help itself. Eden then proposed the expansion of the existing Brussels Treaty organisation (p. 68) and the creation of a

Western European Union (WEU) to include West Germany and Italy. Eden proposed that West Germany should recreate its army and place it entirely under NATO. In return for French agreement to such a West German army, Britain would commit four divisions of troops and a tactical airforce unit to the defence of Europe. In October 1954, the WEU came into being and in May 1955 West Germany became a member of NATO (pp. 227–8).

The Soviet government was frightened by the notion of German rearmament and of the emergence of a born-again militarist Germany committed (at least rhetorically) to reunification. Russia had, after all, suffered two German invasions (in 1914 and 1941) and, it is argued, was justified in fearing a third. This helps to explain why the Soviet government organised the Warsaw Defence Treaty (1955) with her seven European satellites. This Treaty was, in a sense, unnecessary since each of these states had their individual security treaties with Russia. But it did serve to point the division of Europe into the two armed camps, brought about, in this case, by the problem of a divided Germany.

Most Germans wanted to see their country re-united. The Russians on their side appeared at times to be willing to agree to reunification, provided that the larger Germany was demilitarised and belonged to no alliance. They feared that the 50 million inhabitants of West Germany would prove politically, as well as numerically, too much for the 13 million inhabitants of East Germany. A united Germany, free to enter into alliances, might then be a NATO thorn in the body politic of central eastern Europe.

The West Germans refused to accept this limitation. They feared that Russia would use the 'salami technique' against an unarmed and neutralised Germany. They also refused to accept the eastern frontiers of East Germany – that Oder-Neisse line which meant the loss of much of what had been eastern Germany.

The attitude of West Germany towards the Russians and East Germany was encapsulated in what became known as the Hallstein Doctrine, the policy propounded by the West German Foreign Minister in 1955 (p. 195). This said that West Germany would regard diplomatic recognition of East Germany as an unfriendly act, since it would be interpreted as accepting the division of the country. East Germany was not, in West German eyes, a sovereign state.

Documentary evidence

Although Churchill was no longer British Prime Minister, he was an influential and widely-accepted statesman in the post-war world. His 'Iron Curtain' speech (Document 4.1) was, in part, an admission of Allied failure at Yalta (Documents 2.1–3, pp. 36–8) and, in part, a call for a new anti-Soviet policy.

This angered both the British Foreign Secretary, Bevin, and US President Truman (p. 57). However, by the end of 1946 they had both been forced to accept the Churchillian view of post-war development. Truman's 'conversion' was marked by the issuing of the 'Truman Doctrine' (Document 4.2), which led to US participation in the defence of Greece and Turkey in particular. Marshall's offer of aid to devastated Europe (Document 4.3) was another symbol of the emergence of the USA as the leader of the western nations, more particularly when Molotov, on behalf of the Soviet Union, rejected this Aid (Document 4.3b). The Communist coup in Czechoslovakia and the Berlin Blockade (Documents 4.4–6) served to convince US politicians and statesmen that Stalin was intent on enlarging his 'empire' and that, if he was to be 'contained', the USA would have to become ever more involved in European affairs.

Document 4.1

The 'Iron Curtain'

'A shadow has fallen upon the scenes so lately lighted by the Allied victory. Nobody knows what Soviet Russia and its Communist international organisation intends to do in the immediate future. . . . From Stettin on the Baltic to Trieste in the Adriatic, an iron curtain has descended across the Continent. Behind that line lie all the capitals of the ancient states of Central and Eastern Europe . . . Warsaw, Berlin, Prague, Vienna, Budapest, Belgrade, Bucharest and Sofia, all these famous cities and the populations around them lie in what I must call the Soviet sphere, and are all subject in one form or another, not only to Soviet influence but to a very high and, in many cases, increasing measure of control from Moscow. Athens alone – Greece with its immortal glories – is free to decide its future at an election under British, American and French observation. . . . The Communist parties, which were very small in all these Eastern States of Europe, have been raised to pre-eminence and power far beyond their numbers and are seeking everywhere to obtain totalitarian control. Police governments are prevailing in nearly every case, and so far, except in Czechoslovakia there is no true democracy. . . .'

(W. S. Churchill at Fulton, Missouri March 1946)

Document 4.2

The Truman Doctrine

'One of the primary objectives of the foreign policy of the United States is the creation of conditions in which we and other nations will be able to work out a way of life free from coercion. . . . We shall not realise our objectives, however, unless we are willing to help free peoples to maintain their free institutions and their national integrity against aggressive movements that seek to impose on them totalitarian régimes. . . . At the present moment in world history nearly every nation must choose between alternative ways of life. One way of life is based upon the will of the majority and is distinguished by free institutions, representative government, free elections, guarantees of individual liberty, freedom of speech and religion, and freedom from political oppression. The second way of life is based upon the will of the minority forcibly imposed upon the majority. It relies upon terror and oppression, a controlled press and radio, fixed elections, and the suppression of personal freedoms. I believe that it must be the policy of the United States to support free peoples who are resisting attempted subjugation by armed minorities or by outside pressures. I believe that we must assist free peoples to work out their own destinies in their own way. . . . I believe that our help should be primarily through economic and financial aid which is essential to economic stability and orderly political processes. . . . I therefore ask the Congress for assistance to Greece and Turkey in the amount of $400,000,000. . . .'

(President Truman to Congress, 12 March 1947)

Document 4.3a

The effects of Marshall Aid in Britain

'Rations of butter, sugar, cheese and bacon would all have had to be cut by over a third and there would have been less meat and eggs. Cotton goods would have disappeared from the home market; supplies of footwear would have been reduced and tobacco consumption would have been cut by three-quarters. It would have meant even less petrol for private motoring and fewer films, newspapers and books. Shortage of timber would have meant a further reduction in house building, perhaps to 50,000 a year. Most serious of all, our supplies of raw materials for industry would have been affected, and might have brought the unemployment figures up to 1,500,000.'

(*Board of Trade Journal*, 10 October 1948)

Document 4.3b

Bevin, Molotov and Marshall Aid

'General Marshall made his speech in June 1947 at Harvard and the very next morning Bevin picked it up listening to the BBC. He went to the Foreign Office at 8.30 that morning. Bevin had quite a temper. No one was there. His officials arrived at about a quarter to nine and they went over this speech, what it meant, and it was obvious that Britain and France would have to take a lead together. Bevin despatched his officials that very same afternoon to Paris. That led to the meeting of representatives of European countries in Paris. Bevin thoroughly understood what General Marshall had in mind, that Europe should co-operate together in a plan of mutual help. The Soviet Union would have none of it. Molotov would have none of it. He kept insisting: find out from the United States how much they'll give; we'll divide it on the basis that the country that's suffered the most should get the most. Obviously this was the Soviet Union. That, of course, was not General Marshall's idea. The idea was to have a co-operative plan; that through co-operation Europe could be reconstructed and perhaps be made healthier than ever.'

(Averell Harriman, in Alan Thompson, *The Day Before Yesterday*, Granada, 1971)

Document 4.4

The effects of the Czech coup on US opinion

'The Marshall Plan was put up by the Truman administration to the Congress with the strong support of President Truman. Senator Vandenberg played a very important role. He was a Republican, but he was then Chairman of the Foreign Relations Committee of the Senate. I think historians should give him parallel marks with Truman for his support in these principles. The *coup d'état* in Prague was right in the middle of the argument over the Marshall Plan and it was not very clear which way the vote would go. We were all hopeful that we would carry it, but perhaps, by a rather small margin. But the *coup* in Czechoslovakia caused such concern that the Marshall Plan went through a few weeks later with a very large majority.

The blockade of Berlin really broadened the scope of NATO. Certainly the Berlin blockade played a terrifying role, it concerned people very deeply. Of course there was an argument as to whether stern measures were to be taken. General Clay wanted to force the tanks through. We had at that time still a monopoly on nuclear weapons and Truman, undoubtedly, with our approval, decided to go ahead with the air lift and Britain played a very important role. We played in the beginning a parallel, an equal role, but then we gradually took a large per cent of it. I've forgotten just what position Mr Bevin took, but I'm sure Mr Attlee was on the conservative side of that decision.'

(Averell Harriman, in Alan Thompson, *op. cit.*)

Document 4.5

The Berlin blockade

'After the Berlin blockade, it became obvious that one of the big problems was fuel. I think we needed right away about 2,000,000 tons of coal, because there was just a tiny bit of coal available in the city, in the western sectors of Berlin at that point. And the question was how to get that coal, and the next item – food. And this ran into considerable tonnage. In the absence of determination to meet the issue on the ground where it should have been met – mind you, this was a period when we had the atomic bomb and the Soviet Union did not have the atomic bomb – I believe that any thought of the Soviet Union going to war with us over this issue of Berlin was in the realm of fantasy. They couldn't possibly; they were in no condition because of circumstances back home where the destruction had been so terrible. Their population was in no physical or mental condition to permit them going into a war. I find fault with our American joint Chiefs of Staff on that point because they insisted that they had to have eighteen months to prepare because this might lead to an all-out confrontation with the Soviet Union and that was one reason or the reason why we did not meet the issue. All we had, you see, about the blockade of Berlin, was a note addressed to us by the Russian Military Governor saying that the highway would be closed to traffic, because it was in need of repair, for the indefinite future, and then they put a pole across the road with two Mongolian soldiers – and that was a blockade. It didn't cost them a penny, and instead of politely sending them a note and saying thank you very much, but as you are not in a position to give prompt service on the maintenance we will undertake it ourselves, and putting a division with some combat troops and some engineers ready to undertake the maintenance of the highway, we backed away from the issue and resorted to the air lift. Now the air lift was technically a beautiful job, achieved under great difficulties and at great expense. I think we spent over 2,000,000 dollars a month on that thing. The trouble was that we would not stand up on an issue which was very serious, where we had all the cards in our hands – this was the sad feature of that history. General Clay was our Military Governor at that time and we were having a meeting in his office and discussing the question of delivery by air of whatever was needed. The Commander of our Air Force at that time was stationed at Wiesbaden and his name was Curtis Le May. General Clay picked up the phone and called him and said – "Curtis, can you deliver coal by air?" And Le May at the other end of the phone – we could hear the extension – said "Would you repeat the question?" And Clay repeated the question and he said that the Air Force could deliver anything. It was on that basis that the air lift started. The German population co-operated tremendously. That was one of the most astounding features, they worked day and night, sometimes with very little pay and under bad weather conditions and bad food conditions especially. You know, that first winter in Berlin I think probably 20 people a day died from the cold and malnutrition.'

(Robert Murphy, in Alan Thompson, *op. cit.*)

Document 4.6a

US uncertainty

'I think it's important to distinguish between two American approaches to the problems in the post-war world. I think the professionals in the State Department – of whom the outstanding example was George Kennan, who was at that time head of the policy planning staff and wrote the famous article by Mr X in *Foreign Affairs* – didn't believe that the Russians were out for world conquest but did believe that it was necessary for Western Europe to hold the line roughly where the armies had stopped at the end of the Second World War. And, should this happen, the Russian régime would ultimately mellow and come to terms – as I think was right. But of course this was a very sophisticated view to put to a people which had, only a few years earlier, become conscious of the fact there was a world beyond the oceans. And one of the problems, I think, was that those Americans who did become interested in foreign affairs in the post-war period tended to see Communism as an absolute evil, very much in the same way as we in the Labour Party in the 1930s – and still – saw Fascism as the absolute evil. And in some ways, I think the tragedy of this period was that in order to get the Americans committed to a very prudent and necessary strengthening in Western Europe against a spread of Soviet influence, the Americans were easily persuaded by Soviet behaviour in Czechoslovakia and Berlin that the Russians were really out for world conquest in the same sense as Hitler really was out for the conquest of Europe.'

(Denis Healey in Alan Thompson, *op. cit.*)

Document 4.6b

American converts, 1948

'Mr Bevin, during the early part of 1948, had been very anxious to get the Americans interested and, if possible, involved in the defence of Western Europe. With this in mind earlier in the year, he had formed a European alliance (the Brussels Treaty). During 1948 I had been told to try and make progress with the Americans and I made no progress at all. Then quite suddenly, at the beginning of July, I remember, Mr Lubbock, the Under Secretary of State of the State Department, saying to me "Why aren't we making faster progress, it's time we got on?" And the reasons were there had been a Communist coup in Prague in February and then after that, in July, the Berlin air lift. The mood in Congress had changed and in particular Senator Vandenberg, the most important Republican in foreign affairs, had come to see that America could no longer go on in isolation, and therefore Congress and the administration would have won, so negotiations for a North Atlantic Treaty could begin, and they did.'

(Lord Franks in Alan Thompson, *op. cit.*)

FURTHER READING

ADENAUER, K., *Memoirs, 1945–54,* Weidenfeld and Nicolson, 1966–8

ARNOLD-FORSTER, M., *The Siege of Berlin,* Collins, 1979

BALFOUR, M., *West Germany: A Contemporary History,* Croom Helm, 1983

BALFOUR, M., *The Adversaries: America, Russia and the World, 1941–62,* Routledge and Kegan Paul, 1981

BACKER, J. H., *Priming the German Economy: American Occupational Policies, 1945–48,* Duke UP, 1971

BULLOCK, A., *Ernest Bevin: Foreign Secretary,* Heinemann, 1983

CARTER, D., *The Great Fear: The Anti-Communist Purge under Truman and Eisenhower,* Secker and Warburg, 1978

CHILDS, D., *Germany since 1918,* Batsford, 1980

CLAY, GENERAL L. D., *Decisions in Germany,* Heinemann, 1950

DEDIJA, V., *Tito Speaks,* Weidenfeld and Nicolson, 1953

DJILAS, M., *Conversations with Stalin,* Penguin, 1963

HALLE, L. J., *The Cold War as History,* Harper and Row, 1971

HAMMOND, P. Y., *Cold War and Détente,* Harcourt Brace, 1975

LA FEBER, W., *The Origins of the Cold War: a historical problem with interpretations and documents,* John Wiley, 1971

LA FEBER, W., *America, Russia and the Cold War, 1945–1971,* 3rd ed., John Wiley, 1976

MELANSON, R. A., *The Cold War, Vietnam and Revisionism,* Univ. Press of America, 1983

MURPHY, R., *Diplomat Among Warriors,* 1964

SMITH, W. B., *Moscow Mission, 1946–49,* Heinemann, 1950

5

Eastern Europe: the restless empire, 1953–84

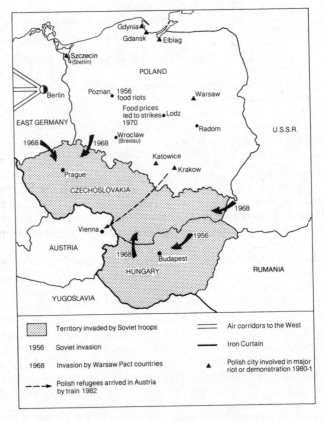

5.1 'The restless Empire' from which Yugoslavia had escaped and in which Russian military might had to be used to ensure political uniformity.

East Berlin, 1953

'Socialist ideas can only triumph when the peoples of Eastern Europe eat like the delegates at this Congress [of the Czech Communist Party]. Love of Communism passes through the stomach.'[1]

Khruschev, June 1954

In April 1953 the political adviser to the Soviet Control Commission in East Germany was called to Moscow. He returned on 5 June to tell the East German authorities that they were going to receive less aid from Russia than in the past and that, if they wanted to develop, they would have to do it by their own efforts.

In June 1953, prices were rising and workers demanded wage increases. At the same time, the government was debating methods of increasing industrial output, the means to that higher living standard already available in the west. Some leaders called for a 10% increase in the workers' 'norm' without any corresponding increase in wages. The governing party's own newspaper, *Neues Deutschland*, argued that the norms would not be raised without the consent of the workers, who were being asked to accept a 10% cut in living standards.

The Party's ideologues insisted that the norms should be raised and this announcement was made on Monday 15 June. Bricklayers, at work on the massive housing project on the Stalinallee, held a protest meeting to demand the withdrawal of the increased norms. On the following day, a junior Party leader told them that the norms would be raised. Within an hour, the whole of the large labour force on the Stalinallee had downed tools to march to the government offices. Other workers joined them and, as they marched, they changed their demands from calls for the abolition of the increased norms to calls for free elections and a new government.

Ulbricht, the Party Secretary, and Grotewohl, the Prime Minister, refused to meet the demonstrators, who were told by the Minister of Mines that the norms would not be increased. This concession was, however, too little and too late. The now radicalised demonstrators called for 'freedom' and for a general strike on the Wednesday, 17 June.

The Red Army moved in during the night; tanks were stationed outside government buildings; Russian infantry were stationed on the border between the British and Soviet sectors; the Peoples' Police were out in force and armed. In spite of this show of force, the strike went ahead throughout the country. The Soviet military administration declared a state of emergency.

There were 10,000 demonstrators on the streets in the early morning. They took over some public buildings, burnt down the Communist Party's headquarters and opened prisons. In spite of attacks by the infantry and police, they continued their demonstration, burning buildings, tearing down the Red Flag at the Brandenburg Gate and disabling tanks with baulks of wood. During the day, they were joined by steelworkers from the Soviet zone steel plant of Hennigsdorf to the west of Berlin; these had had to march through the French zone to join the demonstration.

On 18 June, the Soviet Military Commandant applied emergency regulations. Anyone found demonstrating or holding 'gatherings of more than three people' would be punished by military law. Throughout the day, the courts were busy, condemning people to be shot for having taken part in the demonstration. But the workers did not go back to work. Meanwhile, tanks and troops had to be used in other towns to apply martial law. The German, Max Fechner, Minister of Justice in the East German government, argued that the constitution permitted the right to strike; he was arrested and sent to the concentration camp at Sachsenhausen. In spite of the constitution, Soviet and East German courts continued to punish the strikers, who, slowly and reluctantly, called off their action and returned to work – and to the increased norms.

The 'People's Revolt' of 17 June provided evidence that, eight years after the end of the war, Russia still controlled East German affairs; it was the Russian forces and Russian courts which won the day against the proletariat. It also illustrated the close link between economic, social and political affairs. The workers' grievances were, in the first instance, economic; they resented being asked to produce more for the same wages. This raising of norms had social effects – a reduction in real living standards. However, as the building workers marched on 16 June, they called for greater political freedom. It is this link, of the economic and social with the political, which has led Soviet leaders to reject calls for the economic changes needed to improve the Russian economy.

The rehabilitation of Tito and the 'middle road'

'We sincerely regret what happened and resolutely reject the things that occurred.'
Khruschev at Belgrade Airport, 26 May 1955

Tito had been, until 1948, an ideal 'Stalinist' (p. 47). The Yugoslavian Constitution of 1946 gave the 500,000 members of the Communist Party total control of the country with its population of 17,000,000. The secret police, spies and informers collaborated to arrest thousands of 'capitalists' and 'collaborators with the enemy'; industry was nationalised and the Five-Year Plan of 1947, Stalin-like, concentrated on the development of heavy industry and neglected agriculture, which was forcibly collectivised.

But, as we have seen (pp. 49–50), Tito would not submit himself and his country to Stalin's dictates. His preaching of the 'national road to socialism' led to his expulsion from the Cominform in 1948. He received western aid to help bring about an industrial revolution in his backward country. By 1964 industrial production was five times as great as it had been in 1939 and *per capita* income had risen from 70 dollars to 500 dollars.[2] In 1953, collectivisation was called off; peasants were allowed private ownership but encouraged to form voluntary co-operatives for the purchase of seed and machinery. Workers' councils were set up in industry to provide a form of 'socialist democracy'.

Khruschev wanted to restore unity in the Communist camp and to normalise relations with Yugoslavia. In May 1955, he and Bulganin visited Belgrade where he not only admitted the Stalinist errors of 1948 but accepted the equal status and independence of all socialist states. This 'revisionist' attitude was to be further developed during the historic 20th Party Congress which took place in February 1956 when Khruschev admitted the right of every country to take its own road to socialism, an admission that Russian leaders were not the infallible interpreters of the Marxist truth. In April 1956, the Cominform was dissolved as an indication of Khruschev's intention to abolish Soviet control of other countries' affairs. However, there was more appearance than reality to this seeming withdrawal of control; in 1956, Russian troops invaded Hungary; Comecon remained as a means of economic control; the Warsaw Pact (May 1955) ensured a common foreign policy throughout eastern Europe (Fig. 10.1, p. 217).

The independent-minded Tito refused to join the Warsaw Pact, nor did he join Comecon. Khruschev did not overreact to these signs of independence. Tito was welcomed in Moscow in June 1956 where he praised the honesty which had been displayed at the 20th Party Congress and the denunciation of Stalin (pp. 114–15). And Brezhnev continued Khruschev's attitude towards Tito. In 1962 he visited Belgrade and Tito was invited back to Moscow as signs of good relations between their two countries. It was possible, for Tito and Yugoslavia at least, to retain their independence. Other countries and their leaders would not be so fortunate.

Eastern Europe and the 'Thaw' of 1956

'We already have enough trouble explaining the past after that 20th Congress of the Soviet Party. If I have Cepicka put on trial [for his work as Minister of Justice] the process won't stop there; people will blame the Party and start asking who else was responsible. Go back to your office now, and just forget what you've seen [the files from the Justice Department showing the extent of the purges in Czechoslovakia after 1948].'[3]
First Secretary Novotny to Jan Sejna of the Czech 'Special' Department, May 1956

Khruschev's denunciation of Stalin in February 1956 (pp. 114–15) was revealing not only for what it said but for what it did not say. Khruschev never asked why the system had been unable to prevent Stalin from acting as he did. He did not suggest any remedies for preventing another Stalin from gaining power and committing similar crimes. The speech was, in essence, a series of highly selective revelations and only a superficial explanation of Stalinism.

Outside Russia, a number of people were not satisfied with the conclusions reached by Khruschev; in Czechoslovakia and elsewhere some Party leaders insisted on asking the deeper questions which Khruschev had left unasked. Other Party leaders, such as Novotny of Czechoslovakia, saw the danger of allowing such questions to be raised. Where would it all end? Inevitably, they claimed, with a condemnation of the Party and of the system.

Ulbricht, of East Germany, had been a hard-line Stalinist. He hoped to divert attention from the real questions by continuing, in East Germany, the anti-Stalinist denunciations. In March, he condemned Stalin's written work as no longer to be regarded as Marxist classics.

Jan Sejna had been a life-long member of the Party and had made his way up the ladder so that, in 1956, he was an important member of the Czech hierarchy. In the de-Stalinisation period, he played a part in the overthrow of Cepicka, Minister of Justice in Czechoslovakia who had organised the Stalinist purges during which 1,600 people had been executed. Novotny and other Czech leaders hoped that his overthrow would satisfy Czech demands for an end to the cruelty. Sejna wanted the Party leadership to respond to the demand for a special Congress to bring about a change in the membership of the Central Committee. Novotny was unwilling to follow such a 'democratic' move. Nor would he agree to having Cepicka brought to trial, in spite of Sejna's appeal to him. 'Thus', wrote Sejna, 'he sowed in me the first seeds of disillusion with the Communist system.'[4]

Nor was Sejna alone; throughout eastern Europe there was a 'crisis of confidence' in the system, for there was little change in the leadership of the Communist Parties; the 'Stalinists' continued to hold power in the uncertain days following Khruschev's speech. True, the slight 'thaw' led to greater freedom of speech, of the press, of foreign travel and of religion; the powers of the secret police were reduced and the victims of past purges were rehabilitated.

There was also some economic progress. Russia stopped stripping the satellites for her own benefit. Instead, she started sending out aid. Poland and Hungary were given massive injections of aid and East Germany only slightly less. Although heavy industry was still given priority, there was the development of consumer goods industries, so that television sets, washing machines and other 'luxuries' became available to a wider public.

In the long run, the most significant change was in the field of education. The old guard – Novotny, Ulbricht and others – had been schooled in Moscow and had learned 'the truth' there. In the aftermath of the Khruschev speech and the 'crisis of confidence', there was a loss of the ideological certainty which they, and lesser members of their Parties, had brought to their work. Nowhere was this clearer than in the field of education. The new generation which was educated after 1956 – in schools, universities and technological institutes – had less of that 'ideological certainty' and much more of that questioning spirit which typified the liberalisation which had taken place in economic and social fields. It was these technocrats who were in positions of some power in the 1970s, who brought in the 'socialist market economy' in which managers of state enterprises were given more freedom – to adapt their plans to the national plan, to dismiss inefficient or indisciplined labour, to borrow money for development, to distribute profits among workers and to deal directly with customers at home and abroad.

Poland, 1956–84

'I no longer know how to raise my head. For I have no basis for believing in anything.'[5]

> A letter published by an eighteen-year old Polish student, May 1956

In the 'thaw' following Stalin's death, Poland's Communist leaders made changes in policy and allowed greater freedom to sections of the people. Industry was organised for an increase in the production of consumer goods; there was a slowdown in the collectivisation of agriculture; the police were instructed to call off their terrorism of suspected critics of the system; 30,000 political prisoners were released.

Under this 'New Course', there was increased discussion of the shortcomings of the system. Students and writers became openly critical as they voiced the discontent of the masses. A dedicated Communist, Adam Wazyk, published, in 1955, a 'Poem for Adults' attacking the system which had failed its supporters so that, in his words, 'they lost their faith'. Students' newspapers, such as *Po Prostu*, demanded greater intellectual and political freedom.

It was against this background of criticism that workers at the locomotive factory at Poznan came out on strike on 28 June 1956, in a demand for better pay which turned into a mass demonstration against the government, the Russians and the secret police. Banners were carried with slogans such as 'We want bread and freedom', 'Give us back our religion'; barricades were raised; the Soviet flag was torn down. As in East Berlin in 1953, troops were called to restore order, and 42 people were killed.

The Party leadership was divided as to the policy to be adopted in the light of this uprising. Bierut, the 'Stalin' of Poland, died suddenly while on a visit to Moscow in the summer of 1956. The Russians wanted the Poles to appoint a middle-of-the-roader, Ochab, in his place. He was opposed to major reforms but was willing to make minor concessions, hoping that these would head off the demand for more widespread changes. The small group of hardliners inside the leadership wanted to call on the Russian army, if need be, to help restore order and to suppress the reform movement among students, writers and workers. But this group was small and out of touch with feeling inside the Party leadership. The majority favoured change; they refused to re-elect the Soviet Marshall, Rokossowski, who had been appointed by Russia to be Polish War Minister. Nor did the hardliners find support among the secret police once it had lost its Stalinist leaders.

The small number of 'liberals' in the leadership were prepared to co-operate with the 'middle-of-the-roaders' to bring in what might be regarded as essential, or minimal, changes. On 19 October, the Central Committee of the Polish Communist Party met and co-opted the former victim of Stalinism, Gomulka, and three of his supporters to the Central Committee, which went on to nominate Gomulka for the post of First Secretary. Some voted for him because he was a symbol of both resistance to Stalin and, in his newly-enjoyed freedom, the end of Stalinism (p. 50).

News of Gomulka's nomination frightened the Russians. Khruschev and Molotov flew to Warsaw, having announced the closure of the Polish border and the stationing of Russian troops in Poland. They hoped to force the Central Committee to retain Ochab. But when Khruschev began to address the Committee, he was challenged from the audience. He asked for his critic's identity. 'Gomulka' came the reply, 'First Secretary of the Polish Party'. Khruschev had arrived too late.[6] He then tried to persuade Gomulka not to introduce more liberals into the Politburo and other organs of government. But Gomulka insisted, Tito-like, that Poland would follow its own road to socialism.

Molotov wanted to send in the troops; Khruschev over-ruled him, trusting that Gomulka would realise the relative weakness of his true position. Gomulka introduced a number of major reforms. Political prisoners were released; the victims of past purges of 1945–6 were rehabilitated; Cardinal Wyszynski (p. 54) was allowed to return to his cathedral; existing collective farms were broken up into private holdings; small private shops were allowed to open; factory managers were given more freedom and, as in Yugoslavia, workers' councils were encouraged.

In 1957 there were Parliamentary elections in which there was a choice of candidates and parties; the result was a majority of only 18 for the Communists over the rest.

The Russians allowed Gomulka a free hand because he did not seek to rock the boat too violently. Russian troops were allowed to remain on Polish soil; Poland did not seek to leave the Warsaw Pact; Gomulka did not allow complete political freedom, while he insisted that even the modicum allowed had to be exercised within the framework provided by the communist system. He made it clear that the small gains were not to be a springboard for the launching of more radical programmes. He pointed out that Poland's very existence was under threat so long as West German politicians refused to acknowledge the post-war settlement of Poland's western boundary (p. 25). Poland depended on Russia's support against German claims for the restoration of the pre-war boundary.

Once he was firmly in power, Gomulka then showed that he was much more of a 'Stalinist' than a 'liberal'. He attacked the intellectuals and students whose writings and demonstrations had helped bring him to power. *Po Prostu* was suppressed in October 1957. Some leading intellectuals had their party cards withdrawn, while others, in protest against a new censorship, left the party. With the police and the army under his control, Gomulka could afford to ignore their limited protests, for the intellectuals were no longer in touch with the mass of the people who, in the light of the obvious failure of the 1956 movement, became more apathetic and cynical.

Poland enjoyed some economic development. Gomulka received Russian aid while he was also allowed to accept western credits with which to buy raw materials, capital equipment and consumer goods from the west. With the spread of privatisation in agriculture, there was an increased output, although Polish farming remained relatively backward and unmechanised.

The Catholic Church provided the main problem for the Gomulka government. Even though Gomulka and the Cardinal arrived at a modus vivendi in 1956, the tension between Church and State could not, really, disappear. Both Party and Church laid claims to total loyalty; both Gomulka and Wyszynski claimed to represent Poland's best interests. When the political system failed to come up to people's expectations, an increasing number of Poles, of all classes, looked to the Church for leadership.

While the Church won back the support of many who had once given up their religion in favour of Party membership, the Party failed to develop among the young, while the 'crisis of confidence' affected the strength of the 'faith' of those who remained inside the Party. With the spread of education, there was also the development of a critical student movement, the more free once they were faced with teachers and leaders who had lost that ideological certainty which had once been the hallmark of the 'faithful'. In March 1968, there were student demonstrations in favour of freedom and a more independent national policy. The government, aware of the Czech crisis, (pp. 97–9) adopted repressive measures. Many intellectuals lost their posts; student leaders were arrested and a purge made of those suspected of being disloyal to the Party. A hard-line group even attacked Gomulka, accusing him of not being hard enough on the dissenters. He held on to power, largely because the Russians would not support the hard-liners.

Criticism of Gomulka reached a new peak in 1970. Students and young people generally were opposed to the crushing burden of the inefficient bureaucracy; even in the controlled press there were demands for more freedom. Meanwhile, the economy had lost whatever impetus it had developed in 1956; the State planning system led to the over-production of some goods and a serious shortage of others; the backwardness of the agricultural sector led to food shortages, only relieved by imports from Russia, Canada, the USA and West Germany.

In December 1970, the government faced an internal problem; its revenue was not large enough to cover government expenditure. It decided to make up the shortfall by increasing the prices of a range of goods – including food, fuel and clothing. This announcement led to widespread rioting following strikes by workers at Lodz, Gdansk and Szczecin. At the port of Gdynia, rioters set fire to a Soviet ship, in Gdansk they demolished the Party headquarters. The forces were called out to suppress the outbreak.

Inside the Party, the debate on the riots led to the fall of Gomulka and his replacement by Edward Gierek. He tried to buy peace by cancelling the earlier decisions; food prices were to be frozen for two years; large wage increases were awarded to the lower paid. Industry was to produce more consumer goods, while Gierek spent a good deal of time touring the country inviting discussions on the faults of Polish society. In this more liberal régime, the Church became even more a focal point for discontent and criticism, leading the demand for intellectual freedom and for an end to censorship.

Gierek introduced younger people into positions of authority in State organisations; some of these newcomers were not even Party members. Industry was given more freedom and productivity improved. Western firms were allowed to open factories in Poland, while Polish firms borrowed from western sources to help their own development. In 1973 real wages rose by 24 per cent, industrial production by 33 per cent and agricultural production by 19 per cent. But, in 1973, the country suffered from the first impact of the increased oil prices imposed by the members of OPEC. In the ensuing inflation, the government again faced a financial crisis. In June 1976 Gierek announced large price increases. In the face of widespread rioting, he withdrew the decision and managed to ride out the storm with economic aid from Russia which did not, however, send in her troops. Meanwhile, as western bankers increased their interest rates, Poland found it increasingly difficult to meet the charges on its large overseas debt; the government was forced to cut imports and call a halt to many development schemes. The shortages of everyday goods and the introduction of food rationing led to a sharp drop in living standards. In 1980 there was another upsurge of popular discontent, which started in the shipyard at Gdansk but quickly spread throughout the country. The workers, led by Lech Walesa, created a free trade union movement, Solidarity, in opposition to the government-controlled union movement. Once again, the Church became closely involved, backing Solidarity and attacking government policies. Gierek was driven from power and the Polish

Marshal Jaruzelski was appointed Prime Minister. On 13 December 1981, he imposed martial law on Poland, outlawed the Solidarity movement to which ten million workers belonged, arrested and imprisoned, without trial, many of its leaders and thousands of ordinary members. But the election, in October 1978, of the first-ever Polish Pope, John Paul II, has led to greater international awareness of Poland's affairs, so that the government's freedom of action has been more limited than it would have been in Stalinist days. At the same time, the Russian leaders are reluctant, since the world-wide criticism of their Czech invasion of 1968, to send in troops.

Solidarity was banned, the government claims, more because its leaders were planning a political coup than because of its trade union activities. The signs are that some Poles have moved beyond those leaders who wanted merely to make modest changes to the existing system; many of them have gone beyond the line reached by Dubcek in Czechoslovakia and have been so radicalised that they would appear to be satisfied with nothing less than major political restructuring. Other leaders, notably the new Cardinal Primate, Glemp, fear that the pursuit of these demands will lead, inevitably, to Russian intervention. They hope to be able to negotiate with the Jaruzelski government and bring about modest reforms. But there are signs that many Poles will no longer accept this moderate leadership. In February 1984, the Cardinal removed from Warsaw a priest who had been preaching openly in favour of the now-banned Solidarity movement. The parishioners demonstrated in and out of church against the new Cardinal, condemned by many of them as 'a Communist agent'.

However, the Church remains the focus of intellectual and social activity as well as the centre of opposition to the government and the Communist Party. Party membership has fallen from 3.1 million (in 1978) to just under two million (in May 1984) while youth membership now stands (May 1984) at 260,000, the lowest in the Party's history. It was young people, in Warsaw schools, who organised the opposition to the government decision to ban the display of crucifixes in classrooms. In the so-called 1984 'War of the Crosses', the young people hung crucifixes in dormitories, wore them as personal jewellery and held sit-ins and strikes until the government announced that crucifixes could be displayed in classrooms. The government has announced a package of measures designed to 'resocialise' children said to be suffering from 'demoralisation'. That anti-communist demoralisation is reflected in, for example, the words of a Polish pop-song; 'no goals, no future, no hope, no joy.' It remains to be seen whether a Ministry of Education 'package' will be able to sell Marxism to a disillusioned generation which has publicly, and often, jeered at Party officials and which burns Party propaganda in public demonstrations.

Jaruzelski's campaign against Solidarity took a seemingly democratic turn in June 1984 when nationwide elections were held. The people were invited to vote for candidates for 7,040 regional posts and 103,388 local positions. The outlawed leaders of Solidarity called for a boycott of these elections. They did not want the people to take part in a process which would allow the government to claim that it had the people's support. Thousands of leaflets were printed on underground presses, distributed throughout the country, pasted on stairwells, in lifts and along the walls of subways. In May, some anti-government campaigners in Gdansk freed several pigs, painted red and bearing the slogan, 'VOTE FOR US'. The government's response was to intensify its search for leaders of the underground movement while telling the people that 'those who do not vote should not complain.'

However, the system of voting was designed to make a mockery of the government's claim that the elections would provide opportunity for the people to 'decide their future'. The voting procedure was such that the government was ensured a thumping majority. Voters who were prepared to vote for the government's first choice for the various posts, only had to pick up their ballot paper and put it in a box. Those who wanted to vote for the government's second choice or who wanted to 'write-in' a candidate of their own choice, had to enter a curtained booth. This meant that voters who dissented from the government's approved candidates could be easily identified. In spite of this method of control, the government did not get the 99 per cent turn out and approval which it had looked for, and which, in other Soviet satellites, would be the norm.

Hungary, 1953–84

'This is the Association of Hungarian Writers; we are speaking to all writers' associations and scientific unions of the world who stand for the leaders of intellectual life in all countries. Our time is limited. You know all the facts. Long live Hungary!'[7]

The last broadcast from Radio Budapest on 4 November 1956

When Stalin died in March 1953, Hungary was being governed by the Rakosi-Rajk régime in which 2,000 people had been executed and another 200,000 were imprisoned (p. 46). As in other satellites, so in Hungary; there was a genuflection in the direction of 'the thaw' and writers were allowed a degree of freedom. They formed an Association which they named after Sandor Petofi, a poet and rebel martyr of 1849. The more daring among them criticised the harsh régime and its failure to develop an economy capable of providing a decent living standard. They pointed to the despoiling of the country by the Russians as part of that country's attempt to develop its own economy.

The news of the June 1956 rising in Poland and of Gomulka's accession to power encouraged the Hungarian critics. Khruschev, anxious to avoid another rising on the Polish model, ordered Rakosi to resign (18 July). But the appointment of another Russian protégé,

Gero, did not appease Hungarians' thirst for more democratisation and increased freedom. A bad harvest and a fuel shortage in a wet and cold autumn led to increased unrest and to widespread demands for the removal of Russian troops, one sign of Hungary's subordinate position in the Warsaw Pact.

The slight easing of the régime's repression under Gero served only to weaken the self-confidence of the government while increasing the revolutionary enthusiasm among the intellectuals and students in particular. Ex-prisoners demanded the removal of all the old Stalinists from public life; students demonstrated in favour of democracy and political freedom. On 23 October, the government panicked and imposed a ban on all meetings and demonstrations. The students defied the order and held a monster meeting. The already hated secret police (the AVH) fired on the crowd.

It was this which drew the workers into the struggle; revolutionary committees were set up throughout the country; troops sent out by the government joined the revolutionaries. Khruschev was unwilling to use the Russian troops already in Hungary. The revolutionary movement spread; the secret police disappeared from the streets; government ministers went into hiding; the writers and intellectuals took control of the radio and the printing presses. The pulling down of Stalin's statues throughout Hungary was merely the symbol of the protest.

The Russians, still hoping to organise a government with whom they could work, insisted on Imre Nagy becoming Prime Minister. Nagy had been one of those 'Muscovites' who returned to take a government post in 1945, first as Minister of Agriculture, then, in 1946, as Minister of the Interior before he was replaced by the more ardently Stalinist Rajk. In 1953, with the support of Malenkov, Nagy had replaced Rakosi as Prime Minister. When Malenkov fell in 1955, Nagy was forced from office, and Rakosi, once more in power, expelled him from the Communist Party in November 1955. Increasingly after July 1956, Hungarian writers and ex-prisoners called for his reinstatement as Prime Minister. The Russians bowed to the seemingly inevitable and allowed him to form a Coalition government in which some of the older parties, such as the Smallholders (p. 46), were represented.

Encouraged by Russian acceptance of multi-party government, Nagy demanded the withdrawal of Russian troops from the country; and Hungary's withdrawal from the Warsaw Pact. He also proposed to hold free elections in which parties other than the Communist Party would be allowed to stand.

Nagy had gone much further than Gomulka. Some of his more liberal supporters, fearing a Russian intervention, seemed to have relied on the promise of help which, over the years, had been promised by western radio stations beamed at the east. They refused to moderate their demands as Gomulka had done. Kadar, the First Secretary of the Hungarian Party, left Budapest to set up a new government in eastern

Hungary in opposition to the 'fascist counter-revolutionaries' led by Nagy. Soviet tanks, supporting Kadar, attacked Budapest on 4 November and shelled the radio station and centres occupied by the rebels. 200,000 refugees fled to the West as 15 divisions and 6,000 tanks suppressed the rebellion. Eisenhower, who, with Dulles, had promised that the USA would help 'liberate' eastern Europe from Communism took no action. It is sometimes claimed that the Anglo-French action in Suez helped to distract world attention from the Russian attack on 'free' Hungary. There was no such distraction in 1968 when another Russian government attacked Dubcek's Czechoslovakia. World opinion has little effect on the conduct of governments of the extreme left (Russia) or extreme right (South Africa), although both go to great lengths to attempt to influence world opinion in their respective favour.

The last battle ended on 14 November, by which time some 25,000 Hungarians and 7,000 Russians had been killed. Khruschev and his agent in Hungary, Andropov, appointed Kadar as Prime Minister. He was prepared to serve the Russians by behaving as another Gomulka; there would be no free elections, no democracy and, above all, no withdrawal from the Warsaw Pact.

Kadar's government set about restoring order once the revolution had been crushed by the Russians. Martial law was imposed on the country; the secret police given back their power; strikes were suppressed and workers' leaders imprisoned along with leading writers. Nagy and other members of his former government had taken refuge in the Yugoslav Embassy. Kadar and Andropov promised them that it was safe for them to return to normal life. On 22 November Nagy left the Embassy, was arrested, secretly tried and, with several colleagues, executed. Khruschev was, in spite of all, a Stalinist at heart.

In Hungary itself, Kadar showed himself to be a realist. On the one hand, he took steps not to anger the Russians; on the other hand, once the majority of leading dissidents had been imprisoned, he also took account of the widespread demand for freedom which had been revealed in 1956. He resigned as Prime Minister in 1958, although he remained First Secretary and virtual ruler; he took the premiership again in 1961 and was still in power when Mrs Thatcher visited Hungary in 1984. Modern Hungary is very much 'Kadar's country' and the improvements evident there have to be attributed to his astute ability to get on with the Russians while satisfying some, at least, of the demands of his people.

He benefited from the end of the Russian pillage of Hungary and from the aid which poured in as Russia changed its policies towards the satellites. Between 1956 and 1963 the real income of the people rose by 36 per cent. In 1965, Kadar introduced a new programme to increase productivity and output. There was to be more foreign trade – with east and west. In 1984, over half Hungary's foreign trade is with the west. Investment would be made on the basis of profitability and would be aided by credits obtained from the European Community and western banks. Salaries and wages would depend on productivity. Peasants would be allowed to spend more time on their private plots, and by 1984 over 30 per cent of total output comes from such plots.

In 1984 there was evidence that the Kadar régime had succeeded. The standard of living is much higher than in most other satellites; shops are stocked with food and clothes; streets crowded with privately-owned cars; restaurants full of prosperous workers and their families. The régime has encouraged private initiative, self-improvement and self-enrichment by workers, who work overtime, and by professional people who benefit from private practice. The main losers have been the workers in the old-fashioned heavy industries which remain state-controlled and inefficient.

In the wake of the increases in oil prices announced by OPEC and the higher interest rates charged by western banks for the loans made to the government, there has been a slackening in the rate of growth since 1981. The government has been forced to reduce private consumption (by price increases) as an aid to the drive for exports to earn the much-needed foreign currency. But the acquisitive Hungarians have not reacted as the Poles did to such imposed increases. They have come to terms with the government and its new economic mechanism which has given them 'a people's capitalism', providing them with relatively high living standards. Khruschev was right in thinking that Communism (or acceptance of the system) comes through the stomach (p. 83 and 116).

East Germany, 1953–84

'What is necessary, what is a condition of life for Socialism, and what was lost during the period of Stalinism, is Democracy. Socialism cannot be achieved without Democracy.'
Professor Robert Havemann, at the Humboldt University of East Berlin, 1963

Havemann had been a Communist since 1932 and had been imprisoned by the Nazis. His anti-Stalinist views led to his losing his post at the East Berlin University and being expelled from the Academy of Sciences. But there was no popular uprising against this Stalinist-like behaviour; students did not protest. Ulbricht of East Germany did not allow any of the toleration extended to intellectuals in Poland and Hungary. East Germany was to be the most faithful of Russia's satellites. With 20 Soviet divisions on its soil, there was little danger of a recurrence of the events of 1953.

Ulbricht's government felt the need for Russian protection more than any of the other satellites, because of East Germany's exposed position and because of the unpopularity of the régime which continued to fail to produce living standards comparable to those so evidently enjoyed in West Germany. Alone among the satellites, East Germany enjoyed none of that 'thaw' following Stalin's death, nor, for a long time, did it experience any of the 'liberalising' of the Khruschev era. Until 1971, Ulbricht exercised complete power. His successor, Honecker, has maintained the dictatorship.

In 1962, Ulbricht allowed the introduction of a more flexible economic policy. The East Germans showed that they had the same abilities and will to work as their countrymen in the west. By 1968 East Germany was the country with the highest living standards in Comecon, its industry the best developed outside Russia. Under Honecker the improvement continued. By 1984, the East German GNP was higher than that of several capitalist countries in western Europe. The people are well fed and generally well housed. One in three families has a car. East Germany now produces more than did all Germany under Hitler. Aided by loans from the west, it has become the ninth industrial power in the world.

We have seen in Chapter 4 how the two Germanies came into being, each regarding the other as 'the enemy', neither willing to extend recognition to the other. West Germany's membership of NATO was followed by East Germany's participation in the negotiations which led to the signing of the Warsaw Pact in 1955. As we shall see in Chapter 12 the German problem and, in particular, the problem of divided Berlin, lay at the heart of the troubled relationship between Russia and the western powers. The world was made all too aware of the Berlin problem in August 1961 when the first stages of the Berlin Wall were erected.

Ulbricht realised that there was little chance of economic improvement in the East while its skilled workers and professional people were able to escape, through West Berlin, to the greater freedom and higher wages of the west. Three million people had escaped between 1949 and 1961. During the night of 13 August, units of the East German army, supported by Russian tanks and forces, closed all the crossings from East Berlin to the West; trains were turned back, road traffic halted and East German workmen brought in, first to lay obstacles such as barbed wire, and behind them to build, on land in the Soviet sector, the Wall. The flood of refugees would be halted, forcibly. Over the years the Wall was developed from a temporary structure of concrete blocks to its present state of a complex structure running some 26 miles through the divided city. It has a neat wire-mesh fence, a cement-lined moat three metres deep and four and a half metres wide, and a cleared 'death strip' patrolled from a chain of observation towers. There is also a rampart, guarded day and night, along the 850 mile-long border between East and West Germany.

Ulbricht claimed that the Wall had been built to prevent 'fascist infiltrators' crossing from the West. The sophisticated East Berliners were not fooled. Neither, on the other hand, were many of them foolhardy. Some have tried to escape – and been killed in the process;

others have made the crossing by various hair-raising stunts ranging from parachuting to tunnelling. The majority of East Germans accepted the reality of the situation; there would be no easy method of getting to the West. The improvement in the East German economic performance may be dated from the building of the Wall and, as in Hungary, the 'economic miracle' has been accepted as sufficient payment for the loss of freedom (see also p. 248).

Czechoslovakia, 1953–84

'Beside these rascals, Dubcek stood out as an honest man who sincerely believed that Novotny had to go for the good of the Party. He was a thoroughly decent fellow, very easy to get on with, a man of total integrity, with no personal ambition, but he was unbelievably naive, and his naivety was to cost him his position and nearly his life.'[8]

Novotny had become First Secretary of the Czech Communist party in 1953 (p. 85) and had himself elected President of the Czech Republic in November 1957. He was a dedicated Stalinist, and Czechoslovakia enjoyed little of the 'thaw' which affected the rest of the satellite countries after 1956. There was no rising by Czech writers and intellectuals as there had been in Poland and Hungary. A slight and belated 'thaw' was allowed to develop in 1961–2 but was quickly brought to a halt.

The Party, which had once won 38 per cent of the popular vote (p. 48), became increasingly unpopular. The economy went from bad to worse as the government concentrated on the development of heavy industry and neglected the people's demand for an improved standard of living. In November 1967, there was a series of student protests about living conditions in their hostels in Prague. This was suppressed by the police. That might have been the end of the affair, if there had not been a crisis in the Party leadership.

The Slovaks in the Party had become critical of the way in which the Czech element, led by Novotny, was ignoring internal party democracy and behaving in a more autocratic fashion. In January 1968 this Party crisis came to a head. Novotny was deposed as Party Secretary and replaced by Alexander Dubcek, formerly the First Secretary of the Slovak party. As First Secretary of the Czechoslovakian Party, Dubcek and his Slovak colleagues ushered in a new political programme 'so that every honest citizen believing in socialism and the unity of the country feels that he is being useful and counts for something.' Sejna, one of the Party leaders (p. 103), used the turmoil surrounding the choice of Dubcek to flee from Czechoslovakia; it was clear, he claimed later, that Russia would be bound to intervene. The majority of the Czech people welcomed the changes proposed by Dubcek, who promised that the National Assembly would be more than the mere rubber stamp it had been under Novotny. Censorship of the press ended in March 1968 and reforms were promised for the decentralisation of industry and increased privatisation of agriculture. The government tried to increase its trading links with the west, although Dubcek made it clear, in April, that the government had no intention of leaving the Warsaw Pact.

In March 1968 Novotny was deposed from the Presidency and replaced by Svoboda. He had commanded the Czech Army Corps attached to the Russian army in 1943–4 and had helped to liberate his own country in May 1945. He had been Minister of Defence (1945–50) but suffered in the purges in 1951–2 (p. 51), spending some time in prison before being sent as an accountant to work on a collective farm. Khruschev brought him back into public life. In 1963–5 he was proclaimed 'Hero of the Czechoslovakian Republic and of the Soviet Union'. He seemed a 'safe' person to Russian eyes, while to the Czechs he was a 'hero'. He supported Dubcek's plans for reform after he had taken office as President in March 1968.

However, leaders in other satellites were uneasy. Dubcek's promises of 'more human freedom and respect for human rights' ran contrary to the concept of 'citizen's rights' as understood in the Soviet Union (p. 262 and p. 286). The extension of freedoms – of assembly, of religion, of travel abroad – went too far. The ambition to give communism a 'human face' seemed to be a temporising with the forces of the west, while the talk of 'secret elections' and 'democratic parties' could only encourage what the Russians saw as the 'forces of reaction'.

Dubcek ignored the widespread criticism of his régime by leaders in other satellites. Gomulka, under attack from Warsaw students demanding 'We want a Polish Dubcek', called for the suppression of the 'anti-social elements' in Czechoslovakia. Ulbricht of East Germany, conscious of the common frontier which Czechoslovakia has with West Germany, claimed that the imperialists were trying to detach Czechoslovakia from the eastern bloc by 'ideological subversion'. He also feared that the demand for 'socialism in freedom' being made in Czechoslovakia might be taken up inside his own satellite.

Russia, already facing another kind of revolt in Rumania and Albania (below), was forced to act. In May, Marshal Grechko visited Prague to inform the government that Warsaw Pact troop exercises would take place in Czechoslovakia in June. Throughout June and July, anti-Dubcek propaganda increased in volume and intensity in Russia, Poland and East Germany. Brezhnev, the new Stalinist ruler of Russia, drew parallels between what was happening in Prague in 1968 and what had happened in Budapest in 1956. Warsaw Pact leaders, except those from Rumania and Czechoslovakia, held a series of meetings to discuss the problem. Outside troops were not withdrawn until 3 August.

Dubcek and Svoboda were called to a meeting with the Soviet Politburo during which the Czechs assured the Russians that they had no intention of going over to the western camp, but refused to accept

Russian proposals for the purging of some of the country's leading progressives. The reaction inside Czechoslovakia was predictable. There was increased support, for Dubcek and liberalism, from students and workers. National pride, symbolised by Svoboda, also came to the aid of the liberal movement, which received further support from the visit to Prague of the other 'rebel' leaders – Tito and, from Rumania, Ceausescu.

On 20 August 1968, 650,000 Soviet, Polish, Hungarian, Bulgarian and East German troops invaded Czechoslovakia. The sullen people painted swastikas on the Soviet tanks, a reminder of an earlier occupation of their country. They ran an underground radio and television service which informed the people that on 21 August the Russians had arrested Dubcek. If other prominent Czechs could have been found to form a government, he might have been shot then. As it was, he and Svoboda were taken to Moscow to negotiate a deal. They were forced to accept a permanent Russian military presence and the re-establishment of strict control over all means of communication.

On their return, Svoboda told the Czechs that the alternative would have been 'senseless bloodshed' and ruthless suppression by the invading troops. There was some passive resistance, most notably the suicide by the young Jan Palach who set himself on fire. In April 1969, Dubcek was forced to resign to be replaced by another Slovak, Husak, who was willing to co-operate with the Russians. This latter-day Stalinist purged the Party, trade unions, press, radio, television, schools, universities and law courts. In July 1970, Dubcek was formally expelled from the Party and others of his supporters allowed to resign. By that time, many leading intellectuals had been arrested and some 60,000 Czechs had fled to join Sejna in exile.

The Russians and their hard line allies had won a victory. But at a high cost. For throughout Europe there was a wave of revulsion, most significantly inside Communist parties. Many members resigned; most leaders protested at Soviet interference with developments in another country. It is from this invasion that we have to date the growth of the Euro-Communist movement (p. 213). The Communist parties of France, Italy, Spain and other western countries now claim that, when they win power (by constitutional means) they will look to the interests of their countries and not to the interests of the Soviet Union.

Meanwhile, in Czechoslovakia, the Dubcek-line is maintained by a new generation of intellectuals. In 1977 some of them set up the 'Charter 77' group which campaigns for greater freedoms, such as those outlined in the Helsinki Agreement (pp. 270–3). In 1979, six of the members of this group were sentenced to up to five years imprisonment on charges of subversion or of accepting money from foreign agents. In Czechoslovakia, at least, Stalinism is still the order of the day. This hard-line attitude is illustrated by the nature of the relations between Church and State. Czechoslovakia is recognised as the least tolerant of all the satellites, and the government has, in June 1984, still refused to allow the Vatican to appoint bishops to dioceses whose former leaders have died. There are, currently, eight dioceses without a bishop and the negotiations to try to bring about some rectification of this situation have been long, difficult and unproductive. The Czech Catholics hope that John Paul will visit their country on his way to, or from, Yugoslavia, which he is to visit in 1985. In June 1984, the Czech government has not yet agreed to allow such a visit to take place. They may be fearful of the possible outcome of such a visit by the charismatic leader whose fellow-Poles have provided the Russians and the Polish government with continuing problems.

Rumania and Albania

Albania is the smallest of the satellites of eastern Europe. It has no common frontier with the Soviet Union, and its Stalinist-like leaders came to power without the aid of the Red army. While Russia and Tito were at odds with one another, Albania was a faithful client of Russia's; she needed Russian support in her continuing dispute with Tito over the question of the Albanian minority in the Kosmet region of Yugoslavia. Once Khruschev had become reconciled with Tito, Albania, still more Stalinist than Stalin had been, turned against Russia. She took advantage of the Sino-Soviet split in 1960–1 to align herself with China, who installed a powerful radio transmitter which broadcasts attacks on American imperialism and its 'number one assistants', the Soviet 'revisionists'. She was expelled from Comecon and the Warsaw Pact in 1961, and became increasingly reliant on economic aid from China. In 1978, Chairman Hua ended this aid, part of China's long term strategy of becoming reconciled with Russia.

On pp. 46 and 50 we saw how Gheorghiu-Dej imposed a Stalinist régime on Rumania. In 1956 he supported Khruschev's call for peaceful co-existence and for national variations in socialism. In June 1958, Russian troops were withdrawn from the country, a sign of Khruschev's trust in the dictator. However, Rumania's leaders refused to accept the dictates of Comecon; they wanted to industrialise their country rather than have it be the supplier of oil and agricultural products to other developing Communist states. They were helped by aid from France which, under de Gaulle, was seeking to supplant the USA as the controller of Europe's destinies (p. 177). They also received offers of aid from China as part of that country's dispute with Russia.

In 1964, Rumania's leaders visited Paris and Peking, and in turn received visits from de Gaulle and Chinese leaders. After de Gaulle's visit in 1964, the Rumanian leaders claimed that he had promised military aid if Rumania were attacked by Warsaw Pact troops. Ceausescu, who succeeded to the leadership in 1965, continued Gheorghiu-Dej's independent policy. In 1967, he opposed proposals to invade Czechoslovakia and, when that invasion took place in 1968, he refused to allow Rumanian troops to be used. In 1980–1, Rumania was, again, the odd man out when, alone of the Warsaw Pact countries, she shunned the Pact's attempts to put military pressure on Poland. In 1982–4, Rumania took an even-handed line on the question of nuclear weapons, clearly identifying American and Soviet weapons as equally destabilising. In May–June 1984, while the rest of the satellites followed the Russian line and pulled out of the Olympic Games, Rumania announced that she would send her athletes to Los Angeles.

But Rumania's Stalinist leader has been unwilling to challenge Russia too vigorously. There is no attempt to allow anything like a Solidarity movement to develop in Rumania; there is no move to follow a Dubcek-like line. Rumania remains a member of the Warsaw Pact and of Comecon. The low standard of living inside the country, and the fact that 70 per cent of its trade is with Comecon countries, ensure that, in spite of national feeling and the wish to follow an independent line, Rumania remains solidly inside the satellite system. In June 1984 Ceausescu visited Moscow where he met President Chernenko. The communique used words such as 'businesslike . . . frankness . . .' to describe the talks but did not, as is the case after other such talks, report 'complete identity of views'. But it has to be noted that the main purpose behind the visit was to smooth out trading problems before the meeting of Comecon partners which took place later in June. Rumania remains a Russian satellite, albeit a wild card.

Yugoslavia – after Tito

Tito gained the reputation of being Europe's 'most benevolent dictator'. The people of Yugoslavia's six republics and two autonomous regions did not rise in rebellion in 1956, as did the peoples of Hungary and Poland. With the massive investment coming from the west and with Khruschev's removal of the nagging threat that Russia might intervene against the 'heretic', the Yugoslav people enjoyed a better quality of life than was available to the members of Comecon and the Warsaw Pact.

However, there were cracks even in the Tito-based edifice. Djilas had been a member of the ruling quartet (p. 48) and had, deservedly, gained the reputation of being Yugoslavia's leading intellectual. He became the sternest critic of the system under which, for all his rhetoric, Tito imposed a Stalinist-type control on the country. In the wake of the 'thaw' of 1956, during which Poles, Hungarians and even some Russians voiced their opposition to such control, Djilas demanded more liberalism in Yugoslavia. He protested that Yugoslavia's economic development would never 'take off' unless there was, first, a democratisation of the political system. Tito's response to the criticisms voiced by his one-time collaborator was decisive. Between 1956 and 1966, Djilas spent nine years in prison.

It was a tribute to Tito's 'benevolence' that Djilas was not killed, that he was, ultimately, released from prison and that he was allowed, when released, to continue to voice his criticism and to write his intellectual attacks on Titoism. However, the dictator's control over the country never seemed threatened; there was no Yugoslavian attempt in 1968 to follow the Dubcek line. Western observers were aware of the criticisms expressed by Djilas. They argued that, on Tito's death, Yugoslavia might well face a surge of anti-government activity, that there would be the same sort of 'release' as there had been in Russia after Stalin's death.

Tito died in 1980, when Poland was undergoing the early stages of its Solidarity-based campaign against dictatorship. The probability of a Yugoslav rising seemed the greater because of the deterioration in the economic situation in the aftermath of the oil-price increases of 1979 and the onset of the world-wide depression. However, the country remained politically stable and, in spite of Djilas and other critics, there was no call for a divergence from the Tito line.

In 1984, however, there was fresh evidence that the government was becoming increasingly concerned by the attacks levelled at the system by Djilas and his colleagues. The authorities were all too aware of the continued failure of the economic system; in 1983–4, inflation reached 55 per cent; 14 per cent of the workforce was unemployed; continued deficits in the country's balance of payments were reflected in the £14.2 billion foreign debt. They were also conscious of the way in which the growth of criticism in Poland had, first, been based on the country's economic failure and, second, had led to the threat of Russian intervention. In April 1984, the government ordered the arrest of many of the country's leading intellectuals, although allowing Djilas, 'the grand old man of Yugoslav dissent', to remain at liberty, free to telephone to the west and to be interviewed by western journalists.

The government points to the demand of some of Yugoslavia's regional governments for a return to 'the days of Tito', for, in fact, a neo-Stalinist crackdown on dissent and on leaders of ethnic minorities who demand a further weakening of the powers of the central government. Djilas, on the other hand, continues to maintain that the country's economic problems are inseparable from the weaknesses of the political system. As in Russia, so in Yugoslavia; the *apparatchiks* are unwilling to allow the development of that political 'liberalism' which, Djilas claims, would lead to the emergence of solutions for the economic problems. Such a liberalisation would be a threat to them; even if the result were to be improved economic development, the post-Tito rulers are unwilling to jeopardise their own power. Hence the toughening of internal security and the damage done to Yugoslavia's earlier reputation as the standard bearer for human rights in eastern Europe.

Documentary evidence

Document 5.1

Jan Sejna was a member of the Czech Communist Party when the Soviet-inspired coup took place in 1948. In 1954 he became a member of the ruling Central Committee and began to see at first hand the extent, and effects of, Soviet control of Czech affairs. He fled from Czechoslovakia in 1968 because of his fear that Dubcek's reforms would lead to Soviet military intervention (pp. 97–9).

One leader's 'crisis of faith'

I had learnt that there were two Marxisms; one for the Party leaders and the members of the Central Committee, the other for the Party rank and file and the people. The first kind of Marxism was not what Marx and Engels had taught me; it was simply the bourgeois life of enjoyment.

I had two choices; either to continue to work as a fanatical Communist; or to enjoy life like the other Party leaders; in fact, to cash in on the great deception. I changed more rapidly after 1956 when I had been in the USSR and talked every day with Soviet military leaders. Their lifestyle was the same as that of the nobility in Tsarist days. They treated the poor worse, and spent money with more abandon, than in the West. This was a genuine shock to me, for I had always thought that the Soviet leaders lived as simply as the workers.

The further I advanced in the Communist Party, the more I understood that the Communist system was a self-serving bureaucracy designed to maintain in power a cynical élite. I have written about my campaigns for the Party as a young man before the *coup* of 1948. Even after the *coup* of February 1948 we lived in a continuing atmosphere of crisis and fear that we were surrounded by enemies, as indeed we were – enemies of our own making!

My rustic naivety managed to survive the cynical way in which I was elected to Parliament and to the Central Committee in 1954; but it received the first of a series of shattering blows in 1955. The occasion was a meeting of the Central Committee to discuss agriculture and nutrition. The Government had closed a large number of sugar refineries, a move that obliged the peasants to transport their beet to distant mills for processing.

I criticised Ludmila Jankovcova, Deputy Prime Minister and member of the Politburo with special responsibility for food and agriculture, for this short sighted policy. Jankovcova cornered me at the first coffee break.

'Who gave *you* the right to criticise a member of the Politburo?', she demanded, and continued in a caustic tone, 'You only see the local view, you don't know the national picture.'

'I'm here in Prague to defend the interests of my constituents,' I answered stoutly, 'not to sympathise with your problems.'

This was heresy. Jankovcova was formerly a Social Democrat, but she had learned a lot from her new comrades. 'Your job is not to tell the Party what the masses want, but to explain the Party's policy to the people.'

Novotny adopted a more paternal attitude and took me aside for a few words.

'You must get to know the difference between a local Party meeting and the deliberations of the Central Committee.'

Much more direct advice came from General Zeman, Chief of the Main Political Administration: 'If you want to continue your career, shut up!'

I began to wonder if I really understood Marxism. Nevertheless, it marked the start of my apprenticeship in the mechanics of power and the making of Party policy.

The Russian Army left Czechoslovakia in 1945 and did not return until their invasion in 1968. But after the Communist *coup* of February 1948, the Russians pulled all the strings. For the majority of Czechs, Soviet imperialism was invisible until the tanks rolled again through the streets. Even I had no idea of the degree to which the Russians controlled my country, until I became Chief of Staff to the Minister of Defence.

Soviet control operates at the highest levels of Party and Government. The most comprehensive supervision emanates from the Politburo and the Central Committee of the Soviet Party which constantly guides and monitors the work of its satellites. The Soviet Ambassador in Prague is the representative not only of the Soviet Government but also of the Central Committee of the Soviet Party. He has the power to intervene directly with the First Secretary and with the Heads of Department of Central Committees, as well as all Ministers.

The Russians have their own representatives stationed inside the Ministries of Defence and Interior. In Stalin's time there were KGB advisers in the Ministry of Interior from district bodies right up to headquarters; the senior KGB adviser had an office next door to the Minister. One of Khruschev's reforms in 1957 was to remove the majority of these Soviet advisers from our Army and from the lower levels of the Ministry of the Interior. Their titles were changed to 'Representatives of the Warsaw Pact' and their duties to 'co-ordinating policy at the highest level', but their powers remained the same.

By 1964, Czechoslovakia was beginning to suffer serious inflation as a result of the switch to heavy industry inspired by the Soviet Union, and the huge balance of payments deficit we were running with the USSR. Our massive arms purchases helped to sustain this deficit. The country was choking in bureaucracy because our centralised administration gave powers of decision over the smallest units of production to anonymous Party officials in Prague.

Novotny set up a committee to prepare proposals for economic reform. But there was general dissatisfaction. Intellectuals in the Party were restless at the lack of fundamental freedoms and Party discipline began to suffer. It became difficult to recruit younger people into the Party, whose membership was ageing fast.

(Sejna, J., *We Will Bury You*, Sidgwick & Jackson, 1982, pp. 158–66)

FURTHER READING

ACZEL, T., *Ten Years after: Hungary 1956*, McGibbon and Kee, 1966

ARNOLD–FORSTER, M., *The Siege of Berlin*, Collins, 1979

ARON, R., *The Opium of the Intellectuals*, Greenwood Press, 1957

AUTY, P., *Yugoslavia*, Thames and Hudson, 1965

BROWN, A., AND GRAY, J., *Culture and Political Changes in Communist States*, Macmillan, 1977

CAUTE, D., *Communism and the French Intellectuals*, 1964

CHAPMAN, C., *August 21: The Rape of Czechoslovakia*, Cassell, 1968

COHEN, L. J., AND WARWICK, P., *Political Cohesion in a Fragile Mosaic: The Yugoslav Experience*, Westview Press, 1983

FISCHER–GALATI, S., *Eastern Europe in the 1980s*, Croom Helm, 1981

GARVEY, T., *Bones of Contention*, Routledge and Kegan Paul, 1978
GRAHAM, L. S., *Rumania: A Developing Socialist State*, Westview Press, 1982
GROSSER, A., *Germany in our Time*, Pall Mall, 1971
LAQUEUR, W., *A Continent Astray: Europe 1970–8*, 1979
MIKES, G., *The Hungarian Revolution*, André Deutsch, 1957
MORGAN, R., *The United States and West Germany, 1945–73*, OUP, 1976
PIPES, R., *Soviet Strategy in Europe*, Macdonald and Jane's, 1976
RACHWALD, A. R., *Poland between the Superpowers*, Westview Press, 1983
SCHARF, C. B., *Politics and Change in East Germany*, Westview Press, 1984
SEJNA, J., *We Will Bury You*, Sidgwick and Jackson, 1982
SHAWCROSS, W., *Dubcek*, Weidenfeld and Nicolson, 1970
URBAN, G. R., *Détente*, Temple Smith, 1976
URBAN, G. R., *Euro-Communism*, Temple Smith, 1978

6

The Soviet Union, 1945–84

The régime and its people

'With the disappearance of classes the State will inevitably disappear. Society, which will organise production anew on the basis of a free and equal association of producers, will send the whole State machine to the place where it will then belong; to the museum of antiquities, along with the spinning wheel and the bronze axe.'[1]

Friedrich Engels

Russia had been the last of the major European powers to become industrialised and, in 1917, there was only a small industrial working class on which Marxism was supposed to depend. The success of Lenin and Trotsky in establishing Bolshevik rule in Russia in 1917 ought not to blind us to the fact that, even in 1917, Marxism was opposed by the majority of reformers and revolutionaries in Tsarist Russia. It was seen as one of those undesirable westernising influences (pp. 43–4); most Russian revolutionaries looked for a purely Russian-based revolution; their Slavophilism typified the thinking of people from a wide spectrum of Russian society.

In October 1917, Lenin and Trotsky seized power in the second revolution of that year. Their revolution was based as much on the power of the Red Army as on the weakness of the Provisional Government – and owed little to Marxist 'historical inevitability'. Many Russians, unwilling to be consigned to Trotsky's 'garbage can of history', fought in a civil war in which they were helped by Allied intervention. Lenin created the Cheka, the secret police forerunner to the KGB, to help him overcome his enemies, including the naval garrison at Kronstadt which had been largely instrumental in bringing him to power in the first place.

Having come to power in an unpropitious country (from a Marxist point of view) in an illegal fashion, Lenin then developed a new interpretation of Marxist philosophy. He taught the virtues of 'democratic centralism'. The basic organ of the post-Lenin Communist Party is the local cell, a handful of members in a given army unit, institution or factory. Each cell elects a representative to the town committee (or soviet) which elects representatives to a provincial soviet and so on until one reaches the Party Congress. This meets every five years; it elects a Central Committee to carry on the day-to-day work of running the Party; that Committee elects the Politburo which, in Lenin's time, consisted of only five people.

The Communist Party is the only political party in the USSR; government rests entirely in its hands. It claims that the system is democratic since people, at the base, play a part in the choosing of representatives. At the same time, it claims that the system is 'centralist' since each lower body has to obey the decisions of higher bodies. In this way, the Politburo controls the activities of all the organisations in the Party and government structure. Under Lenin, Stalin and Brezhnev a single person dominated the Politburo (Document 6.1).

Kerensky had foreseen this development. In June 1917 he had said of Lenin's attempted coup; 'Out of the fiery chaos that you wish to make will arise, like a phoenix, a dictator.' But, with the constitution of 1918, and subsequent constitutions in 1924, 1936 and 1977, the Communist Party has endeavoured to clothe Party supremacy and the dictatorship with democratic clothes. The law-making body of the USSR is the Supreme Soviet. This is made up of two chambers: the Soviet of the Union has about 750 members representing all the constituencies; the Soviet of the Nationalities is composed of 32 members from each union Republic, 11 from each Autonomous Republic and one from each National Area, about 630 members in total. These two Chambers elect a Praesidium of 33 members under the chairmanship of the President who ranks as Head of State.

As with the Communist Party, so with the State structure; people at the constituency level of the village, city and collective farm elect members to the Supreme Soviet who, as we have seen, elect the Praesidium. Since the only political party in Russia is the Communist Party, all the members of the Praesidium are Communists as are all the members of the Supreme Soviet. Indeed, most of the members of the Politburo will also be members of the Praesidium.

The Supreme Soviet meets only for a few days each year and then simply approves the items presented to it by the Communist Party Secretariat. The Praesidium appears to have more power; it is in session throughout the year; it issues decrees and interprets the Constitution. But it has no control over Ministers who are, in turn, supervised by the Politburo, which controls the decision making and action of all government departments.

All members of the Praesidium, Politburo and Council of Ministers will have served a long apprenticeship in the Party's service. Their promotion will have depended on the goodwill of the head of whatever section of the cellular structure they were serving at any time.

In most references to the country in this book, the word 'Russia' has been used. The correct title, of course, is the Union of Soviet Socialist Republics. There are now fifteen such Soviet Socialist republics, of which the Russian Republic is the largest in size and population. In theory, any of the Republics has the right to secede from the Union. But the system is geared to ensuring that no such strongminded and independent opposition could ever come to power in any Republic.

The War, 1941–5

'You have only to kick in the door and the whole rotten structure will come crashing down.'

Hitler to Runstedt, 1941

Between 1928 and 1941, Stalin had driven Russia into forced industrialisation, arguing that 'We are fifty or a hundred years behind the advanced countries. We must make good this distance in ten years. Either we do so or we go under.' Evidence of his success, in certain fields, is provided by the following table:

Production figures, in millions of tons

	1928	1932	1937
Oil	11.7	22.3	28.5
Pig iron	3.2	6.2	14.5
Steel	4.0	5.9	17.7
Coal	35.4	64.3	128.0

The output of electricity also increased (in billions of kw hours):

5.05	13.4	36.2

During this period there was a consolidation of industries in European Russia and a vast expansion in the number of industries beyond the Urals. This latter region escaped the long period of German occupation after 1941, but much of European Russia was conquered and destroyed. At the height of their success, the Germans occupied one-third of Russia and 'ruled' over 60 million Soviet citizens. While many people in western Russia had welcomed the invading Germans as 'liberators', the majority obeyed Stalin's command that they wage 'total war'. Animals were killed, crops and buildings destroyed by the retreating Russians. This 'scorched earth' campaign added to the damage done by German planes and artillery.

People in many Russian cities and towns also suffered. Many cities, such as Kharkhov, Kiev and Minsk, were almost totally destroyed. The people of Leningrad endured a siege from August 1941 until January 1944. Under the command of Zhdanov, the people endured continual bombing, and constant shortages of food and other supplies; one million died, 632,000 of them from starvation (p. 87). At Kiev, where the Germans murdered over 33,000 Jews at Babi Yar, the famine was so severe that, even after the city had been re-taken by the Russians, the people took things into their own hands; law and order broke down as roaming bands hunted the devastated area of the Ukraine. The MVD (forerunner to the KGB) was called on to crush these 'bandits' and other food rioters in cities such as Kharkhov.

But, for the Russian government, the war was not all loss. Millions of Russians rushed to join the Communist Party during the 'Patriotic War'. Stalin appealed to ancient Russian tradition and history, comparing Hitler with Napoleon, and allowed the appearance of works praising older Russian heroes, such as Peter the Great, Suvorov and Kutuzov. He allowed more freedom to the Russian Orthodox Church so that religion, too, came to the aid of the Party.

By 1945, steel production was only half of what it had been in 1937, and agricultural output was down to 60 per cent of its pre-war level. This was the result of enemy action, the general dislocation, the lack of skilled workers, the failure of the transport system and the consequent shortage of food. These factors affected output everywhere so that, for example, output in the undamaged Baku oilfields fell to half its pre-war level.

During the war there were none of the purges, arrests and trials that had plagued Russia in the 1930s. With, additionally, the appeals to patriotism, the freedom allowed to the Church, and the diminished role of the once-powerful political commissars in army and factory, there was good reason for the Russian people to hope that 'after the war' everything would be better than it had been in the 1930s. Millions of Russian soldiers had served in the army which first conquered and then occupied Germany. To them, even in the harsh conditions prevailing in that devastated country (p. 19), there appeared to be a superfluity of housing, food and consumer goods. Stalin and Zhdanov knew that in 1814–15 another Russian army had occupied areas of Western Europe. From its ranks there had arisen that Decembrist conspiracy which had threatened the autocracy of Alexander I. Stalin and Zhdanov ensured that there would not be a repeat performance (p. 44). Once the war was over, strict measures were taken; indoctrination was strengthened and thousands of potential 'thought criminals' imprisoned or executed.

The threat from 'cosmopolitanism' and 'westernisation' was the greater because of the territories gained by Russia as a result of the war; Lithuania, Latvia, Estonia, Eastern Poland, Bessarabia, Moldavia, East Prussia, Carpatho-Russia, Karelia, Petsamo, Tannu Tuva, the Kurile Islands and Southern Sakhalin. There were millions of new citizens to be re-educated and incorporated into the Soviet system.

The people in western Russia who had collaborated with the Germans were transported to be re-settled in the Soviet east. During the war, Stalin had recalled the patriotism of Tsars such as Peter the Great. For many Russians, Stalin was the latter-day version of the tyrannical rulers of the past. Like them, he annihilated his enemies, and claimed a monopoly of political power. He was part of that Russian continuum which makes Russia radically different from the West.

Stalin's last years, 1945–53

'We cannot for one minute forget the basic fact that our country remains the one socialist state in the world . . . victory doesn't mean that all dangers to our state system and social order have disappeared. Only the immediate danger which threatened us from Hitler's Germany has disappeared.'

President Kalinin, speaking in August 1945

In the immediate post-war years, many Russians endured what has been termed 'a crisis of faith'.[2] The returning soldiers, with their tales of German 'wealth' and with captured booty to prove it, hoped that life in post-war Russia would be different to what it had been; Stalin had other ideas. He saw his first task as the re-building of Russian industry, mainly to provide for a strong military machine. Old industrial centres were rebuilt and new industrial areas opened up and developed. These new industrial centres attracted millions of people from the country-side; Sverdlovsk became a major centre; Revda a major mining town; Polevskoi a new manufacturing centre. For the 'immigrants', life was hard with a shortage of housing and food. But for Stalin these new centres were signs of Soviet success, also reflected in the output of Russian industry.

Production figures in millions of tons (see also p. 108)

	1945	1950	1953
Oil	19	38	53
Steel	9	27	38
Coal	149	260	320

The output of electricity also increased (in billions of kw hours):

	43	87	133

These impressive figures mask the fact that Russian planners seemed unaware of the new techniques being adopted in western countries, in, for example, the production of steel. They also ignored the many new industries on which most western countries based their post-war development, such as the petro-chemical and plastics industries. Nor did they pay much attention to the needs of Russia's major industry – agriculture; they continued to produce the old-fashioned heavy trac-tors, and did not produce anything like the lightweight but powerful tractors being produced in the West.

During the war, there had been a fairly liberal attitude towards agriculture; peasants had been allowed to spend an increasing amount of time on their private plots which had grown in size. After the war, largely under Khruschev's influence, there was a reduction in the number of collectives; these were merged into much larger units. In

1947 there were 250,000 collectives, by 1950 only 125,000 and by 1952 only 94,000. The planners assumed that the larger units would be more efficient and productive. In fact there was, for many years, a shortage of machinery and fertilisers so that output rose, if at all, only slowly.

The success of the industrial development was due largely to the massive aid from the west – the raw materials taken at nominal prices from the satellites in eastern Europe (p. 51), the contribution of the two million German prisoners of war, and the goods and equipment taken from Germany, Manchuria and other places as reparations. Without this 'aid' the Russian recovery would have been much slower. Even as it was, the Russian people had to pay dearly for the concentration on heavy industry. In the expanding towns, millions of people lived in shanty suburbs and the housing shortage remained the biggest social problem in Russia. Conditions were no better in older cities and towns. The British Military Attaché in Moscow wrote: '[in Moscow] all houses, practically without exception, show lights from every window after dark. This seems to indicate that every room is both a living room by day and a bedroom by night. There is no place in overcrowded Moscow for the luxury of eating and sleeping in separate rooms.'[3] In 1977, on a visit to Russia, my son told his Russian friends that each of my children had his or her own bedroom. 'Nobility', whispered the old grandmother in the overcrowded room where she lived with her extended family.

Throughout Stalin's last years (and for years after) the standard of living for the majority of people hardly improved. Housing, food, clothing and other necessities of life were both difficult to obtain and poor in quality. One reason for this was the investment in heavy industry which grew twice as fast as the Gross National Product and three times as quickly as did personal consumption.

This failure to match western progress was one of the reasons for the post-war 'crisis of faith' and for the resurgence of Stalinist terrorism. Once again, Stalin took on the role of Ivan the Terrible. In 1937–8 some thousand men and women had been shot each day in Moscow alone; after the war Stalin, now corrupted by power, once more revitalised the secret police and gave Beria a free hand.

During these years Stalin behaved like an oriental despot. There was no Party Congress between 1939 and 1952; there were few meetings of the Central Committee; the Politburo was his tool (Document 6.1). In 1952, he called the Nineteenth Party Congress when a new Central Committee was elected. At the same time, a new purge seemed to be planned; there were rumours that a number of Jewish doctors had poisoned some of the now dead Russian leaders. Before that purge could get under way, Stalin died on 5 March 1953 (Document 6.2). The death of the man who had dominated life for so many years, who had controlled the vast empire for so long came as a shock to many Russians; 'The whole of Russia wept. So did I. We wept sincerely with grief and perhaps also with fear of the unknown.'[4]

Khruschev's climb to dictatorship, 1953–7

'Stalin abandoned the method of ideological struggle for that of administrative violence, mass repressions and terror. Arbitrary behaviour by one person encouraged arbitrariness in others. Mass arrests and deportations of many thousands of people, execution without trial and without normal investigation created conditions of insecurity, fear and even desperation.'[5]

Khruschev, in 1956

Nikita Khruschev (1894–1971) was one who had served Stalin and had been promoted up the Party ladder as a reward. He had fought with the Red Army during the Civil War before working for the Party in Kiev and, later, in Moscow where, in 1935, he became secretary of the Moscow Regional Committee, working closely with the Mayor of Moscow, Bulganin. From 1938 to 1947, he was mainly concerned with Ukrainian affairs, playing his part in the stamping out of Ukrainian national feeling (p. 108). He was Prime Minister of the Ukrainian Soviet Republic from its liberation until 1947; in 1949 he was appointed to reorganise Russian agriculture (p. 110). At the time of Stalin's death, he was a member of the Party Praesidium.

On Stalin's death, the Central Committee appointed Georgi Malenkov as Party First Secretary and Prime Minister. It seemed as if he was destined to be the new Stalin, with all the levers of power in his hands. Khruschev was named as Senior Party Secretary with his supporter, Marshal Zhukov, as Minister of Defence. Within a few weeks, the Central Committee had voted to 'release' Malenkov from the key position of Party First Secretary, arguing that he was fully occupied by his duties as Prime Minister.

In July 1953, a mere three months after Stalin's death, Malenkov ordered the arrest of Beria, the head of the secret police. It was Khruschev who explained to the other members of the Central Committee that Beria was plotting to achieve supreme power and their liquidation. Beria was taken to a military barracks where Marshal Konev presided over a court martial which tried him on charges of spying for the West, the murder of thousands and of plotting against the leadership. He was sentenced to death and shot by a military firing squad. Khruschev took advantage of Beria's fall to purge the KGB and to appoint General Serov in his place.

Malenkov launched a campaign to raise living standards by the manufacturing of more consumer goods. In August 1953, he announced agricultural reforms, including the abolition of tax-in-kind which Stalin had imposed on the peasants' private plots. The Kremlin, which the paranoiac Stalin had ordered closed, was re-opened to the public. An investigative commission was set up to study the evidence of illegalities which had emerged during Beria's trial. In the more relaxed atmosphere of this post-Stalin 'liberalisation', Malenkov allowed the production of books, films and plays showing the 'dark' side of life in Soviet Russia. The bell-wether Ilya Erhenburg published a short novel, symbolically called *The Thaw*, which gave its name to the period.

In 1953, 1954 and 1955, Khruschev was busy building his own power base while also undermining Malenkov's. In 1954, for example, he called for a clamp down on the rising flood of critical literature. When Malenkov claimed that war with the West would mean the destruction of the world, Khruschev argued that it would only 'end in the collapse of the world imperialist system.' When Malenkov claimed, as a result of his agricultural reforms, that 'the whole country is fully supplied with grain', Khruschev said 'grain production does not cover all the needs of the national economy' and showed that Russia had fewer cattle in 1955 than in 1916. He called for agricultural reform to be handled by the Party (under his direction) and in March 1954 he launched his 'Virgin Lands' scheme for the farming of huge areas of marginal land in Kazakhstan (Fig. 6.1a, p. 120) and Southern Siberia.

Khruschev was appointed First Party Secretary at the September 1953 meeting of the Central Committee. Like his mentor, Stalin, he used this position to consolidate his hold on the Party apparatus. He persuaded the Stalinist 'old guard', Molotov and Kaganovich, that Malenkov was leading the Party and country to disaster. He persuaded the military that concentration on consumer goods would weaken the nation's defences; he showed the bureaucrats running the conservative industrial ministries that a switch from heavy to light industry would weaken their relative position in the hierarchy of power; he persuaded the *apparatchik* that the economic reforms would have undesirable political and social repercussions.

Malenkov was a colourless personality and a weak leader, who did not take the steps needed to thwart Khruschev, who had shared his belief in the need for the increased production of consumer goods and for those agricultural reforms which, in turn, would call for increased output of machines, steel and chemicals. In February 1955, he was deposed from the post of Prime Minister. His successor, Marshal Nikolai Bulganin, the military's representative on the Politburo, appointed him to be Minister for Electrical Energy. Bulganin had worked with Khruschev in Moscow in 1935. 'Mr K and Mr B' became well-known in the West where they presented what appeared to be a more acceptable face of communism.

Back in Russia, Khruschev was busily engaged on strengthening his position. He organised a witch hunt of Malenkov's supporters in the provinces, had one of his own supporters, Shepilov, appointed editor of *Pravda* and persuaded the Central Committee to criticise Malenkov in July 1955 for opposing a rapprochement with Tito. The military, the planning chiefs and the *apparatchik* welcomed the new concentration on heavy industry, which, however, was accompanied by more invest-ment in agriculture, a drive to build more houses, the offer of higher minimum wages and better working conditions. Khruschev continued Malenkov's policy of de-Stalinisation. While the rift with Tito was patched over, relations were established with West Germany, and Adenauer invited to visit Moscow. In 1955 and 1956, five million prisoners were freed from labour camps or had their sentences commuted to exile.

But until January 1956 there was no criticism of Stalin. Certainly, his name was mentioned less on radio and appeared less often in the press. But the Stalinist 'hardliners' would not permit overt criticism. Khruschev and other 'liberals' were also aware that such criticism might have incalculable effects on Russian society. In January 1956, however, *Pravda* launched an attack on 'little Stalins' who in the provinces and in industry abused their power, and resented any criticism of their lack of achievement. When the Twentieth Party Congress opened in February 1956, there had been no decision to condemn Stalin. Khruschev's six-hour long opening speech dealt with many problems. He adopted the very attitudes which a year before he had condemned in Malenkov. War, he said, was not inevitable; western communists might take the parliamentary road to power; light industry must develop quickly. It was this speech which first roused the hostility of the Chinese communists who condemned such 'revisionism' of Marxist-Leninist doctrine (p. 252).

It was Mikoyan who, on February 17, first criticised Stalin's rule and his attack on Party leaders who had been condemned by the autocrat as 'enemies of the people'. Mikoyan called on the Congress ('the most important since Lenin's death') to undertake a complete re-think of its position as regards the recent past. Only then did Khruschev make that 'secret speech' which was published in the West but which has never appeared in print in Russia itself (Document 6.3). This condemnation had major repercussions in eastern Europe (Chapter 5) and affected Sino-Soviet relations (Fig. 6.1), so that it may be said to have played a part in the changed relationships between the West and the two communist superpowers. But the condemnation was limited in its scope. There was, for example, no attack on the system which allowed a Stalin to come to power and to exercise such control. Nor did Khruschev make any attempt to rehabilitate the old Bolshevik leaders who had been executed by the now-condemned autocrat.

In spite of the Party's best efforts, knowledge of the 'secret speech' did leak out.

> 'Something approaching a crisis of conscience appears to exist among many Soviet young people. They were raised to believe that Stalin was all-good and all-wise; the recent revelations about him have caused many to develop doubts, not only about Stalin but about his successors as well.'[6]

In eastern Europe, the anti-Stalinist mood led to the rising in Poland (pp. 87–8) and the more serious revolution in Hungary (pp. 93–4). It is not surprising that Khruschev was attacked by the Stalinist 'hardliners' on the Politburo and in the Central Committee. Until June 1956 he had seemed to be gaining power. The Stalinist, Kaganovich, had been moved to a junior government post, Molotov replaced as Foreign Minister by Khruschev's supporter, Shepilov. Within days of these moves came the uprising in Poland and the appearance of student unrest in Moscow itself.

Students at Moscow University put up transcripts of BBC Russian Service bulletins about the Hungarian uprising. Party lecturers were heckled at factory meetings and wallposters appeared in the naval academies of Kronstadt and Vladivostock.

In November 1956, Khruschev adopted a harder line. He had 200 student leaders expelled from Moscow University and warned the rest that if they did not like life in the University, 'you can go out to work and others will come and study in your place.' He had the press run a campaign against 'rotten elements' and 'demagogues' who were seeking to destroy the Party's image. In December 1956, the Central Committee heard criticism of Khruschev, whose policy had allowed such 'elements' to feel free to criticise. He was not overthrown, although he suffered a series of minor defeats. Molotov was put in charge of Party propaganda and ideological work; 'Zhdanovoism' would ride again. Malenkov saw some of his supporters promoted in the wake of criticism of Khruschev's economic policies, while he himself was given more prominence in the Committee than he had received for some time.

Khruschev was not slow to learn. 'We are all Stalinists', he claimed at a reception held in the Kremlin on New Year's Eve. In January he called Stalin 'a model Communist', while Stalinism he described as 'a willingness to fight for proletarian interests'. However, he maintained his attempts to improve Russian industrial efficiency. In February 1957, he proposed the creation of about a hundred regional councils (*sovnarkhozy*) in place of central planning commissions. But this liberalisation was condemned by the Politburo in June 1957 by seven votes to four. Khruschev then decided to play 'the democratic card' by presenting his case before the Central Committee. His friend, Marshal Zhukov, used airforce planes to fly in Khruschev's supporters to this Committee meeting.

The Central Committee reversed the Politburo's decision and approved Khruschev's plans. It also criticised Malenkov, Molotov and Kaganovich for being an 'Anti-Party Group' and dismissed them, along with Pervukhin and Saburov, from their posts. Only Molotov refused to vote for his own condemnation; the rest of the Committee was unanimous. Malenkov was sent to run a power station in the Urals; Molotov became ambassador to Outer Mongolia; Kaganovich was given a junior post. A year later, in August 1958, Khruschev dismissed the other two who had voted against him, Bulganin (from whom he took over the post of Prime Minister) and Voroshilov. Khruschev now held all the levers of power in his hands.

The Khruschev years, 1957–64

'You cannot put theory into your soup or Marxism into your clothes. If, after forty years of Communism, a person cannot have a glass of milk or a pair of shoes, he will not believe that Communism is a good thing, no matter what you tell him.'

Khruschev

The son of a mine worker and educated late in life, Khruschev married the daughter of a Ukrainian farmer and seemed, to many western outside observers, to be a peasant at heart. He was, from 1917 onwards, a convinced Marxist, and became, as we have seen, a ruthless Stalinist.

However, he had an informal manner, appearing to be 'cosy', if sometimes ridiculous. This did not please more serious-minded communists. While waiting for him at the railway station in Prague in 1962, the Secretary of the Czech Central Committee remarked cheerfully; 'Now we shall have some fun again. Comrade Khruschev is a great one for cracking jokes.' The Soviet Ambassador retorted; 'Do you think that the First Secretary of our Party should be a clown?'[8]

This visit to Prague was only one of many visits which Khruschev made outside Russia. He visited Poland, Yugoslavia, China, India, Burma, Afghanistan, Egypt, Britain, France, Austria, Scandinavia and the USA. Such travelling would not be remarkable in a western statesman-politician. It is a reminder of Russia's isolationism, and of her leaders' suspicion of the West, that Khruschev's journeys were noteworthy.

Many people hoped that his accession to supreme power would lead to a change in domestic and foreign policy (p. 252). Many western commentators have suggested that a change did take place. If it did, it was a change in degree and not a change in kind. There was, as we have seen, no rehabilitation of Stalin's victims. There was, on the other hand, Khruschev's own ruthless climb to power – on the back of the Army and on the broken careers of many of the old guard. His clownish behaviour may have disguised this ruthless trait: 'he wore his charm like the grass used to hide animal traps.'

In his domestic policy, Khruschev followed, at first, the very policies for which he had condemned Malenkov. The power of the secret police waned further; the labour camps held fewer prisoners; there were fewer arrests and no major purges. In 1956, following the denunciation of Stalin, Pasternak was completing *Dr Zhivago*, and Dudintsev's novel *Not By Bread Alone* was about to be published – with its condemnation of the new Soviet middle class with all its graft, greed, careerism and corrupt privileges. Students at universities throughout the Soviet Union were publishing critical articles in magazines and putting up wallposters condemning the system. There were other outward signs of the inward effect of 'the Thaw'; drainpipe trousers, jeans, open sandals, winklepicking shoes and flowered shirts were worn by Russian youth who sought to imitate western youth not only in dress but in critical questioning of their elders and of authority. In 1957, Moscow was the scene of an International Youth Festival, and Russian youth learned to imitate the Americanism of pop culture. Tourism was increased under a more liberal régime. In place of the few hundred who had visited Russia in 1953, there were 13,000 American tourists in 1959. To the hardliners, many now out of power, this 'cosmopolitanism' seemed a high price to pay for the much-needed western currencies used to buy western technology.

But Khruschev was unwilling to allow 'liberalism' to run anything like a full course. In his condemnation of Stalin he had said; 'We cannot let this matter get out of the Party, especially not to the press. We should know the limit. We should not give ammunition to the enemy.' And when things looked like getting out of control, Khruschev was as ruthless as any Stalinist could have wished. The students at Moscow University were quickly silenced (p. 115); Pasternak's *Dr Zhivago* was never published in Russia. In Hungary, he was coldblooded and ruthless; he personally ordered the seizure of the Hungarian leader, Imre Nagy, and his subsequent execution (p. 94). He did little to reduce the pervasive influence of the KGB in Russia, although he tried to bring it more firmly under his control.[9]

The anti-Stalin campaign continued. In the 22nd Party Congress in 1961, one delegate told how Lenin had appeared to her in a dream, complaining about the decision to place Stalin's embalmed body in the Mausoleum in Red Square. 'It is unpleasant for me to be side by side with Stalin who brought so many problems upon the Party.' Stalin's body was removed, in yet another tactical move in the 'game' in which Stalin was attacked while the Party and the system was left untouched. For the labour camps still existed – at Kandalakskaya in the north-west, at Dubroviag near Moscow (with 19 camps in a massive complex), at Guryveka, Tomsk and Memerevo in Central Russia and Talaya and Magadan in the east, all part of that 'Gulag Archipelago' described by Solzhenitsyn.

The superficial, often temporary, and always merely cosmetic changes which Khruschev allowed, made little change in the system of government. It was, therefore, relatively simple for Brezhnev to make other small changes – again, in degree and not in kind – to bring back the Stalinist apparatus in force in the 1970s.

Khruschev planned an increased production of consumer goods as a way of making the system more acceptable. Defence plants were made to turn out motor cars and radio sets; the production of leather shoes, woollen fabrics and knitted clothes doubled between 1953 and 1963; the output of refrigerators rose from 49,000 to nearly one million. These large increases still left Russia very far behind the West in terms of production of such goods. In housing there was a similarly limited improvement; the target was raised so that the allowance per person was 6.8 square metres instead of the previous 4.67 square metres.

Khruschev's development of a consumer-orientated society was condemned by the Chinese who accused him of 'practicism' and of wanted to create a 'goulash society'. Khruschev also led Russia into the second industrial revolution. Stalin had concentrated on the old staple industries, especially coal, iron and steel. Khruschev started the switch to an economy based on oil, natural gas and water power. By 1961, the Soviet Union was the world's second largest oil producer behind the USA; by 1963 she was producing 243 million tons, of which 66 million tons were being exported. The vast reserves of natural gas discovered in Siberia were exploited, and in 1963 the first huge pipeline was constructed from fields near Bukhara to the industrial towns of the Urals.

But the wellbeing of the Soviet economy depended, as always, on the agricultural sector. In 1957, Khruschev launched his campaign to promote the growing of maize, to plough up grassland, to popularise peat compost and to 'catch up the United States in the production of meat and milk.' The Ten Year Plan, inaugurated in 1959, called for impossible rates of growth. Undaunted, Khruschev unveiled in 1961 plans to surpass America 'in all fields' and promised that some goods and services would be provided free in 1980. He continued with his earlier schemes for the consolidation of collectives into huge farms (p. 110) and by 1964 there were only some 50,000 agricultural complexes. While he tried to ensure an increased delivery of machinery and fertilisers, he also reduced collective farm quotas and paid a higher price for their deliveries, and relaxed restrictions on the private plots.

In agriculture and industry, Khruschev's policies enjoyed early success. The Virgin Lands produced two massive harvests. Twice as many houses were completed in 1958 as in 1955; the output of cement, coal, oil, electricity and steel grew rapidly – by 1963 Russia produced more steel than Germany, France and Britain combined. Khruschev could claim that his liberalisation worked; that, while the over-centralisation of the past had held things back, his insistence on regional, as opposed to central, control provided more incentives to management and men.

But the improvement was of short duration. In fact, the Russian government was trying to do too much with its scarce resources. The military insisted on increased spending on defence; spending increased by one-third between 1959 and 1963. In the competition for resources between 'guns and butter', the 'guns' won, so that there were never enough resources for the implementation of Khruschev's bolder plans for consumer goods industries. The rate of industrial growth fell, from 13 per cent in 1954, to 10 per cent in 1958, and to 7.5 per cent in 1964.

And the falling rate of growth of the GNP was even more significant. It had been 10 per cent in 1958, when the Soviet GNP was about 44 per cent of the American; in 1961, growth rate fell to 6.5 per cent, and in 1963 to less than 3 per cent. Russia was not going to overtake the Americans at this rate.

Why, apart from increased defence spending, did Khruschev fail? The Virgin Lands scheme led to soil erosion as the fertile top soil was swept away. The whole enterprise was a disaster. Elsewhere, the lower ranks in the Party bureaucracy and in the government machine had never welcomed the industrial plans which Khruschev introduced so enthusiastically; they were reluctant to make the changes demanded, and the dead hand of this bureaucracy helped ensure that his plans would not be fully implemented. Those plans depended, to a large extent, on local initiative and on increased productivity on the part of individual workers, managers and plant. Khruschev might have ensured this initiative and productivity if he had been prepared to allow greater freedom to management – if he had, in fact, allowed the appearance of a market economy. This, however, would have had political repercussions; western concepts of 'freedom' might have been dragged in on the coat tails of economic freedom.

Instead, Khruschev tried to generate initiative from the centre. In 1962, regional and district Party Committees were divided; one half of a committee looked after industry while the other half looked after agriculture. The number of such controlling committees was halved, which meant that the committees controlling the economy did not match the pattern of committees exercising political control. At the same time, with the creation of the larger agricultural units (p. 118), the administrative boundaries of agricultural districts were changed, and these coincided with neither political borders nor industrial-committee structure. It is little wonder that the *apparatchik* were either alienated or bewildered.

The military were angered by the reduction in the size of the armed forces – there being three million fewer servicemen in 1963 than in 1956. The call for increased spending on space development and new missiles led to this fall in manpower. The navy was, relatively, neglected as more attention was paid to rocket development and missile construction. The military were determined to switch leaders in the hope that this would lead to a change of policies.

The Party ideologists had been angered by Khruschev's re-definition of Marxism and his hopes for 'peaceful co-existence', and they were concerned that his overtures to the West would lead to Russia being contaminated by 'cosmopolitanism'. They argued that his de-Stalinisation had brought about the crisis in Poland and Hungary. Many blamed him for his conduct during the quarrel with China (Figures 6.1a, 6.1b) and for the 'adventurism' of the Cuban affair (pp. 248–51).

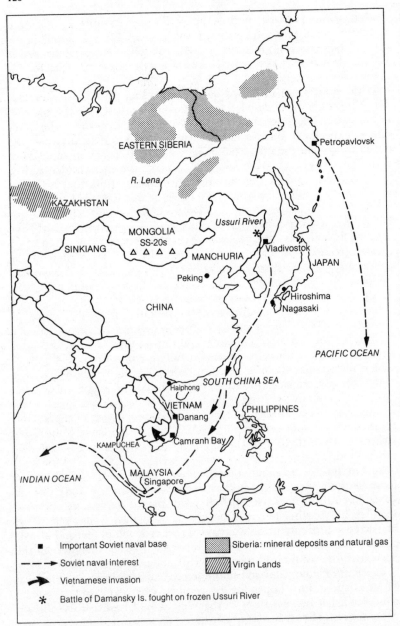

6.1a Russian and Chinese interests clash along the border and in Vietnam, which forces Russia to maintain defensive and offensive forces in the Far East.

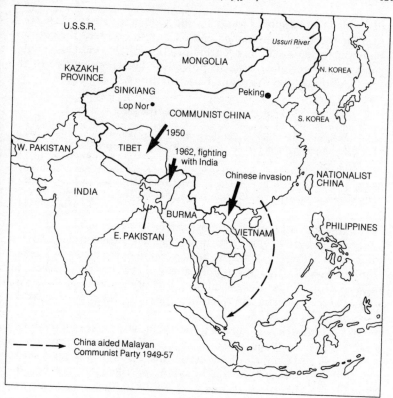

6.1b Chinese expansionism.

Khruschev played a part in his own downfall by the way in which he treated his closest supporters. In 1957, he had been saved by Zhukov's actions at the time of the 'Anti-Party' group's activities (p. 115). Barely a year later, while Zhukov was on a visit to Yugoslavia, he was dismissed by Khruschev, who had been persuaded by the KGB that the Marshal was becoming too powerful and seeking an even stronger position. Another of his strongest supporters had been his former mistress, Madame Furtseva, First Secretary of the Moscow Party, who had used her great influence to Khruschev's benefit in 1957. In 1960, she became Minister of Culture and lost her influence as the leader of a powerful local party.

On the other hand, Khruschev trusted Brezhnev, whom he made his First Deputy in the Party and Supreme Soviet. But it was Brezhnev who organised his mentor's downfall. In October 1964 Khruschev was on holiday in the Crimea. He was summoned back to find the Politburo in session. Brezhnev, as acting Chairman, told him that the Politburo had decided that he should resign for the good of the Party. As in 1957, Khruschev took the fight to the Central Committee. Here, the vote was unanimously against him; even his brother-in-law, Grechko, voted against him. Brezhnev came to power as the representative of the interests of the KGB, Army and Party machines.[10]

The Brezhnev years, 1964–82

'Improvement in the well being of the working people is becoming a more and more urgent requirement for our economic development itself.'

Brezhnev, 1971

'We use the advantages offered by foreign economic arrangements to have additional possibilities of carrying out our economic plans, to increase the efficiency of production and to accelerate scientific and technological progress.'

Brezhnev, 1977

Brezhnev was a Ukrainian whose career had been advanced by his compatriot, Khruschev. In 1950, he was elected to the Supreme Soviet; four months before Stalin's death he was appointed to the Party Central Committee and he joined the Politburo in 1957. In 1960, he became President of the Soviet State while also becoming Khruschev's deputy in the Party hierarchy. In October 1964, he became First Party Secretary.

As in 1953, the Party seemed determined in 1964 to prevent too much power falling into one person's hands. Khruschev's position as Chairman of the Council of Ministers (i.e. Prime Minister) went to another Party stalwart, Alexei Kosygin. In 1960, he had become Deputy Prime Minister so that he was, as it were, the natural inheritor of Khruschev's seat. In fact, Kosygin's was very much a titular post; Brezhnev used his position as Party Secretary to become the principal ruler in what was nominally a collective leadership. Although Kosygin remained in his post until 1980, Brezhnev used the revision of the Constitution in 1977 as the opportunity to take for himself the post of President in succession to Podgorny, who was forced to retire.

There was, certainly at first, little evidence of changes in policy; Brezhnev tended to pursue policies similar to Khruschev's in industry and agriculture. There was, however, one major shift; there was an end to de-Stalinisation. Indeed, in April 1965 Brezhnev praised Stalin and Zhdanov, an indication that he intended to maintain their attitude towards 'cosmopolitanism' and dissent.

In 1966, the 23rd Party Congress produced no surprises, no major shifts in policies. At the 24th Congress in 1971, Brezhnev announced that he was going to enlarge the Politburo which controls the work of the Party between the meetings of Congress. In 1973, he published his decisions. Out went those whose loyalty he doubted; in came three newcomers who would be dependent on him: Marshal Grechko, the Khruschev brother-in-law who had voted against his relative in 1964, became Minister of Defence; Andrei Gromyko, the long-serving bureaucrat who was Foreign Minister; Yuri Andropov, the head of the KGB, and the first security chief to be in the Politburo since the days of Beria.

The new and larger Politburo had 21 members and alternative members; six of these were among the 11 secretaries of the Central Committee who, with the rest of the 400 or so members and alternative members of that Committee, were rarely convened. Inside the all-powerful Politburo, Brezhnev had an inner group of senior members who, under his control, ran the country. It was a major criticism of the system that this group was made up of old men when it was first constituted in 1973 so that, with the passage of time, Russia came under the rule of a gerontocracy which seemed more determined to hold on to power than with using that power for improvement in the Russian way of life.

In the industrial field, the new leadership proposed reforms which Khruschev had advocated in his latter years in power. Russian economists had long argued that efficiency and productivity would only improve if ways were found of combining centralised planning with a market economy. In September 1965, Kosygin announced a series of reforms which made profitability the main indicator of industrial efficiency. Enterprises were allowed to use part of their profits to make bonus payments to workers and management; managers were given more freedom as centralised controls were relaxed.

But these reforms did not go far enough; they did not allow the free play of market forces. Nor were they, modest though they were, properly carried out. Between the proposing and the implementation of the reforms was the bureaucracy, conservative in nature, and self-interested in maintaining the status quo.

The reforms did not lead to any radical increase in the quantity or quality of consumer goods available to the Russian people. The success of the bonus schemes, and calls for increased productivity, depended on the appearance of more consumer goods on which to spend the increased earnings. Between 1968 and 1971 there were a few signs of success, and light industry grew more rapidly than heavy industry. But, after 1971, the old order was restored as the military exerted their influence. Khruschev had called the military 'the metal eaters'; after 1971 they, and their heavy industry bureaucratic allies, ensured that their interest took first place. The share of heavy industry in total output rose from 68 per cent, under Stalin, to 72 per cent under Khruschev, and to 74 per cent under Brezhnev in 1979.

And this growth in the share taken by heavy industry was being made in an economy which was slowing down. The industrial growth rate fell from an average of 8 per cent in the 1950s to 3.7 per cent in 1980, while the target for the Five Year Plan announced in 1981 was the lowest since 1945.

It was against this background of failure that, in July 1979, the Central Committee passed a resolution calling for the implementation of the 1965 reforms. Further evidence of the admitted failure of the system was provided by Tikhnov, Prime Minister after Kosygin's death in 1980. This elderly protégé of Brezhnev's told the 26th Party Congress that the Russian economy had reached an impasse. The days when it could expand by adding new workers (from the countryside) and by developing new resources were over. Increased growth had to come from increased efficiency. But, as Andropov was to point out a year later, this efficiency depended on a workforce which, he said, was guilty of drunkenness, absenteeism, indiscipline and laziness.

There was a similar story of failure in agriculture. In concentrating on the development of heavy industry, Stalin had tended to ignore the most important of Russia's industries, agriculture. He had forced collectivisation on an unwilling people, killing off the kulaks, the more enterprising farmers, so that the collectives were run by the unsuccessful farmers. Khruschev had further enlarged the size of the individual collectives on the notion that 'big is beautiful' (p. 110). He had made a heavy investment in agriculture – irrigation, mechanisation, fertilisers and new breeds of seed – but the organisational weakness of the system prevailed over such attempts at improvement. The drought of 1963 forced Russia to buy grain abroad. This, together with the evident failure of the Virgin Lands scheme (p. 119), had been the final nail in Khruschev's coffin.

Brezhnev tried to solve the agricultural problem with increased investment, so that about one-third of all Russian investment in the 1970s went into agriculture. But, like Khruschev, Brezhnev had no success. In 1972, the weather prevailed over the planners, the grain crop was 18 million tons lower than in 1970, and Russian buyers went into world markets to buy the grain needed for animal foods as well as for flour-making. Their incursion played a major role in driving up the prices of wheat and maize, which led to an increase in the rate of inflation throughout the western world (Fig. 7.5, p. 152). To try to alleviate this problem, the US government released grain from its surpluses to sell, cheaply, to the Russians.

In 1975, a combination of drought, rain and frost led to a major agricultural failure. The harvest was 80 million tons lower than the crop of 1974 and 65 million tons short of what had been planned. To prevent the possibility of there being another Russian-induced inflation in the western world, the US government forbade American sellers from dealing with the Russians. The Russians were told that they would not be allowed to use the world market only when their own crop failed. Instead, the US government forced the Russians to agree to buy, on commercial terms, six million tons of wheat and maize every year for six years. In addition, when US supplies were plentiful, the Russians would be allowed to buy another two million tons on the market, and more still by special arrangement with the US government.

The dependence of Russia on 'capitalist grain' was ironic in view of the claims made, in Russia and China, for the success of the collective scheme of state ownership. In Hungary and other satellites, the rulers had learned the lesson of failure more quickly. There, the collectives had been broken up into smaller units so that the earnings of the individual farmworker were related to his labour. The Russians rejected such private enterprise schemes, fearing the political consequences which might follow. However, further poor harvests led Brezhnev to announce in 1977 that production on private plots was to be encouraged. In 1981, restrictions on the private ownership of livestock were lifted, banks were authorised to give loans of up to £2,000 for private farming and the area of private plots was increased. The kulaks' successors were to be encouraged. Or so it seemed. However, the collective-minded leadership at the top and the self-interested bureaucracy below ensured that such reforms were never fully implemented; they became mere tinkering with the existing and inefficient system. In spite of foreign imports, bread-rationing has to be introduced in many towns when the harvest fails. The forty million working on the collectives are unable to produce the food needed, and Russia has to depend on the output of the less than four million who work on US farms.

Nor was it only foreign food that was imported. To try to increase the output from Russian industry, Brezhnev sought aid from the West. Mining equipment was bought from the USA; Fiat experts were brought in to modernise Soviet car production lines. In May 1973, Brezhnev visited West Germany in search of technical aid and capital investment. Imports from capitalist countries rose from 2.5 billion roubles in 1970 to 3.4 billion in 1974 and 10.8 billion in 1976. Chemicals and petro-chemicals, ships, transport, mining, food processing, computers, photocopying, aerospace and steel-making, were among the list of imports. Sometimes the import took the form of a complete plant with or without a licence for local manufacture; sometimes the imports were only components. Additionally, there was technical help for the erection and operation of the plant supplied, so that there were Frenchmen, Americans, British and Germans working in construction sites and industrial complexes throughout Russia. Western banks have opened offices in Moscow to provide for the financial arrangements following from this increase. For Russia cannot afford to pay for multi-billion dollar imports, and western financiers have to arrange credit deals to help finance the development of Russian industry.

Between 1972 and 1976 the Soviet Union borrowed over 11 billion dollars from the West; by 1980 this debt had more than doubled, while the cumulative debt of the Comecon countries as a whole had risen to over 80 billion dollars.

The attempts by Khruschev and Brezhnev to increase the output of consumer goods has had a limited success. There are more privately owned cars in Moscow; an increasing number of Russians now have television sets and a washing machine; those who do not yet possess these luxuries dream of doing so. To the western visitor life in Moscow may appear to be colourless, inefficient and shoddy (Figure 6.2); to the average Russian, life in the Brezhnev era was incomparably better than it had been in Stalin's time. In an increasingly large number of families, the wife goes to work so that there are two incomes to the household. This enables the family to buy luxuries such as a television set; it also qualifies working women for the state pension which is only available to former workers, for there is no old age pension as such.

Perhaps the most noticeable thing about Brezhnev's Russia was the poor quality of housing. He had claimed that, by 1980, every family would have its own flat. However, almost a quarter of Russian towndwellers still live in communal apartments, in which several families each have a room and share the kitchen and lavatory.

During his brief 'reign' (November 1982–February 1984), Andropov drew attention to some of the causes of the failure of the Russian system. He accused the labour force of too frequent absenteeism, which caused losses much greater than those caused by strikes in western countries. Even when it was at work, he said, the workforce spent only half its time actually working. The rest of the time it spent shopping or queueing for tickets for games or cinemas. Management has little, if

6.2 *Pravda*, in 1980, making fun of the state of the inefficient Russian railway system. 'Now they've bloomed, next year we shall have fruit.'

any, control over this inefficient workforce; to dismiss a worker is almost impossible. In 1970, Brezhnev introduced new labour laws under which it was possible for guilty workmen to be executed for 'economic crimes'. But there is little evidence that such draconian measures changed anything. Andropov, in 1982, still complained of labour's failure.

He also drew attention to the problem of alcoholism. One cause of this problem is that there is little else other than drink on which to spend money. Another cause is that heavy drinking is accepted by the majority of Russians as being 'natural'; children are taught to drink from the age of seven, according to one Russian survey. In 1979, one commentator argued that 'it would be naive to expect tremendous results in only sixty-two years'. Alcoholism is yet another part of the Russian continuum.

The demand for, and chances of, change

'The basic necessity for economic reform, including the establishment of greater economic independence for state enterprises, decentralisation of planning and the introduction of elements of a mixed economy, appears incontrovertible. However, any such reforms, inevitably affecting the very foundations of the totalitarian economic and social structures, are very unlikely at the present time.'[11]

Dr Andrei Sakharov, March 1980

Sakharov is one of the leading Russian dissidents. His critique of the system is one with which, in part at least, Russia's leaders would agree; from Khruschev to Chernenko, they have called for 'economic reform'; they have, in varying degrees, tried to provide 'greater economic independence for state enterprises, decentralisation of planning and the introduction of a mixed economy'. But, as Sakharov pointed out, economic structure is, as everywhere, intertwined with the social and political systems. To reform any one of the three, leads, inevitably, to the need for, and inevitability of, reform in the other two. From Khruschev to Chernenko, Russia's leaders have been held back from making the necessary reforms because they have feared the political consequences.

During his short reign, Andropov made tentative steps towards reform of the Party structure. Some of his protégés were promoted to the Politburo in place of some 'Brezhnev men'; in the regions, there was some response to his call for a revitalisation of the Party leadership, as many party chiefs were replaced by men of Andropov's choice, so ensuring him control of the Party Central Committee on which these chiefs serve. Andropov called for efficiency, expertise, discipline and personal responsibility. He invited some to take 'honourable retirement' on account of age, an ironic call from a sixty-nine year old and ailing leader.

He died in February 1984, before these changes had been fully implemented and before there had been time to see whether, if implemented, they would have made any considerable difference. In any event, these were, in Sakharov's terms, not far-reaching reforms; they were, at best, a Khruschev-like attempt to tinker with the machine and not far-reaching reforms of 'the very foundations of the totalitarian . . . structures'.

But the demand for economic reform goes on, and with strong support from all the major organs of the system. The military, 'the metal-eaters', want economic improvement to ensure the availability of the technological hardware they demand as they face the USA challenge. With the new leader, Chernenko, as Chairman of the Defence Council, they may feel assured of having their voices heard at the highest level. Chernenko has indicated that, in part at least, he is an Andropov man; he has talked about 'slackness, irresponsibility' and the need for the 'serious re-structuring' of the economic machine.

The Party ideologues also demand improvement. They re-echo Khruschev's demand for the system to produce the goods demanded by the people (p. 116), a demand which is even stronger in 1984 than it had been in 1956, as the people have developed rising expectations and also have increasing evidence of the much higher standards being enjoyed, not only in the 'capitalist' West but also in some satellite countries, notably Hungary and East Germany (Figure 6.2). Chernenko spoke for this element in the structure when he declared: 'We expect from our economic executives more independence at all levels, a bold search and, if necessary, a well-justified risk in the name of increasing the effectiveness of the economy and ensuring a rise in the living standards of the people.' Chernenko and the ideologues are aware of the political apathy and 'crisis of faith' common among the generation now labelled 'Grandchildren of the Revolution'. This generation, now in its teens, demands western music and clothes, western films and consumer goods; the grandchildren of the present-day Russian leaders, with access to western goods, are the very ones who most show this attitude towards the West, with their acquisition of such simple things as scarves and discs.

Another group among the ideologues, sharing Zhdanovite views (p. 44), is less certain about this development. They fear that such 'cosmopolitanism' may lead, on one hand, to lack of political commitment or, on the other hand, to a demand for the freedom enjoyed in the West, which led to the emergence of that youth culture which Russian youth is now eager to make their own, if only by adoption. 'What goes on in the leadership is remote from our lives,' said a young engineer on the day of Andropov's funeral,[12] indicating the apathy of some, while Sakharov's supporters typify those who call for the greater freedom.

Given the memory left by Stalin's massive terrorist campaigns, and even taking into account the 'Thaw' under Khruschev's more 'liberal' régime, it is surprising that a dissident 'movement' exists in Russia. The number and importance of such dissidents increased in Khruschev's later years, if only because they were disappointed with the failure of his talked-of reforms of the system. Most of the dissidents began where Khruschev left off; they accepted the Soviet system but wanted it to become more efficient. In that sense, Andropov and Chernenko might claim 'we are all dissidents now'. However, the dissidents called for an advance on Khruschevism. Led by such distinguished men as Roy Medvedev, they call for a 'liberalisation' of the system, for a 'democratisation' which would, they claim, ensure the better reali- sation of the social goals. They argue that only such liberalisation and popular control will overcome the dead hand of the bureaucracy which is currently responsible for society's malfunctions. They want open debate inside the Party in which people with skills and knowledge would have their voices heard.

Some of those who followed Medvedev in his early protest in 1970 have moved on, and left him and his 'collaborators with the system' behind. Led by such men as the distinguished scientist, Andrei Sakharov, these radicals call for an overall reform of the political, economic and social system so as to ensure, among other things, the enjoyment in the Soviet Union of those human rights taken for granted in the West. Intellectuals call for an end to censorship; the religious- minded want freedom in which to practise; Jews, in particular, call for this freedom and for the right to have more than the one synagogue permitted them in Moscow.

Brezhnev dealt harshly with such critics. Sinyavsky and Daniel were sentenced to several years in labour camps for criticising the system by publishing their forbidden books abroad. Solzhenitsyn was awarded the Nobel Prize for Literature in 1970 – for works published abroad but not published in Russia. Like Pasternak, he did not go to receive his Prize, but later left the Soviet Union to become a critic not only of the Soviet system but also of 'godless' capitalism as found in the West.

Under this kind of censorship, critics of the system developed an underground literature or *samizdat* which was passed from hand to dissenting hand. In these works, the critics discussed the reforms that were needed, informed Russians of what was happening abroad and of the fate of critics inside Russia. Medvedev and other writers of *samizdat* make five or six carbon copies of their work and pass them on; others then make more copies and so the volume of work grows. Some *samizdat* are smuggled to the West and form parts of broadcasts through the Russian services of the BBC, the Voice of America, Radio Liberty and Deutsche Welle so that far more Russians hear of the dissidents' views than would ever read the *samizdat*.

In 1970, Russian dissidents 'went public' and formed the Moscow 'Committee on Human Rights' to monitor the way in which the Russian government honoured the agreements it appeared to have made at Helsinki (pp. 270–3). The Committee acted as a centre of pro- test against the treatment of dissidents and of help to those who were in trouble. It helped organise their defence while also calling for legal reform. The Committee learned to use foreign correspondents in Moscow as avenues for spreading their ideas, while some of its members maintained contact with friends in the West via telephone and letter.

The Brezhnev government tried to stamp on the dissident movement. In 1966, pro-Jewish demonstrators at Babi Yar (p. 108) were arrested and imprisoned; in 1968, Tartars, protesting in Moscow because they were not allowed to return to the Crimea, were arrested and shipped to Siberia; in the same year, Pavel Litvinov (grandson of the Russian Foreign Minister from 1930 to 1939) was arrested for demonstrating against the Russian invasion of Czechoslovakia. At his trial, he appealed to the Russian Constitution which, in Article 125, guarantees freedom of speech 'in the interests of socialism'. In 1970 Andrei Amalrik, author of *Will the Soviet Union Survive until 1984?* (published in 1970) was jailed for the second time. It was he who wrote of the process of 'putting their opponents into mental hospitals' as 'the most disgusting thing this régime does'.

The arrest of the famous and less famous went on, and, by 1977, most dissidents had been imprisoned, exiled or expelled. The West knows something of the conditions endured by the more famous, such as Sakharov – in 1984 under house arrest 500 miles from home. It knows little, if anything, of the nameless mass of the prisoners in the still-flourishing Gulags. In its treatment of its political opponents, the communist government apes the behaviour of its Tsarist predecessors, as also in the policy of registration, which is a development of the Tsarist system of the internal passport. To live in Moscow, Leningrad, Kiev and other cities, one has to be registered as a citizen of one of them. Registration can be acquired by birth or by marriage; many marriages are arranged to provide such registration for ambitious men and women from the provinces. In May 1975, Brezhnev announced that, for the first time, Russian villagers would be free to leave the collectives on which they were born. The government would issue them with an internal passport, a form of identity card, which would allow them to travel freely, for the first time, as citizens of towns had long been able to do. But to be deprived of that passport, or, as in Sakharov's case, of the right to register as an inhabitant of Leningrad, Moscow or Kiev, condemns the citizen to a form of imprisonment 'without tears'; this gives the authorities a form of control over potential dissidents.

The majority of Russian citizens accept the system, for they know no other. This is brought home in conversation with Russians. My Intourist guide insisted that there were 'only five' dissidents in the Soviet Union; one of my hosts refused to believe that Britain did not have military conscription, while another 'knew' that my account of unemployment benefit payments was a lie. Perhaps more frightening was the 'watchdog' in the hotel who tried to stop Russians coming to my room to talk over a drink. A censored press, radio and television, a controlled literature and the absence of opportunities for opposition to make its voice heard, all help to explain the blinkered view of the West which is common. The Communist Party insists on this environment; its role is defined in the 1977 Constitution introduced by Brezhnev:

> 'The Communist Party of the Soviet Union is the leading guiding force of Soviet Society and the nucleus of its political system. The CPSU exists for the people and serves the people. Armed with the Marxist-Leninist teaching, the Communist Party determines the general prospects for society's development and the line of the domestic and foreign policy of the USSR, gives guidance to the great creative endeavour of the Soviet people and places their struggle for the triumph of Communism on a planned and scientific basis.'

It is to be understood that, in return for the Party's acting as the mainspring of all that affects him, the citizen has the duty of obeying the Party, of fitting his plans to those established by the Party. 'Human rights' are understood to be the right to work, to security of employment and of a roof over one's head. Neither the Party nor the majority of the Russians have any concept of human rights as they are understood in the West. This, as we shall see, has led to great misunderstandings about dissidents and their treatment, and about détente, which many in the West would wish to link with a development of human rights in Russia and with more toleration there of dissidents. The leading dissident, the Nobel Peace Prize winner, Andrei Sakharov, began a fast on 2 May 1984 in an effort to gain official approval for his wife's request to be allowed to receive medical treatment outside the USSR. Sakharov was already in trouble with the Soviet authorities for his dissident campaign in favour of human rights (pp. 127ff). He has been living in exile in the city of Gorky since 1980, and it was from Gorky that news trickled through to his friends in the West that, in June 1984, Sakharov was either very ill because of his fast, or, indeed, had already died. Many leading diplomats and statesmen took up his cause whenever they met a Soviet leader. President Mitterand, the then-chairman of the EEC's Council of Ministers, appealed to the Soviet government, claiming that Sakharov's death 'would be such a shocking thing that it would affect relations between the Soviets and any country'. His appeal was dismissed on the grounds that the Sakharov case was 'an internal affair'. In mid-June, the Australian Foreign Minister was in Moscow for two days of talks with his Soviet opposite number, Andrei Gromyko. At the end of the talks, he asked Gromyko about the state of Sakharov's health. In an angry reply, Gromyko snapped; 'We will not be told how to deal with the Sakharovs by other countries.' Nor, clearly, does Russia intend to translate human rights into terms which can be readily understood in the West.

Documentary evidence

Milovan Djilas (Document 6.1) was a close friend of Tito's and one of the quartet which ruled Yugoslavia after 1945 (pages 48 and 101–2). He shared Tito's opposition to Stalin's attempts to extend Soviet influence in eastern Europe. Djilas had met Stalin many times and was aware of the cruelty of the Stalinist régime, although he himself had helped Tito to carry out Stalin-like purges of opponents in Yugoslavia and was, himself, to become a victim of such purges. Stalin's death in 1953 saved the Soviet Union from another massive purge (Document 6.2); most of those named in the account by the US reporter were to feature in Soviet history after 1953. Beria was assassinated by his erstwhile colleagues, who feared him much as Stalin had done; Mikoyan, marked down by Stalin in 1953, led the denunciations of his former 'boss' in 1956; Khruschev's condemnation of Stalin (Document 6.3) may be seen as a political ploy by an ambitious ex-Stalinist rather than as a call to a return to 'principles . . . democracy . . . legality . . .' (p. 133).

Document 6.1

A meeting with Stalin, 1945 (see also p. 21)

'An ungainly dwarf of a man passed through gilded and marbled imperial halls, and a path opened before him; radiant, admiring glances followed him, while the ears of the courtiers strained to catch his every word. . . . He knew that he was one of the cruellest, most despotic figures in human history, but this did not worry him a bit, for he was convinced that he was carrying out the will of history. . . . Poets were inspired by him, orchestras blared cantatas in his honour, philosophers in institutes wrote tomes about his sayings, and martyrs died on scaffolds crying out his name. His power, absolute over a sixth of the globe, was spreading farther and farther. This convinced him that his society contained no contradictions and that it was superior to every other society in every way. He joked, too, with his courtiers – 'comrades' – I, too, was swept up by Stalin and his witticisms. But in one little corner of my mind and of my moral being I was awake and troubled; I noticed the tawdriness, too, and could not inwardly accept Stalin's manner of joking – nor his deliberate avoidance of saying a single human, comradely word to me.'

(Djilas, M., *Conversations with Stalin*, Penguin, 1965, p. 95)

Document 6.2

A new purge, 1953

'I will be frank and say that the hair rose on the back of my neck when I read this statement and the editorial which accompanied it in *Pravda*. . . . It was quite apparent that Russia stood on the brink of a reign of terror beside which that of the 30s would seem trivial. . . .

It took no analytical ability to see two obvious and immediate targets of this campaign. One was Beria, chief of the security forces. The other was the Jews . . . Each new batch of provincial newspapers that was brought into my office reported new scandals, new exposures, new arrests. . . .

The target quickly broadened out, Khruschev was involved, because his Party chiefs were being attacked. . . . Mikoyan was involved deeper and deeper, because of the alleged scandals in the trade organisations. And Malenkov was dragged in, because in one city after another, his Party lieutenants were implicated.

But, most deeply and dangerously of all, was implicated that dry, pedantic little man who had survived so much before, Vyacheslav Molotov. . . .

As February wore on, the terror deepened in Moscow. Every day the rumours circulated. There had been arrests in *Tass*, the news agency. The head of the agency, Palgunov, a man known for years to be very close to Molotov, had vanished . . . arrested. Madam Molotov (a Jewess) had disappeared . . . banished to Siberia. . . . Arrests in Moscow University. . . . Arrests in the Academy of Sciences. . . . More Jews dismissed . . . Protectors of Jews arrested. . . . Arrests in the Central Committee. . . .

Who in the Politburo could feel safe by late February? No one, I thought. Not Molotov. Not Malenkov. Surely not Beria. . . . There wasn't a safe name on the list.

And what of Stalin himself? In the pink of condition. . . . Good health, lively mind. That was the verdict of three foreigners who saw him in February. . . .

Only Menon, (the Indian Ambassador) had one strange thing to report. . . . Throughout the interview, the old man kept doodling wolves. . . . And presently Stalin began to talk, too, about wolves. Russian peasants, he said, knew how to deal with wolves. They exterminated them.'

(Harrison Salisbury in *Daily Telegraph*, 17 January 1955)

Document 6.3

Stalin, by Khruschev, 1956

'Comrades! . . . Quite a lot has been said about the cult of the individual and about its harmful consequences. . . . The cult of the person of Stalin . . . became at a certain specific stage the source of a whole series of exceedingly serious and grave perversions of Party principles, of Party democracy, of revolutionary legality. . . .

Stalin . . . absolutely did not tolerate collegiality in leadership and in work and . . . practised brutal violence, not only toward everything which opposed him, but also toward that which seemed to his capricious and despotic character, contrary to his concepts. . . .

Stalin abandoned the method of ideological struggle for that of administrative violence, mass repressions and terror. . . . Arbitrary behaviour by one person encouraged and permitted arbitrariness in others. Mass arrests and deportations of many thousands of people, execution without trial and without normal investigation created conditions of insecurity, fear and even desperation.

Stalin showed in a whole series of cases his intolerance, his brutality and his abuse of power. . . . He often chose the path of repression and annihilation, not only against actual enemies, but also against individuals who had not committed any crimes against the Party and the Soviet government. . . .

Many Party, Soviet and economic activists who were branded in 1937–8 as 'enemies' were actually never enemies, spies, wreckers and so on, but were always honest communists; they were only so stigmatised, and often, no longer able to bear barbaric tortures, they charged themselves (at the order of the investigative judges – falsifiers) with all kinds of grave and unlikely crimes.

This was the result of the abuse of power by Stalin, who began to use mass terror against the Party cadres. . . . Stalin put the Party and the NKVD up to the use of mass terror when the exploiting classes had been liquidated in our country and when there were no serious reasons for the use of extraordinary mass terror. The terror was directed . . . against the honest workers of the Party and the Soviet state. . . .

It has been found that all the cases of so called 'spies' and 'saboteurs' were fabricated. Confessions of guilt of many arrested and charged with enemy activity were gained with the help of cruel and inhuman tortures. . . . Many thousands of honest and innocent communists have died as a result of this monstrous falsification of such 'cases', as a result of the fact that all kinds of slanderous 'confessions' were accepted, and as a result of the practice of forcing accusations against oneself and others. . . .

It is clear that these matters were decided by Stalin . . . He was the chief prosecutor in these cases. Stalin not only agreed to, but on his own initiative issued arrest orders. . . .

Stalin was a very distrustful man, sickly suspicious. . . . Everywhere and in everything he saw 'enemies', 'two-facers' and 'spies'. Possessing unlimited power, he indulged in great wilfulness and choked a person morally and physically. A situation was created where one could not express one's own will. When Stalin said that one or another would be arrested, it was necessary to accept on faith that he was an 'enemy of the people'. . . . What proofs were offered? The confession of the arrested. . . . How is it possible that a person confesses to crimes that he has not committed? Only in one way – because of application of physical methods of pressuring him, tortures, bringing him to a state of unconsciousness, deprivation of his judgement, taking away of his human dignity. . . .'

(Khruschev's address to the Twentieth Party Congress, February 1956)

FURTHER READING

BLOCH, S. AND REDDAWAY, P., *Soviet Psychiatric Abuse*, Gollancz, 1984

BROWN, A. AND KASER, M., *The Soviet Union since the Fall of Khruschev*, Macmillan, 1975

BROWN, A. AND KASER, M., *Soviet Policy for the 1980s*, Macmillan, 1983

CONQUEST, R., *The Great Terror*, Macmillan, 1968

CONQUEST, R., *Kolymann: The Arctic Death Camps*, Macmillan, 1978

CROSSMAN, R., ed., *The God that Failed*, Hamish Hamilton, 1950

DUMORE, T., *Soviet Politics, 1945–53*, Macmillan, 1984

EDMONDS, R., *Soviet Foreign Policy, 1962–73*, OUP, 1975

GARVEY, T., *The Bones of Contention*, Routledge and Kegan Paul, 1978

KHRUSCHEV, N., *Khruschev Remembers*, Penguin, 1971

LYONS, E., *Our Secret Allies: The Peoples of Russia*, Arco, 1954

MCCAULEY, M., ed., *The Soviet Union after Brezhnev*, Heinemann, 1983

MEDVEDEV, R., *Khruschev*, Basil Blackwell, 1982

MILLER, J., *Life in Russia Today*, 1969

MOONEY, J. P., *The Soviet Superpower*, Heinemann, 1982

MUNTING, R., *The Economic Development of the USSR*, Croom Helm, 1983

RUBENSTEIN, A. Z., *Soviet Foreign Policy since World War II: Imperial and Global*, Prentice-Hall Int., 1983

SHORT, P., *The Dragon and the Bear: Inside China and Russia Today*, Hodder and Stoughton, 1982
SOLZENITSYN, A., *The Gulag Archipelago (1918–56)*, Fontana, 1974
WESTWOOD, J. N., *Russia since 1917*, Batsford, 1979
ZINOVIEV, A., *The Reality of Communism*, Gollancz, 1984

7

Developments in Western Europe, 1945–84

Economic planning

'Men only accept change in the face of necessity; and they see that necessity only when confronted by crisis.'[1]

Jean Monnet

In 1942 Sir William Beveridge wrote of the need to create 'a better world than the old world. . . .' (p. 15). That 'old world' had been represented, perhaps at its worst, by the Great Depression of the 1930s. In that decade, world trade was one-third smaller than it had been in the 1920s and, in the worst years, one-quarter of the British workforce and one-third of the German was unemployed. That world-wide depression had had many causes. In 1919, J. M. Keynes had highlighted one cause in his *The Economic Consequences of the Peace*. He prophesied that the demand for reparations and the repayment of war debts would cause many countries to have deficits in their balance of payments, deficits which were traditionally tackled by cuts in imports (p. 15). Cuts in one country's imports lead to cuts in other countries' exports and to the 'export of unemployment'. The history of the 30s proved Keynes's point (p. 15). Politicians seemed incapable of producing policies to increase employment (at the national level) or increase world trade (at the international level.) They were dominated by the *laisser faire* philosophy which called for the free working of market forces which 'in the long run' had improved the world economy over the centuries. Keynes, more radical than most of his fellow economists, noted that 'in the long run, we are all dead.'

In the 1930s, he pointed to the waste of resources resulting from the depression and the opportunities for raising living standards that were being lost. He called for governments to use their powers to control the level of investment and spending, and to create credit, which would encourage investment and spending, even if this led to budget deficits. He 'invented' the now-familiar Public Sector Borrowing Requirement, the result of post-war governments having adopted many of his ideas.

During the Second World War, Keynes was appointed financial adviser to the British government; many of his young 'disciples' gained influential positions. During the war, governments were forced to take a dominant role in economic affairs. They controlled national resources so that essential industries would produce the goods needed to fight the war; manpower was directed into the forces or essential industry; commodities were rationed; government agencies organised bulk purchasing of commodities overseas; commissions prepared reports on how post-war governments might ensure that 'better world' and, because of wartime experiments, all such reports called for a great degree of government participation in the economic and social life of the nation.

One result of this wartime study by the British and other Allied governments and by resistance movements was the emergence of demands for National Economic Plans. The British did not go that far. But in the Netherlands, Norway and France (pp. 170–1) there were schemes for government, employers and trade unions to join forces to draw up 'indicative' plans. While no plan could ensure success, the very existence of such plans influenced the investment programmes of industrialists and provided guidelines for governments, and for housing authorities, while their investment decisions helped to make the plans self-fulfilling.

The call for an increased role for the state in economic and social affairs appealed to many intellectuals in western Europe who had long been critical of the injustices produced by the private enterprise system. Many of these had become either members of the Communist Party or fellow-travelling supporters of that Party. In France (p. 168) and Italy (p. 204), communism appeared to be the legitimate heir of the resistance movements and the one most likely to fulfil the hopes of the young for a more just society. There was a variety of International Congresses – of artists, or writers, of intellectuals – in the post-war period at which leading personalities appeared as critics of western society and advocates for western Communist Parties. Purblind, these intellectuals chose either to ignore or even to defend the policies adopted by Stalin and Zhdanov (p. 44) against fellow-intellectuals in Russia and eastern Europe, and against the human rights of the peoples of the Russian 'Empire'. Many western intellectuals had invested much of their moral capital in the Soviet system, which they had praised in the inter-war period; it was difficult, if not impossible, for them to adjust their views without considerable loss of face. For many, their personal *amour propre* was more important than compassion for Stalin's victims; they lacked the will to recognise the unwelcome truth. In 1945, George Orwell's manuscript, *Animal Farm*, was rejected by twelve British publishers, because they did not believe that such an obvious attack on Stalin and Stalinism could become a saleable book. In France, David

Rousset was attacked when, in 1949, he called for an examination of conditions in Soviet concentration camps. Rousset had been a founder-member, with Sartre and Camus, of a left-wing movement in Paris. His fellow-members condemned him in 1949: 'With whom are you – with the people of the Soviet Union, building a new society, or with their enemies?' It was to be many years before western communists felt free to take an independent line, the line taken by Tito, who was condemned by the western intellectuals when he broke with Stalin.

Economic recovery, 1945–55

'Marshall Aid was the blood transfusion which sustained the weakening European economies and gave them strength to work their own recovery.'[2]

OEEC, June 1951

In 1945, many observers feared the onset of a depression even greater than the one which had followed the First World War. In 1945 Europe was a 'rubbish heap' (p. 15). By the end of 1946 things were little better; in France and Belgium output was only 20 per cent of what it had been in 1938; in Germany it was only 15 per cent of that pre-war level. Europe was producing only half the steel it had produced in 1938. With its industries unable to produce sufficient for the export market, Europe was able to import all too little; so that rationing continued (p. 20).

The disastrous winter of 1946–7 led to a serious fuel shortage. Widespread blizzards and up to 16 degrees of frost prevented miners and railways from getting coal supplies to industry. Factories and power stations shut down. The Germans were saved from starvation when the British government released 112,000 tons of wheat and 50,000 tons of potatoes from Britain's own small stockpile. In 1946–7 the British had to endure the rationing of bread and potatoes, something which they had not had to suffer even during the war (Figure 7.1).

If Europe was to recover, there had to be a massive importation of capital goods and raw materials from the only source of plenty – the USA. But Europe did not have the dollars to buy these goods and materials; her export industries could not earn enough to pay for these as well as for the food and other necessary imports. It was Marshall Aid which enabled Europe to get out of this 'chicken-and-egg' situation (pp. 60–2).

The effects of this Aid were quickly apparent. Between 1948 and 1958 overall output went up by 25 per cent. The output of steel went up by 70 per cent, of cement by 80 per cent, while the output of oil-based products was trebled. By the end of 1951 European output was 35 per cent above the 1939 level, exports were up by 95 per cent and Europe could pay its way in the economic world.

One reason for that growth in exports was the devaluation of European currencies against the dollar. This lowered the price of

"*Now don't forget—anyone hanging around with a wistful look in their eye—let 'em have it—bing, bang!*"

7.1 The artist Giles's view of the food shortages in Britain in 1947. Bread rationing was imposed *after* the end of the war, an indication of the problems facing post-war Europe.

exports to the USA – and led to increased sales. On the other hand, devaluation was inflationary since it put up the price of imports – of food and raw materials in particular. This led to demands for wage increases and to widespread strikes, often fomented on Stalin's orders by the European communist movement (p. 62). The inflationary spiral was given a further twist by the onset of the Korean War (p. 74). The USA and Britain increased their defence spending; materials which might have gone to make peacetime goods had to be used to make weapons and munitions. The demand for and price of raw materials rose sharply (Figure 7.2) which led to an immediate increase in the cost of living.

The end of the Korean War in 1953 led to a fall in demand and in prices. Europe needed to export less of its industrial output to pay for its imports of foods and raw materials. By 1955, overall output was 50 per cent greater than it had been in 1951 and far in excess of the pre-war level. This industrial success was matched by the success of the export drive so that 'the dollar gap', which had been a feature of the immediate post-war years, ceased to be a major problem.

And if the 'dollar gap' disappeared, so, too, did that pessimism which had been a feature of those post-war years when the harsh economic climate had matched the uncertain international climate of the Cold War. In the 1950s, the 'Thaw' internationally and the much improved

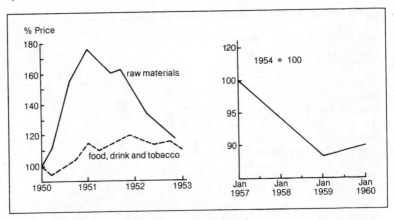

7.2 Import prices rose sharply because of the Korean War, but fell sharply once that war had ended. The fall in prices provides one explanation for the emergence of the 'affluent society' in Europe.

economic situation helped to produce an optimism. Germany and Italy had 'economic miracles'. Macmillan told the British in 1957 that they had 'never had it so good'. The improvement in the economic outlook was due, in part, to the success of the various national plans, whose success was such as to force the reluctant British to create the National Economic Development Council (NEDC) in 1961. It was also due to the adoption of many of Keynes's ideas; governments spent vast sums of money on social investment (in housing, schools and welfare developments), on industrial developments (in nationalist industries such as gas, electricity, coal and rail) and on military development. This government spending both created employment directly and stimulated industrial development (and employment) and consumer spending (by those employed by government).

Industrial investment was continually rising as firms expanded their capacity and adopted modernisation schemes to meet the rising demands from consumers and from the export market. The growth in free trade, following on the activities of GATT (p. 15) and from the successes of the EEC and, to a lesser degree, of EFTA, contributed to the growth of overall trade. The rise in Europe's population may be seen as both cause and effect of the improved economic situation (Table 7.1).

The economic expansion led to an increased demand for labour. This was met, at first, by the increase in the numbers of married women returning to work. This affected the incomes of millions of families, whose subsequent rising living standards led to increased demand for labour to meet the increased consumer demand.

The changing role of women in the economy led to the development of a variety of movements under a general heading of 'women's liberation'. There were demands for equality of pay and of job-

Population (in thousands)

	1950	1966	Natural increase (1960–5) (annual average)
Belgium	8,600	9,500	+0.7
Czechoslovakia	12,300	14,200	+0.7
France	41,700	49,400	+1.2
West Germany	n.a.	59,600	+1.2
Hungary	9,300	10,100	+0.4
Italy	46,300	51,900	+0.7
Netherlands	10,100	12,400	+1.3
Poland	24,800	31,600	+1.3
Rumania	16,300	19,100	+0.8
Spain	27,800	31,800	+0.8
Sweden	7,000	7,800	+0.6
Switzerland	4,600	6,000	+1.8
United Kingdom	50,000	54,900	+0.6
Yugoslavia	16,300	19,700	+1.1
Soviet Union	180,000 (approx)	227,000 (approx)	+1.7

Table 7.1

opportunities, and for girls to be given the same educational opportunities as their brothers. As women became accustomed to the prospect of a working career there were demands for more efficient methods of contraception and, in the 1960s, for legal abortion.

But the demand for labour could not be satisfied even by the employment of over half of all the married women in Europe. It became necessary for industrialists to seek to attract immigrants to fill the gaps in the labour force. North Africans poured into prosperous France; Turks and Eastern Europeans found work in West Germany which also absorbed, without difficulty, the millions who fled from East Germany; Britain welcomed coloured immigrants from the Commonwealth. This influx of foreign labour led to social friction and compelled governments to pass a variety of laws aimed at preventing the emergence of overt racialism. Economic development was not without its social strains.

The affluent society, 1955–65

'In continental Europe the decade of the 1950s was brilliant, with growth of output and consumption, investment and employment surpassing any recorded historical experience, and the rhythm of development virtually uninterrupted by recession.'[3]

National planners and the Keynesians in control of national economic affairs could claim credit for their policies. Table 7.2 shows the percentage average yearly growth of the Gross National Products of the main European countries between 1948 and 1963:

Belgium	3.2	Holland	4.7
France	4.6	Italy	6.0
Germany	7.6	United Kingdom	2.5

Table 7.2 (Source: OECD)

Germany and Italy had started from a low economic base, their economies having been more severely affected by the war. Their rate of progress was greater during the middle and late fifties; between 1959 and 1961 the Italian rate of growth was 7.5 per cent.

There was, generally, a continuation of the rate of expansion in the first half of the 1960s as can be seen by the following table showing the average annual rate of increase of the Gross National Products between 1960 and 1965:

Italy	5.1
France	5.1
Germany	4.8
United Kingdom	3.3

Table 7.3 (Source: OECD)

This continued expansion baffled the Marxists in East and West who had long argued that capitalism had shown in the 1930s that it was incapable of development. Some of them claimed that the system was being invigorated only by military expenditure, which was to ignore other causes for the boom, such as government intervention through taxation manipulation and monetary policy, and increased free trade in the world as a whole and in EFTA and the EEC in particular. And the capitalist-industrialists were contributing to their own success by maintaining a high level of investment (and spending on capital equipment); in France, Germany and Italy investment averaged between 20 and 24 per cent of the GNP while in Britain, the laggard in this as in much else, investment took some 16 per cent of GNP.

One major effect of this widespread economic growth was an ever mounting affluence. Increasingly, Europeans began to enjoy a way of life that had hitherto been enjoyed only in the USA. New suburbs sprang up as private industry catered for the newly prosperous; car ownership became commonplace, with the two-car family becoming more than a Hollywood-centred dream; tourism became the opportunity for the development of major new industries as millions of Europeans learned to take holidays abroad. Industry and the private consumer became major users of cheap energy as, between 1951 and 1971, petrol prices fell in real terms by 17 per cent and electricity prices fell by 43 per cent. Such price changes, and falls in the prices of most imports, helped to contain the inflationary pressures caused by high government spending and workers' success in getting ever-higher wages.

This inflationary pressure was accompanied by balance of payments problems for some countries, notably Britain and France, Belgium and Denmark. In 1957–8 governments of these countries had to adopt restrictive measures to lessen the pressures on their currencies, the result of adverse balance of payments. But even during this 'recession', growth averaged 2 per cent throughout Europe. The international collaboration presaged by the foundation of the International Monetary Fund (p. 15) served the world well; there was no relapse into the habits of the pre-war world, no seeking to 'beggar my neighbour' by attempts at autarky.

Between 1948 and 1972 world trade increased by an annual average of 7.3 per cent while world output increased by an annual average of 5.0 per cent. There was sufficient liquidity in the international system to finance this increased trade without creating, at least in the 1950s, any sense of alarm. The USA had been the first generous contributor to that improved liquidity; its Marshall Aid dollars had served Europe well. The cash reserves of multi-national corporations, banked in one financial centre or another, served to lubricate the system, as did the piled up Euro-dollars after 1958. The Euro-dollar market had its origins in the fears of the Russians and the Chinese that the US government might, in an international crisis, freeze their holdings in the US. They invited European banks to hold the dollars they earned from trade with the US. The Federal Reserve in the USA contributed to the growth of this market when, in 1959, it fixed the interest which US banks could pay on time-deposits, while leaving alone the interest earned on dollar deposits in foreign banks. In 1959, such deposits paid one-quarter per cent above the rate permitted inside the USA. As a result, London banks began to bid for dollars which they re-lent to clients in the USA. When, in the 1960s, the US balance of payments remained in deficit, there was always a plentiful supply of dollars in this Euro-dollar banking system.

The Bretton Woods agreement had established an exchange rate system under which exchange rates of currencies of member countries were to be fixed in the short term, but would be variable in response to structural changes in countries' balances of payments. This meant that some currencies became suspect, leading to currency speculation which harmed some countries' economies. However, the net effect of speculation was to move international funds and to increase international liquidity. If Britain, for example, defended its own currency, it could do so by selling part of its foreign exchange reserves which, bought by some other country, became available for use in the international system. Britain was forced to devalue the pound in 1949 and 1967, while France underwent a series of devaluations between 1947 and 1965 (Figure 7.3). Such devaluations were often the last step; governments preferred to try to rectify the currency situation by restrictions on domestic economic development. A sign of the success

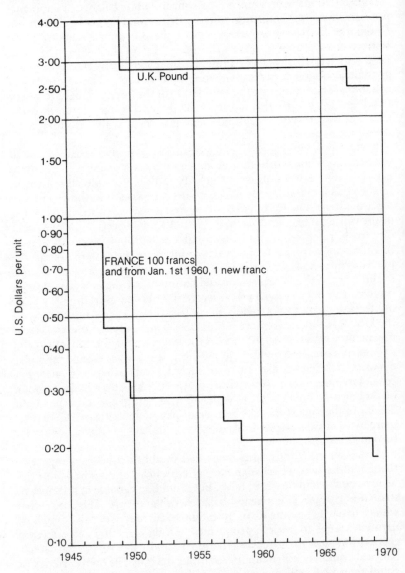

7.3 The official devaluations of the pound sterling and of the franc after 1945. (See Fig. 7.4 for the fate of the 'floating' pound.)

of the Germany economy was the revaluation which took place in 1961, as the government sought to cut down on the imbalance of earnings over expenditure in an effort to avoid the inflationary pressure which would follow from a piling up of national reserves.

The growth in each country's GNP and in the volume of world trade is reflected in the following table which shows the rise of European industrial production after 1945 (with 1958 being taken as the base year with an index of 100):

	1938	1948	1952	1959	1963	1967
USA	33	73	90	113	133	168
West Germany	52	27	61	107	137	158
France	52	55	70	101	129	155
Italy	43	44	64	112	166	212
Holland	47	53	72	110	141	182
Britain	67	74	84	105	119	133

Table 7.4 (Source: OECD)

But these overall figures mask structural changes: the old, staple industries declined in relative importance, and sometimes, in absolute terms. Coal, for example, was increasingly displaced by oil and other fuels and the run down of the European coal industry started in the late 1950s. Crude oil imports had risen from 17 million tons in 1929 to 450 million tons in 1967. Pits were closed down throughout Europe; the British coal industry, the most important in Western Europe, had produced nearly 300 million tons in 1914, whereas output fell from 196 million tons in 1964 to 175 million tons in 1975. The substitution of cheap oil for expensive coal was to lead to an overdependence on foreign imports – and to a crisis in the 1970s.

Other old industries declined – steel, for example, became less important a contributor to GNP than chemicals. Other new industries expanded; the growth of the European automobile industry was a major feature of the post-war world. In 1963 Germany became Europe's largest producer, exporting over one million cars of its output of 3 million cars; Britain and France were producing 1.5 million and 2 million cars respectively while the Italians, newcomers to the industry, were producing one million cars in 1963.

The oldest industry, agriculture, prospered in the post-war world. Increasingly mechanised, supplied with fertilisers by the expanding petro-chemical industry and aided by governments which provided financial assistance to farmers, the output of this industry increased dramatically. By 1957, European output was one-third greater than it had been in 1938. Europe produced most of the wheat and meat which it required; and produced surpluses of potatoes, sugar, vegetables and dairy produce. And this expansion of output was achieved with a falling labour force; in 1970 the labour force was only about one-third of what it had been in 1938 – the displaced workers being rapidly absorbed in the expanding industries in Europe's towns and cities.

There was a decline in the use of, and profitability of, railways everywhere as people travelled short distances by road and used the expanding airlines for longer distance travel. The development of air travel also crippled passenger carrying shipping which had been a feature of the inter-war world. But then only the well-off travelled in search of leisure and work; in the air-carrying days, travel became commonplace.

Tables 7.2–7.4 show that Britain was the poorest performer in every European league table. In the early 1960s there was a plethora of publications to explain 'What's Wrong with Britain'. There were, it seemed, as many causes for the British decline as there were economists. The class structure, poor management, the educational system, the progressive tax system, trade union reluctance to accept change, overmanning, a low level of investment coupled with investment in the wrong things, all came in for blame. There were calls for widespread reform, some of which were answered. The government set up the NEDC in 1961; it set up the National Incomes Commission at the same time, hoping to produce a wages-policy which would stem inflation. Management courses were started at colleges and polytechnics; schemes to help people accept redundancy were meant to lead to the end of overmanning.

But a major burden carried by Britain was the need to maintain the level of sterling in the face of currency speculation and balance of payments deficits. This burden was not jettisoned until the 1970s when it was agreed to allow exchange rates to 'float' in response to the working of the market economy.

The end of the post-war era? 1965–72

'In an educated community of nations, in an age with such opportunities as the present, it is appalling that this counter-revolution of falling expectations should set in. It is not caused by any slowing down in the rate of accumulation of man's knowledge, or productive capacity, or technical innovation; it does not need to take place.'

The Economist, 18 December 1968

In a later section (p. 159) of this chapter we will examine some of the political effects of both rising affluence and the 'counter-revolution of falling expectations'. We will see that, even as Macmillan was telling the British that they had 'never had it so good', there appeared John Osborne's *Look Back in Anger* (1956), a play which appeared to reflect a movement against the smug complacency of the affluent society. There was, at the same time, the beginnings of the creation of a 'New Left' formed by intellectuals and students who claimed that the obvious improvements in living standards were only cosmetic changes which masked the reality – that there was still a rigid class structure in which the rich few manipulated the relatively poor majority.

In the early 1960s the first post-war children became teenagers. Born and bred in an atmosphere of 'rising expectations', led to assume the inevitability of full employment, the children of prosperous homes, these teenagers were both the cause and effect of social change. Manufacturers saw them as a new, large and prosperous market – for clothes, magazines and, above all, for music. In Britain, there were 'The Young Meteors' such as Mary Quant, the fashion designer, and Tommy Steele, the British answer to America's Elvis Presley. In 1963, this youthful 'revolution' was typified by the success of the Beatles whose appearances attracted mass audiences and whose records were bought in their millions.

The success of the relatively few, plus the persuasive propaganda of the manipulating advertisers and manufacturers, persuaded almost everyone that there was a 'Brave New World' waiting for young people to explore and develop. They challenged conventional authority by their behaviour – in dress and sexual freedom – and that authority became increasingly incapable of meeting the challenge. Teachers, parents and even the Churches allowed the young an ever-growing licence. Even in the most rigid structure, the Catholic Church, there was an outbreak of 'protestantism' and 'free thinking' in the wake of the Church's Second Vatican Council which completed its work in December 1965.

These social effects of the 'revolution of rising expectations' came to fruition in the 1960s. But it was during that same decade that the 'revolution' came to an end. In 1963–4, Italy went through a major economic crisis following on a period of large deficits in its balance of payments; France, was forced to devalue the franc in 1963 and again in 1968–9 in efforts to cure its balance of payments problem; in 1964, Britain had a deficit of £800 million on its balance of payments, which was to force the incoming Labour government to renege on its electoral promises and to adopt restrictive measures – increasing taxation, tightening bank credit and hire purchase terms and cutting government expenditure on the social services (p. 167). Even Germany had its setbacks, and the 'economic miracle' came to an end in 1966–7.

The continuing weakness of the British economy was to be a major factor in bringing to an end that post-war period of ever-expanding trade. At Bretton Woods the pound sterling and the dollar were named as key currencies, with the pound to be made freely convertible into what were then scarce dollars. In 1959 sterling became freely convertible and it was 'Bretton Woods at last'. But by 1964 the pound sterling was obviously declining rapidly and was not equal to the role which had been forced on it. This gave the dollar an increasing importance as the single key currency.

Under the Bretton Woods system all currencies had fixed their parities in relation to the dollar. With the dollar convertible into gold (at 35 dollars to an ounce of gold) this linked all currencies to gold, and related all exchange rates to that precious metal. If the dollar was to be the single key currency, the world had to be ensured of a sufficient supply of dollars, for countries to hold in reserve and to use to pay their international debts. However, the supply should not be so large as to create over-large surplus balances, which might impair confidence in the dollar. The US balance of payments ought to be either in easy balance or, at worst, only in slight deficit, to create this confidence.

But from 1959 onwards, the US had ever increasing large deficits on its balance of payments. Its current account (the balance of trade plus the balance on invisible services) was normally in surplus; between 1964 and 1973 the average surplus was 2.8 billion dollars. But this annual surplus was more than offset by adverse capital items; in 1970 this adverse item was 9.8 billion dollars, in 1971 it was 29.8 billion dollars. This was mainly the result of three major factors: overseas investment by US companies, overseas aid provided by the US government and, particularly, expenditure on the Vietnamese war. Since these capital items could not be paid for out of current earnings, there was a decline in the national gold reserve, a piling-up of surplus dollar holdings abroad and, after 1968, increasing doubt about the dollar's future.

The doubt was increased by the development of the Euro-dollar market which had expanded in the 1960s as US banks set up branches in Europe to escape from the restrictions imposed on them at home. By 1970 there were 30 such institutions (often a consortium of US banks acting co-operatively) providing billions of dollars in loans. When, in 1970 and 1971, the Nixon government lowered domestic interest rates – as part of the priming of the economy in the run-up to the Presidential election – there was a massive outflow of US capital seeking a more profitable home in the Euro-dollar market.

Every deficit has a surplus somewhere else to offset it. The surpluses which offset the US deficits were shared by West Germany, Japan and a few smaller countries. In 1967 the British had been forced, by their continuing deficit position, to devalue the pound sterling and to borrow heavily from the IMF. This agency compelled the Labour government to tackle its payments problem and cut its deficits. The British had to endure another massive credit squeeze and further cuts in the amount of government spending on housing, schools, hospitals and other public works (p. 167). The result was a rise in the level of unemployment. But the 1967 devaluation pushed up import prices. To curb the inflationary effects of those rises, the Labour government had to take further restrictive action with the sharpest credit squeeze since 1945 and, in 1968, an equally sharp increase in taxation. In spite of this, Britain suffered from inflation as prices rose, in 1970, by some 18 per cent. The pound, it was clear, would have to suffer a further devaluation.

This evident failure by one of the key currencies threw more weight on to the dollar, the other, and more important, key currency. The problem of the world surplus of dollars could have been tackled in several ways. The countries holding those surpluses (Germany and Japan in particular) could have revalued their currencies upwards, so making likely an increased spending on cheaper (dollar) imports. The USA might have followed the British example and devalued the dollar, leading to increased earnings from cheaper exports; but Nixon would not make such an announcement as he prepared for the Presidential election. The surplus-holding countries could have expanded their economies to provide better markets for US (and other countries') goods; but the Germans had too vivid a folk memory of the inflation of the 1920s to allow them to undertake such a liberalisation. The deficit could have been attacked by US cuts in quotas and tariff restrictions on imports; but this would have run contrary to the GATT arrangements.

In August 1971, following the election, Nixon announced a raising of the American gold price, which effectively devalued the dollar by 8 per cent and a surcharge of 10 per cent on US imports. Additionally, there

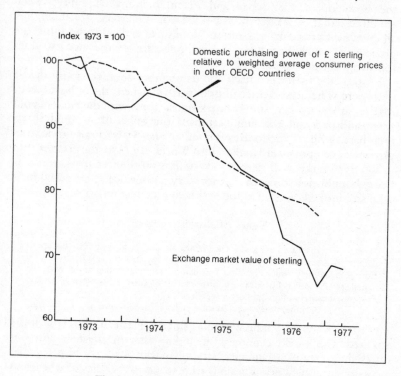

7.4 The fall in the value of the pound sterling, 1973–7.

were to be cuts in overseas aid. Germany and Japan protested at the imports surcharge. In negotiations, Nixon got these countries to accept a revaluation of their currencies; the mark went up by 13.6 per cent against the dollar; the Japanese yen by 16.9 per cent; the franc by 8.6 per cent and the already embattled pound was revalued aginst the dollar by 8.6 per cent while the US price of gold was raised from 35 dollars an ounce to 38 dollars.

But this proved to be merely a holding operation. In 1972 and 1973, the US continued to have large deficits; Germany, Japan and other countries continued to gather in large surpluses, while the pound became weaker until in June 1972 the British announced that, in future, the pound would be allowed to float; there would be no fixed rate of exchange. While this led to a sharp fall in the value of the pound (Figure 7.4), it also increased the pressure on the dollar, which was suffering from the same 'disease of deficits' which had led to the end of sterling's attempts to maintain a fixed rate. In February 1973, the US announced another 10 per cent devaluation of the dollar; in March 1973 representatives of the fourteen leading industrial countries met in Paris to discuss the problem of the dollar and of international liquidity. They announced that, in future, there would be floating rates of exchange for all the world's currencies. Bretton Woods had ended. So, too, had the prosperity which had been the main feature of the twenty years following the end of the war.

In 1974, the IMF freed itself and its member countries from the tie with gold. The official price of gold was abolished, the obligations of IMF members to make some of their transactions with the Fund in gold was abolished and the Fund returned one-sixth of its gold to its members, while it auctioned off another one-sixth to raise money to provide development aid to the Third World. By 1980, the price of gold in the free market had risen to 600 dollars on the free market; it was being bought not so much by monetary authorities as by individuals who still looked on gold as the best hedge against inflation.

Years of shock, 1973–9

'The survey produced stark evidence of the decline of Europe. No European country ranks as the leading source in any technology area. In most fields, the top European country – usually West Germany – ranks a distant third with the panellists. All other European countries virtually cease to register as widely recognised sources of technology leadership.'

Comment on a special survey, *Wall Street Journal*, 31 January 1984

In 1972, while the pound was being floated (Figure 7.4) and the dollar attacked, the world economy, including that of Western Europe, suffered a major inflationary shock. In the wake of the Russian incursion into the world's grain market (p. 124), the price of wheat and maize, animal feed and meat shot up. As a result of the failure of the coffee crop in Brazil and the sugar crop in Cuba, the prices of these two

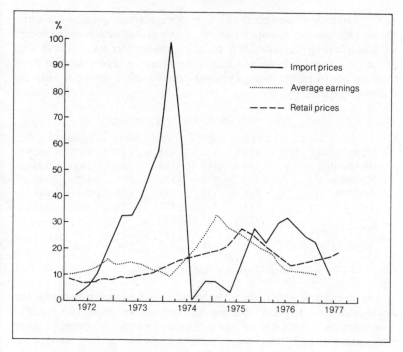

7.5 The impact of the increases in the prices of imports into Europe – particularly of oil.

commodities also rocketed. Between 1972 and 1974, prices of these various items rose on average by 16 per cent (Figure 7.5).

In 1973 worse was to come. The Israeli victory in the Yom Kippur War of October 1973 brought an embargo by the Arab oil states on supplies of crude oil to industrial countries. This brought swift restrictions in oil-based energy supply and a great increase in its cost. This embargo was soon replaced by cartelised supply arrangements under the Organisation of Petroleum Exporting Countries (OPEC) and by December 1973 the price of crude oil was about 150 per cent above its October level. Thereafter the price of crude oil continued to rise; by the end of 1974 it was 300 per cent up on its pre-October War level; by 1979 it was a staggering 20 times that level. It is a reminder of an age which has disappeared to note that in 1973 'petrol prices in Britain shot up from 35p a gallon to about 70p a gallon'. In 1974, the British motorist learned to cope with petrol at £1 a gallon and has since waited for the appearance of the £2 a gallon tag.

More important than the effect on the private motorist was the effect on the economy as a whole. The petro-chemical firms use oil as a raw material, turning it into paint, plastics, fibres and animal feedstuffs. The price of all these had to go up in line with the increasing oil prices. Oil is the fuel for most of Europe's industries, which had developed in the era of falling energy costs. Their costs of production rose in line with increasing energy costs, and final prices rose to accommodate those rising costs of production. This inflationary effect can be seen in the following table:

Consumer prices 1972–7 (1970 = 100)

	1972	1973	1974	1975	1976	1977
Austria	111	120	131	142	153	160
Belgium	110	118	133	150	163	174
France	112	120	136	152	167	181
Ireland	118	132	155	186	220	241
Germany	111	119	127	135	141	147
Italy	111	123	146	171	200	231
Netherlands	116	125	137	151	165	176
United Kingdom	117	128	148	184	215	249

Table 7.5 (Source: OECD)

The initial spiral was given continual twists by workers, in highly organised and powerful trade unions, seeking to keep their wages in line with the externally created inflation. In various countries there were attempts to develop wages policies, either by agreement with the unions or, where that was impossible, by government rulings. Some of these policies had short-term successes and workers accepted, say, 10 per cent pay increases while inflation was at, say, 15 per cent, in the hope that in a subsequent year the level of inflation would fall. But none of these attempts to control wages had any lasting success; indeed, the evidence was that, after the short-term 'successes', the workers managed, in 'unsuccessful' years, to force employers to pay above inflation rate increases – and so give the spiral an even sharper twist. In the 1950s and 1960s, people had appeared to be alarmed by inflation rates of 3, 4 and 5 per cent. In the 1970s they became accustomed to rates of 10, 15, 20 and 25 per cent.

This post-1973 inflation eroded savings as represented by building society accounts and pension schemes. It also pushed up the price of servicing state welfare schemes – pensions and other benefits. To try to attract more money into savings – needed by governments to help balance their budgets and by housing associations to provide funds – interest rates had to be pushed up to historically high levels. The British, for example, endured rates of interest of 15 and even 17 per cent. This affected the willingness of industrialists to spend money on investment; they could earn more simply by placing their profits in the money market.

Another major effect of the increased oil prices was seen in the balances of payments of the oil-importing countries. In 1964, the pound sterling had come under fatal pressure because of a deficit of £800 million. The following table shows how the increase in oil prices affected the balance of payments in some countries:

Current balances of selected countries, 1973–6 in billions of dollars.

	1973	1974	1975	1976
France	−0.1	−4.8	1.1	−5.0
Italy	−1.2	−6.6	0.9	−1.7
Japan	0.1	−4.5	−0.4	3.9
United Kingdom	−1.2	−7.8	−2.8	−1.1

Table 7.6 (Source: IMF 1977)

All the oil-importing countries had to spend a higher proportion of their earnings (personal and national) on oil. This left less to be spent on non-oil products. Governments had to concern themselves with the effect of this on balances of payments; individuals in each country had to be concerned, primarily, with the effect on personal consumption. As people spent less on non-oil products, there was a fall in consumer demand, and the onset of the trade depression which has remained a feature of the world economy since 1973. Government attempts to cope with deficits in the payments' accounts deepened the depression. Attempts had to be made to limit imports of oil and non-oil products. Credit restrictions, higher taxation, higher interest rates, all added to the deflationary effect of an already existing tendency to lower consumer spending and led to a deepening of the depression. This can be seen in the following table:

Annual percentage changes in real output, 1971–6

	1971	1972	1973	1974	1975	1976
France	5.3	5.7	5.4	2.3	0.1	5.2
West Germany	3.0	3.4	4.9	0.4	−2.5	5.7
Italy	1.6	3.1	6.9	3.9	−3.5	5.6
Japan	7.3	9.1	9.8	−1.3	2.4	6.3
United Kingdom	2.0	3.1	6.1	−0.1	−1.6	1.5

Table 7.7 (Source: IMF 1976)

The rise in output in 1976 was due, in large part, to the increased spending by the OPEC countries, or by their making their increased earnings available, through the western banking system (including the vastly inflated Euro-dollar system) to borrowers who could put the money to profitable use. Table 7.8 overleaf illustrates the growth of the OPEC countries' earnings.

The potentially disastrous effects of the piling up of surpluses in the OPEC community was partially offset by international co-operation. In January 1974, the IMF issued guidelines which recommended that the deficit countries should not try to overcome their problem by deflation (although many adopted some deflationary policies) but that

Current balance situations, 1973–6 in billions of dollars

	1973	1974	1975	1976
Major oil export	+ 6.2	+67.4	+34.7	+41.0
Industrial countries	+11.1	−11.2	+18.6	− 1.4
Non-oil primary producers –				
more developed	+ 1.3	−14.3	−14.8	−14.3
less developed	−10.9	−29.5	−38.2	−25.8

Table 7.8 (Source: IMF 1977)

they should finance the deficits by borrowing from the OPEC countries. These countries, for their part, were unable to spend the money which they received. They welcomed the opportunity to make further profit from their success in having pushed up the oil prices. Forty-two per cent of their surplus income went into the Euro-dollar market, 35 per cent was invested in the short-term money markets in

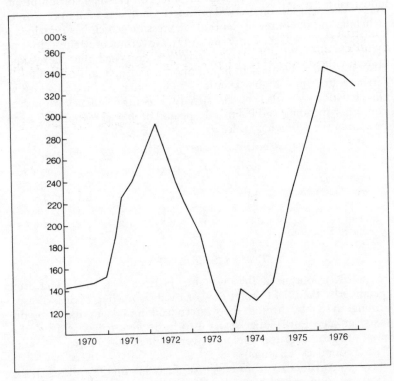

7.6 The level of unemployment in British manufacturing industry, 1970–6. Similar graphs could be drawn to illustrate the situation in every other country in Western Europe.

the USA and Britain. Most of this money was re-lent so that, for example, Britain, Italy and France met their deficits (totalling 23 billion dollars) by borrowing on the Euro–dollar market, so that they actually increased their official reserves in 1974 in spite of adverse balance of payments deficits.

After 1976, the OPEC countries began to spend their surplus income on various forms of development. This brought more OPEC money back into international circulation so that, again, the worst effects of the price increases were averted. There were, of course, observable effects of the depression; the level of unemployment in all European countries continued to rise in the second half of the 1970s; governments were forced to spend increasing sums on social security benefits (Figure 7.6). However, for those who had a job, the late 1970s proved to be a period of growth and prosperity. While the price of oil continued to increase (reaching a high mark of 35 dolars per barrel in 1979), wage rates continued to rise at an even faster rate. In real terms the price of oil fell in industrialised countries, as can be seen in Figure 7.7.

The rate of inflation showed no sign of falling, and the prices of industrial goods continued to rise. This had an effect on the prices paid by OPEC importers for their development schemes. They had to pay more for their projects than had been first planned in 1974–6. At the

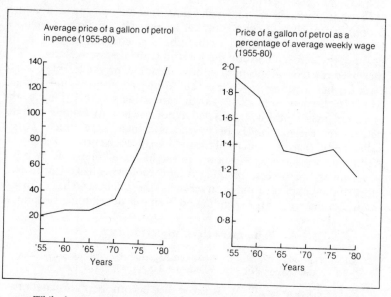

7.7 While the nominal price of petrol has risen since 1955, its real price has fallen steadily, indicating that wages have risen more steeply than oil prices and that the oil exporting countries have had to suffer, as they are forced to pay inflated prices for their imports from the manufacturing countries.

same time, the industrial slow-down led to a sharp fall in demand for oil in the industrial countries. But while that fall was developing, so, too, were new sources of oil, so that the suppliers' nightmare became a reality: an increasing supply met a falling demand. The result was a fall in prices from the high level of 35 dollars a barrel to what became a new, if shaky, price of 27 dollars a barrel. The problem which this created for the oil producers is illustrated by the Nigerian example. Nigeria had planned an output of 3 million barrels a day when the price was 35 dollars a barrel. This would have provided a daily income of 105 million dollars. In 1983, Nigeria was selling only 1½ million barrels per day and at 27 dollars, giving a daily income of 40 million dollars. Industrial and social development had been planned on the expectation of 105 million dollars; these had to be sharply cut back in the light of the much lower income, particularly when that smaller income had to be spent on industrial goods which were increasing in price. The collapse of the Nigerian economy in 1983 was a sign that OPEC was not all-powerful.

Even worse was the effect of the oil price increase on Third World countries. These were affected in three principal ways. Firstly, most of the primary producing countries are over-dependent on a single commodity – copper in Zambia, coffee in Brazil. World demand for primary products fell as a result of the depression and these countries had smaller export earnings.

Secondly, people in under-developed countries spend a higher proportion of their small income on oil than do people in developed countries; oil is the source for lighting and cooking as well as for heating; the kerosene tin and the paraffin lamp are essential items. The increased price of oil meant that these already deprived people became even further deprived, even less able to buy consumer goods, which added to the depressed state of their national economies. Finally, the governments of these countries had to borrow heavily to cope with the deficits on their balances of payments which were much worse, collectively, than the deficits of the industrialised countries (Table 7.8). As interest rates rose, in response to the increased demands by other government borrowers, these Third World countries had to spend even more of their export earnings on servicing these debts and had even less foreign exchange left for spending on desirable development schemes.

The growth of uncertainty

Getting from Here to There: A Policy for the Post-Keynesian Age. The title of a book by W. W. Rostow, Macmillan, first published in USA 1978, in UK 1979.

The US economist, W. W. Rostow, had become best known for two books which he published in 1952 and 1960. The first, *The Process of Economic Growth*, was re-published in 1978-9, partly as a counter-blast to a book called *The Limits to Growth* which had first appeared in 1970 and whose gloomy forecasts were amply reinforced by the experiences of the following decade.

Keynes had proposed increased government spending, easier credit and manipulation of taxation as remedies for the unemployment which was common in the 1930s. In the 1970s the levels of unemployment reached 1930s proportions; indeed, the high levels of unemployment remained a feature of European economies for much longer than they had in the 1930s, when, after peaking between 1932–3, unemployment slowly fell. There was little fall in European unemployment, even by 1984.

But no government, now, believes that the Keynesian recipe could work. Indeed, the British had tried to 'spend their way out of the depression' in 1971–3 when the money supply was first expanded. Although the money supply continued to expand, there was no fall in the level of unemployment, and it was a socialist Prime Minister, Callaghan, who had to tell the Labour Party Conference in 1977 that new ways had to be found of tackling the unemployment problem.

The oil-induced depression accentuated existing trends, one of which was the long-term decline of the old, traditional industries – coal, iron and steel and shipbuilding. Not only was there a falling demand for the products of these industries; there were also new sources of supply from the developing world. Brazil, Korea and even Vietnam could produce cheaper steel in more modern plants, and their products replaced Europe's to take an increasing share of the world's markets.

Europe had also failed to take a leading role in the development of the new industries, the computer-based and high technology industries. These industries were centred on the Pacific, with Japan, Singapore, the Philippines, Korea and Taiwan as major producer countries. The centre of gravity of the industrial world had shifted from the mid-Atlantic (based on the USA and Europe) to the mid-Pacific (based on the USA and Asia).

Britain had been the first to experience the decline of the old industries; she was the first to cut the output of coal and to close steel plants. The rest of Europe followed the British example in the late 1970s and in the early 1980s. In Europe, as in Britain, there was industrial unrest as workers were forced out of the traditional industries of the Ruhr and Saar and joined the lengthening unemployment queues.

In Britain and Germany the electorate returned conservative governments to govern their countries. Mrs Thatcher's 1979 electoral promise was to bring down the rate of inflation. Chancellor Kohl won power in 1982 with a similar set of harsh promises; for it was clear that bringing down the rate of inflation would have painful repercussions on domestic and international economies. The French, perversely, chose a left-wing government to cope with the problems of the post-Keynesian age. Mitterand, who became President in 1981, initially indulged in a Keynesian bout of tax-cutting, increased government spending and extension of government activity as hoped-for cures for France's unemployment. Within a few months he was forced to accept the realities as perceived by Thatcher and Kohl: taxes were increased; French people were forbidden (for a brief period) to take holidays abroad, in attempts to save foreign exchange; the franc was devalued and, in 1984, Mitterand presented to the economic world the same 'monetarist' face as was provided by Thatcher and Kohl, and saw the conservative right gain electoral successes in French local elections.

In the Keynesian age, European governments, responding to the call for 'a better world' (p. 15), had introduced a variety of welfare schemes which had been extended during the 1950s and 1960s. In the prosperous years, when growth was the accepted norm, these benefits could be paid for without a deal of trouble. The following table illustrates the problem facing welfare-providing governments in depressed Europe:

	Social spending as % of GDP		Annual growth rate of real GDP	
	1960	1981	1960–75	1975–81
Belgium	17	38	4.5	3.0
France	13.4	23.8	5.0	2.8
Germany (West)	20.5	31.5	3.8	3.0
Holland	16.3	36.1	4.5	2.0
Italy	16.5	29.1	4.6	3.2
UK	13.9	24.9	2.6	1.0

Table 7.9 (Source: OECD)

If existing schemes are maintained, and if spending is maintained to match expected rates of inflation, total social spending will increase – on pensions (for an aging population), and on health (on those longer-surviving pensioners), even though less will have to be spent on education (because of the fall in the birthrate).

If European economic performances do not improve, the burden of such spending will increase in real terms. One hopeful sign is the belated recognition by the countries in the EEC that the technological revolution is in full swing. In 1984 the EEC set up a European Strategic Programme for Research in Information Technology (ESPRIT) costing £1 billion, to examine ways in which Europe might catch up, at a late stage, on developments in micro-electronics, software technology, advanced information processing and office and factory computerisation. Information technology is a growing sector of the world economy; in 1983 the growth was over 8 per cent. It is expected that, by 1990, some 5 million people will be employed in this relatively new sector. In 1983 EEC countries bought 30 per cent of all such products, but produced only 10 per cent of world output, leading to a deficit of over £4 billion. In 1973, the EEC countries had a trade surplus in high technology; they have not retained their leadership in the newer and faster growing fields.

Also in 1984, ministers from EEC countries started to co-operate on the production of schemes for tackling the problem of unemployment. There were, in February 1984, some 33 million unemployed in the EEC, some 9 per cent of the workforce. This is an increase of 14 million over the 1979 level, and to return to that level will require the creation of some 18,000 new jobs every day for the rest of the 1980s. But the early evidence from ministerial conferences was that there were deep divisions between the radicals of 'The New Right', who would hope for greater flexibility and adaptability by workers, and the workers' representatives who see 'wages flexibility' as code words for reductions in living standards. In March 1984, steelworkers on the Ruhr begin a massive strike in protest against the closure of redundant plant; in Britain, miners organised a long strike in protest against the closure of uneconomic pits. There is not much sign of 'flexibility'; rather there is much of 'what I have I hold', and hold all the stronger because of the uncertainties which now prevail throughout a relatively declining Europe.

Alienation – the result of affluence?

'Among the possible sources of alienation in western democracies . . . is the new democratic Leviathan itself . . . a product of long evolution and hard struggle, welfare-oriented, centralised, bureaucratic, tamed and controlled by competition among highly organised élites, and, in the perspective of the ordinary citizen, somewhat remote, distant and impersonal.'[4]

R. A. Dahl, 1966

The alienation of which Dahl wrote was expressed, in 1966, in the main, only by a relatively small group of intellectuals. In Britain, France and Germany there was a growing discontent with the prosperous societies created in the late 1950s. In the early 1960s a small intellectual 'New Left' gained support among the rapidly expanding university student populations of these booming countries. Some of this élite were 'bored' by prosperous Europe; others attacked the 'welfare-oriented' states which, they claimed, had done nothing to change the reality of the political and economic power-structures. A significant minority of students regarded higher education mainly as an opportunity to become better-armed with criticism of the very society which had created that opportunity. Influenced by the 'New Left', which was divorced from the traditional socialist parties of Europe, they condemned those parties as vehicles for the maintenance of the *status quo*. Leaders and led in this 'New Left' ignored the fact that the vast majority of workers (for whom they claimed to speak) welcomed their *embourgoisement*; they ignored, too, the electoral proofs of the tendencies of the prosperous workers to switch voting patterns, so that conservative governments continued to win power in prosperous Europe. The 'New Left' argued that the working class had become corrupted by prosperity, and that only the radicalised students understood what were the workers' best interests.

The anger and frustration of this 'New Left' was deepened by the behaviour of the leaders of the traditional socialist parties. In Germany, for example, the Social Democrats produced the Bad Godesberg programme in 1959 (p. 195). The Party abandoned its Marxist past, renounced 'pacifism' by accepting the case for German re-armament, announced that nationalisation was only one of several possible methods of controlling the economy and chose the young, pragmatic Willy Brandt as its new leader. This was condemned by the 'New Left' as showing that the German socialists had chosen political expediency, rather than political principles, as the guideline for future action. The fact that this switch led to electoral success in the 1960s did nothing to assuage the anger of the 'New Left' which had come to regard the electoral process as part of the 'fraud' of the system.

There were similar changes in policies by the socialist parties in Britain and Italy. The Italian Socialist Party entered into an alliance with the moderate wing of the Christian Democrats (p. 10); in Britain, Gaitskell tried to get the Labour Party to renounce its devotion to nationalisation. His failure to win this struggle for 'the soul of the Party' only served to hide the fact that the Party was on its way to becoming the pragmatic party which, under Wilson, would, when in power, pursue policies which the 'New Left' would condemn as being 'typically Tory'. In the late 1970s, the 'New Left' made inroads into the British Labour movement and succeeded in getting the policy-making Conference to adopt left-wing, socialist-oriented policies (p. 168). This was a major cause of the formation of the Social Democratic Party, led by four former Labour ministers. This had also been the fate of the Dutch Labour Party; in 1970, a right-wing group broke off from the increasingly left-wing Labour Party to form a distinct party at the 1971 election.

The continued success of Europe's conservative parties and the evidence of 'treachery' by pragmatic socialist parties were among the reasons for the alienation of a variety of groups throughout Europe. In 1968, for example, a European-wide student movement seemed to aim at the overthrow of the political system. Amsterdam, Berlin and Paris were the main centres for student activities; the students' rising in 1968 in Paris was one cause of de Gaulle's fall from power (p. 179). The major flaw of such student activity was that it had little notion, if any, of what it wanted other than to destroy the existing political, economic and social system. It failed to become a major political force; some of its leaders fell back into everyday life once the heady days of 1968 were over; others entered into the traditional political process and became members of one or other of the older political parties. A small number formed extremist, terrorist organisations, the most notorious of which were the Baader-Meinhof gang (so named after two of the leaders) in Germany (p. 198) and the Red Brigades in Italy (p. 213). By 1984, these had either been wiped out or had deteriorated into self-centred bands more interested in enrichment than in philosophy.

German students were angered at the continued success of the Christian Democrats who provided West Germany with 'Chancellory Democracy': Adenauer (until his retirement in 1963) had seemed all-powerful as he made the post of Chancellor the dominant one in West German politics (p. 188). French students were roused as much by de Gaulle's presidential style of authoritarianism as by the failure of the socialists to present a credible alternative. In Britain, too, there was increasing comment on the increasing power of the prime minister; throughout the 1960s there were claims that Britain suffered from prime ministers who regarded themselves as quasi-Presidents. The fall of Wilson in 1970 and the collapse of the Heath government in 1974 showed that there was not much truth to such claims. However, the attention which the media paid (and pays) to the leaders of the political parties lends credence to the notion that in many western democracies the leader of a political party is more than *primus inter pares*. And the behaviour of some leaders provides evidence to support the claims of their critics. In France, there was the 'style' of the Giscard government; in Britain, there was the emergence of 'Thatcherism'.

But even the most pretentious of leaders found that political reality was stronger than even their critics supposed. On assuming power, they found that the bureaucracy was a powerful machine which could, in some cases, stultify government policy. And, beyond the bureaucracy, there were the realities of the national and international economies. Mitterand, of France, might have wished, after 1982, to be the left-wing leader of the socialist-communist alliance (p. 183). He was forced, in 1984, to adopt an increasingly right-wing stance as he grappled with France's economic problems. Unemployment and inflation did not disappear with the accession of a left-wing President who was, additionally, forced to accept the economic need to cut the size of the French steel and coal industries, much as the right-wing Thatcher had done in Britain. And in left-wing-led France, as in right-wing-led Britain, the cost of living continued to rise as did the level of taxation as governments paid for the welfare provisions resulting from earlier legislation (p. 158).

The failure of the democratic system to provide the panaceas which left-wing optimists had hoped for, led to the emergence of three different forms of political activity. On the one hand there has been the development of single-interest groups campaigning for such things as protection of the environment ('ecology' became an in-word in the 1970s) and for women's rights. Then there has been the tendency to direct action. Trade unionists, for example, have used the industrial strike as a political weapon; in 1974, British trade unionists caused the downfall of the Heath government and led Heath to announce that Britain was 'ungovernable'. In 1979, widespread strikes by workers against the policies of the Labour government were among the causes of that government's defeat in the 1979 election. In 1984, workers in France, Germany, Belgium and Britain used the strike weapon as a protest against government decisions to scale down the size of the coal and steel industries in those countries. Increasingly, it seems, and in many countries, workers refuse to accept the decisions of elections and the policies of governments.

For a short period the most serious challenge to the democratic system seemed to come from the emergence of regional parties. The Basques of northern Spain had maintained their hostility to the centralised state and had employed terrorism as part of their campaign (p. 217). In 1968, the Catholics of Northern Ireland were drawn into terrorism as part of their campaign for equal civil rights. Terrorist activities have been used only by fringe elements of the Scottish Nationalist Party and Plaid Cymru which campaign for Home Rule for Scotland and Wales respectively. Similar movements have disrupted political life in Belgium (where the Walloons fight with the Flemings), Brittany (with a Celtic-tinged notion of local autonomy) and Switzerland (where the Catholics fight for equality with the Protestants).

Dahl's critique of western democracies (p. 159) appeared in 1966. Since then, as has been shown, alienation has affected even more groups, so that it is possible now to perceive a loss of faith in western democracy similar to the loss of faith in communism which is widespread throughout Russia and Eastern Europe. We have also seen that the international monetary system has failed to live up to the great hopes that were expressed by the authors of the Bretton Woods agreement of 1944. This failure has, in turn, been one cause for the emergence of the problem caused by the massive debts of countries such as Argentina, Brazil, Mexico – and the Soviet bloc. In fine, the Europe of the mid-1980s faces a series of seemingly insoluble problems nationally and internationally. There is no room, now, for the optimism of the early 1960s, and, it seems, there can only be a further alienation of people from the normal democratic process. How that alienation will develop, and how society will cope with it, will be matters for future historians.

FURTHER READING

FLORA, P. AND HEINENHEIMER, H. J., eds. *The Development of Welfare States in Europe and America*, 1981

GIMBEL, J., *The Origin of the Marshall Plan*, 1976

HINDELBERGEN, C., *Europe's Post-War Growth*, 1981

LAQUEUR, W., *A Continent Astray: Europe, 1970–78*, 1979

MCINNES, N., *The Communist Parties of Western Europe*, 1975

MENDELSOHN, M. S., *Money on the Move*, McGraw-Hill, 1980

MILWARD, A., *The Reconstruction of Western Europe, 1945–51*, Methuen, 1984

OECD ECONOMIC SURVEYS (published annually)

POSTAN, M. M., *An Economic History of Western Europe, 1945–64*, Methuen, 1967

ROSTOW, W. W., *Getting from Here to There: A policy for the post-Keynesian Age*, Macmillan, 1979

SAMPSON, A., *The Seven Sisters*, Hodder and Stoughton, 1981

SCAMMEL, W. M., *The International Economy since 1945*, Macmillan, 1982

SCHONFIELD, A., ed., *International Economic Relations of the Western World, 1951–71*, OUP, 1976

8

Britain and France, 1945–84

BRITAIN

Considerations of space have dictated a less full coverage of Britain than of the other major European states. On the one hand, students of British history need more detailed studies than could be provided in an introductory survey of European history. On the other, however, references to Britain elsewhere in this book require, at least, a summary of post-war British domestic history.

The election of 1945 marked the return to party politics after rule by wartime coalition governments. Labour governments (1945–51, 1964–70, 1974–9) have alternated with Conservative (1951–64, 1970–4 and 1979–   ). Because of wartime promises, the influence of Keynesian economics and the need to gain electoral popularity, there was, until 1979, general agreement on the aims of British governments – full employment, rising living standards, a developing welfare state and industrial expansion and modernisation.

In 1945, the Attlee government's freedom was limited by severe economic problems. Resources had to be devoted to the rebuilding of much that had been destroyed or damaged during the war. Other resources were needed for the modernisation of old industry and the development of new. Such demand for resources led, immediately, to increases in the volume and value of imports. Britain's ability to pay for her imports was limited by the loss of £3 billion of overseas investments, the wartime acquisition of heavy overseas debt and by the difficulties of rebuilding the export trade in a war-shattered world (Figure 8.1). The devaluation of the pound in 1949 lowered export prices and helped the export drive (Figure 7.3, p. 144). However, it also increased import prices and added to the inflation already sparked off by the over-high demand for men and materials. This inflation was worsened by increases in world prices following the outbreak of the Korean War (Figure 7.2, p. 140). The Labour government made its own position

OLIVER

8.1 The artist, Low, shows Selwyn Lloyd, British Chancellor of the Exchequer, trying to persuade British workers that they cannot have 'more', because of the demands made by the IMF and European banks that Britain bring her inflation rate down. This cartoon might have been drawn at any time from 1945 to 1980 with a variety of Chancellors playing the part of the unwilling doler-out.

even more critical by its decision to undertake a vast rearmament programme (p. 139). This further increased the demand for already over-scarce resources.

To try to solve part of its problems, the government imposed charges for some Health Service facilities. This led to a Cabinet split, ministerial resignations and electoral defeat in 1951. Churchill's government benefited from the fall in world prices following the end of the Korean War in 1953 (Figure 7.2), and from the increased output from industries developed after 1945. These favourable changes allowed the government to end rationing, lower taxes and encourage economic expansion. Under Eden and, later, Macmillan, Conservative governments enjoyed the economic boom of the 'fifties (Document 8.2). This led to increased demands for labour; married women were encouraged to return to work while immigrants from Commonwealth countries were attracted to take jobs which the affluent British were unwilling to do.

The expansion also led to continuing inflation and recurrent crises in the balance of payments (Document 8.1). Attempts to solve these twin problems led to a 'stop-go' cycle. In the 'go' period, interest rates were lowered, wage increases allowed and economic expansion encouraged. In the 'stop' period of the cycle, there were high interest rates, cuts in government spending, attempts to limit wage increases and a slow-down in the rate of economic expansion. In the 'stop' period there was also high unemployment and electoral unpopularity. In 1961 Mac-millan tried to find alternatives for the crude 'stop' policies. He set up NEDC in the hope that this would lead to a planned expansion of the economy; he set up the National Incomes Commission hoping that this would ensure controlled increases in wage rates. He applied to join the EEC, hoping that membership would provide a spur to the economy and a means of enlarging British exports.

In 1963, in the wake of the failure to gain admission to the EEC, the government tried 'a dash for growth'. Taxes were lowered and

8.2 How the artist, Vicky, saw the retreat by left-wing parties from their socialist path. Britain's Labour leader, Attlee (in hat) is shown in the cartoon along with Morrison (in glasses), Gaitskell, Wilson (with pipe), Shinwell, Bevan, Cripps and Jay. But socialist parties in France, Germany and Italy made British-like changes in policies in the hope of winning electoral popularity. 'The death of socialism' was one of the prices to be paid for electoral affluence.

modernisation encouraged in the hope that the consequent rises in imports would be more than matched by rises in exports. The upshot was a deficit of £800 million in the balance of payments. In 1964 a Labour government, under Harold Wilson, tended to imitate the policies tried by Conservative predecessors (Figure 8.2). A Department of Economic Affairs was intended to 'plan' economic expansion; a Prices and Incomes Board was to regulate increases in prices and incomes. At first, there was an encouragement of expansion and a free-for-all in wages negotiations. The twin problems of inflation and deficits on trade worsened. Britain had to apply for a large loan from the IMF to meet its deficit. The IMF insisted that Britain tackle the problem of inflation. The government then adopted the 'stop' policies of previous governments. Interest rates went up, government spending was slashed, wages frozen and charges by nationalised industries increased. In 1967 the pound was devalued again as an aid to exports – but at the cost of a further twist in the inflationary spiral (Figure 7.3, p. 144). In the 1970 election campaign, the Heath-led Conservatives promised to reduce prices 'at a stroke' – and won the election.

Between 1970 and 1972 the Conservative government reduced government spending, lowered taxes and encouraged industrial invest-ment. When these policies failed to produce the desired economic growth, the government adopted radically different policies (Figure 7.6, p. 154). Government borrowing was enlarged, interest rates lowered and private borrowing encouraged in the hope that the economy could be forced into a credit-based boom. The pound was 'floated' by a government which hoped that a falling pound would help exporters (Figure 7.4, p. 149). However, the most immediate outcome of credit expansion and a floating pound was a rise in the level of inflation. This forced the government to bring in a wages policy which, in turn, led to a miners' strike in 1973–4. The government seemed incapable of governing and it lost the 1974 election.

Heath's problems had been worsened by the increases in oil prices in 1973. Further increases in these prices in the 1970s affected the freedom of Labour governments. There were deficits in the balance of pay-ments, more loans from the IMF, further IMF-inspired cuts in spending and attempts to tackle the problem of inflation (Figures 7.4 and 7.5, pp. 149, 151). Restrictive policies and high unemployment (Figure 7.6, p. 154) led trade unionists to accept Labour proposals for limitations on the rate of wage increases. These helped to bring down the level of inflation. They also lowered workers' living standards. In 1979, trade unions refused to accept further limitations on wages. In the public sector, there was a series of damaging strikes which led to government unpopularity and to the Conservative victory in the 1979 election.

Since 1979 the Thatcher governments have maintained their attack on inflation in spite of the consequent rise in the level of unemploy-ment. They have tried to bring down the level of taxation and to lessen the role of government in the economic and social life of the nation. The electoral unpopularity of such policies has been offset by the support gained during the Falklands War and by the continuing decline in the fortunes of the Labour Party, which seems more intent on internecine war than on finding alternatives to existing government policies.

FRANCE

1940–6

'All my life I have kept alive in myself a certain idea of France . . . I early came to believe that France had an eminent and exceptional destiny . . . I am convinced that France is really only herself when she is in the front rank. France cannot be France without greatness.'

Charles de Gaulle

The humiliation of the defeat of 1940 and the collaboration of the Vichy government left major scars on the French psyche. De Gaulle was a junior general who escaped to England where he set himself up as the leader of the Free French forces. Many regarded him as a traitor who had run away; others feared that he was primarily interested in self-seeking. He was 'endured' by Churchill and Roosevelt who, however, did not consult him before holding a wartime summit in Casablanca – part of the French Empire over which de Gaulle claimed to 'rule'. Nor was he invited to attend this or any of the other wartime conferences; the Anglo-Saxons were to pay, later on, for this treatment of the proud general.

In June 1944, de Gaulle set up a Committee of National Liberation in Algiers to provide France with the framework for a government once the Germans had been driven out. In August 1944, the Allies allowed him to lead the triumphal entry into liberated Paris. In September he set up a new government which the Allies formally recognised in October 1944. Its 22 members consisted of much that was 'old' and some that was 'new'. Thirteen of the ministers represented political parties; two of them were communists, one of whom, Tillon, was a well-known leader of the underground resistance movement.

The French resistance movement had developed a programme for post-war development and in 1944 had issued a Resistance Charter which called for a reconstruction of French society in which the dignity of everyone would be recognised, 'a more just social order', and the reorganisation of the economy in the general interest and not just for the benefit of a favoured few; it listed the rights of workers, called for a Beveridge-type system of social security, the nationalisation of many private monopolies and the right of workers to share in economic policy-making within industries and firms.

The Communists had a good deal of influence in the resistance movement – its members providing roughly half the total membership of that movement. During the war they had won a major foothold among the peasants and the trade union movement, while the middle class, with its support for Vichy, had shown (said the Communists) that it was unfit to rule the new France. The militant and successful Party might have seized power in 1944–5, just as Communists did in the liberated areas of eastern Europe. De Gaulle persuaded the leaders of the resistance movement, including the Communists, to accept the leadership of the Provisional Government, and got the leaders of local resistance groups to hand over power to local administrators appointed by that Provisional Government which included Thorez, the Communist Party leader, once he had returned from his wartime 'exile' in Moscow.

In August 1945 the leaders of the Vichy government – Pétain, Laval and the other collaborators – were tried; some 800 of them were executed (although Pétain was merely imprisoned) and another 40,000 were imprisoned. Additionally, there were acts of revenge carried out in different localities as people got their own back on petty collaborators.

There was a return to political activity throughout the period July to September 1945. The Communists, with some 900,000 members, were the largest single party and were held in high esteem for their work in the resistance movement. The Socialists, who had co-operated with the Communists in that resistance movement, now feared being swallowed up by the stronger, Moscow-orientated Party. The Mouvement Republicaine Populaire (MRP) was a new party led by left-of-centre Catholics such as Bidault and Schuman. It gained its support from the traditionally conservative and Catholic regions such as Normandy, Brittany and Alsace. There was no strong right-wing party, not surprisingly in view of the links between the right and the German occupying forces after 1940. There was also a fall in support for the once-powerful Radical Socialist Party, the pillar of the Third Republic but now left without a political base since the extreme left of the political spectrum was occupied by the Communist Party, while the moderate socialists led by Mendès-France and the moderate right MRP filled the major section.

In October 1945, the French people went to the polls to elect a Constituent Assembly. The Communists (26 per cent), Socialists (24 per cent) and the Catholic MRP (25 per cent) gathered three-quarters of the votes. The Assembly drew up a constitution for a Fourth Republic which, however, was rejected by the voters in a referendum. A fresh and more conservative constitution was approved in a second referendum by a majority of one million – although some 8 million voters abstained.

This constitution had much in common with that of the Third Republic. The Legislature consisted of two chambers – the National Assembly and the Council of the Republic (the Upper House). The President, the head of state, was to be elected for seven years by both

Chambers. He was to appoint the Prime Minister, who had to be a Member of Parliament who could command a majority in the National Assembly (the Lower House). In 1945, the three major parties combined to elect de Gaulle as the first President in post-war France.

De Gaulle had not approved of the new constitution; it did not provide the President with sufficient powers and, he thought, it would lead to the fragmentation of the major parties into warring factions each seeking power for its own sake. As head of the Provisional Government, (August 1945–October 1945), he had approved of the fundamental economic and social reforms. Mines, railways, power stations, Air France and most banks were nationalised; a social security system was established and a planning commission appointed, under Jean Monnet, to plan the modernisation of French industry. This Commission produced the first of its Five Year Plans in 1946.

As head of state after October 1945, de Gaulle formed his first government in November 1945. This included five leading Communists. However, relations between the politicians and de Gaulle were uneasy. On 20 January 1946 he called a Cabinet meeting, appeared in full uniform and announced his resignation. He claimed that the transition from war to peace was now over and that the politicians could govern without him.

The end of the Fourth Republic, 1946–58

'Faced with problems too hard for the régime to tackle, France has, for the last twelve years, followed a disastrous road. In the past, the country from its very depths entrusted me with the task of leading it to salvation. Today, with new ordeals facing it, let the country know that I am ready to assume the powers of the Republic.'

Press statement issued by De Gaulle, 15 May 1958

The war had been a costly one for France. Two million French men and women had been taken to Germany to be used as forced labour or placed in concentration camps. Many had died or had been executed; those who returned were often too broken to be able to play a full part in the nation's economic life after 1945. Bombing, and the fighting which followed the Allied invasion in June 1944, led to the destruction of many French ports on the northern coast and to many cities and towns being severely damaged; one-fifth of French houses were damaged; two-thirds of the railway stock destroyed and one-half of livestock killed. A French War Damages Commission estimated that the war had cost France some 45 per cent of its total wealth. This was the background against which Monnet's Planning Commission had to work. Marshall Aid was welcomed (pp. 60–3 and because of its economic problems France played a leading role in the various movements for European integration (Chapter 11).

Economic recovery was rapid, in spite of the failure of politicians to provide the stability which would have aided that recovery. The system of proportional representation encouraged a return to the fragmentation of parties so that no single party could gain a majority in the National Assembly. Between 1946 and 1958, France had 24 governments and it is not surprising that there was little continuity of policy on such issues as social reform and, in particular, inflation which, in 1951 and 1952, ran at the rate of 15 per cent a year.

Largely because of Monnet's Planning Commission and because of large investments in the immediate post-war years, economic recovery was rapid. Industry was back to its 1938 level by 1948; agriculture was back to the pre-war level by 1950 in spite of the severe winter of 1946–7 (p. 138). The franc was often devalued (Figure 7.3, p. 144) in attempts to cope with inflation and as an aid to the drive to promote French exports.

However, the politicians made little contribution to this recovery. In May 1947, the other parties formed an alliance to drive the Communists from the Coalition Government. In return, the Communists led damaging strikes at the Renault nationalised factories (p. 62) and, when Marshall Aid began to arrive, organised major demonstrations against this Aid and the US presence in Europe. Thorez was a loyal Muscovite. His tactics, however, served to alienate many French voters who saw Stalinism at work in eastern Europe. The moderate government's use of military force to crush the strikes by three million Communist-led workers and supporters was widely approved.

The onset of the Korean War in 1950 (p. 74 and Figure 4.2, p. 74) hampered the French recovery. The US demanded that her European allies increase their military strength which led to increased demand for military equipment and to inflation. Import prices, too, rose steeply (Figure 7.2, p. 140) which in France, as in Britain, added a further twist to the inflationary spiral.

In June 1951, the French went to the polls to elect a fresh National Assembly. The elections showed a distinct switch of political allegiances. The Communists emerged as the main recipient of working class votes; the Socialists who had been so powerful in 1945, suffered from their involvement in government. The once-powerful MRP also suffered, as many of its former supporters drifted back to their traditional position of supporting more conservative parties. A new party, founded by de Gaulle in April 1947, the Rassemblement du Peuple Français (RPF) was, according to de Gaulle, less of a political party and more of a 'movement' with social as well as political overtones. It quickly gained political credibility, partly because of the leader, partly because of the policies he advocated (anti-American as well as anti-German). In October 1947, the RPF won 40 per cent of the vote in local elections; in 1951 it had 120 Deputies in the Assembly. Some of his more ardent supporters urged de Gaulle to organise a *coup d'état* and seize power. He refused, since he wanted any régime which he might head to have the dignity of legitimacy. The RPF, which presented itself as a Catholic party, made further inroads into the

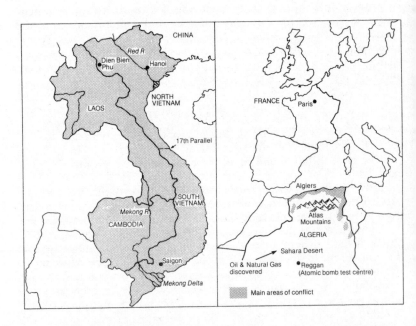

8.3 The French fought bitter wars to try to hold on to colonies in (a) Indo–China and (b) Algeria.

support of the MRP which declined rapidly.

However, the support for de Gaulle ebbed rapidly: in 1947 the party had won 52 council seats in Paris; in 1953 it had only one; by 1953 the RPF had split into left-wing and right-wing (more conservative) factions, whose members were drawn into one or other of the successive coalitions which governed France after 1952. In July 1955, de Gaulle admitted that the RPF had failed to perform as he had hoped and announced that he was retiring from public life.

Meanwhile, the coalition governments, usually led by a Socialist (such as Guy Mollet) or a Radical (such as Mendès-France), had to cope with the costly and increasingly futile colonial war in Indo-China (Figure 8.3a and pp. 244–5). It was a Radical-Gaullist-Socialist coalition led by Mendès-France which finally negotiated the end of that war in 1954 (p. 245). This retreat from empire angered some right-wingers and people with links with the officer class in the retreating army. However, Mendès-France pleased these people by sending more troops to Algeria to bring the revolt by the Muslim Nationalists to an end. This angered the left-wing members of the Coalition and Mendès-France was forced to resign.

In the elections to the Assembly in 1956, the Communists emerged as the strongest party with some 25 per cent of the seats. Another alienated group was represented by fifty supporters of a right-wing demagogue, Pierre Poujade, whose anti-intellectual, anti-socialist and anti-European policies were supported by small shopkeepers and businessmen whose profits had been hit by rapid inflation. The Radicals, under Mendès-France, supported the Socialists, led by Guy Mollet, who became Prime Minister, hopeful of solving the Algerian problem. In February 1956, Mollet went to Algiers where the white settlers organised a large and hostile demonstration. This frightened Mollet from pursuing his plans for a peaceful solution to the problem. He was further driven into an anti-Muslim attitude by his anger at Nasser's nationalisation of the Suez Canal (p. 94). Nasser was thought to be responsible for providing aid and comfort to the Algerian rebels. Mollet persuaded Eden to co-operate with France and Israel in the Suez adventure aimed at the overthrow of Nasser.

Mendès-France refused to support the more warlike policy after May 1956. Several leading Socialists also resigned from the Party as Mollet became increasingly conservative and authoritarian. This made him a prisoner of the conservative right, who, however, organised his downfall when he proposed a reform of the tax system in 1957. The conservatives refused to take power, fearing the unpopularity that would be bound to be attached to any government trying to deal with the Algerian problem (Figure 8.3b). Several younger Socialists or Radicals were given chances to form governments; most of them had a short ministerial life. In May 1958, while the Algerian rebels held down some 500,000 French troops at a cost of more than £1 million a day to the French taxpayer, the politicians wheeled and dealed to such effect that France had no government for four weeks. Pierre Pflimlin, a moderate left-wing leader of the small MRP, was given the chance to form a government. But the Algerian settlers feared that he might try to make peace with the rebels, and on 13 May 1958 they rose in rebellion with the support of most army units. They took control of the government and administration of Algeria and set up Committees of Public Safety in the major towns of the colony. The Pflimlin government fell and the Paris-based politicians tried again to organise a ministry. Some hoped that de Gaulle could be attracted back to political life; others wanted the army to impose French rule on Algeria; only a minority wanted to agree a peace with the Algerian Muslims. Meanwhile, the rebels gained control of Corsica, and there was a rumour that the Algerian-based army was going to organise an invasion of Paris from the air.

On 1 June the desperate Assembly turned to de Gaulle and offered him a blank cheque if he would only return to lead the country. The army, in Algeria, assumed that he would be 'their' man; the rebel settlers thought that he would not abandon them to Muslim rule; the right-wing politicians saw in de Gaulle the one who could impose law and order again; the left remembered how his government had set about urgent social and economic reform in 1945–6. De Gaulle was, in a sense, all things to all men – or so they preferred to believe.

De Gaulle had come to power, as he had always wished, legitimately. The discredited politicians of the Fourth Republic gave him six months during which he could rule as he wished while he drafted a new constitution.

The de Gaulle years, 1958–68

'It is apparent that he will not play second fiddle to the United States. He has destroyed Fascism in Algeria and in France; now he believes he can deal with the Communist Party in the same way. It is up to our French comrades to see that he fails.'

Khruschev, August 1961

De Gaulle formed a government drawn from every shade of political opinion except the Communists and Poujadists, while he set about writing a new constitution. Now that he had a free hand, he gave France a constitution that was a mix of the French parliamentary tradition and of the US presidential system. While retaining the National Assembly, de Gaulle reduced its powers. It met for only six months in the year; it could, for example, delay a money bill for up to 70 days, after which the government had the power to impose taxes by decree. The government had the power to decline the Assembly's debating timetable, while the President had the power to dissolve the Assembly and, in an emergency, to assume emergency powers.

He abolished the system of proportional representation in favour of the British system of single member constituencies. However, there was a system of two-tier voting; if no candidate emerged from the first round of elections with a clear majority, the weakest candidates had to retire to give the voters a straight choice for the second round.

The President was to name the Prime Minister and other ministers, none of whom were to sit in the Assembly, although they had to get its approval for their policies. A vote of censure on the government required a majority of the whole Assembly and even then the government need not necessarily resign.

De Gaulle presented this constitution to a referendum in September 1958; 84 per cent of the electorate voted, with 74 per cent approving the presidential-style constitution of the Fifth Republic. In the election for the Assembly which followed, the new Gaullist Union pour la Nouvelle Republique (UNR) won 188 seats, just over one-third of the seats; the MRP, which supported de Gaulle, increased its representation for the first time since 1946, while the old Independents and other right-wing groups won a quarter of the seats. The main losers in the elections were the parties of the extremes. The Poujadists faded away as their supporters turned to the UNF; the Communists, in spite of maintaining a large voting strength, gained only ten seats, less than 2 per cent of the total in the Assembly. The two-tier system of voting had been designed by de Gaulle especially to ensure that the Communists would gain fewer seats than their electoral strength had won for them in the old system of proportional representation. The Socialists also suffered, but they won some 40 seats so that they became, for the first time, the chief representatives of the left in parliament.

On January 8 1959, de Gaulle was formally proclaimed President of the Fifth Republic. He appointed Michel Debré as Prime Minister, a post he held until 1962. He was followed by Pompidou who was replaced by Couve de Murville in 1968. But although these three were men of great ability, de Gaulle remained not only head of state but also leader of the government, so that the Prime Ministers were often no more than mere administrators of de Gaulle's policies.

De Gaulle had been brought to power because of the Algerian crisis; by 1962 those who had most clamoured for his recall were to be the most disappointed by his Algerian policy. During 1958 and 1959 he held unofficial talks with leaders of the Front pour la Libération d'Algérie (FLN), while he allocated larger sums for the economic development of the colony and increased the numbers of Muslims in positions of authority. He also weeded out unreliable officers in the army in Algeria. In September 1959, he announced that, four years after the fighting was brought to an end, the Algerians would have the right to determine their own future. This angered the white settlers but failed to satisfy the leaders of the FLN who continued their guerilla war. In January 1960, he recalled the leader of the army in Algeria, Massu, fearing that he was unwilling to obey presidential wishes. Some army units rose in revolt, hoping that de Gaulle would fall as easily as had the Fourth Republic. De Gaulle obtained emergency powers from the Assembly and was helped when the bulk of the army in Algeria remained loyal. In November 1960, he announced that independence for Algeria was inevitable, and this led, in April 1961, to a major military revolt led by General Salan. De Gaulle appealed to the people and the army to remain loyal; the revolt collapsed and a number of its leaders were arrested. A referendum of the French people showed that three-quarters of them approved de Gaulle's Algerian policy, which led a handful of settlers and army officers to form the OAS (Secret Army Organisation), which used terrorist methods in its anti-de Gaulle campaign. However, he continued to hold talks with the leaders of the FLN; in March 1962, independence was negotiated and in July 1962 Algeria became an independent state.

De Gaulle had freed France from the costly burden of trying to retain a colony against the wishes of the majority of its inhabitants. Even the Communists approved of his anti-colonial settlement for which they had been calling since 1945. The elections of 1962 were a triumph, in which his supporters won an outright majority in the Assembly, something that no party had done since the Third Republic was set up in the 1870s.

In France as in Britain and Germany, political popularity was, in part, due to economic success. While the politicians had tried to cope with the problems of the colonial wars, Monnet's Planning Commission (p. 170) had maintained its role of supervisor and instigator of economic change and progress. Five-Year Plans appeared on time (the sixth being published in 1970), and, in spite of the politicians, modernisation of industry and agriculture went ahead. Some 40 per cent of the French people had worked on the land in 1940 whereas, in 1968, only 17 per cent did so. The 'displaced' workers went to work in the booming industrial towns, providing France with the industrial base which paid for the developing welfare state in which, for example, there was a vast expansion of educational opportunity.

The industrial expansion and the social security system were two more burdens (along with the huge military expenditure in Indo-China and Algeria) which weakened the franc. In 1958 there was yet another devaluation (Figure 7.3, p. 144) just before de Gaulle came back to power. This had the effect of cheapening French exports (which rose by some 30 per cent in 1958–9), so that the export trade provided some 16 per cent of the French GNP. France was able to benefit from the creation of the EEC (Chapter 11) and one result of the improved trading position was that France built up massive gold reserves.

While de Gaulle coped with the Algerian problem, economic growth continued. Between 1959 and 1963, under the influence of the Planning Commission, about 22 per cent of the nation's GNP went into investment, while that GNP grew at between 4 and 7 per cent a year. By 1964 the per capita GNP was one-quarter higher than it had been in 1958, whereas, for example, the British per capita GNP had risen by less than one-fifth. It is not surprising that, under de Gaulle, France gave the appearance of being a booming and optimistic nation with its new industries, many in newly developed regions, where modernised farming provided increased volumes of produce.

There were, not surprisingly, several weaknesses in the economy: there was too little allocated to housing development; too few hospitals and schools were built; land prices rocketed, so that there were high social costs to be paid for urban and industrial development; France continued to have too many businesses and industries dominated by the small family firm with too little resources for the development that was called for.

De Gaulle himself caused economic problems with some of his policies. His insistence on a French nuclear force (*la force de frappe*) (Document 8.3) was inflationary, while it also meant that men and materials were diverted from more productive sectors into the armaments sector. There was also the decision to expand old, staple industries, notably coal and steel. While this was popular with the workers in those industries, it did mean that future French governments were left with a larger problem than need have been the case.

One reason for maintaining these old industries was de Gaulle's concern for the high rate of unemployment in France. In 1968, there were some half a million out of work, a higher proportion of the working population than in any European country except Britain. But coal, steel and the railways had to be maintained at a high cost, and these subsidies contributed their own twists to the inflationary spiral, so that France suffered a higher inflation rate than did her neighbours.

Cost of living indices

	Germany	France	Italy	Britain	Holland
1958	100	100	100	100	100
1962	108	110	109	112	106
1965	118	132	130	125	122

De Gaulle's constitution provided France with a political stability she had not enjoyed since 1871. This may be seen as one of his major contributions to his country. He, himself, might well have preferred to be remembered as the leader who had restored France to a position of influence in the wider world. His efforts in this field led him, immediately, into conflict with America and Britain, whom he blamed for his wartime humiliations (p. 168) and for their too easy acceptance of the terms of the Yalta agreement, which he saw as the cause of the crisis in central Europe.

Soon after becoming President in January 1959, de Gaulle met Dulles, the US Secretary of State, who wanted to treat France as if she were merely another European state, such as Germany and Italy. De Gaulle wanted France to be treated as a world power. To underline his disagreement with the Americans, de Gaulle ordered the withdrawal of all French naval units from the NATO Mediterranean Command. He also made it clear that he did not approve of the American control of European defence. He claimed that they had neither the experience nor vision required; he wanted Europeans to play a larger part in their own defence so that Europe would not be dependent on the US deterrent (Document 8.3). His disagreement reached its culmination in 1966 when he took France, partially at least, out of NATO (Figure 10.1, p. 217), claiming that France was at least the equal of the USA and would not be treated as if she were a minor state in a US-dominated alliance. Because of this withdrawal, NATO had to move its headquarters from Paris to Brussels.

Another of de Gaulle's major ventures was the development of close relationships with West Germany. He and Adenauer had led their country out of a period of crisis and had restored national self-respect and hope; both had a vision (if different) of the future of Europe, and while Adenauer's reliance on the US was at odds with de Gaulle's hopes for a more independent Europe, both men had the ability to overcome their prejudices in the interests of their respective countries. They had their first meeting in 1958, largely at the instigation of Bidault and Robert Schuman, both members of the MRP, and the men who were responsible for the development of de Gaulle's foreign policy. The meeting of the two leaders signalled, some thought, the end of the traditional Franco-German enmity. However, the two leaders found themselves at odds about the future of Europe. Adenauer was an ardent supporter of the European Community; de Gaulle had threatened, before coming to power, to tear up the Treaty of Rome. De Gaulle had a vision of a Europe 'from the Atlantic to the Urals' (Document 8.4) in which France would be the dominant member along with Russia; Adenauer, with his anti-Russian attitudes, preferred the unification of Western Europe.

The two leaders met frequently in 1959, 1960 and 1961, preparing the climate for the signing of the historic Treaty of Franco-German Friendship on 22 January 1963. By this time, de Gaulle had become a supporter of the European Community, although he refused to see it as the precursor to a united Europe, preferring to see it as a *Europe des États* in which each state would retain its sovereignty (p. 233). By 1963, too, de Gaulle had vetoed Britain's application for membership of the Community (Figure 11.1, p. 235), claiming that Britain would be merely a stalking-horse for the USA as it tried to impose its control on Europe. In 1958, before Britain had become converted to the notion of entering the Community, de Gaulle had proposed to Eisenhower and Macmillan that the future military and defence strategy of Europe should be the responsibility of a troika of France, the USA and Britain. The Anglo-Saxons had rejected his proposal, confirming de Gaulle's view that Britain was, in reality, a client-state of the more powerful USA. In 1963 he refused to sign the Partial Test Ban Treaty (p. 257) and went ahead with the development of a French nuclear weapon and the *force de frappe* which could deliver it.

The success of his domestic policy (with continuing rises in GNP and standards of living), coupled with his successful foreign policy, by which France became more widely respected, won popular approval. In the presidential election of 1964 he gained 44 per cent of the vote while Mitterand (the candidate of the Socialist-Communist Federation) gained 39 per cent and Lecanuet, the candidate of the centre, gained only 15 per cent. Lecanuet represented those who were critical of de Gaulle's foreign policy, with its anti-US overtones, and of his unfavourable attitude to the hoped-for integration of Western Europe. There were other critics who pointed to the high cost (one billion dollars a year) of the independent nuclear deterrent, while younger voters became irritated by his authoritarian behaviour. In 1967, the parliamentary elections provided evidence of the growing criticism. The Gaullist share of the vote fell to 38 per cent as, in the wake of the slowdown in the economy, wages grew too slowly.

In May 1968, Paris was one of the main centres of the European-wide student revolt (p. 160). French students first demonstrated against the failure of the university authorities to provide sufficient new facilities for the greatly increased number of undergraduates. The university authorities failed to meet student leaders, who then turned their attention on the government which, they claimed, had the power to improve matters. The government's reply was to turn out various police forces to quell the demonstrators. The subsequent riots saw workers siding with the students (whom they had, at first, ignored) in demands for wage increases. Workers took over factories, and rioters took over the streets of Paris. The leaders of the political opposition – Communists, Socialists, Mendès-France and Mitterand – jumped on the bandwagon as the government seemed to be incapable of coping with the violence which went on throughout May. It seemed that de Gaulle would be forced to resign. On 29 May, he left Paris to consult with the general commanding troops in West Germany. Assured of their loyalty, he returned to Paris to announce that, since he was popularly elected, he would not be driven to resignation. He dissolved the Assembly, fixed 23 June for new elections and called on his supporters to '*Aidez moi*'. Within minutes of his broadcast, a million of his conservative supporters were on the streets, workers ended the occupation of their factories and the students evacuated the universities which they had occupied. Central and local forces arrested known leaders of the uprising, extremist student groups were banned and the 'revolution' had died down. In the June elections, all the left-wing parties lost votes as Gaullists scored overwhelming victories.

However, the subsequent wage increases, the loss of production because of the near month-long strikes and the loss of confidence in the franc led to a financial crisis, and de Gaulle had to ask for international aid. As a price for this aid, he was forced to impose drastic economies which, in November, led to sporadic outbreaks of violence and unrest.

De Gaulle often appeared to be more concerned with foreign than with domestic affairs. His antipathy to the Anglo-Saxons may help to explain some parts of his policies. But his determination to exercise a major role on the world's stage was based on his notion of the 'French mission'. He angered the USA by recognising the government of communist China and by his criticisms of US policy on Vietnam. He had been almost alone among western leaders in criticising Israeli policy in the Middle East, particularly at the time of the 1967 Arab-Israeli War. He had held a series of meetings with the leaders of the Soviet Union and the various members of the Warsaw Pact, claiming that he would lead the way to détente and, he said, to the gradual 'liberalisation' of the régimes in eastern Europe. His reputation as an expert in foreign affairs suffered in August 1968 when the Russians ordered troops from eastern Europe to invade Czechoslovakia (p. 99). This threw doubts on his claim that NATO did not need US backing, for who, other than the US-backed NATO, would save West Germany or, indeed, France, if eastern European forces invaded the West?

Early in 1969, de Gaulle announced plans for reforms of the Senate and of regional government. He put these proposals to the electorate in a referendum which he turned into a vote of confidence in himself. The dissatisfaction with the government's economic policies, and the concern about the direction of de Gaulle's foreign policy, help to explain why 12.5 million voted against him and only 10 million for him. Having lost his referendum – and vote of confidence – de Gaulle resigned. In the subsequent presidential election, his former Prime Minister Pompidou (whom he had dismissed in the aftermath of the May Days of 1968) emerged from political retirement to win the votes both of the Gaullist faithful and of the mass of uncommitted voters. The parties of the left failed to unite behind a single candidate, and their fragmented vote enabled Pompidou to win and so helped to ensure a continuation of the broad pattern of Gaullist policy.

The years of decline, 1969–84

'To conserve foreign currency and to try to cure the French balance of payments problem, President Mitterand has forbidden French people from taking holidays abroad.'

Newspaper report, 1982

Georges Pompidou had been Prime Minister from 1962 to 1968 when he was dismissed by de Gaulle, who used him as a scapegoat in the post-May Day attempt to regain popularity. He had, in those years, been regarded as the heir-apparent to 'the great Charles', and, with the left-wing groups badly divided because of the events of May 1968, Pompidou won the presidential election which followed de Gaulle's resignation. He did not gain an outright majority in the first ballot and needed a run-off to ensure his entry into the Elysée Palace.

He appointed Chaban-Delmas as Prime Minister, a move calculated to win for Pompidou the support of the die-hard Gaullists, who feared that the President was not a fervent Gaullist. Indeed, Pompidou did away with some of the extravagances of the old régime. He also shared with his Prime Minister the belief in the need for economic progress and social and economic reform. The franc was devalued to make the economy more competitive, costly projects were discontinued and France moved closer to NATO although she did not rejoin the alliance. Pompidou smoothed the path for Britain's entry into the EEC (p. 236) as another indication that he was not planning to be a pale imitator of de Gaulle.

For the first three years (1969–72) of Pompidou's government the economy improved, and, with the opposition parties bitterly divided, Pompidou appeared to be in a strong position. In the local elections of 1971, the Gaullists made great gains while the more moderate parties of the centre lost votes to them and to the other extremists, the Communists. Giscard d'Estaing's attempt to forge a coalition of centre-right groups had failed. The parties of the left, too, were in disarray after the 1969 presidential election when both the Communist and the old Socialist Party put up candidates which split the working class vote, with the Communists gaining 21 per cent of the total vote while the Socialists gained only 5 per cent. In 1971, a new Socialist Party emerged. The leader of this new party, François Mitterand, worked for an agreement with the Communists, claiming that only if the left combined did it have a chance to win power. In 1972, the two parties signed a manifesto which established the Union of the Left.

As the parties of the centre came together again and those on the left re-formed, the Gaullists (UDR) tended to break into warring factions. There was a public scandal which forced the Prime Minister to resign to make way for Pierre Messmer. His government had to try to cope with the world-wide inflation which followed the American decision to sell grain to the Russians (p. 124 and Figure 7.5, p. 151 and with the effects of the first of the major increases in oil prices (Figure 7.7, p. 155). Messmer's government adopted conflicting policies, trying at the same time to overcome inflation without limiting economic growth. The franc, like the pound sterling, was floated but this had little beneficial effect on the economy. The French, like others in western Europe, suffered because of the recession which followed the increases in oil prices.

The political effects of the failure of the economic policy were seen in the results of the general election of 1973. There was a decrease in the Gaullist vote, although, with the support of lesser political parties, it was still the dominant party. There was a large increase in the support for the Communist-Socialist bloc, whose candidates campaigned on a united front demanding a monthly minimum wage, retirement at the age of 60 on full pension, a 40-hour week, the nationalisation of financial institutions and large industrial combines, and the abolition of France's nuclear armaments.

Pompidou, already a sick man, decided to accept the need for social reform. In the autumn of 1973 a national minimum wage was introduced, retirement at the age of 60 was made easier, workers' participation in their firms' decision-making and in profit-sharing schemes was encouraged by legislation and exhortation. These socialist-like decisions angered many of the die-hard Gaullists while they encouraged the broad left which saw, in this imitation of their own earlier demands, a legitimising of their claim that only left-wing policies could really cope with France's problems.

Other politicians saw Pompidou's adoption of left-wing policies as a betrayal of the country's best interests. The centre-right coalition, for which Giscard d'Estaing had worked, gained increased support, on which Pompidou had to depend to ensure the passage of legislation. When Pompidou died in April 1974, Giscard was the candidate put forward by the Gaullist-Centre bloc. The Communist-Socialist bloc united behind the candidature of Mitterand who won 43 per cent of the vote. It was a sign of the division of opinion, and of the decline of the appeal of Gaullism, that Giscard defeated Mitterand by only 300,000 votes in a second ballot, when Mitterand gained 49.19 per cent of the vote while Giscard gained some 50.8 per cent.

Giscard appointed Jacques Chirac as Prime Minister to appease the Gaullists, who were annoyed by the reduction in the number of Gaullists in the Cabinet from ten to five. Giscard repudiated many of the old Gaullist policies; press and film censorship was ended as was illegal telephone tapping. He also introduced some modest reforms: the national minimum wage was increased in a bow to the left. But when he tried to push through a modest capital gains tax, Giscard met stiff resistance from the rich and from the Gaullist right wing. Nor did he have more success in his efforts to deal with the problems of inflation and recession. This recession reached a peak in the summer of 1975 when more than a million were unemployed and when industrial production had fallen by more than 10 per cent in a year. Giscard dismissed Chirac and appointed an economics professor, Raymond Barre, in the hope that he might be able to cope with the problems of the economy. One effect of this change was to promote further divisions inside the ruling group: Gaullists grouped around Chirac in antipathy to Giscard, who had already lost the support of the right. Only a fear of a left-wing take-over prevented a complete breakdown in the ruling alliance.

In 1976, the Union of the left made considerable gains in the local elections, and in the municipal elections of March 1977 they gained 52 per cent of the total vote. By then Barre's economic plan (introduced in September 1976) had begun to bear some fruit. Inflation was down, industrial production rose by 10 per cent and the GNP increased by about 5 per cent. But the franc was still under pressure, falling by 17 per cent in value in 1976 against the German mark. The balance of payments, too, remained in deficit (by 6 billion dollars in 1976 as in 1974) and the rate of unemployment remained high. The explosion of the French nuclear bomb in 1976 gave little comfort to other than the extreme right.

Given the failure of some, at least, of the economic policies, the divisions in the centre-right coalition and the progress made by the left in local and municipal elections, many observers foresaw a left-wing victory in the election of 1978. But from the jaws of victory, the Communist Party snatched defeat. They decided to break their alliance with the Socialists. They had seen how Mitterand's Socialist Party had won electoral popularity (gaining some 22 per cent of the vote in 1976). The Communist Party feared that, under a Mitterand Presidency, the Socialists would gain increasing support and would supplant the Communists as the major party of the left. Rather than this, the

Communists preferred to plough the lone furrow, even if this led to permanent opposition. For there was little evidence to suggest that the Communist Party would be able to turn their electoral power (some 25 per cent of the popular vote) into political influence.

The division of the left-wing enabled the coalition to hold on to power after 1978, in spite of the divisions in its own ranks. Mitterand used this electoral failure to persuade the Communists that, in spite of their fears of a resurgence of socialist strength, the policies which the Communists wished to see implemented depended on the left gaining political power, which, in turn, could come about only with the re-creation of the Communist–Socialist Federation. Marchais, the Communist leader, managed to get the Party's support for this Mitterand-inspired 'renewal of the Left'.

In May 1981, Mitterand won the presidential election and became the second socialist President of the French Republic (the first having been Alexandre Millerand, 1920–4), and the first to have been directly elected by the people. The Communists, who won only 44 seats in the General election, nonetheless gained their political reward; there were Communists in the Cabinet for the first time since 1947 (p. 171). Mitterand proceeded to honour his promises – to the Communists, to his own supporters and to the electorate – by introducing the socialist programme on which the Federation had agreed. Many firms were nationalised, the minimum wage increased, public works schemes started in the hope of bringing down the high level of unemployment, and increases made in social security payments. Left-wing coal miners welcomed both the decision to expand, by one-third, the output of their industry and the increased wages offered to the expanded workforce.

In May 1984, Mitterand, looking back over his first three years in office, talked of the 'socialist achievements': the laws abolishing capital punishment and humanising the system of justice, the democratising of the shop floor, the improvement in the status of women and the decentralisation of the administration of France. He was equally proud of the nationalisation of large sectors of industry and banking, of his 'Third World' foreign policy, and of reforms such as the lowering of the retirement age to 60, the 39-hour week and the fifth week of paid holidays.

Like every good politician, Mitterand was selective in his observations on the events of the three years under review. For, within a year of taking office, Mitterand had been forced to change policies, and radically. His expansionist reforms had alarmed the financial world and the value of the franc fell sharply, leading to an increase in the size of the French balance of payments deficit. This deficit was further increased by a sharp rise in French imports, stimulated by the increased spending power of those who gained from Mitterand's social reforms. The rate of inflation, too, rose sharply, so that many people suffered a fall in living standards. In his 1984 review, Mitterand admitted 'the black side': an increase in foreign indebtedness, heavy imports, the high rates of interest and the low rate of economic growth. He also acknowledged the high level of unemployment, 'one of the government's hardest problems,' which he hoped, in 1984, to combat by modernising the economy. But that very modernisation, coupled with a decline in economic activity, has been a major cause for the fall – by nearly 50 per cent – in, for example, the demand for French coal. The miners, who had supported Mitterand in the electoral campaign in 1981 and who had gained their reward once he had taken power, had been forced to accept cuts in output, a drop in the numbers of miners employed and a series of pit closures, in spite of long and bitter strikes in which 'their' government sent the armed police into action against strikers.

By May 1984, Mitterand had adopted a centre-left stance, rejecting what he called the 'economic liberalism' of Thatcherism and Reaganomics, which he dismissed as 'an illusion', but also rejecting 'collectivism' favoured by his Communist allies, which he condemned as 'a trap'. In place of the two extremes, he wanted to promote a mixed economy in which private and public sectors co-operated. This 'moderate' position is attacked by the right (composed of Gaullists and Giscardians) which, Mitterand claimed, wants to increase French resources and wealth but has no interest in equalising their distribution. His policies are also attacked by the left which, he said, 'wants to distribute without bothering about producing. When it has been explained to me how to distribute what we are not producing and how to win markets, starting at home, with industries 20 years behind their competitors, I may start being interested.'

The various U-turns which Mitterand had made between his victory in 1981 and the interview of May 1984 had angered and dismayed many of those who had voted for him. Communist supporters at the grass-roots level demanded that their elected representatives should withdraw from the government and cease supporting a 'right-wing' government. Socialist supporters complained that they had not voted for Mitterand in order to see him implement the policies which they associated with Giscard and Raymond Barre. In 1982 and 1983, local election results showed a decline in electoral support for both Communist and Socialist candidates. But Communist ministers were trapped; if they resigned, would this make Mitterand any the more eager to switch to the left again? If the Socialist-Communist government fell, would it, perhaps, be replaced by one with more inclination to the right?

Their position, and that of the socialist President, was made the worse by the results of the EEC elections in June 1984. The Socialist Party gained only 20 per cent of the votes – roughly the same as they had gained in the early 1970s. The Communist Party, which had won 20 per cent of the votes in the 1979 EEC elections, received less than 10 per cent in 1984. The government, it seemed, was supported by less than one-third of the electorate. The various factions of the right did better, although, since they gained only some 42 per cent of the total vote, they could not claim the ability to form a majority government. The most surprising outcome of the June 1984 elections was the emergence of a hard-right party, similar in policies and in its working-class support to the British National Front. Only the future will tell whether Mitterand can regain the support which took him to power in 1981, whether the fractured right can combine behind one leader (Giscard? Chirac? Barre?) and gain the increased support needed to win power, or whether the emergent right-wing National Front will hold the balance of power in a France which tries to come to terms with the realities of economic life.

Documentary evidence

In the 1930s, Robert Boothby (Document 8.1) had been one of the few Conservative MPs to support Keynes's calls for increased government spending as a solution to the problem of large scale unemployment (pp. 136–7). Dalton, the Chancellor of the Exchequer in the Labour government until 1947, put Keynes's ideas into practice (pp. 136–7) and the Labour government was praised by Boothby in 1949 when he told the Young Conservative Conference that the country had gone through 'the greatest social revolution in its history.' Keynesian policies were maintained by Conservative governments in the 1950s and the social revolution seemed set to become a permanent feature of British life. However, it was Boothby who led the call for some reconsideration of Keynes's ideas because 'excessive public expenditure' (Document 8.1) had led to the onset of the two problems which have plagued almost all post-war governments in Britain – inflation and deficits on the balance of payments. Not until the 1970s were governments willing to accept the need to abandon Keynesian ideas.

The determined independence of mind of General de Gaulle is illustrated by each of the Documents 8.3–4. Called to power by those who hoped that he would be able to preserve *Algérie Française*, he negotiated the independence of that former colony. However, he then set about asserting the rights of France to have its own independent nuclear weapons as well as a *force de frappe* to deliver the weapons if need be (Document 8.3). Some critics saw his anti-NATO and anti-US policies as his revenge for the way in which the Anglo-Saxons had treated him during the war. De Gaulle claimed that he was more interested in asserting French rights than in trying to right old wrongs. He hoped to make France more influential than she had been since 1945. Part of that policy was his attempt to make bilateral deals with the Soviet Union. Even here, however, his independence of mind is revealed (Document 8.4) for he was prepared to use undiplomatic language when talking with Khruschev while, at the same time, outlining his vision of a 'Europe' much more embracing than the smaller 'Europe' of the Community of which he was an uneasy member.

Document 8.1

Britain's overspending, 1956

'What are the four main causes of our present trouble? The greatest has been excessive public expenditure ever since the war. I am oppressed by the expenditure on defence. This has been an expenditure not of £10 million or £20 million, like the bread or milk subsidies, but of hundreds of millions of pounds, absolutely wasted.

On my second point I may not carry all Hon. Members with me. A system of progressive taxation on earned income which is the greatest hamper to our economic advance.

Thirdly, the actions of employers and workers who are responsible for determining rates of wages and the prices which inevitably follow, by bidding up for higher wages, in conditions of full employment. Employers have tried to bribe labour away from one industry to another, and the trade unions have been tempted – I do not altogether blame them – to take advantage of full employment to force up wages to heights which the economy cannot stand.

I now come to excessive imports. The most significant are coal, steel and feeding stuffs, all of which we should be producing ourselves in far greater quantities. Sooner or later we shall have to cut our dollar imports to the level of our dollar earnings.'

(Lord Boothby, *My Yesterday, Your Tomorrow*, 1962)

Document 8.2

All middle class now? 1959

'High incomes have enabled most of the British people to enjoy a way of life that was inconceivable in the 1930s and unobtainable in the 1940s. Increasingly, the largest firms were mass-producing goods appealing to working-class as well as to middle-class people. The mass-consumption of such goods has helped to lessen old class distinctions based on housing, dress and means of travel. Less than a decade previously, cars, holidays abroad and television were considered the perquisites of a minority of the middle class. Before the war, in many working-class areas, the home had few amenities. An individual's life often centred around communal meeting places – the street, the pub, the fish and chip shop, the cinema, the union, the chapel or perhaps the Co-op hall. But now, in new homes, the living room has become more attractive than the pub, and everywhere television provides more entertainment than the cinema. A car or a motor cycle and sidecar is a focus of family life as well as a symbol of prosperity; it is not necessary to wait for a works charabanc trip to go to the seaside.

A significant number of skilled workers may be called class hybrids – working class in terms of occupation, education, speech and cultural norms, while becoming middle class in terms of income and material comforts. With the disappearance of many of the most overt distinctions between middle and working class, the sense of class conflict has been reduced.

The last ten years have eroded some of the traditional foundations of Labour strength. Full employment and the welfare state have made the well-paid worker much less dependent on his trade union or on the Labour Party than before the war. At the bench, a man may still be plainly working class, but in his new home, in his car, or out shopping, his social position may be more difficult to assess. He may well think of himself as a consumer first and only secondly as a worker. Wages of up to £80 per week have taken a number of skilled manual employees far away from pensioners and other members of the working class.

A New Town resident could even tell an interviewer: "There aren't any poor now. . . . Just a few – in London." '

D. E. Butler and Richard Rose, *The British General Election of 1959*, 1960

Document 8.3

De Gaulle on French defence, 1959

'The defence of France must be in French hands. If a nation like France is obliged to make war, it must be its own war; its effort must be its own effort. This means that for France the system known as "integration", which the free world has followed up to now, has had its day. . . . It goes without saying that our strategy must be combined with that of others. For it is more than likely that in the event of a conflict we should find ourselves side by side with allies. . . . But let each play his own part! The consequence is that we must provide ourselves over the next few years, with a force capable of acting on our behalf, with what is commonly known as a "strike force", capable of being deployed at any moment and in any place. The basis of this force must obviously be atomic weapons.'

(De Gaulle, 16 September 1959)

Document 8.4

De Gaulle to Khruschev, 1960

'But you shout at the top of your voice of peaceful co-existence, you heap blame on Stalin retrospectively at home, you were Eisenhower's guest three months ago and today you are mine. If you don't want war, don't take the road that leads to it. . . .

We must seek the solution, not by erecting monolithic blocs, face to face, but on the contrary by starting work in turn on *détente*, *entente* and co-operation within the framework of our continent. We shall thus create, between Europeans, from the Atlantic to the Urals, relations, links, an atmosphere which will, firstly, remove the virulence from German problems, including that of Berlin, next will lead the Federal Republic and your Republic of the East to draw together and join up, and finally will hold the Germanic whole bound in a Europe of peace and progress where it will be able to make a fresh start.'

(De Gaulle, 24 March 1960)

FURTHER READING

Britain

ATTLEE (LORD), *A Prime Minister Remembers*, Heinemann, 1961
ATTLEE (LORD), *As it Happened*, Heinemann, 1954
BACON, R., *Britain's Economic Problem: Too Few Producers*, Macmillan, 1978
BARNET, JOEL, *Inside the Treasury*, André Deutsch, 1982
BARTLETT, C. J., *A History of Post-War Britain, 1945–74*, Longman, 1977
BULLOCK, A., *Ernest Bevin: Foreign Secretary*, Heinemann, 1983
BRUCE-GARDYNE, J., *Mrs Thatcher's First Administration*, Macmillan, 1984

BUTLER, D. AND KAVANAGH, D., *The British General Election of 1983*, Macmillan, 1984

CROSLAND, S., *Tony Crosland*, Coronet Books, 1983

DALTON, H., *High Tide and After*, Frederick Muller, 1962

FOOT, M., *Aneurin Bevan*

HARRIS, K., *Attlee*, Weidenfeld and Nicolson, 1982

HOLMES, M., *The Labour Government 1974–9*, Macmillan, 1984

MADGWICK, P., *The Territorial in United Kingdom Politics*, Macmillan, 1982

SAMPSON, A., *The Changing Anatomy of Britain*, Hodder and Stoughton, 1982

THOMAS, H., *The Suez Affair*, 1967

WILSON, H., *The Labour Government, 1964–70*, Weidenfeld and M. Joseph, 1971

France

ARDAGH, J., *The New France*, Penguin, 1977

CRAWLEY, A., *de Gaulle*, Collins, 1969

CROZIER, B., *de Gaulle: Statesman*, Eyre Methuen, 1973

EHRMANN, *Politics in France*, 1976

FREARS, J. R., *Political Parties and Elections in the French Fifth Republic*, 1977

HANLEY, D. L., et al., *Contemporary France*, 1977

JOHNSON, R. W., *The Long March of the French Left*, Macmillan, 1981

PICKLES, D., *The Fifth French Republic*, Methuen

9
West Germany and Italy, 1945–84

WEST GERMANY

The new Germany, 1948–9

'The "climate" in Germany was becoming such that he* had grave doubts as to whether he would be able to approve a constitution and the subsequent formation of a Western German government. . . . Germany, and particularly the Ruhr, was being allowed to come back too quickly.'[1]
*General Koenig, French Military Governor of Occupied Germany, November 1948

In Chapter 4 we saw why and how 'Germany . . . was being allowed to come back' and how, in spite of French reservations, the new state of the German Federal Republic, or West Germany, was created. A Parliamentary Council met at Bonn on 1 September 1948 to draw up a Basic Law or constitution for the new state (pp. 72–3). That Basic Law was approved by the Council on 8 May 1949, and by the Military Governors, including Koenig, on 12 May.

In earlier chapters we have seen some of the problems that confronted the people and government of this new state. Wartime destruction p. 15 and Document 1.2) had meant a dislocation of economic and social life. While recovery did take place at a rapid rate – hence Koenig's 'grave doubts' – there were still one and a half million unemployed men in West Germany in 1949 and the flight of refugees from Eastern Europe (Figure 2.1, p. 24) meant that some 10 million East Germans had to be fitted into life in the new state.

The Basic Law provided for the creation of a Federal Germany, consisting of ten Länder each of which retained authority over some aspects of people's lives: education, culture, religious affairs, police, local government and internal administration. The Federal, or Central Government, was given control of currency and coinage, weights and measures, posts and telecommunications and, later on, over foreign affairs, defence and trade relations with foreign countries.

There are two houses in the West German parliament. The Bundestag is the Lower House and its members are elected by popular vote. As with the Senate in the USA, the Upper House of the West German parliament, the Bundesrat, is the recognition of states' rights. However, whereas in the USA each state elects two senators, in West Germany the number of delegates representing each Länd varies according to the size of population. Each Länd sends a minimum of three delegates; states with populations between two and six million send four, and states with populations over six million send five delegates. This Upper House is more powerful than the Bundestag and its members (all of whom are Länd ministers) vote according to the decisions of their own Länd governments. All legislative proposals have to be examined by the Bundesrat in draft form and before they are submitted to the Bundestag. Bills passed by that Lower House have to be approved by the Upper House before they pass into law.

After the First World War, the authors of the Weimar Constitution had provided for the popular elections of a President who was given great constitutional powers. In 1949 the authors of the Basic Law avoided this mistake. The West German President is elected for five years by the Federal Meeting, made up of all the members of the Bundestag and an equal number of delegates elected by the state parliaments on the basis of proportional representation. While the President is the head of state, he cannot, on his own authority, appoint or dismiss a Chancellor. He cannot choose Cabinet Ministers, dissolve the Bundestag or rule by decree in a state of emergency. Presidents of West Germany have none of the power enjoyed by their Weimar predecessors; nor are they as powerful as the Presidents of the USA. Their powers tend to be those of a temporary constitutional monarch.

The new constitution gave much more power to the Chancellor than had been given to his Weimar predecessors. He chooses the Cabinet and, with these ministers, decides policy. The Bundestag may pass a vote of no confidence in the Chancellor and his government but it is required, in such a situation, to simultaneously elect a successor and ask the President to dismiss the former Chancellor. As long as a Chancellor is the leader of the strongest party in the Bundestag, it is unlikely that one can be dismissed, except in exceptional circumstances.

The Basic Law allowed for the creation of a Constitutional Court, rather on the model of the US Supreme Court with the task of interpreting the constitution. It also allowed for the formation of political parties with certain safeguards. The Law banned parties which 'seek to impair or destroy the free democratic order or to endanger the existence of the Federal Republic of Germany. . . .'[2] To prevent the proliferation of parties which had weakened the Weimar Republic, half the members of the Bundestag are elected by proportional representation, and half by the simple majority system, and no party can be represented unless it gets at least 5 per cent of the total votes.

The election of 14 August 1949 to the first Bundestag was contested by nine political parties. In Chapter 4 (pp. 70–2) we saw how the larger parties had emerged, first in the Soviet zones and, slowly, in the other zones of occupied Germany. In August 1949 none of these parties won an overall majority. The Christian Democrats (CDU) gained 7.3 million votes (31 per cent), the Social Democrats (SPD) led by Schumacher gained 6.9 million votes (29.2 per cent) and the Free Democrat Party (FDP) gained 2.7 million votes (11.9 per cent). The Communists, who had been one of the largest parties in the Weimar Republic, gained only 1.3 million votes (5.7 per cent). 21.1 per cent of the votes went to candidates of seven smaller parties – representing the old Centre (Catholic) Party, the Bavarian Party and right-wing groups.

The Christian Democratic Union benefited from the greater proportion of Catholics in Federal Germany as compared with the Weimar Republic. This gave it a solid base. Its representatives formed majorities in Länd governments and on the Economic Council and had already shown an ability to govern and to help Germany to recover. It was, in the main, a conservative party. However, its representatives and supporters included trade unionists and others who wanted social reform as well as 'liberals' and capitalists who favoured a free enterprise system.

The Social Democrats had the right to be best pleased with the result of the elections of August 1949. The SPD had been a large party in pre-Hitler Germany. But in August 1949 it was cut off from the centres of its earlier strength, many of which were now in the Soviet Zone. It also had to pay, in electoral terms, for its adherence to Marxism which, in spite of Schumacher's outspoken opposition to Russian policy in eastern Europe, allowed opponents to smear the SPD with the 'Russian bogey'.

The indecisive result of the elections meant that there was no obvious candidate for the post of President; nor was it certain who would become Chancellor. Adenauer (leader of the CDU) persuaded the left-wing members of his party to ignore their opposition to the 'liberalism' of the FDP and the right-wing tendencies of the German party. He organised a coalition vote for Professor Heuss for the post of Federal President. Heuss, in return, proposed Adenauer for the post of Chancellor. This proposal was carried by only one vote, that of Adenauer himself. By hindsight, we know that Adenauer became a powerful Chancellor, a respected 'European' and world statesman. Few would have suggested such a future for him in 1949; most would have suggested that the Federal Republic would suffer, as had Weimar Germany, from a series of weak governments.

The Adenauer years, 1949–63

'Without him no Coal and Steel Pool, no Common Market, and no Euratom. Without him the dream of a United Europe would not have become a reality.'
Paul Spaak, Belgian Prime Minister, on Adenauer

In the newly elected Bundestag, the CDU had 139 seats, the SPD 131, the FDP 52, with the remaining 80 seats going to smaller and regional parties. In the elections of September 1953, the CDU gained 45 per cent of the vote and a clear majority of seats in the Bundestag. The minor parties suffered most, and while the SPD maintained its level of support, (28 per cent) they did not get through the '30 per cent barrier to credibility'. Adenauer's conservative CDU benefited from the decline in the vote of the smaller parties and from the European-wide trend to conservatism in the 1950s. West Germans had seen the events of June 1953 in East Berlin, and preferred Adenauer's conservatism to the Marxism of the SPD. In 1956 the Russian treatment of the Hungarians (pp. 92–4) was the background against which the West German parties opened the electoral campaign for the 1957 elections. In these elections, the CDU won over 50 per cent of the vote and, with 270 seats, an absolute majority in the Bundestag. Adenauer's party assimilated several small moderate and right-wing parties, so that in the elections of 1961 there were only three parties putting up candidates. Only the FDP prevented the two major parties from taking all the parliamentary seats between them.

These electoral successes were a tribute, in part, to the character and leadership of Adenauer himself. He was, by nature, a conservative, so that there was, say some critics, too little social reform and too little expansion of education where the introduction of religious oriented schools created difficulties. He was, it is said, too rigidly anti-communist and anti-Russian. He regretted the division of Germany but refused to accept neutrality as the price for unification; Adenauer, a Rhinelander, was too much oriented to the west to accept this Russian demand. His anti-communism led him to support, in 1956, the banning of the German Communist Party. In fact, the Communist Party was a declining force so that it was, perhaps, a mistake to have given it this 'martyrdom'. Indeed, if it had been allowed to exist – and decline – it might have been used as an illustration for the failure of communism to attract votes.

On the other hand, Adenauer has been accused of having been 'soft on Nazism'. In 1951 a militant, neo-Nazi movement called the Socialist Reich Party (SRP) won a number of seats in state elections. Adenauer, fearing the resurgence of Nazism, asked the Constitutional Court to ban this undemocratic party. The ban was issued in 1952 on the grounds that the SRP did not accept the democratic principle, that it deified Hitler, condoned Nazi mass murders and called for the abolition of all other political parties. However, in 1953, Adenauer appointed Theodor Oberlander (a representative of the small Refugee Party which had 27 seats in the Bundestag) as Minister of Refugees. Oberlander had been an 'Eastern expert' of the Nazi party and a member of the SS. His appointment aroused a storm of protest to which, eventually, Adenauer bowed, so that this ex-Nazi was dismissed. Not so other former Nazis. Hans Globke was Adenauer's closest associate and confidant. He was a lawyer who was co-author of the official commentary of the Nuremberg Race Laws of 1935. Adenauer refused to dismiss him in spite of public protest. Other ex-Nazis served in Adenauer's government which continued to pay pensions to ex-Nazis, such as Admiral Raeder and Kassler, once the commandant of the Sachsenhausen concentration camp.

The government continued the occupation powers' policies of bringing Nazi war criminals to trial and of de-nazification – the weeding out of former Nazis from public posts. However, both processes moved slowly, much more slowly than, for example, they did in East Germany. Indeed, thousands of war criminals were known to be at large in West Germany, many employed in government service.

Adenauer was also accused of being too autocratic, and his period of government has been dubbed 'Chancellor-democracy'. He refused to take political opposition into account. He disliked independent personalities (who were often forced to resign) while retaining, himself, the self-confidence which he shared with men such as Churchill and de Gaulle. Like them, he was less concerned with economic matters than with foreign affairs. He left the running of the economy to Ludwig Erhard (p. 66), who believed in a social market economy. And it was Erhard who was credited with the 'German economic miracle' when, between 1953 and 1960, the West German GNP grew by about 60 per cent (as compared with an average rate of growth of 37 per cent in the countries in the OEEC), and when living standards rose by 58 per cent (compared with the OEEC average of 34 per cent).

There were many reasons for Erhard's success. In spite of the heavy destruction of wartime Germany, Allied bombing had left many industrial plants untouched. Erhard, who insisted on a laisser-faire economic system, stated that the so-called 'miracle' was due to the 'honest efforts' of the German people. There is no doubt that the Germans worked hard and for long hours, enjoying the benefit of not having to pay tax on overtime earnings. But there were other more important reasons for the 'miracle'. West Germany was the fourth largest recipient of Marshall Aid, which allowed her to buy new machinery and raw materials from the USA. There was, too, the stimulus to the economy provided by the demand for reconstruction, and by the existence of a pent-up demand created by the war and the period of hardship after 1945. The West Germans also benefited from the ban on German re-armament; they had no army until 1955 (pp. 73–6), so that the men and materials and taxes which might have gone to military use could be devoted to economic recovery. Erhard deliberately kept taxation at a low level while managing, at the same time, to provide subsidies to help industrial development.

The influx of refugees from the east, while it created economic and social problems, also brought some economic gains. Among the refugees were millions of skilled workpeople, willing to add their contribution to the recovery of West Germany. And while the refugees added to the numbers of unemployed (one million in 1955), this tended to weaken the power of the already weak trade union movement. The leaders of this movement tended to be more responsible than were leaders in Britain and France, more aware of the national need and more amenable to appeals to maintain low industrial costs. Under guidance from the British TUC, the West German union movement had been organised on an industrial, rather than on a craft, basis. This meant that there were only sixteen unions, one for each major industry. These unions were willing to reach, and to honour, legally binding wages agreements. The growth, under the law, of workers' participation in the decision-making in industrial firms, tended to provide workers with a better insight into the needs of their firms and industries, so that they more readily accepted innovation and change.

After 1958 German industry benefited from its membership of the EEC, as it had benefited earlier from its part in the ECSC (pp. 225–6). Unemployment fell to half a million in 1959, and below the level of unemployment in Britain in 1961. German industrial progress was the key to social reforms such as the income related system of retirement pensions introduced in 1957, which put West Germany ahead of most other countries in this field. Germany also had an enviable house-building record, providing some 500,000 new houses a year from 1953 to 1960, whereas the British rarely managed to live up to Macmillan's demand for '300,000 houses a year'.

We have seen (pp. 73–6) that West Germany was allowed to rearm and to have an army (albeit under NATO control). Some more nationalistic-minded Germans welcomed this partial return to normality. Others regretted the return to militarism, fearing that, as in the past, the leaders of the armed forces would exercise political influence (although the Germans were forbidden a new General Staff to avoid such an abuse of power, of which the old had been guilty). The new Bundeswehr was made as different as possible from the old Reichswehr, which Hitler had renamed the Wehrmacht. Its soldiers were trained for defence and not attack; it was treated as a citizens' army rather than an élite as in the past.

As Spaak indicated in his praise of Adenauer, the German Chancellor had played an active role in the European movement. He was, too, active in the wider field of foreign affairs. In 1950, the Allies allowed the West Germans to have their own diplomatic representatives; in 1951, West Germany was admitted to the Council of Europe and was a founder-member of the ECSC (pp. 225–6). In July 1951, the 'state of war' was officially ended, in spite of the absence of a peace treaty. In March 1952, Russia suggested that the four wartime Allies should consider the question of a peace treaty and of the reunification of

Germany. They hoped to turn West German opinion against the proposal that West Germany become a member of the EDC (p. 75). The western Allies refused to accept any such proposal as long as Russia refused to allow free elections in East Germany; Adenauer shared this opposition to Russia's advances while she sustained the 1950 Treaty signed by East Germany and Poland confirming the Oder-Neisse line as a boundary.

In 1955, West Germany joined NATO (p. 69), and between 1956–8 she played a major role in the creation of the EEC. This put West Germany firmly in the western and anti-Russian camp. Adenauer's visit to Moscow in 1955 was aimed at examining the possibilities of German unification and negotiating the return to West Germany of the prisoners of war still held in the Soviet Union. Adenauer established diplomatic relations with Russia. However, any further progress was limited by what came to be known as the Hallstein Doctrine. In December 1955, Hallstein, the Federal Foreign Minister, made it known to all neutral and non-aligned countries that West Germany would regard diplomatic recognition of East Germany as an unfriendly act, for it would be interpreted as an acceptance of the division of the country. Adenauer claimed that only West Germany had the right to represent Germany and that East Germany was not a sovereign state. This remained the policy of West Germany until 1966.

The building of the Berlin Wall in 1961 (pp. 96) was evidence that Adenauer's policy towards East Germany had failed. By this time, too, there was more widespread criticism of the long-serving Chancellor, and in the elections of September 1961 the CDU's share of the vote fell to 45.3 per cent (and 242 seats). The SPD increased its share to 36.4 per cent (and 190 seats), while the FDP increased its share to 12.7 (and 67 seats). A coalition between the CDU and the FDP was formed, but Adenauer was forced to promise that he would retire within two years.

The most important result of the 1961 election was the growth in support for the SPD. Following its defeat in the 1957 elections, the party had examined ways of making itself more popular with the electorate. Younger leaders argued that the party's insistence on sticking to its Marxist stance allowed Adenauer to link the party with the East German system. They argued that, in a country where religion was important, the party had to abandon its public antipathy towards the churches. Schumacher had helped promote some of these younger, more pragmatic-minded leaders. He had also encouraged the recruitment of middle-class members, such as Helmut Schmidt, and welcomed the influx of emigrants such as Willy Brandt and Ollenhauer who were more pragmatic than 'native' members of the SPD. Increasingly, too, since 1951, Schumacher had played down the SPD's antipathy towards the churches, so that the changed programme adopted at Bad Godesberg in 1959 ought to have come as no surprise. That programme called for a 'free partnership' between the party and the churches, for the protection and encouragement of private owner-ship of the means of production, and for a more positive attitude towards national defence. Some saw this as the betrayal of socialism (Figure 8.2); others saw it as a coming to terms with political reality. The party adopted the young, charismatic and world-famous Mayor of West Berlin, Willy Brandt, as its candidate for the Chancellorship, another indication of its wish to sever its Marxist links. While it did well in the 1961 elections, it failed to win power; too many middle-class people preferred to vote for the middle-of-the-road FDP than to support the 'working-class' SPD.

Almost as soon as he took office again, Adenauer faced a major political crisis. His Minister of Defence was Franz-Josef Strauss, the leader of the Bavarian Christian Socialist Union (CSU), part of the CDU governing group. Many suspected that Strauss was more right-wing than was good for democracy. In 1962, the magazine *Der Spiegel* published what Strauss claimed were military secrets. This leading weekly had long been critical of government policy and, in particular, of Strauss. In October 1962, Strauss took the lead in seizing an edition of the paper and arresting its editor along with leading journalists. He did not use the regular legal channels; he did not even consult the Minister of Justice, a member of the FDP. Five FDP ministers resigned in protest against what they claimed were Strauss's illegal actions. FDP members of the Bundestag indicated that they would withdraw their parliamentary support unless Strauss were dismissed. His resignation allowed the crisis to simmer down, but his antipathy towards Adenauer, coupled with the FDP's continued suspicions of Adenauer's devotion to democracy, meant that the old man's last years in power were marked by increased criticism, and concern as to the nature of the future leadership of the CDU and, by implication, of the government.

The SPD comes of age, 1963–84

'Twenty years is enough; the time for repentance is over.'
Willy Brandt, Chancellor, October 1969

Strauss's resignation ensured that Adenauer's successor, in 1963, would be the supervisor of the 'economic miracle', Ludwig Erhard. In view of his past success, his relative failure as Chancellor is somewhat surprising. Certainly, he suffered from the constant carping of Adenauer, who remained a member of the Bundestag and Chairman of the CDU, and who accused Erhard of being too soft on the Reds. In addition, Erhard's accession coincided with the slowdown in the rate of growth of the Germany economy. There was in West Germany, as elsewhere in Western Europe, a decline in the coal industry as cheap oil became a more widely used fuel. The resulting unemployment in the Ruhr, where some 250,000 miners lost their jobs between 1958 and 1967, was held against the new Chancellor.

Erhard's reputation also suffered from the struggle inside the Bundeswehr between the traditionalists and the democrats. There were those, such as ex-Admiral Heye, Parliamentary Commissioner of the Armed Forces in 1964, who claimed that the armed forces were becoming 'a state within a state', beyond supervision by politicians. On the other hand, there were those, such as General-Major Grasney, deputy commander of the West German army in 1969, who claimed that political supervision by the Bundestag and its Commissioner ought to be abolished along with the 'citizen in uniform' concept of the German soldier.

Meanwhile, the SPD tended to concentrate on 'image' rather than on policy, hoping to woo the Catholics and the middle class. The FDP grew increasingly unpopular, sharing the blame for the problems facing the government of which its leaders were part. In the elections of 1965 the FDP vote slumped; it gained only 9.5 per cent of the vote and some 49 seats in the Bundestag. The SPD improved its position, gaining 39.3 per cent of the vote and some 202 seats. This did not provide it with the hoped-for majority. The CDU/CSU emerged once again as the strongest party with 47.6 per cent of the vote and 245 seats. Once again, but only with considerable difficulty, the FDP was won into a coalition with the CDU, and Erhard remained as Chancellor.

But this coalition was short-lived. The economic situation did not improve; in 1966 there was a recession and West Germany's GNP grew by only 1 per cent. In 1967, there was an increase in the level of unemployment which had consistently fallen throughout the Adenauer years. This created strains inside the ruling coalition, strains which were increased by the differences over foreign policy. Was Germany to go along with de Gaulle's concept of a 'Europe from the Atlantic to the Urals' (Document 8.4), which would require a new attitude towards East Germany, the 'lost territories' and the Soviet Union; or was Germany to continue its support for the Atlantic Alliance and perhaps suffer a lessening of the warmth of the newly won friendship with France?

Several leading members of the CDU argued that Erhard was too weak a Chancellor; the leaders of the FDP refused to agree to a proposed tax increase in 1966, and withdrew from the coalition. For two months the still-young democracy faced a crisis, as the CDU tried to find a clear-cut successor to Erhard whose name could be put to the President. There was a second feature to the crisis. Was the CDU to try to woo the FDP back into the coalition or was it to seek a coalition with the SPD? Such a 'grand coalition' ought to provide the best solutions for the country's economic problems and help to produce a positive foreign policy. After two months of politicking, Kiesinger, the CDU minister, President of the state of Baden-Wurttemberg, was elected as Chancellor and the two major parties agreed to form a grand coalition.

The SPD welcomed this opportunity for entry into the 'corridors of power' which would show the electors that the party was not only capable of ruling but of 'drawing the carriage out of the mess'. One feature of 'the mess', and a reminder to older Germans of the crisis of 1929–32, was the rapid growth after 1964 of an extremely right-wing National Democratic Party. In 1965, it gained 2 per cent of the votes (600,000) in the Federal elections. In 1966, it gained increasing shares of the votes in Länd elections in Hamburg and Hesse, in both of which it gained representation in the regional parliaments. After the formation of the grand coalition, the NDP's electoral success was increased as it gained seats in more Länd parliaments. Overall, some two million West Germans voted for this neo-Nazi party, which called for stronger government under a strong President, a turning away from concern for the recent past and a return to Germany's 'traditional' values, with a strong army able to deter every possible enemy. The failure of the western Allies to achieve German reunification, the success of Gaullist ideas in France, the deepening of the economic recession in 1966–7 and the resentment against foreign workers, all played a part in helping the new party to grow.

Fortunately, the grand coalition was a successful combination. The economic situation improved, so that there was an increase in the number of foreign workers employed. More importantly, there was a marked shift in foreign policy. Willy Brandt, Vice Chancellor and Foreign Minister, launched his *Ostpolitik*, a new approach to East Europe and the Soviet Union. This is discussed more fully in Chapter 13.

In 1968, the coalition government had to face the students' unrest which was a result of the emergence of a new generation of left-wing oriented students (pp. 160–1). This growth had been encouraged by many developments. Catholic students were affected by the 'liberalism' of the Vatican Council; others were angered by Adenauer's autocratic methods, by the *Spiegel* Affair, and by the failure of the government to resolve the reunification problem; some students were drawn into action by the government's failure to provide decent conditions for the increasing number of the student body; others were caught up in demonstrations against nuclear weapons and against the US part in the Vietnam War. There were diverse reasons for the student unrest which, following the uprising in Paris in May 1968 (p. 179), turned into street demonstrations claiming to be an extra-parliamentary opposition to the grand coalition. In Germany, as elsewhere, the students failed to develop a coherent organisation, and their pretensions were ignored by the government. More serious was the emergence, after this, of highly organised terrorist gangs, such as the Baader-Meinhof group, which used murder and terrorism during their anti-government campaign. Determined action by the government, and the deaths and arrests of many of the terrorist leaders, saw a decline in this activity in the 1970s.

More immediately, the grand coalition welcomed the evidence that the revival of the NPD was a short lived affair. By the end of 1969, it had ceased to be a factor in German politics. It gained no seats in the Federal elections of 1969, in which the CDU gained the largest share of the vote (46 per cent) and the largest number of seats in the Bundestag (242). The SPD broke through the 40 per cent barrier for the first time since 1949, gaining 42 per cent of the vote and 224 seats. The FDP share of the poll slumped to 5.8 per cent which gained it only 30 seats. The results showed that the SPD had gained increased support among the young and among professional people. In an increasingly urbanised West Germany, where social mobility was as important a factor as it was in Britain (Document 8.2), these voters paid less attention to the church and more attention to Brandt's claim that 'We'll create the modern Germany'. It was significant that these SPD gains were made in spite of Brandt's softer line towards Russia, and in the wake of the brutalities of Russia's invasion of Czechoslovakia (pp. 98–9).

Kiesinger offered to hold talks with the leaders of the FDP and the SPD, hoping to hold on to power in an even grander coalition. However, the FDP offered to support Brandt, who became Chancellor in October 1969. The SDP-dominated coalition pursued a series of policies which won electoral approval, as was shown in the elections of 1972 and 1976. There was wide support for Brandt's *Ostpolitik* (p. 259), which he was careful to balance by an Adenauer-like support for the Atlantic Alliance and for the EEC. There was a welcome for the economic improvement which followed the revaluing (upward) of the mark, which made imports cheaper and helped the international community overcome the monetary crisis following the devaluation of the pound (pp. 144 and 167) and the continuing weakness of the dollar. The government increased social security payments and spending on educational development, while the school-leaving age was raised to sixteen, as in Britain. As in Britain, too, the voting age was reduced to eighteen, while a law was passed to encourage wider share ownership by workers. Brandt opened the debate on co-determination, the rights of employees to be informed and to be heard about matters concerning their place of work. The Co-determination Law came into effect on 1 July 1976, and, in the 650 major companies in West Germany, the number of employee representatives on the boards was increased from one-third to one-half.

Brandt carried through these changes in foreign and domestic affairs in the face of opposition from the CDU and of criticism within his own party. In October 1970, three members of the FDP defected to the CDU, which lowered Brandt's parliamentary majority; in 1971 and 1972 some members of the SPD defected in opposition to the *Ostpolitik*. In April 1972, the Budget was rejected by one vote, following which there were more defections from the SPD; these led Brandt to get himself defeated in a vote of confidence, so that in September there had to be fresh elections.

Brandt was certain that his policies were right and would gain electoral approval. Although right-wing members of the SPD defected during the election campaign, and although there were doubts about the government's ability to deal with the problem of terrorism, the election results justified Brandt's optimism and shocked the CDU/CSU. The SPD gained 45.9 per cent of the vote, and 230 seats; the CDU/CSU gained 44.8 per cent of the vote and 176 seats; the FDP had 8.4 per cent of the vote and 42 seats – an electoral approval for their support for the Brandt-led coalition. For the first time the SPD had outstripped the CDU/CSU.

Brandt did not enjoy his triumph for very long. In April 1974, one of his personal assistants, Gunter Guillaume, was arrested as an East German spy. Brandt took personal responsibility for this failure in his own office and resigned, although he remained in the Bundestag and as chairman of the SPD. The Bundestag elected Helmut Schmidt as Chancellor of the SPD/FDP coalition. It was the Schmidt government which had to cope with the recession that followed the first major increase in oil prices in 1973–4. While Germany did not have as high an inflation rate as other European countries (in 1975 it was only 6 per cent), it did suffer from a nil rate of growth of GNP in 1974 and from a 3 per cent fall in GNP in 1975. Although there was a 5.5 per cent growth in 1976, unemployment remained above the one million mark and, with the mark remaining Europe's strongest currency, there was less investment, and German exports became expensive so that, for example, the car industry was severely hit. Since the job of one German worker in five depended on export trades, the world-wide depression, which lasted throughout the rest of the 1970s, meant that many Germans began to fear continued unemployment. The high birth rate of the 1960s meant that there would be an increasing number of teenagers coming on to the job market in the later 1970s and in the 1980s. The Schmidt government offered school leavers apprenticeships worth £100 a month; successful apprentices could choose from over 450 trades. In 1980, only 7 per cent of German school leavers were unemployed or in unskilled jobs.

In the 1976 elections, the CDU/CSU emerged with 48 per cent of the vote. The SPD/FDP allies remained in power, the SDP having gained 42.6 of the vote and the FDP 7.9 per cent. The failure of the CDU to win enough support to take power was due, in part, to its failure to find a sufficiently attractive leader. Strauss might have been the strongest personality, but too many people – inside the CDU and in the electorate at large – distrusted his temperament.

The Schmidt government pushed through the Co-determination Law (above), and was responsible for a number of social reforms; there was a reform of the marriage law, and abortion was made easier. The government also continued to tackle the problem of unemployment. In 1982, for example, the government proposed to spend £2,860 million on the creation of new jobs, in spite of which unemployment went beyond 1.9 million. However, other reform proposals were blocked by the CDU-dominated Bundesrat, representing the Länder. The government also came into conflict with the unions, which no longer regarded investment as a major priority; they demanded larger wage increases, which added to the threat of inflation and further hampered the recovery of Germany's export trades.

In spite of violent opposition inside the CDU, Strauss was chosen as the candidate for Chancellorship in 1980. In spite of the continued weakness of the economy and of inflation, and in the face of Catholic opposition to the reforms concerning marriage and abortion, Schmidt and his FDP allies held on to power. However, Schmidt became increasingly unpopular inside his own party, and with younger voters, because of his pro–American stance. He insisted that Europe needed to have US missiles, as counterweights to the growing threat provided by Russian missiles based in eastern Europe. He also roused opposition with his decision to increase German dependence on nuclear power – an opposition which was crystallised in the 1982 elections in the so-called 'Green Party' which won slightly more than 5 per cent of the vote and so was entitled to send 28 members to the Bundestag. This party, founded only in 1979, attracted support from people from most parts of the political spectrum. Some saw it as a vehicle for a peaceful attack on the 'outmoded' class system; others used it as a medium for their anti-Americanism. Ex-Communists and people who had previously supported movements such as the Friends of the Earth, conservationists and anti-nuclear bomb campaigners, all shared membership of this party whose main campaign, and the one which won it its electoral success, was against the siting of Cruise and Pershing missiles in West Germany. But, in spite of the Greens, the missiles arrived and the opposition was taken up by the Social Democrats once they had driven Schmidt from leadership after the defeat in the 1982 election. The CDU Chancellor, Kohl, a Catholic who had been Prime Minister of the Rhineland-Palatinate after 1969, was a moderate, unlike Strauss, and he lacked the experience which Schmidt had gained in the 1970s. However, by 1984 he has emerged as a strong leader, if not in the Adenauer mould; as the Green Party breaks up in disarray and as the SPD seeks a new and acceptable leader, he provides in Germany, as does Thatcher in Britain, proof that right-wing governments may be better able to cope with the problems of the recession than left-wing governments, such as Mitterand's in France. But with over 2 million unemployed and with workers violently resisting attempts to slim down the steel and coal industries, West Germany is no longer the dominant force it was in the Adenauer years.

The immediate reason for the calling of the 1982 elections was the decision by the leaders of the FDP to abandon their alliance with Schmidt and the SPD and to give their support to the CDU, now led by

Kohl. Since 1974, the FDP had shared power; their leader, Genscher, had been Foreign Minister and Deputy Chancellor – high rewards, one might think, for gaining a small, if decisive, share of the popular vote. But, in September 1982, Genscher thought that his political future, and that of his FDP colleagues, would be more assured in an alliance with Kohl and the CDU than with the increasingly unpopular Schmidt.

In the event, Genscher appeared to have gambled correctly: Kohl's CDU won the largest share of the popular vote and welcomed the FDP into a coalition; Genscher retained his twin posts of Foreign Minister and Deputy Chancellor, a reward for his ability to walk the tightrope between the two large parties. The victory of the CDU in 1982 was due as much to the internal divisions inside the SPD as to the voter's support for CDU policy. From 1982, the SPD wasted valuable time and lost electoral support as it agonised over the issue of the siting of cruise missiles. The belated acceptance of Schmidt's policy allowed some to hope that the 'temporary' and 'poor' Kohl might be driven from office.

However, as is often the case, the 'office made the man' and Kohl became the dominant leader. His long-standing friendship with Genscher enabled the leaders of the coalition to make their alliance work. This did not please all members of the FDP. Five leading officials and over 10,000 individual members had left the Party when Genscher had abandoned Schmidt and the SDP. This decline was reflected in a fall in electoral support for the junior partner in the CDU-FDP coalition. In local and state elections in 1983 and 1984, the FDP share of the vote slumped; in six of the Länd elections, the FDP failed to gain the 5 per cent of the vote required for parliamentary representation. Some blamed Genscher for this electoral collapse, noting his tendency to down-play the traditionally liberal FDP's ideological identity. Said one official, 'We've lost votes, we've lost membership, and worse, perhaps, we've lost self-confidence.'

Meanwhile, Kohl has had to grapple with a series of problems, some of which have been self-imposed. His Economics Minister, von Lambsdorff, had to resign and face trial over a political-contributions scandal. His Defence Minister, Manfred Worner, aroused a good deal of public hostility when he sacked a leading general for alleged homosexuality, only to be forced to retract the accusation and to admit that the dismissal had been 'a mistake'. Kohl sponsored a bill to grant amnesty to some 3,000 West German businessmen and political figures accused of making illegal tax-deductible contributions to political parties. Genscher had promised to support this measure. However, a rebellion in the diminished ranks of the FDP forced him to backtrack on his promise, which compelled Kohl to withdraw the bill. This embarrassed the government, which was shown to have an uncertain touch. The ambitious Strauss might hope to take advantage of Kohl's unpopularity, while the decline in support for the now divided Green

Party may portend an improvement in the electoral chances of the SPD.

But in West Germany, as in Britain and France, the government's major problems in 1984 are linked to the economy. There are now some two million unemployed in Germany, where the month-long strike by metalworkers points to the unwillingness of workers to accept the realities of economic life. The government may wish to run down the coal and steel industries; the workers are determined to resist this long-term decline. German businessmen and industrialists are no longer as confident as they were of their ability to challenge the world. 'Everywhere,' I was told, 'there is Japan.' They fear that Germany will never again be the dominant force, in economic and in political terms, that she was under Adenauer.

ITALY

The return to democracy, 1945–8

'Another group with a radical programme was a new Party of Action . . . a 'third force' between the popular front and the conservatives. These "actionists" were second only to the communists in their contribution to the Resistance and so held considerable authority in the years 1943–5. Their leaders were . . . greatly respected for their courage and integrity . . . Ferruccio Parris, Carlo Sforza. . . . Their hostility to the monarchy, to the Church and to Bonomi's government was far more . . . uncompromising than that of Togliatti [the Communist leader].'[3]

The war accentuated the problems facing Italy which was, in 1939, only semi-developed, with half its people engaged in a poor form of agriculture. It had no mineral resources and had not become as industrialised as other states in Europe. There had been some development in the North – Fiat at Turin, Olivetti in Ivrea and, at Milan, the giants Pirelli, Edison and Montecanti. Because the governments of Italy had normally been dominated by northerners, the South was kept overtaxed and under-invested to provide the funds for northern industry. Some two-fifths of the Italian people lived in the South (i.e. South of Rome), enduring a life in which they had less than half the per capita income of the northerners, and where some one-quarter of the people were illiterate.

The war had brought tremendous damage to agriculture, to buildings, shipping and internal communications. In 1945, agricultural production was 40 per cent, and industrial production 25 per cent, of the low pre-war level. State expenditure exceeded revenue and the country suffered from a high rate of inflation; in 1947 the wholesale price index was 55 times its pre-war level. With 2.5 million people without work, in a country which lacked foreign exchange, the outlook was bleak.

During the war there had been an active resistance movement. In

1945 there were about 250,000 fighters in northern partisan groups, and the Italian Committee of National Liberation included representatives of all anti-fascist parties. For many peasants and workers this was their first experience of political activity; since Italy had been united in 1861, they had had little political influence. In their radicalised groups, they developed policies for post-war Italy: schemes for the end of hardship, privation and insecurity. They tended to disregard the ideas of old or conservative and liberal politicians (who had done nothing for them); they hoped for a great alliance of all left-wing progressive forces which, it was hoped, would gain sufficient electoral support to win power after the war.

The Communists were the largest single group in the anti-fascist resistance movement. Although their leader, Togliatti, spent the war in Moscow, party activists controlled the trade union movement and a great part of the resistance movement. They argued that the Party had the answers to Italy's economic and social problems. They claimed that the workers and peasants could gain political power only by voting for Communist Party candidates when elections were called, claiming that the older parties tended to provide only for the social and economic well-being of industrialists and landowners.

Togliatti had become a Communist while a student at Turin University. In 1935 he had become Secretary of the Comintern (p. 26), living in Moscow and working with Stalin and the other leaders of the world movement. When he returned to Italy in 1944, he found a Communist Party of some 400,000 members; by 1948, he had recruited some two million members into what was the largest Communist Party outside Russia. Indeed, with its support in the partisan movement and among the industrial workers, the Communists might have carried out a coup in 1945. But Togliatti refused to adopt the policy favoured by some of his supporters. The failure of the Communist rising in Greece (pp. 57–60), and the presence of Allied troops in Italy, persuaded him that a Communist uprising would be quickly crushed. He preferred to work within the legally established political system.

Italy's oldest political party was the Socialist Party which, as in Germany (p. 71) and France, had its roots in Marxism. The party had failed to achieve political power in the past and, to many young voters, it appeared to be merely one of the old, discredited political movements, lacking the dynamism of the younger movements – the Communists on the extreme left and the Christian Democrats on the centre-right. The Italian Socialists hampered their own development by internecine fighting, with the maximalists (who wanted quick revolutionary change) willing to work with the more radical Communists, while the reformists argued for a gradual change, to be obtained by working within the existing system. The former group was led by Nenni (willing to co-operate with Togliatti and open to the accusation of being a 'fellow traveller') while the more moderate group was led by Saragat, who was to found the Social Democratic Party in January 1947.

Italy's newest mass party was the Christian Democratic Party, which was, however, by way of being the heir to a long tradition of social Catholicism. It is, perhaps, surprising that a Catholic party had not emerged previously as a dominant factor in Italian politics: 99 per cent of the electorate were, nominally at least, loyal Catholics. But the working classes in Italy, as in France, had been 'de-Christianised', and preferred to support the utopian communists, while the better-off Catholics preferred to safeguard their own interests through right-wing parties. In 1945, the leader of the Christian Democratic Party was de Gasperi, who had been a member of the Italian parliament in the 1920s and who had spent the war years as a Vatican librarian. He campaigned to reduce the control which the Church had, traditionally, exercised over Catholic parties and voters; he accepted the calls for social reform which came from the resistance movement, pointing out that many of their demands had been made in Papal Encyclicals and by pre-war Catholic members of parliament.

In December 1944, the moderate socialist, Bonomi, formed a Popular Front government, in which Togliatti's Communists played their part. This government was opposed by the new Party of Action which hoped to be a 'third force' between the Popular Front and the conservatives. The failure of the Popular Front government to deal with the manifold problems of wartime Italy led to its replacement, in June 1945, by a government formed by Parri, leader of the Party of Action. He called for the implementation of the demands made by the resistance movement, asked Italians to abandon their traditional parties and to support his radical social and political programme. This alarmed leaders of parties of both the left and right. Togliatti's Communists and de Gasperi's Christian Democrats co-operated to bring down the Parri government in November 1945.

As the head of the largest single party, de Gasperi then formed a coalition government, containing Christian Democrats, Socialists and Communists. Togliatti was Minister of Justice, responsible for the freeing of many political prisoners and for the decision that there would not be, in Italy, any war-crime trials. The willingness of the Communists to share power in a coalition was on a par with the behaviour of the Muscovite-led parties in Eastern Europe. Perhaps Togliatti hoped to employ the 'salami technique' (p. 45) which had brought Communists to total power elsewhere.

In June 1946, the Italians voted to abolish the monarchy, in an election which also chose the representatives for Italy's first constituent assembly. The three major parties obtained three-quarters of the vote; the Christian Democrats had 35 per cent, the Socialists 21 per cent and Togliatti's Communists 19 per cent. The constitution which was drawn up was heavily influenced by the Communists and by the earlier demands of the Action Party. The country was to be a republic, in which there would be 20 regional governments and a bicameral central legislature which, the constitution said, would be obliged to produce a series of reforms: industrial trusts were to be broken up or brought under government supervision; some industries and utilities would be nationalised; there would be land reforms and the introduction of a system of progressive taxation. The Communists insisted on a system of election by proportional representation which, they thought, would gain them more seats than would be won in the British system of direct elections to single-member constituencies. The Christian Democrats, having made these concessions to the left, won constitutional approval for the position of the Church; the Lateran Treaty of 1929 was incorporated in the constitution, which also decreed that there would be no civil marriages and no divorce, while the Catholic religion would be taught in all state schools.

The Coalition Government formed in December 1947 saw the economy slowly improve. De Gasperi campaigned to widen the base of support for his Christian Democratic Party, appealing for support from conservative industrialists and middle-of-the-road 'liberals', whom he frightened with the threat of a Togliatti take-over. He was helped when, in January 1947, Saragat led a breakaway from the Nenni-led socialist movement, claiming that his Social Democrats would support a democratic government. De Gasperi then expelled the Communists from his cabinet in May 1947, and governed with the parliamentary support of the Saragat socialists.

The new republican constitution came into operation in January 1948 and elections were held in April. The coup in Czechoslovakia (pp. 48–51) damaged the electoral fortunes of the Communists, while pro-de Gasperi propaganda was produced by the Church and, through emigrant Italians, by the US government, which was already committed to providing Marshall Aid to help Italy's economic recovery (pp. 60–2). The Christian Democrats gained 48 per cent of the vote and 53 per cent of the seats in the Chamber, while Nenni's socialists and the Communists together obtained only 31 per cent of the vote. This provided de Gasperi with an overall majority; it also marked the defeat for Parri's 'third force actionists' who had campaigned for a secular, radical and egalitarian Italy. The country was sharply divided between the forces of the extreme left and those of the Catholic centre-right.

Economic miracle and political instability, 1948–62

De Gasperi, a devout Catholic, became Prime Minister in May 1948. Right-wing Christian Democrats hoped that he would lead a strongly Catholic and anti-liberal government. De Gasperi himself was a moderate, somewhat to the left of centre. He realised that Italy's economic and social recovery would be the faster if he could heal that split between Church and secular society which had existed since the state was founded in 1861. He was careful, therefore, to include non-Catholics in his government. This pleased the left wing of his party, which was also supported by the non-revolutionary socialists, republicans and liberals whose leaders were in the Cabinet.

This 'broad church' government ensured that de Gasperi retained the premiership, although warring between factions (inside his own party and inside his coalition) meant that he was forced to form and re-form ministries. He led eight governments between 1948 and 1953; after 1953, political instability became worse, so that the average life of governments between 1953 and 1970 was only nine months. There was, however, no danger to the political supremacy of the CDP. The Communists and the Nenni-led revolutionary socialists failed to win sufficient electoral support, so that there was no alternative government.

It was, then, the Christian Democrats who supervised the recovery of Italy after 1948. In imitation of Monnet's Planning Commission (p. 171), the Italians had their Committee of Reconstruction which laid down the outlines for economic development. The expulsion of the Communists from the government in 1947, and the success of de Gasperi at the elections in 1948, ensured that the USA continued to pour aid into Italy, which helped its economic recovery, shored up the lira and, by helping to promote prosperity, lessened the danger of social unrest. Italy had its Erhard-like figure. In 1947, Luigi Einaudi became governor of the Bank of Italy and then Budget Minister. Like Erhard, he supported economic freedom and financial orthodoxy. A severe financial squeeze brought down the level of inflation and improved the overseas value of the lira. Although this led at first to high unemployment and to a fall in industrial development, by 1948 Einaudi's policies had succeeded, so that the post-1948 development took place against the background of a strong lira and a low rate of inflation.

By the end of 1948, industrial production was back to its 1938 level. By 1950, agricultural output had also reached its pre-war level, in spite of the severe winter of 1946–7 (p. 138) and widespread droughts in 1949. The reforming government had adopted several means to improve agriculture – production grants, guaranteed prices and the beginnings of the redistribution of land, so that inefficiently run large estates were broken up (by compulsory purchase) in favour of small peasant holdings.

Index of Italian industrial production

1948	63	1961	200
1953	100	1963	241
1958	141	1966	285

(Source: OECD statistic annually)

Italy's recovery was given a major boost by the discovery of natural gas in the Po valley. This gave Italy a domestic source of power and lessened the need for the expensive and imported coal which was a drain on the balance of payments. The gas discovery was made by the Oil Exploration Agency run by Enrico Mattei. By 1950, his Agency was producing nearly 7 billion cubic metres of natural gas a year. He used the income from the sale of gas to promote other industrial developments – chemicals, cement, textiles, tourism, nuclear energy and newspapers. In 1953, oil was discovered in eastern Sicily, another valuable contribution to Italian development and to easing the strains on the balance of payments.

Mattei and other industrialists were helped by the existence of a large pool of labour. Fiat, Pirelli and other firms quickly became among the best known in Europe. The prosperity of industrial workers led to the development of Italian-based consumer industries which led to the export of scooters, refrigerators and such items as coffee-making machines. Italy became, for the first time a major exporter of manufactured goods. By 1967 every third refrigerator produced in Europe was of Italian origin.

Most of this development took place in the North, where the standard of living in the 1960s was as high as that of most industrialised countries in Europe. By 1968, one out of seven Italians owned a car, the same proportion as in Britain. Italians had as many television sets and telephones per thousand of the population as did the French. However, 36 per cent of the Italian people lived in the backward South, where they accounted for less than 25 per cent of the GNP and where major development projects failed to make much improvement. Many of the people were illiterate – the product of centuries of neglect. When millions of them migrated to the industrial North, to France, Germany and Britain, they were forced to take the lowest paid jobs. Attempts to improve the social awareness of the people of the South – by people such as Danilo Dolci – were thwarted as much by the ignorance, superstition and backwardness of a people who suffered from 'a poverty of desire', as from the strong socio-political control of the Mafia.

Between 1950 and 1970, the Italian government, Italian firms, the European Investment Bank and the World Bank co-operated to provide the infrastructure of a modern state in the regions south of Rome. Irrigation schemes, railways, roads, steel and chemical works, schools, hospital and agricultural services were provided, and the land reform Act of 1950 provided the peasants with smallholdings. However, improvement was slow, and the gulf between North and South widened. The Church, which had controlled people's lives with relative ease when Italy was an agriculturally backward country, regretted the development of the modern Italy, where the socially mobile professional classes and the geographically rootless migrants tended to lose their contact with and respect for the teachings of the Church. The demand, in later years, for civil marriages, divorce and easier abortion, were signs of the failing influence of Catholicism over large sections of Italian society.

Other, older, Italian habits remained. There was the growth of an over-large bureaucracy, which tended to slow down the pace of development. By the end of 1967 some £3.4 billion of state money allocated to economic development had not been spent, the plans for the spending being locked into some red tape controversy. Nor was the Mafia the only corrupting influence; the tradition that one helped 'the family', ensured that officials and politicians provided friends and family with contracts and public funds whenever possible, whatever the effect. The system of taxation was such that even the moralistic Church argued that it was not a sin to falsify tax returns.

Throughout this period of industrial and social change, the Christian Democrats retained political control, another illustration of the conservative mood of prosperous Europe (pp. 159). De Gasperi was Prime Minister until 1953 (he died in 1954) and, as a fervent 'European', he took Italy into NATO, the Council of Europe and the ECSC. After his retirement the Christian Democrats lacked a leader with the capacity to hold together the coalition of warring factions. In June 1953, there were new elections for the Chamber of Deputies, in which the Christian Democrats won 261 (instead of 304) of the 590 seats in the Chamber.

The main losers were the Nenni-led revolutionary socialists who were linked, in the public mind, with the Communists. Their moderate supporters left them to support the Social Democrats; their more extreme left-wing supporters left to support the Communist Party. There was the emergence of right-wing, even pro-monarchist, parties which tended to draw votes away from the Christian Democrats. In face of the hostility of the parties of the left, the Christian Democrats had to rely on the parliamentary support of the parties of the right. The internal divisions within the governing party – with its own left, centre and right – meant that none of de Gasperi's successors enjoyed a long tenure in power. Between 1953 and 1960, six men held the office of prime minister for short periods.

This coming and going created political instability, which meant that the problems and issues facing Italy were rarely tackled and never brought to a successful conclusion, since there could not be any long-term planning. In the summer of 1960, there was a series of strikes and anti-government demonstrations organised by the left in the industrial cities of the North. As in Paris in May 1968, it seemed that Italy faced a revolutionary situation. This threat forced the ruling party to close ranks behind Fanfani, leader of the moderately left-wing section of the party. He led a government which included three former prime ministers and which was drawn, in the main, from the centre-left of the party.

Fanfani claimed that reliance on support from the right had made the party unpopular and had created the climate for the emergence of a threat of revolution. He called for an 'opening to the left', an alliance between the Christian Democrats and the Socialists. This would provide stable political leadership, draw the teeth of the potential revolutionaries and allow the development of a programme for social and economic reform. In 1956, in the wake of the Hungarian uprising (pp. 92–4), Nenni had broken his links with the Communists. By 1960, he accepted the need for an alliance with the Christian Democrats, another illustration of the tendency for European socialists to adopt moderate policies and attitudes.

In 1961, the two parties formed coalitions in several local governments (e.g. in Milan and Genoa), in spite of the opposition of the Church. In 1963, they agreed to come together at the national level for the first time since 1947, to try to provide Italy with political stability. The Socialist Party was as divided on this issue as were the Christian Democrats; some left the party to join the Communists, others remained in the party hoping to re-convert it to the purity of traditional thinking.

The advance of the left, 1963–84

'. . . the Italian way to socialism involved a search for a new rapport with groups that face the same problems of work, peace and aspirations to social justice.'
Luigi Longi, leader of the Italian Communist Party, March 1964

The Christian Democrats gained only 38 per cent of the vote in the elections of 1963 (and only 39 per cent in the 1967 elections), the Communists gained 25 per cent (and 27 per cent in 1968), while Nenni's still-revolutionary socialists gained only 14.5 per cent of the vote, doing much less well than had been expected. Saragat's Social Democrats already supported the Christian Democratic-led governments. In 1963, Nenni agreed to join a Fanfani-led coalition in which he was appointed deputy Prime Minister. This left-centre coalition's programme showed the influence of the Socialists, in its proposals for economic planning (with a detailed Five Year Plan), educational reform, and agricultural and regional development. Nearly £1 billion was allocated to education, in the hope of improving the country's record in this area, which showed that school places were available for only two-thirds of the children aged between eleven and fourteen.

But the historic coalition was only partially successful. Many of Nenni's supporters saw his co-operation with Fanfani as the death of socialism (Figure 8.2) and drifted to the Communists, who remained antagonistic to co-operation with the Christian Democrats. On the other hand, the conservative wing of the CDP disliked the 'opening to the left' and could not rid themselves of the influence of a Church that, in spite of John XXIII, remained frightened of the Communists who, it was clear, had an attraction for some Socialists. Even after 1963, there were still warring factions in the Legislature, which, for example, had to hold 24 votes in 1964 before arriving at an agreement as to who was to be President. This intra-party and inter-party wrangling meant that, again, there were frequent changes of government, so that no long-term planning could take place and no proposals for long-term reforms could be pushed to their conclusion. So, in spite of manifestos and programmes, there was too little reform of the universities, little regional development, no reform of the antiquated and time-wasting civil service or of the social security system. Nor could the successive governments produce the much needed reform of the tax system, while the schemes to tackle the problem of the Mafia remained, until 1970, mere proposals.

In spite of political instability, there was a continuation of industrial progress and of a rise in living standards, although the South continued to lag far behind the North, in spite of repeated promises to make the South 'the California of Italy'. There was, consequently, a continued growth of a socially mobile middle class and the development of a more free-thinking and less Church-dominated attitude. The accession of a 'liberal' Pope, John XXIII, in 1958, had played a part in this liberalisation. His two encyclicals, *Mater et magister* (1961) and *Pacem in Terris* (1963) spelled out the Church's support for democracy, for social welfare, social justice and the mixed economy, in which state owner-ship and economic planning would be vital. In *Pacem in Terris* he argued that even 'false' movements, such as communism, could be productive of good.

And while John XXIII was trying to force Catholics to 'turn to the left', the Italian Communist Party under Togliatti (who died in 1964) and his successor, Longi, was undergoing a radical shift. The erstwhile Stalinist, Togliatti, announced that there was a specifically 'Italian way to Socialism'. What he had earlier condemned in Tito (p. 49) and Gomulka (p. 50) now became the conventional wisdom. The Party's programme contained most of the proposed reforms which the centre-left had failed to achieve – regional decentralisation, reform of the educational and taxation systems, the suppression of the Mafia, and equal pay and legal rights for women. The Party abandoned its demands for nationalisation in favour of workers' participation in the affairs of their industries and firms. There was also a new approach to foreign affairs, with support for the 'capitalist' EEC and a playing down of the earlier opposition to the US-dominated NATO. But most radical of all was the changed policy towards the Catholic Church. The work of John XXIII and of the Vatican Council was praised, as indicating that co-operation between groups of all shades of political opinion was possible and desirable.

This moderation on the part of the Communists had its electoral effects in May 1968. The Socialists lost votes (being blamed for their part in the failure of the government) while the Communists had a sharply increased vote. The centre-left coalition was shaken; the internecine warring intensified, so that between May 1968 and the end of 1970 there were five governments. Outside parliament, discontent grew and exploded into massive strikes in 1969, as well as in a wave of student riots after the model of May 1968 in France. The causes of the unrest were many and varied. Students were angered by the failure to reform the universities. There were some 1.7 million unemployed, partly, it was argued, because too much of Italy's investment went into unproductive spheres at the dictates of the over-large and corrupt bureaucracy. Italy had a higher inflation rate than Britain, long the leader in the 'inflation league', and her industrial costs were three times as high as those of Germany, one of her main competitors in the EEC. And while there were strikes by judges, teachers and civil servants as well as by industrial workers, there was also a flight of capital as the moneyed classes lost faith in the coalition government, many of whose officials were put on trial for currency speculation and the misuse of tax revenue for political purposes.

The government survived this storm, and in 1970 produced some long-overdue reforms. Regional governments for fifteen of the country's twenty regions came into existence, the coalition partners winning power in twelve of the newly selected governments, while the Communists won outright power in Emilia, and shared power with the Socialists in Tuscany and Umbria. There was also the legalisation of divorce, in spite of strong opposition from the Vatican and, in response to nationwide strikes, the promise of subsidised housing for the poor on a large scale, and of a state-financed health service.

Because of its own oil resources (p. 208) Italy was not as badly affected as most countries by the first of the major increases in oil prices (Fig. 7.7, p. 155). Indeed, in 1974, the Italian GNP grew by 6 per cent. But the effect of the increased oil prices on the European economy as a whole was the cause of a fall in that GNP (by 4 per cent) in 1975, when Italy had a deficit on its balance of payments of 8 billion dollars and had to call for loans from the IMF and from Germany. In 1975–6, the economy recovered, with the GNP growing in 1976 by 4 per cent, and in 1977 Italy had a surplus on its balance of trade for several months. However, with wage increases of around 30 per cent, and in the absence of any British-style wages policies (pp. 166–7), the rate of inflation was rising and lasting recovery seemed impossible.

A major cause of the economic crisis was political instability. In 1974, for example, Italy had three successive governments, which precluded any attempts to produce even temporary solutions to the crisis. That crisis, coupled with the failure of the centre-left coalition, led to the growth in the popularity of the Communists, the party which, by definition, could not be blamed for the political 'mess' or for the economic crisis. In the regional elections of June 1975, the Communists gained over one-third of the total vote; in Milan, Naples, Turin and Florence, Popular Front coalitions formed the local governments.

The inability of the politicians – of all shades – to form a stable government, and the consequent failure to produce even partial solutions to Italy's economic ills, increased the number of people who became alienated from the normal political process. The students' rising, the massive strikes by workers of all classes and the continued apathy of the people of the South were illustrations of this alienation. More serious, perhaps, was the emergence of quasi-military groups proposing extreme right-wing solutions and, in response, the growth of the extremist Red Brigades – both of which were prepared to use violence and terrorism to achieve their ends. The Red Brigades had a carefully organised campaign of kidnappings and assassinations, of judges, prosecuting lawyers and political leaders. The murder in 1978 of a former Prime Minister, Aldo Moro, led to a wave of public indignation which provided the background against which the police and legal authorities acted more successfully in their campaign against the extremists. A series of arrests led to a fall in terrorist activity, although the reluctance of jury members to condemn the arrested terrorists hampered the authorities.

Although the Communists condemned Moro's assassins, they were linked, in many people's minds, with the extremists responsible for the murder. Like the Communists, the Red Brigades and their followers were frustrated by the failure of the political system to produce solutions to Italy's economic and social problems. In 1972, the Party had formally endorsed the leadership of Enrico Berlinguer, who had, in fact, been its unofficial leader during Longi's latter years. Berlinguer developed Togliatti's concept of distancing the Italian Party from the Soviet Union. In the late 1960s, he had refused to accept the Russian demand that the Italian Party should join in the excommunication of Maoist China. Like Togliatti (p. 211) he insisted on the 'national way' to socialism, with each Communist Party free to choose its own line of development. Berlinguer had condemned the Russian invasion of Czechoslovakia in 1968 (p. 99) which he thought ought to have been free to develop its own brand of socialism. In 1975 Berlinguer tried to organise a 'Euro-Communist movement' which would have brought together the various Communist Parties of Western Europe. While this was condemned as 'heresy' by the Russians, it failed to gain the support of the two other large Parties – in France and Spain – so that the 'movement' never achieved the success that Berlinguer had hoped for and which many observers had feared.

His moderate and Italian-based leadership proved to be electorally popular. In 1970, the Party gained total or partial control in several regional governments (p. 212). In 1973, Berlinguer called for 'a historic compromise' whereby the Communists would join in a grand coalition with the Christian Democrats. This call was inspired, in part at least, by the assassination of Chile's Marxist President, Allende. Berlinguer argued that Allende's failure was largely due to the narrow political base on which he had relied: a coalition between the Christian Democrats and the Communists would provide a broad base on which, he claimed, it would be possible to build a new Italy. The Christian Democrats rejected this offer, seeing in it a 'salami' approach (p. 45).

The Communists continued to gain electoral approval in regional elections in 1975, following which they joined the Socialists in Popular Front coalitions in several regions (p. 213). The central leadership of the Socialist Party, which had been in the governing coalition along with the dominant Christian Democrats, was alarmed at the growth in the Communist vote. The Socialists withdrew from the coalition, which led to the fall of the government in January 1976. In the ensuing elections, the Christian Democrats gained some 39 per cent of the vote and Berlinguer's Communists some 34 per cent. The main losers were the parties of the centre and of the centre-left, including the Socialists. Andreotti, the new Christian Democratic Prime Minister, asked for, and obtained, the tacit support of the Communists, who were given a say in the formation and implementation of domestic and foreign policy. Under the terms of the IMF loan (p. 212), the government was forced to adopt a stringent credit squeeze; the Communists, unlike the socialist opposition, accepted the need for such a policy which, by 1980, saw the lira recover and the Italian balance of payments achieve a healthy surplus.

In December 1977, Berlinguer raised the question of the formation of a 'grand coalition' again. He wanted a more formal partnership with the Christian Democrats, with the Communists being given some Cabinet posts. This angered some of the Party's supporters in the country, and Berlinguer abandoned this 'path to power'. But this still left him, and the parliamentary Party, with the taint of indulging in a selfish quest for office. In the elections of June 1979, the Communist share of the vote declined for the first time since the war; they polled 30 per cent and took only small comfort from the larger decline in the vote for the Christian Democrats, whose share fell to 33 per cent. The main gainers in these elections were the Socialists, who had campaigned against the government's economic record.

Their success led Berlinguer to propose a 'leftist alternative', with the Socialists and other left-of-centre parties. But this offer, too, was rejected and Italy continued to have a succession of weak, Christian Democratic-dominated governments, which failed to produce even partial solutions to Italy's economic ills, so that even more people became alienated from the political process. In the 1983 elections, the Christian Democrats and the Communists maintained their share of the vote, with the socialists as the third largest party. The Christian Democrats were unable to agree on which of their warring leaders should form a government. Anxious to assuage the increasingly left-wing electorate, they turned to Bettino Craxi, the leader of the Socialists, and offered to co-operate with him. Craxi managed to form a government in which five parties of the centre-left share office, with their main aim being, it may appear, to keep the Communists from gaining power. In spite of his electoral rhetoric, Craxi has been compelled to adopt the same orthodox policies as were followed by his Christian Democratic predecessors. The first socialist Prime Minister of Italy has been forced, like his fellow-socialist in France, to accept the harsh realities of economic life.

FURTHER READING

Germany

ADENAUER, K., *Memoirs, 1945–54* Weidenfeld and Nicolson, 1966–8

balfour, m., *West Germany*, Croom Helm, 1968

BRAUNTHAL, G., *The West German Social Democrats, 1969–82*, Westview Press, 1983

BURDICK, C. B. et al, eds., *Contemporary Germany, Politics and Culture*, Westview Press, 1983

CALLO, D., *The German Problem Reconsidered*, 1978

CHILDS, D., *From Schumacher to Brandt*, 1966

CHILDS, D., *East Germany*, 1969

CONRADT, D., *The German Policy*, 1978

DORING, H., ed. and SMITH, G., ed., *Party Government and Political Culture in Western Germany*, Macmillan, 1982

GRAF, W. D., *The German Left Since 1945*, CUP, 1976

HAHN, W., *Between Westpolitik and Ostpolitik*, 1975

HANHARDT, A. M., *The German Democratic Republic*, Johns Hopkins UP., 1978

HANREDIER, W., ed., *Helmut Schmidt: Perspectives on Politics*, Westview Press, 1982

KLOSS, G., *West Germany: An Introduction*, Macmillan, 1976

PRITTIE, T., *The Velvet Chancellors*, 1979

SCHWEITZER, C. C. et al., eds., *Politics and Government in the Federal Republic of Germany: Basic Documents*, Berg Publications, 1984

TILFORD, R., ed., *The Ostpolitik and Political Change in Germany*, 1975

Italy

FRANKEL, H., *Mattei: Oil and Power Politics*, Faber and Faber, 1966

GRINDROD, M., *The New Italy*, OUP, 1955

HALES, E. E. Y., *Pope John and His Revolution*, Eyre and Spottiswoode, 1965

KOGAN, N., *A Political History of Post War Italy*, Praeger, 1965

PANTALEONE, M., *Mafia and Politics*, Chatto and Windus, 1966

RUSCOE, J., *The Italian Communist Party 1976–81: On the Threshold of Government*, Macmillan, 1982

WILLIS, F. R., *Italy Chooses Europe*, 1971

10

The countries of Southern Europe, 1945–84

This brief examination of five countries is justified by the political developments which took place in some and by the significant, if relatively minor, roles which others played in the wider European scene.

In 1945, Spain was universally treated as a pariah. Condemned at the UNO, where a Stalinist Pole introduced the condemnatory resolution, she was excluded from the new European organisations, such as OEEC and NATO, and not allowed to receive Marshall Aid. The 'liberals' in charge of European affairs were unwilling to forgive Franco for having taken aid from Hitler and Mussolini during the Civil War (1936–9) which brought him to power. They ignored his neutrality during the Second World War, preferring to draw attention to the nature of his police state with its ban on political activity, its censorship laws and secret police.

During the 1950s, Franco's Spain was brought in from the cold. The USA needed naval and air bases on Spanish soil and, as a quid pro quo, provided economic aid. Tourists, the offspring of the European economic boom, poured into the country, their foreign currency providing a welcome addition to Spain's earnings. Spain was admitted to UNO in 1955 and to the OEEC in 1958.

Increased foreign earnings allowed economic improvement to take place. As elsewhere, there was an interplay between economic and social improvement on the one hand and the growing demand for political change on the other. The need for political change became even clearer in 1962 when Franco applied for membership of the EEC. He was told that there had to be more liberalisation before the application could be considered seriously. In 1966 came the new constitution; the Organic Law changed the political structure and provided for a sharing of power between the Head of State and a partially-elected Parliament. This failed to satisfy liberal priests (influenced by the discussions at the Vatican Council and by the writings of Pope John XXIII); nor did it satisfy the increasing number of students who enjoyed the freedom provided by the abolition of the censorship laws. Workers, now free to form trade unions and to strike, Basques and Catalans anxious to obtain local autonomy for their regions, and younger officers in the influential Army all, in their own ways, demanded more political change.

Franco died in 1975. He had named Prince Juan Carlos as his successor. But few observers expected that the new King would be allowed a peaceful reign. He appointed Alfonso Suarez as Prime Minister. He announced that elections would be held in 1977, by which time over 200 political parties had been formed. Many people assumed that this would be the signal for that anarchy which had wrecked Spain in the early 1930s; others expected that either the right wing or the Communists would attempt to seize power. Meanwhile, the economy suffered from the internal and external effects of the oil-price increases. It is, then, all the more remarkable that in spite of problems and

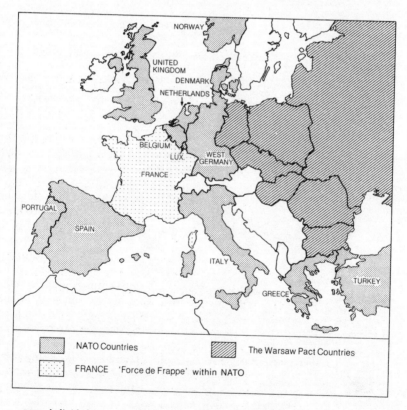

10.1 A divided Europe, in which only Ireland, Sweden, Switzerland, Austria and Yugoslavia are not linked to either NATO or the Warsaw Pact.

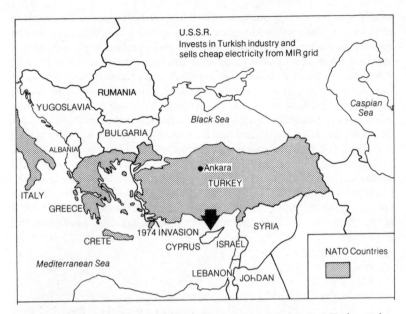

10.2 The eastern wing of the NATO alliance comes under strain as Turkey and Greece maintain their dispute over Cyprus (Fig. 10.3). Russia has tried to take advantage of this situation to further her traditional interests in this region (see Fig. 2.1, p. 24).

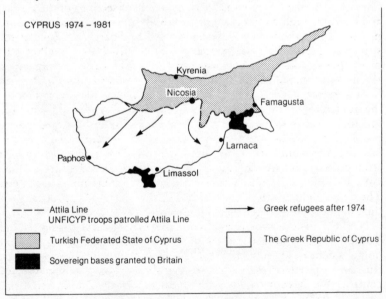

10.3 A divided and often warring Cyprus.

contrary to expectations, Spain moved smoothly from dictatorship to democracy. Suarez and, later, his Socialist successor, Gonzalez, tackled the country's economic problems; they led Spain into the EEC; they defeated right-wing attempts to seize power.

Portugal, too, has seen 'the democracy' succeed. By 1945, Salazar had enjoyed thirteen years of autocratic rule. However, unlike Franco's Spain, his Portugal was not excluded from the world scene. Portugal was a founder-member of NATO, the OEEC and, later, of EFTA. It was evident that, in spite of the autocracy, Portugal had few of the trappings of a real police state.

Portugal's weak economy depended to a great extent on trade with, and wealth from, its African colonies, Angola and Mozambique. In the 1950s, about half the nation's budget went to maintain the armed forces fighting against nationalist guerillas in these colonies. Salazar retired in 1968 to be succeeded by his former right-hand man Caetano. In 1969 he allowed free elections to take place. During the election campaign there were calls for greater democracy, a liberalisation of Portuguese life, colonial freedom and the release of political prisoners from jail. In 1974 the Caetano dictatorship was overthrown by a group of military officers led by General Spinola but effectively controlled by a left-wing extremist, Lt. Col. Carvalho. The extremism of this junta led to a second military coup by a group of radical but less left-wing officers. In September 1974 they set up a government which allowed political exiles to return and permitted the formation of political parties. Carvalho and the Communists seized control of sections of the media, and Portugal seemed to be on the threshold of a civil war. In elections in April 1975, the moderate Socialists, led by Soares, emerged as the strongest party. The Communists were unwilling to allow the moderates to take power; in November 1975 they staged a coup which failed to gain much support; people had been alienated by the Stalinist line taken by the Portuguese Communists and had been won to support the moderate reforms offered by Soares. He has succeeded in holding together a series of coalition governments, in spite of the economic problems facing the country in the wake of the oil-price increases. He has also overcome the Communist-led terrorist movement which attempted to prepare the country for another military coup. In June 1984, its leader, Carvalho, was arrested along with his main supporters. The fragile democracy survives. NATO's western wing is secure – for the time being.

NATO's eastern wing is less secure: two of its members – Greece and Turkey – are at loggerheads with one another. Greece, the ancient home of democracy, was the scene of a savage civil war after 1945 when Russian-inspired forces fought with British-supported Monarchists for control. We have seen how the Truman Doctrine followed from Britain's withdrawal from Greece in 1947 and how, after the Tito-Stalin quarrel, Greek Communists received less aid. After a dozen or so feeble governments had failed to provide the firm and reforming administrations which the country needed, General Papagos formed a conservative party which won a majority in the elections of November 1952. Papagos and his conservative successor, Karamanlis, succeeded in restoring the economy, with massive aid from the USA. Karamanlis resigned in protest at his King's visit to Britain in 1963 while Greece was in dispute with Britain over the Cyprus question. The King appointed a moderate socialist, Papandreou, as Prime Minister. In 1964 his party won a majority in the election and set about building on the economic base created by Karamanlis. He also introduced a series of 'liberal' reforms; political prisoners were freed; free education was provided for all children up to the age of fifteen. But his liberalism frightened conservative forces in the army. He was also opposed by the new King, Constantine II, who distrusted his Prime Minister and was anxious to make his own mark on Greek history. In July 1965 he drove Papandreou from office, in spite of his majority in Parliament. The ensuing political unrest forced the King to call fresh elections in April 1967. A junta of army officers, fearing that Papandreou would win power again, seized power on the eve of the elections. At first the King collaborated with the junta; in December 1967 he tried a coup of his own; when this failed, he went into exile. Papandreou was imprisoned; released because of ill-health, he died in January 1968. His son had already been driven into exile.

The junta remained in power for seven years, turning Greece into a police state. Their behaviour was condemned by the European Commission on Human Rights; they were deprived of US economic aid; Greece was forced to resign from the Council of Europe, but was allowed to remain a member of NATO. Students' risings were put down, often savagely. But a crisis over a student rising in 1973, coupled with criticism for the government's mishandling of the Cyprus affair, led the country to the brink of civil war in 1974. In July 1974 the armed forces relinquished power and Karamanlis returned to power. He won a majority in the elections of November 1974 and for six years battled with the economic problems facing the country while trying to find a solution to the Cyprus question. That problem also plagues the socialist government which came to power after elections in July 1984.

The Cyprus issue involves Greece and her NATO partner, Turkey, which had been ruled by the autocratic Ataturk until 1938, when he was succeeded by his Prime Minister, Inonu. In 1945 he signed the UN Charter and promised that Turkey would become a democracy. Inonu remained in power until 1950 when the first free elections were held. He received aid from the USA under the Truman Doctrine, more aid under the Marshall Plan and was a member of OEEC. In 1950 Menderes's Democratic Party won a majority of seats and he became Turkey's first democratically elected Prime Minister. Fearing Russian aggression, he took Turkey into NATO in 1952 and supervised the slow economic improvement of the country. Millions of Turks went to work in booming West Germany, and their earnings provided a welcome addition to the other foreign earnings which helped Turkey buy the goods needed for her economic development. That development was slow, was hampered by inflation and a growing population, and was one cause of the discontent felt by religious leaders (fearful of the 'paganism' of the west) and by peasants (opposed to the growing domination of industrial towns), and of the criticisms of a vocal middle-class which criticised the wastefulness of some of the projects on which aid was spent.

In April 1960 Menderes tried to set up a dictatorship. He was overthrown by a military coup in May 1960. Unlike their Greek counterparts, the Turkish officers did not set up a permanent government; they drew up a new constitution (approved by a referendum in July 1961) which led to elections being held in October 1961. Demiral led the Socialists to victory in elections in 1961, 1965 and 1969. Economic recovery continued in the wake of increased aid. Economic planning was introduced and three successive development plans have maintained a degree of economic progress. Students rioted in 1968 in imitation of their western counterparts, wanting more rapid modernisation of their poor country. In the 1970s there was a wave of terrorist outrages conducted by political groups anxious to destabilise the country. In 1980 the army once again overthrew the government which seemed incapable of coping with the terrorists. A new constitution was produced and, in 1982, Turkey returned to the democratic fold.

The new government has turned to Russia for help; there are joint Russo-Turkish industrial enterprises, while Russia provides cheap electricity from her national grid. Some NATO leaders fear that this will lead to further weakening of their eastern wing, already in some disarray because of the Cyprus question.

In 1945 Cyprus was a British Crown Colony in which four-fifths of the population was Greek and one-fifth was Turkish. The Greek majority wanted Enosis, 'union with Greece'. There were pro-Enosis riots in 1948 against a new constitution which did not provide for institutional links with Greece. In 1953, a Greek Colonel, Grivas, and a Cypriot religious leader, Makarios, formed a new Enosis movement. In 1954, British troops were withdrawn from the bases along the Suez Canal. Cyprus became more important to Britain and NATO as a military base in the eastern Mediterranean. Britain assured its allies that there was no chance of the island ever gaining its independence.

This was the signal for an outbreak of terrorism by the Grivas-led movement whose military wing was known as EOKA. In 1956, Makarios was arrested and exiled to the Seychelles by a British government seeking to put down EOKA. In 1957 he was released and took part in the negotiations which, in 1960, led to the setting up of the independent republic of Cyprus. Civil and political offices were shared out among the population on racial lines, with four-fifths of the positions going to Greek Cypriots and the rest to Turkish Cypriots. This did not end the terrorism; EOKA turned its attention to Makarios and the new government. There were also clashes between the two racial groups which led, in 1964, to the despatch of a UN peace-keeping force. In 1967, the Greek junta tried to infiltrate troops into the island. This caused the Turkish government to threaten an invasion. Under US pressure, the Greeks withdrew their forces. The Turkish Cypriots saw this as a victory for themselves; in 1970 they set up an unofficial Parliament of their own in northern Cyprus and refused to accept the legality of the Greek-dominated Parliament in Nicosia. This led to a fresh outbreak of EOKA-led terrorism aimed against Makarios, who fled into hiding after his palace had been attacked by aircraft sent from the Greek mainland by the Greek junta. The Turkish government sent troops to Northern Cyprus to guard the Turkish Cypriots there. By mid-August this invading army had captured two-fifths of the island which it declared a Turkish Federated State, from which Greek Cypriots were driven Fig. 10.3.

This invasion and partition took place in spite of the presence on the island of some 3,000 troops of the UN peacekeeping forces. It was the cause of bitter divisions inside NATO, whose eastern 'wing' was the weaker for the dispute. Turkey believed that its NATO partners had pro-Greek tendencies; this helps to explain the decision to look towards Russia for aid and trade (p. 221). Makarios returned to the divided island and tried to heal the racial breach in discussions throughout the winter of 1976–7. He died in the summer of 1977, and his successor as President was Kyprianou. It was he who continued the negotiations with the Turkish Cypriots led by Denktash, the virtual 'ruler' of the northern portion of the divided island where, in 1983, the Turkish Cypriots announced their own form of Unilateral Declaration of Independence, proclaiming that the northern portion of the island was now an independent republic.

FURTHER READING

CLOGG, R., ed., *Greece in the 1980s*, Macmillan, 1983

FOLEY, C., *The Legacy of Strife: Cyprus from Rebellion to Civil War*, Penguin, 1964

GALLAGHER, T., *Portugal: A Twentieth-Century Interpretation*, Manchester Univ. Press, 1983

GRAHAM, R., *Spain: Change of a Nation*, M. Joseph, 1984

LEWIS, B., *The Emergence of Modern Turkey*, OUP, 1968

MONZELIS, N., *Modern Greece*, 1978

POLYVIOU, P., *Cyprus: Conflict and Negotiation, 1960–80*, Duckworth, 1981

PRESTON, P., ed., *Spain in Crisis*, 1976

SAMPEDO, J. L. and PAYNO, J. A., *The Enlargement of the European Community: Case Studies of Greece, Portugal and Spain*, Macmillan, 1983

11

The integration of Western Europe, 1945–84

The tentative years, 1945–50

'We're not making a machine, we're growing a living plant, and we must wait and see until we understand what this plant turns out to be. Nevertheless, we've lit a fire which may blaze or it may go out . . . the embers may glow and then one day they may spring to light again.'[1]

Churchill, 1949

In the winter of 1945–6, Europe was indeed that 'rubbish heap' of which Churchill was to write in 1947 (p. 15), with its flood of refugees and shortages of clothing and fuel. No single European nation could match the economies and defence systems of the superpowers.

Pessimists thought that Europe's day was over. Optimists argued that the 10 per cent of the world's population which lived in Western Europe should be able, in unity, to play a major role in world affairs.

They agreed that no single European state would succeed in isolation from the rest. Europe's recovery would be that of 'the European family'.

So, in the European 'rubbish heap', there developed afresh the 'European idea'. From widespread discussions there emerged two views of 'a united Europe' and two different paths towards the desired end. Some wanted a confederal Europe, what de Gaulle was to call *L'Europe des patries*. This would be a loose association of independent states whose representatives would meet for joint discussions and to plan joint action in certain fields. It would be a functionalist affair; a limited unity would be caused by the need for joint action at certain times and for specific ends.

The limited view of these minimalists was condemned by the maximalists who wanted a European federation. In their 'United States of Europe', states would surrender their sovereignty in certain fields to supranational organisations with power to take decisions binding on the member states. These federalists pointed to the federal systems of the USA which allowed states' rights on certain issues while giving the federal government overall power in matters of trade, foreign policy and defence.

It was possible to distinguish national attitudes towards the 'European idea'. The majority of spokesmen from West Germany, France, Italy and the Benelux countries supported the creation of a federal Europe. On the other hand, the majority from Britain and the Scandinavian countries favoured the creation of a looser confederation.

It was a Frenchman, Jean Monnet, who earned the title of 'father of Europe'. Monnet had been a consultative economist for the League of Nations after 1919. He had supported Briand's proposal in 1929 for some 'sort of federal link' between the states of Europe. Monnet had prepared plans for such a 'link' but Europe's statesmen refused even to discuss them. During the Second World War he had worked with de Gaulle and prepared the Monnet Plan for French post-war development (p. 170–1). It was the limited success of that Plan which convinced him that Europe needed to consider, again, proposals for closer economic and political collaboration.

Monnet supported the work of Robert Schuman, Prime Minister of France from November 1947 to July 1948 and, perhaps more importantly, Foreign Minister from July 1948 until January 1953. We shall see that Schuman made a number of far-sighted proposals, some of which were implemented, for European collaboration.

Monnet and Schuman were members of the French government which negotiated the first post-war Treaty. In the Treaty of Dunkirk (March 1947) (p. 68) Britain and France agreed to take joint action in the event of an aggressive threat from Germany, a reminder of the continuing fear of Germany. More significantly, in the Treaty the two governments agreed to constant consultation over economic matters of joint concern. Belgium, Holland and Luxemburg set up a customs union, Benelux, which became effective on 1 January 1948 (p. 68). This abolished internal barriers to free trade inside the union, which led them later to agree to the free movement of capital, goods and people between their respective states.

Robert Schuman was Prime Minister of France when the Dunkirk Powers (Britain and France) signed an alliance with the Benelux countries on 17 March 1948. In this Treaty of Brussels the five states promised to provide each other 'all military and other aid and assistance' if any one of the five were under armed attack in Europe. The Treaty also provided for quarterly meetings of Foreign Ministers, a Permanent Military Committee, and several economic and social sub-committees to further the idea of a Western European Union. We will see below how that Union emerged; we should note here that the creation of the Brussels organisation was stimulated by the crisis over Czechoslovakia (pp. 48–9); the five nations saw Russia, and not Germany, as the main threat to Europe's peace. In Chapter 4 we saw how that Russian threat had led to the creation of NATO (Figure 10.1) in 1949. In each of these defensive alliances, but particularly in NATO, the member states have ceded part of their sovereign control of their defence forces.

Functionalists regarded such concessions of sovereignty as pragmatic steps necessary for the functioning of the treaties and alliances. Federalists, who wanted even more concessions of national sovereignty, hoped that these functionalist concessions would lead, inevitably, to the further concessions they sought. The creation of the OEEC (p. 62) was welcomed by both functionalists and federalists. The former saw it as essential if Marshall Aid was to be distributed so that Europe's economic recovery could be furthered. The latter saw it as yet another step towards that confederation at which they aimed. OEEC called for joint planning which, in the event, led to economic expansion, the removal of trade quotas and currency convertibility. Such proofs of the benefit of what might be termed 'federal activities' were used by federalists to further their cause.

Britain would not accept such enlargement of the work of OEEC. Bevin had helped to create the Organisation. But he also argued that Britain's Commonwealth ties meant that she had to be interested as much in world trade as in European trade. When some members of OEEC proposed the creation of a customs union (along the Benelux model) Britain made it clear that she was opposed to this next logical step in development. The Conservative Opposition, led by Churchill, attacked the Labour government's coolness towards plans for European integration. In 1949 Monnet proposed the merging of the British and French economies. The Labour government turned it down. They also turned down Monnet's plan for the merging of the coal and steel industries of Western Europe.

It was Robert Schuman who proposed the adoption of Monnet's plan. We have seen that, after 1948, the West German economy had begun to develop. France had not yet lost her fear of a resurgent Germany. Would a revived Germany be, again, a threat to France and to European peace? Could the desired German recovery take place without a revival of Germany's heavy industry? Could that industry recover without, at the same time, providing the means for the re-militarising of West Germany? The Monnet plan provided for the integration of German heavy industry with that of France, Belgium, Luxemburg and, he hoped, Britain. Bevin refused to take part in the discussions of the plan which Schuman put forward in May 1950. The Labour government was about to nationalise the British steel industry and they did not wish to see it pass under the control of the sort of supranational authority Schuman proposed. (Document 11.1).

The European Coal and Steel Community (ECSC) was set up by the Treaty of Paris, April 1951, signed by France, West Germany, Italy and the Benelux countries. It created Europe's first supranational body, with Monnet as the first President of its High Authority and its headquarters at Luxemburg. Monnet urged member countries to consider not merely national interests but the common European interest during their discussions (Document 11.2). Europe's first community was highly structured. The High Authority consisted of nine experts, appointed by the six governments for a period of six years. They were not responsible to the appointing governments but as 'members of the Community' were called on to think as 'Europeans' and not as Germans, Frenchmen or whatever. A Permanent Secretariat administered the Authority's orders and a Court of Justice (of seven international lawyers) interpreted the Authority's decisions. There was a Consultative Assembly made up of the representatives of the six countries already meeting in the Council of Europe (below). This Consultative Assembly could hand on recommendations to the Authority and could dismiss that Authority – but only with a two-thirds majority in the Assembly. Foreign and Economic Ministers from the six countries worked closely with the Authority; in their Council of Ministers they could discuss, but not block, decisions made by that Authority.

Under Monnet's chairmanship the Authority helped old-fashioned firms to modernise and stimulate the output of steel. It widened its scope to take into account the housing of workers and social security provisions for workers in heavy industries. As men moved freely across national boundaries there had to be supranational decisions about such housing and welfare schemes. In this 'salami technique' method Monnet persuaded politicians and diplomats to think on 'European lines'.

Some politicians had, earlier, taken what they hoped would be a 'political road' to integration. In 1946, having made his 'Iron Curtain' speech in the USA (p. 57 and Document 4.1), Churchill went to Zurich where he called for the setting up of 'a kind of United States of Europe'. He supported the work of his son-in-law, Duncan Sandys, who organised the International Committee of the Movement of European Unity in 1947. Many optimists hoped that Britain would help create a democratically elected European parliament. In May 1948 the first Congress of Europe met at the Hague. Here the advocates of political unity set up a permanent Assembly, the Council of Europe, which met in Strasbourg. This was an unofficial body of 130 members, consultative in character, whose meetings were mainly devoted to discussion of human rights and cultural relations. The Labour government refused to support moves to provide this Assembly with any power nor would it support moves for closer political co-operation. Monnet saw the Assembly as a useful talking-shop: 'The thing is to bring people together round a table and make them talk about the same thing at the same time.'

Many people hoped that, with Churchill back in power in 1951, Britain might provide a clearer lead. But they were to be disappointed.

Churchill saw Britain as playing a role in each of three intersecting circles – Europe, the Commonwealth and the rest of the world. In 1949 he was a delegate to the Council of Europe; in 1950 he proposed to that Assembly that there should be a United European Army under a single Minister of Defence. But once back in power in Britain, Churchill showed that he had little intention of living up to his own rhetoric.

A European Army?

'[Churchill] himself proposed the creation of a United European Army under a single Minister of Defence. I think he felt that he might *be* that Minister of Defence.'[2]

While Schuman was organising the supranational Coal and Steel Community, his Prime Minister, René Pleven, proposed a supranational European Army. As with the Coal and Steel Community, so too with this proposal for a European Army; the stimulus was provided by the rapid growth of the West German economy. Could Western Europe provide a united opposition to the threat of Russian aggression without allowing West Germany a part in the defence of Western Europe?

Churchill was not the only statesman calling for the creation of a European Army. The USA, deeply committed to the Korean War (p. 74), called for a European integrated force, under a centralised command and with a German component. Pleven was conscious of widespread French opposition to German re-armament. But he appreciated the valuable contribution which Germany might make to the defence of Western Europe. He proposed that a united European Army should be created from small national contingents – no national unit should be larger than a battalion. There would also be a common budget and supranational control in a European Defence Community (EDC). Inside this EDC, German remilitarisation could be permitted and controlled.

In October 1951 Churchill became Prime Minister of Britain and the 'Europeans' in Britain and on the Continent hoped that he would live up to his own promises. In November 1951 his Home Secretary, Maxwell-Fyffe, told the Council of Europe that Britain supported the concept of the EDC, although she would want to negotiate the terms under which it would come into being. But, as he was making favourable comments about the proposed EDC, the Foreign Secretary, Eden, was announcing in Rome that Britain would not join an EDC 'on any terms whatever'.

Churchill, in whom great hopes had been placed, allowed Eden to have his way. However, Pleven went ahead with his European negotiations. The Treaty to establish the EDC was signed in Paris on 27 May 1952 by France, West Germany, Italy and the Benelux countries, the six countries that were about to enter the ECSC. But there were powerful voices in opposition to this federalist proposal. In France, for example, there were fears of German militarism. From his retirement de Gaulle campaigned against the EDC which he dismissed as 'higgledy-piggledy' and 'stateless' and as being the result of US cajoling of the dependent Europeans. Many Frenchmen wanted a British presence as a necessary counterweight to the feared German force. In its absence, the French parliament refused to ratify the Treaty on August 30 1954. The EDC was thus destroyed before it came into being.

Dulles of the USA had been increasingly impatient with the French dithering over the EDC. In December 1953 he had threatened 'an agonising reappraisal' of America's relations with Europe if the European Army did not come into being. In August 1954 there was a real danger that the Atlantic alliance might crumble. Eden, who saw himself as Europe's leading 'Atlanticist', was forced to perform a *volte face* to keep Dulles from living up to his threats and, at the same time, to ensure a German contribution to Europe's defence. He proposed that West Germany should be allowed to re-arm, should join the Brussels Treaty Powers (p. 68) in a Western European Union and place her forces under NATO command. In return for a French agreement to German re-armament, Eden proposed that Britain would station four divisions and the Tactical Air Force in Europe for as long as the European powers wished. The French agreed (Document 11.3). Eden had been forced to make a commitment that he had refused to make earlier when it might have saved the EDC. Germany now had that national army which would have been denied her in the EDC.

Creating the Economic Community, 1955–8

'Britain sent an official from the Board of Trade, Mr Bretherton. He was told to make the Europeans understand that if they were up to their supranational tricks they could not expect Whitehall to take them seriously.'[3]

In 1955 both federalists and functionalists could claim partial success for their different policies. The federalists used the ECSC to show that it was possible to create supranational authorities and to persuade nations to cede part of their sovereignty. However, they were all too conscious of their failure to persuade the nations to accept the EDC with its supranational command, budget and authority. The functionalists could point to the success of the OEEC which had got rid of quota restrictions and barriers between members. Production, consumption and trade in Western Europe had all developed rapidly since 1948, and the Western Europeans were reaping the benefits in swiftly rising standards of living. However, they had to concede that the OEEC did not deal effectively with tariff barriers, and there was a widespread feeling among OEEC members that this hurdle had to be surmounted in a functionalist manner.

There were major differences as to how this should be done. The British, particularly, wanted a quick dismantling of tariff barriers inside the OEEC. The six members of the ECSC wanted to go much further. They wanted to create a Customs Union, as a step towards the formation of a closely knit Economic Community with common economic, financial and social policies, with political federation as its ultimate goal. They had seen the technological benefits accruing from their supranational ECSC; they realised that the same technological imperative called for closer economic collaboration in other fields.

In 1955, in the aftermath of the failure of the Pleven Plan, the members of the ECSC instructed their Foreign Ministers to examine schemes for closer economic collaboration. At a meeting in Messina (June 1955), they set up a committee under the chairmanship of the Belgian Foreign Minister, Paul-Henri Spaak, to 'examine the possibilities of expanding their existing community into an economic association based upon free trade, joint social and financial policies, the abolition of restrictive trading practices and the free movement of capital and labour.' The report of Spaak's committee was debated by the member countries, who then agreed to the Treaty of Rome on 25 March 1957. The European Economic Community came into being on 1 January 1958. Its first aim was to abolish tariffs and other restrictions on trade between the member states of this more-than-customs union. The Community would also, as a customs union, establish a common external tariff against trade with the rest of the world. These two processes would be completed, by a pre-agreed timetable, by 1970 and would lead, naturally, to both economic integration and political federation, the EEC, to 'its progenitors, being involved primarily 'in politics and not in economics'.[4]

The EEC was headed by a nine-member Commission (later thirteen) appointed by the governments of the member states 'for their general competence and of indisputable independence'. The Commissioners are appointed for four years and are responsible only to the Community. They work with, but not under, the Council of Ministers. The Commission initiates policy proposals and is responsible for the day-to-day administration of the Community. Its decisions become part of the domestic regulations of the member states and are enforced by national law courts. Member states have ceded part of their sovereignty to this non-elected and supranational body.

The Council of Ministers is a changing body, its membership depending on the issue being discussed. Sometimes it is the Ministers of Agriculture who meet, sometimes the Ministers of Finance. Ministers of Transport, Education and Technology will meet when the issue being discussed involves their respective departments. In this Council, the Ministers represent their various national interests as distinct from the Community interest represented by the Commission. The Council exercises some control over the Commission, since it is the Council which has to approve the decisions of the Commission before these can be implemented.

The Community has a European Parliament – not to be confused with the Council of Europe (p. 226). Until 1978 the members of this Parliament were nominated by their national parliaments; since 1978 there have been direct elections to this European Parliament. It has more powers than the Consultative Assembly set up in 1948. It can dismiss the Commission; the Commission is bound to consult it about plans and decisions; and it can question the Commission and individual Commissioners. The 'European' nature of the Community is emphasised by the creation of 'European' blocs, as members of right-wing groups from the member states tend to sit and vote together as do the members of the various socialist groups.

The European Court of Justice has to interpret the treaties which created the Community, and to hear cases involving individuals, firms, governments, the Commission and the Council of Ministers. British workers have taken trade unions and employers before the Court to appeal against their dismissal by firms under 'closed shop' agreements. Decisions in favour of the dismissed workers – and many other decisions in other fields – have led to the creation of a body of 'European law' which is binding on member states.

Britain and the EEC, 1955–73

'If the UK were to join such a Customs Union, the UK tariff would be swept aside and would be replaced by a single common tariff. Such an arrangement would be wholly disadvantageous. We could not expect the Commonwealth to give preferential treatment to our exports if we had to charge them full duty on their exports to us.'[5]

Macmillan, 26 November 1956

The members of the EEC made rapid progress. The customs union feature of their plans was achieved on 1 July 1968, eighteen months ahead of schedule. All customs duties on industrial goods were abolished and the common external tariff established. The EEC has negotiated with other countries in GATT to cut the level of this external tariff since 1968.

The success of the EEC was reflected in the growth in the trade of each of the member states.

People in EEC countries enjoyed a continually improving standard of living in this period. The real wages of workers increased by 69 per cent in Holland, 66 per cent in West Germany, 55 per cent in Italy and 46 per cent in Belgium. The level of unemployment fell from 2.4 million in 1958 to 1.6 million in 1968 and during that period the Community took in millions of 'guest workers' from Turkey, North Africa and from the UK. The European Investment Bank was set up in 1958 to provide investment in underdeveloped areas of the Community (such as southern Italy) and to finance projects which serve the interests

Annual rates of Growth of Trade, 1955–68

Country	Exports of goods and services		Imports of goods and services	
	by value	by volume	by value	by volume
USA	6.6	5.5	6.7	6.3
UK	4.8	3.2	5.2	4.1
Belgium	8.0	7.2	8.2	7.2
Holland	7.6	7.6	8.0	8.5
France	9.2	7.9	10.8	10.0
Germany (West)	9.9	9.0	10.5	10.9
Italy	13.4	14.2	11.8	12.6

(Source: National Accounts of OECD Countries, 1955–68,
Paris: OECD, 1970.)

of the Community as a whole rather than the interests of one or two states in particular.

In June 1967 the European Community came into being through the merger of the executive bodies of the three existing communities, the ECSC, the EEC and Euratom. Member states wanted not only closer economic links, but also closer political links.

There were many other signs of closer integration. There was the beginning of a transport common market by which national licences were replaced by Community road licences, freight charges were regulated and working conditions for drivers laid down. There was a free movement of labour across national boundaries, in what has been called 'a common labour market'. The Community advises member governments on the training, housing and provision of welfare services for migrant workers and has established a European Social Fund for the re-training and re-employment of Community workers.

In some of these developments, and in discussions aimed at producing a common European currency, the Community had moved outside the terms of the Treaty of Rome. Its supranational and European-minded leaders were using the *functional* opportunities provided by the Community to promote their *federal* ideas. But the Treaty of Rome had laid down that there had to be a common policy in agriculture. Negotiations for a Common Agricultural Policy were bitter and long. France in particular saw the Community as an opportunity for its farmers to sell their produce in the industrial Community in general and in Germany in particular. The politicians in France, Italy, and, to an extent, in Germany, had to take more account of the farming vote than did politicians in, say, the UK. If the Community produced beneficial results in the industrial sector it was important for these politicians to ensure similarly beneficent results in the agricultural sector.

The basic provisions of the CAP were as follows. (1) Free trade within the Community in agricultural products. (2) Common prices for most commodities. (3) Protection by minimum import prices for

European-produced commodities through import levies on agricultural imports. (4) The Community purchase of any surpluses so as to ensure the guaranteed prices to be paid to farmers. (5) These surpluses to be stored at Community expense or diverted to export markets through export subsidies.

This CAP guaranteed farmers a price for produce; it provided no control over the volume of output. Indeed, the guarantee encouraged farmers to maximise incomes by increasing output. And since prices tended to be fixed at a level which suited the least efficient farmers, the more efficient became rich while producing vast surpluses. The Community became notorious for its 'mountains' of beef and butter, its 'lakes' of milk and wine. More importantly, the CAP swallowed up over two-thirds of the Community's income, and two-thirds of the CAP's funds were used to provide for the purchase and storage of surplus food.

In 1955–6 Britain, still then the richest European state, had been invited to take part in the Messina talks. In November 1956 Macmillan explained Britain's objections to the proposed 'customs union'; Britain's system of imperial preference would have to end if Britain adopted the 'union's' common external tariff. He might also have argued that Britain's agricultural support system would have to be abandoned if the UK became subject to the CAP.

In May 1957, after the Rome Treaty had been ratified, the British government tried to set up a wide Free Trade Area (FTA). This would have included all the members of the OEEC, with the proposed Community acting as a single unit on behalf of its six members. They were invited to join the proposed FTA as a single bloc and to abolish the common external tariff on industrial goods as regards trade with other members of the proposed FTA. Britain proposed that agriculture should be excluded from the FTA (so allowing Britain the luxury of cheap food from the Commonwealth). She also proposed that the FTA should have the minimum of structural organisation; there would be no Commission, Court of Justice or Council of Ministers. It would, in effect, be a common market for industrial goods only.

The Europeans saw this as a device by which Britain would gain access to a tariff-free Europe for her industrial goods while denying Europe access for its agricultural produce. Members of the Commission saw the proposal as a device for dividing Germany and France; Germany might be attracted by the tariff-free British market for her industrial goods, while France would be angered by the denial of that British market for her agricultural produce. In 1958 the EEC rejected the British proposal. Britain then established the European Free Trade Area (EFTA) with Portugal, Norway, Sweden, Denmark, Switzerland and Austria as her partners. The 'Seven' signed their Treaty in November 1959 and EFTA came into operation in May 1960.

But by then Macmillan had decided that Britain had to join the EEC.

President Kennedy had told him that if Europe remained at 'Sixes' and 'Sevens' the USA would tend to favour the 'Six' rather than the less important 'Seven'. Macmillan had also become conscious of the continuing growth in the economies of the 'Six' and the relative failure of the British economy to grow. In 1960–62 there were many critical reports and publications on the general theme of 'What's wrong with Britain?' (p. 146). Macmillan adopted a number of policies to try to improve Britain's economic performance. Planning belatedly came into fashion with the creation of the National Economic Development Council (NEDC); the planning of incomes was to be tackled by the National Incomes Commission (NIC).

In July 1961 Macmillan announced that he wanted Britain to join the Community. Negotiations opened in November 1961, with Edward Heath leading the British team. Many Community politicians welcomed this move. Some looked for Britain to provide a counterweight to de Gaulle who had made himself the master of the Community. Others, more far-sighted, hoped that Britain would help ensure the Community's development of a democratic framework as it progressed towards closer political integration. President Kennedy also welcomed Britain's decision. He saw the enlarged Community as better able to provide for its own defence – albeit in alliance with the much stronger USA.

Heath's negotiations with the Community brought out the difficulties facing Britain. He tried to force the Community to allow Britain a 'special position' as regards her Commonwealth imports. This angered many Community leaders who saw this as an attempt to 'square the circle', an attempt to create the British-desired Free Trade Area from which agriculture would be excluded. De Gaulle was to write later: 'In the middle of 1961 the English launched a new offensive. Having failed, from the outside, to prevent the birth of the Community, they now plan to paralyse it from within.'[6]

There were many Europeans who saw de Gaulle as a major opponent of the 'European idea'. He was violently opposed to its supranational institutions and to the aims of the Europeans for political fusion. In April 1962 he had proposed that the only form of political collaboration should be through regular meetings of the heads of state. In May 1962 he denounced the idea of a supranational Europe; he talked only of 'a Europe of the nations'; 'I do not believe that Europe can be a living reality without France and her Frenchmen, Germany and her Germans, Italy and her Italians.'

De Gaulle had also been prepared to wreck the Community in defence of French interests. In the autumn of 1961 he instructed the French ministerial team to quit the EEC if they did not get an agricultural agreement to suit French interests. He got his way, and in January 1962 the ill-fated CAP was agreed. In May 1962, five of his ministers resigned from his government because of his outspoken opposition to the demand for progress towards a political union in a United States of Europe. In 1965 France withdrew from the Community for seven months (below).

Britain, like de Gaulle, did not want Europe to become a federation. Macmillan shared de Gaulle's opposition to the supranational pretensions of the President of the Commission, Walter Hallstein. But de Gaulle did not want Britain even as a potential ally in the Community. He had enough difficulty in imposing French leadership on Germany; he could not hope to impose it on Britain as well. Moreover, he saw Britain as America's 'Trojan horse' in Europe. Macmillan might have overcome that problem by cutting relationships with the USA. He did the very opposite. He met de Gaulle in December 1962 to learn that France would block Britain's proposed application to join the EEC. The General said that, if Britain joined, the character of Europe would change; many smaller nations would apply and would join. The Community would then become merely part of the Atlantic trading system, too large for him to control, too disparate to suit French interests. Macmillan left this unhappy meeting to go to Nassau to meet Kennedy, who offered Britain the Polaris sea-to-ground missile as a substitute for the cancelled Blue Streak missile. Macmillan, in return, endorsed the US project for a multilateral nuclear force – a NATO fleet of Polaris-armed ships and submarines, with mixed crews and mutual vetoes on the use of nuclear weapons. Macmillan returned to London in triumph. The Nassau meeting had confirmed the 'special relationship' in which he saw himself playing the role of paternal tutor to the young President.

De Gaulle saw it otherwise. The agreement merely confirmed his suspicions that Britain was a pawn in the US attempt to gain more control over European affairs. On 14 January 1963 he called a press conference and announced that he would veto Britain's application to join the EEC (Document 11.4 and Figure 11.1). There were many in Britain who welcomed this announcement. Right-wingers had feared that British membership would lead to a weakening of Commonwealth ties. The Labour Party, under Gaitskell's leadership, had described the application as a turning of the British back on a thousand years of history. But it was another Labour leader, Wilson, who, as Prime Minister, made the next attempt to join the EEC, only to have that attempt thwarted by de Gaulle in 1967.

By then, the Community had lost much of its initial enthusiasm for closer political ties. Under de Gaulle's influence it had become, instead, a battle ground where national interests were defended and fought for. De Gaulle's contempt for the supranationalists was clearly illustrated by 'the Soames affair' of 1969. Christopher Soames was the new British Ambassador to France. De Gaulle told him that he had no faith in the Community which he would like to see evolve into a looser form of free trade area. He proposed that discussions should be held with Britain

NON!

11.1 De Gaulle blocks British entry into the EEC, because of Britain's 'special relationship' with the USA.

with a view to the creation of a larger European economic association which should be controlled by a small inner council consisting of France, Germany, Italy and Britain. This conversation was revealed to the world when, in February, Prime Minister Wilson told the German Chancellor, Kiesinger, exactly what had taken place. The mutual recriminations between Germany, France and Britain drowned the chorus of protest from the smaller members of the EEC whose views had not been sought by the ambitious General.

De Gaulle resigned in April 1969. His successor, Pompidou, let it be known that France would welcome a fresh British application to join the Community. Edward Heath, Prime Minister after the Conservative victory in the election of June 1970, made that application. Negotiations opened in which Britain and three of her EFTA partners (Ireland, Denmark and Norway) worked out the terms on which they might join the Community. They signed the Treaty of Accession in January 1972. In September, the Norwegians withdrew their application after a referendum had shown that a majority of Norwegian voters were opposed to membership. Britain, Ireland and Denmark became members of the EEC (and European Community) on 1 January 1973, some eighteen years after Britain had turned down the opportunity of playing a leading role in the initial discussions at Messina (p. 232). In June 1975 British voters showed in a referendum that they supported Britain's membership of the enlarged Community, which became even larger when Greece was admitted as a member in 1981, and promises to become larger still when Spain and Portugal join in 1986 (Figure 11.2).

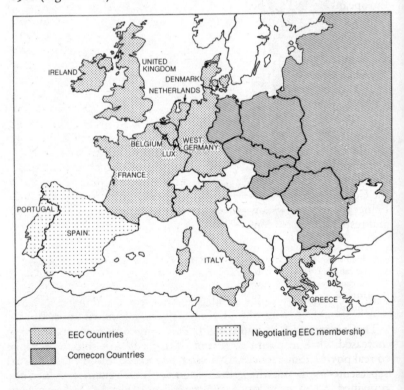

11.2 Another view of divided Europe (see also Fig. 10.1, p. 217) showing how economic 'alliances' confirm political and ideological divisions.

The crisis-ridden Community

'Mrs Thatcher today faces one of the sternest tests of her foreign policy so far when she may have to decide in Brussels whether to press for justice for Britain over the Common Market budget or to be held to account for the possible break-up of the EEC.'[7]

We have noted the 'crisis of faith' in the communist bloc (pp. 86–7, 103–4, 114–5), and we have examined the 'loss of faith' in the western bloc which had once believed in Keynesian solutions to economic problems (pp. 156–7). There has been a similar turn of events in the EEC. It has lost its initial drive towards closer political federation. It has degenerated into a trading club, in which the member states do their best to safeguard their national interests. There does not seem to be anyone, now, urging that 'European idea' which inspired Monnet, Schuman and Hallstein.

Since 1979 it has become the norm for French representatives to condemn Britain, represented by 'the Iron Maiden' as being 'not European-minded', as being too concerned for what benefits she is, or is not, getting from membership of the Community. The headline at the start of this section indicates that even British newspapers have fallen for the French line. In fact, Britain behaved, in 1984, as France had done when led by de Gaulle. In 1965, de Gaulle withdrew all French representatives from Brussels and announced a French boycott of the Community. 'Europe had come to a full stop.'[8] At issue then was the question of French freedom to sell her surplus wheat to Russia without the permission of the Commission. Hallstein, the President of the Commission, had proposed that it, and not the Council of Ministers, should take charge of the agricultural budget and that it should be responsible not to the Council of Ministers but to the European Parliament. De Gaulle attacked this attempt to enlarge the powers of the Commission. On 9 September 1965 he declared his refusal to allow France to be 'ruled by some sort of technocratic body of elders, stateless and responsible to no one'. That speech ended with a threat:

'There is no doubt that it is conceivable and desirable that the great undertaking which the Community represents should one day be got under way again. But that can take place, probably, only after a period of time the length of which no one can foresee. Who knows, in fact, if, when and how the policies of each of our partners . . . will finally come round to facing the facts which have just been demonstrated once more.'

De Gaulle got his way in 1965. The Commission's powers were not increased; the European Parliament did not receive a fillip to its claims to real power; the Council of Ministers, in which national interests are represented and in which each member government has a veto, remained the powerful organ which de Gaulle wanted it to be.

In Hallstein's time the European Parliament had consisted of members nominated by the national parliaments of the various member states. In June 1979 the nature of that Parliament changed. Four hundred and ten elected members replaced the 198 members nominated by the nine parliaments. This enlarged Parliament, directly elected by the people of the Community, has, if slowly, flexed its muscles and has begun to demand that it should be given the powers of a 'real' parliament – control over the executive (the Council of Ministers) and of the administration (the Commission). It is likely that these demands will grow stronger. This is more likely to happen if leading politicians from member countries become Euro-MPs.

In 1965 Hallstein and de Gaulle were driven to their 'constitutional clash' by French manipulation of the CAP. And it was that CAP which, in 1984, was the root cause of the clash between the British and other members of the Community. We have seen the CAP system encourage overproduction, which requires high payments from the Community Fund to farmers, as well as high costs for storage of the surpluses. Member states contribute to the Fund by an agreed formula: they pay one per cent of the amount collected by VAT in each of their countries plus the import levies on food and other nominated imports from outside the Community. Britain, as one of the world's largest importers, pays a high proportion of the total Fund. But with British farming being relatively small, her farmers receive a small proportion of the money spent on the CAP. And because that CAP takes more than two-thirds of the total Fund, there is little left over for other desirable objectives, such as those listed by the Economic and Social Committee which wants to help regenerate depressed areas in the Community, including depressed areas in Britain.

	Net receipts or payments £	Per head of population £	Gross Domestic Product as % of EEC average
Belgium	152m	16	107
Denmark	177m	35	126
Germany	1.2bn	20	123
Greece	411m	42	44
France	11m	–	114
Ireland	439m	125	58
Italy	970m	17	71
Luxembourg	155m	421	108
Netherlands	182m	13	111
UK	1.2bn	22	98

When the heads of the Community governments met at a summit at Athens in September 1983, it was clear that the Community would be bankrupt by the middle of 1984. The spending on the CAP had outrun the Community Fund's ability to pay. Some members wanted the heads of government to agree to an increase in each member's contributions. Mrs Thatcher argued that this was a recipe for the sort of overspending which had led Britain and other countries to financial disaster. With her belief in the need to bring inflation under control in Britain and in 'a strong currency' it was not surprising that she opposed the apparently reckless proposals being made by her partners.

It was largely because of her insistence on firm monetary control that, in 1984, the Council of Ministers and the Commission made the first real attempt to deal with the CAP. There were announcements that, in 1984, the CAP would pay for less beef and less milk than it had paid for in 1983. Farmers would have to cut their output. The CAP was going to try to limit the demands it made on the Community Fund.

This realistic approach to the problem of the CAP was a cause of the breakdown of the Athens Summit which ended in failure in March 1984. The Irish Prime Minister insisted that his country ought to receive 'special consideration' and be allowed to produce more than its allocation of milk so that its farmers would continue to receive the £1 billion 'milk cheque' from the CAP. It is probable that Mitterand of France welcomed this breakdown, for he could not have looked forward to facing angry French farmers with the news that they, too, would receive smaller cheques from the reformed CAP. The Irish 'walk-out' from the Summit meant that no decisions could be taken about other monetary issues. These included Thatcher's demand that the Community live up to an earlier promise by giving back to Britain part of what had been agreed was her 'overpayments' in previous years. That agreement has now been cancelled. She also demanded that the Community should create and agree a formula by which the contributions of member states could be fixed. Under her proposals, Britain would be asked to make a smaller contribution (£200–300 million) than the £1.2 billion she had been making in the 1970s.

In July 1984, there was another EEC summit at Fontainebleau. Mitterand, of France, wanted an agreement which would allow the expensive CAP to continue. His main political opponent in France, Jacques Chirac, called for the expulsion of Britain from the EEC. It was Britain, said Chirac, which was holding back the Community from solving its problems. Mrs Thatcher, for her part, was anxious to reach a solution to the seemingly everlasting round of confrontations between Britain and her EEC partners.

So it was that a compromise solution was arrived at: Britain abandoned her entrenched position and accepted less by way of rebate than she had formerly demanded, but could claim that she would, in future, pay much less into the Community's funds than she had been paying. The lobbyists for CAP persuaded each member country to pay 1.4 per cent of the amount collected by VAT into the Community's funds. This would allow an increase in expenditure on the CAP, although a smaller increase than would have been the case without the earlier decision to cut the output of milk.

So, as so often in the past, there were, in July 1984, no winners and, perhaps, no losers as the Community reached yet another compromise. De Gaulle did not take France out of the Community in 1965. In 1984, the Community did not follow Chirac's advice and expel Britain. If there was a 'loser' at Fontainebleau it was 'Europe'. In 1965 it was de Gaulle, in 1984 it was Thatcher and Fitzgerald (of Ireland) who put national interest above Community interests. There has been, as we saw on p. 237, a loss of faith in 'Europe'.

Documentary evidence

Hjalmar Schacht had been Hitler's Minister for Economics. He arranged a number of trade and currency deals with countries in Central and Eastern Europe, which enabled German trade and industry to develop. Like fellow-Ministers in other countries in the 1930s, Schacht had been concerned with the economic well-being of his own country; in a 'beggar-my-neighbour' policy, the politicians of the 1930s (the 'Schachtian' decade – Document 11.2) had ignored the effects of their internal policies on other countries. In post-war Europe, Jean Monnet (Document 11.2) and his disciples such as Schuman (Document 11.1) persuaded European politicians to consider problems and policies in a transnational way. The British Labour government was the least European-minded of the European governments; it refused to join in discussions which led to the formation of the Coal and Steel Community (Document 11.1). Some had hoped that, when Churchill led the Conservatives to victory in 1951, Britain might again take the lead in Europe. However, Churchill's pro-European rhetoric had misled such optimists. Britain blocked attempts to form a European Defence Community (p. 227), only to be forced, under pressure from the USA, to perform a *volte face* (p. 228). Anthony Nutting, (Document 11.3), was a supporter of Eden – at least until Eden led Britain into the anti-Arab War in 1956. It is doubtful if Eden deserved the title of 'brilliant negotiator' (Document 11.3).

De Gaulle was aware of Britain's lukewarm attitude towards 'Europe' and although he was not a fervent supporter of the Monnet-Schuman concept of a United Europe, he used his power to block Britain's first application to join the Community in 1963 (Document 11.4).

Document 11.1

The Schuman Declaration, 9 May 1950

'Placing the whole of Franco-German coal and steel output under a common High Authority, in an organisation open to the participation of the other countries of Europe. The pooling of coal and steel production will immediately provide for the establishment of common bases for economic development as a first step in the federation of Europe, and will change the destinies of those regions which have long been devoted to the manufacture of munitions of war, of which they have been the most constant victims. . . . This transformation will make possible other joint actions which have been impossible until now. . . . The solidarity thus achieved will make it plain that any war between France and Germany becomes not only unthinkable, but materially impossible.'

Document 11.2

A Dutch view of Monnet's method

'Some of the delegates, formed in the tug-of-war of economic negotiations of the "Schachtian" decade (1933–9), at first believed that they were being simply tricked when, during meetings, they saw the little group of Frenchmen around Monnet disagreeing among themselves just as much as with other delegations. How could one negotiate one's nation's special interest in orderly fashion against another's, if the inviting delegation seemed to have no clear view of the national interests it wanted to defend? But Monnet's method was so contagious, the attempt to find solutions for common problems instead of defending simply one's own national interests was so liberating and exhilarating, that none of the chief delegates resisted this new approach for very long. Monnet thus succeeded in creating out of these hard-boiled negotiators a group of ardent Europeans, many of whom later came to Luxembourg and Brussels to make the Community work.'

(Max Kohnstamm, 'The European Tide' in *A New Europe?* ed. Graubard, S.,
Houghton Mifflin Co. 1964)

Document 11.3

Anthony Eden negotiates with the French, 1954

'When the French threw out the European Defence Community there was no institution available whereby the Germans could be brought into the Western community. Eden set off around all the various capitals in the countries that had negotiated the European Army Treaty. He left the French till last because he knew that there lay the principal opposition. He put it to the French that the Germans should be made members of the West European Union and admitted to NATO with the national army. The French didn't like this at all. I was present at the meeting with Mendès-France when Eden, Gladwyn Jebb and myself put this to the French. They sat us in a corner of a room and Mendès-France and all his advisers ranged in front of us. There we were cornered, and I could see Eden's back stiffening against the wall. He was determined not to give the one concession which he had up his sleeve, which Mendès-France knew he had up his sleeve; namely that the British would guarantee to the French that we would be there in the West European Union with an army on the continent of Europe until the end of this century. This is what they hoped we would give for the EDC. We wouldn't give it to the European Army because this would mean putting our army into a European setting, but we would keep our army on the continent of Europe to hold the hand of the French. Eden knew that if he gave the concession at that particular meeting, then Mendès-France would pocket it and say, "thank you very much" and come back for more. So all through that meeting Eden refused to give a single thing. He said, "It is for you, the French; you rejected the only alternative, it's for you to bring the Germans in. Now you must agree to my proposal that they should be brought in to the West European Union and through that into NATO. You refused to make an army with them; all right, they will have to come in with a national army of their own." It wasn't until one meeting later when he got Mendès-France to come to London that he finally made the concession. By this time Mendès-France was almost on his

knees begging for this thing, and then it was all right. Eden was a brilliant negotiator.'
(Anthony Nutting in Alan Thompson, *The Day Before Yesterday*, Granada, 1971)

Document 11.4

De Gaulle says 'No', 1963

'Thereupon Britain posed her candidature to the Common Market. She did so having earlier refused to participate in the communities we are building, after creating a free trade area with six other states and, finally, after having put pressure on the Six (for the long negotiations on the subject have not been forgotten) in order to prevent a real beginning of the Common Market. Then England applies for membership, but on her own conditions.

This confronts the Six, as well as England, with considerable problems. For England is insular, maritime, linked by trade, markets and food supply to very different and often very distant lands. She is an industrial and commercial nation and her agriculture is relatively unimportant.

In short, the nature, the very situation which are England's differ profoundly from those of the continentals. . . . For example, England imports foodstuffs cheaply from the two Americas or from the former Dominions, while granting considerable subsidies to English farmers. The system adopted by the Six deals with agricultural products within the Community as a whole, fixing prices, forbidding subsidies and requiring each member to pay to the Community the amounts saved through purchasing foodstuffs from outside the Community.

How can England be brought within this system? It has sometimes been thought that our English friends . . . were agreeing to change their ways to the extent required. . . . How far is it possible for Britain to accept a truly common tariff? . . . for this would involve giving up all Commonwealth preferences . . . and treating as null and void obligations entered into with the Free Trade Area. Can she do this?

It cannot be claimed that this question has been answered.'
(Press conference, 14 January 1963, from *The Annual Register*, 1963)

FURTHER READING

ARBUTHNOTT, H., AND EDWARDS, G., eds., *A Common Man's Guide to the Common Market*, Macmillan, 1979
BELOFF, N., *The General Says No*, Penguin, 1963
CAMPS, M., *European Unification in the Sixties*, New York, 1967
COOMBES, D., *The Future of the European Parliament*, PSL, 1979
CRAWLEY, A., *De Gaulle*, Collins, 1969
CROZIER, B., *De Gaulle: The Statesman*, Eyre Methuen, 1973
FELD, U. J., *The European Community in World Affairs*, Washington, 1976
HALLSTEIN, W., *United Europe: Challenge and Opportunity*, London, 1962
HOLLAND, S., *The Uncommon Market*, Macmillan, 1979
HU, Y. S., *Europe under Stress*, Butterworth, 1982
KITZINGER, U. W., *The Challenge of the Common Market*, 1982
KITZINGER, U. W., *Diplomacy and Persuasion*, Thames and Hudson, 1973

LAQUEUR, W., *A Continent Astray: Europe, 1970–78*, 1979

LODGE, J., *Institutions and Policies of the European Community*, Frances Pinter, 1983

MARQUAND, D., *Parliament for Europe*, Cape, 1979

PAXTON, J., *The Developing Common Market*, Macmillan, 1976

SCAMMEL, W. M., *The International Economy since 1945*, Macmillan, 1982

SWANN, D., *The Economics of the Common Market*, Penguin, 1978

TRACEY, M., *Agriculture in Europe*, Granada, 1982

TWITCHETT, C. and K., eds., *Building Europe*, Europa Publications, 1982

12

Europe between the super-powers, 1953–73

The 'Thaw', 1953–61

'That Paris summit meeting (1960) happened largely because of Mr Macmillan. Eisenhower didn't have any faith in it . . . but was persuaded to go along.'[1]
'The summit failure revealed very starkly the clash between the two giants and the fact that the honest broker . . . had very little beyond . . . words to use.'[2]

Eisenhower became US president in January 1953, two months before Stalin's death (March 1953). He hoped for a working relationship with the Russians, and the Korean armistice (July 1953) led to an easing of tensions between the superpowers. However, his Secretary of State, Dulles, was suspicious of those of the President's advisers who looked for opportunities for détente. Dulles called for containment (as Truman had (p. 60)) and for Communism to be 'rolled back', if possible.

In 1953 the Russian-backed North Vietnamese were defeating their French imperial masters (p. 172). The USA was involved in this struggle, providing assistance to France amounting to one billion dollars in 1954 alone. But events proved that technological mastery and superiority of fire power were not enough. In May 1954 the communist forces won the decisive battle of Dien Bien Phu. Earlier, Dulles had suggested that this latest communist advance might be halted, and the Soviet power 'rolled back', by the use of atomic bombs. Anthony Eden, Foreign Secretary in Churchill's Conservative government, persuaded Dulles that such 'brinkmanship' might lead to that major confrontation with Russia which the West had carefully avoided since 1945. Eden found an ally in the new French Prime Minister, Mendès-France, who appreciated that France could not afford to continue the Indo-China War and that it was in the best French interests to sign a peace treaty with Ho Chi-minh.

The foreign ministers of Britain, France, the USA, Russia and communist China met at Geneva where, after a two-month long conference, the map of Indo-China was re-drawn. In July 1954 Laos and Cambodia became independent, the 'Geneva Powers' guaranteeing their neutrality. They were to be, said Eden, a 'protective pad' around

Vietnam, which was divided along the 17th degree of latitude into North and South Vietnam. Ho Chi-minh was to rule the communist state of North Vietnam while a non-communist government would hold power in the South. Within two years all foreign troops were to leave the two states, which would then hold free elections and be re-united under a government of their own choice. With hindsight, we know that this 1954 Agreement did not solve the problem of Vietnam, which became the cockpit in which the superpowers fought another, more savage and longer, vicarious war.

The Geneva Agreements were hailed as a major breakthrough in international relations. Eden took advantage of the 'Geneva Spirit' to propose to Russia a package consisting of a demilitarised zone of Central Europe to include Germany and a security pact. He managed to get the Russians to agree to the Austrian State Treaty (May 1955) which provided for the withdrawal of occupying troops from Austria, which became independent within the frontiers of 1937, and for the Austrian parliament to pass a law pledging Austria to permanent neutrality (p. 31).

This Treaty marked a major policy shift by the Soviet Union, which had earlier opposed attempts to conclude such a settlement. Many western observers hoped that it signified Russia's willingness to disengage troops holding the line of the 'Iron Curtain', but, on the day after signing the Austrian Treaty, the Russians and her satellites signed the Warsaw Pact which ensured the continued presence of the Red Army in Central Europe.

In spite of the Warsaw Pact, Eden hoped to take advantage of the new diplomatic climate to arrange a treaty for Germany along the lines of the Austrian Treaty. In July 1955 there was a summit meeting in Geneva when Eisenhower met Khruschev and Bulganin, Eden and the French Prime Minister, Edgar Faure. This was the first meeting between the leaders of Russia and the USA since Potsdam, ten years before. The conference was conducted in a friendly atmosphere, giving rise, again, to talk of 'the Geneva Spirit', a relaxation of the Cold War tension. However, the conference failed to achieve anything of substance; there was an agreement on cultural exchanges (and, presumably, the end of 'Zhdanovism' in Russia), and a tacit under-standing that both sides had their own interests in the Far East, where the USA had already adopted South Vietnam as a client state (p. 251). The South East Asia Treaty Organisation (SEATO) had been signed in September 1954 by representatives from Australia, Britain, France, New Zealand, Pakistan, the Philippines, Thailand and the USA which regarded it as an Asiatic counterpart to NATO.

The Geneva Conference also recognised that in the age of the hydrogen weapon, war had become so terrifying a prospect that it was better to live with the status quo than to fight to alter things. Macmillan, British Foreign Minister, summed things up with his quip, 'there ain't gonna be no war'.

In 1956, Eisenhower put forward his 'open skies' plan under which the powers would allow 'spy planes' from other countries to overfly their territory in order to verify the size of opposing military forces. Russia would not agree; she saw this as an attempt by western powers to intrude on Russian affairs. On the side of the USA, too, there was still the policy of 'containment', declared by Eisenhower in January 1957 in words reminiscent of Truman's: '. . . the United States has a deep involvement and responsibility in events that may lead to controversy in every part of the world, whether they touch the affairs of a vast region, the fate of an island in the Pacific, or the use of a canal in the Middle East.' The next year US marines landed in the Lebanon to prevent a pro-Nasser attempt to seize power.

Khruschev's opening speech at the 20th Party Congress had outlined his 'revision' of Russian foreign policy (p. 114). War was not inevitable with the capitalists; co-existence was desirable; in the age of the hydrogen bomb there would be no winners. But Khruschev spoke also of co-existence 'between states having different social systems' which, inevitably, would continue their struggle for supremacy. In May 1958 Khruschev addressed the representatives of the Warsaw Pact gathered in Moscow and outlined 'the tactics' which the socialist bloc should pursue.

> 'I say "tactics" advisedly, because the basic purpose of Communist strategy remained the same – the domination of the world by Communism, as represented by the USSR. The purpose remains, and will remain, constant through every change of leadership; only the tactics vary.'[3]

Or, as Khruschev said to western diplomats in November 1956, 'We will bury you.'

Between the 1956 speech and the 1958 outline of 'tactics', a plan for the creation of a zone free of nuclear weapons in Central Europe was proposed by Rapacki, the Polish Foreign Minister, in a speech at the United Nations in October 1957. Poland, Czechoslovakia, East and West Germany would be 'nuclear free' zones in which there would be neither manufacture nor stockpiling of nuclear weapons. Rapacki proposed joint inspection by NATO and Warsaw Pact states to ensure observation of the plan. The USA and Britain rejected the plan, claiming that it would favour the Soviet bloc countries with their greater number of conventional weapons. Their opposition was reinforced by the West Germans, who distrusted the proposal that the plan should be followed by direct talks over the future of the two Germanies and their relationship with each other.

In spite of this western rejection of a Russian tactical plan, representatives of the major powers gathered again at Geneva in July 1958 to discuss the problem of detecting nuclear explosions. Another Geneva Conference opened in October 1958 to discuss methods of providing safeguards against a surprise attack. By this time the superpowers were rivals in space technology. Russia had launched the original earth satellite (Sputnik 1) on October 4 1957 and the USA had launched its first scientific satellite, Vanguard 1, on 17 March 1958. The potential for mutual destruction had increased; the need for détente was the greater.

Khruschev and Bulganin visited Britain in April 1956 to contact Macmillan, in whom 'Khruschev believed he had found a natural ally' in his search for peaceful co-existence.[4] The two shared, for different reasons, the belief that a summit meeting might lead to wider agreement on, for example, disarmament. Macmillan had succeeded in re-building that 'special relationship' between Britain and the USA which had been badly damaged by Eden's Suez adventure. He accepted the stationing of medium-range missiles in Britain; he welcomed the US decision to allow the transfer to Britain of information, nuclear materials and non-nuclear components of atomic weapons. He used this new-found relationship to urge on the US the need to discuss disarmament with the Russians.

In 1959 Khruschev visited the USA, partly to address the UN General Assembly, partly to meet Eisenhower at Camp David. In spite of US revulsion at the suppression of the Hungarian revolution in 1956 (pp. 92–4) and Dulles's hesitations (p. 244), it was agreed that a summit meeting should be held in 1960. Apart from disarmament, the summit would, it was hoped, lead to a settlement of the German question. In November 1958 Khruschev had threatened that Russia would uni-laterally decide the future of Berlin by supporting the seizure of West Berlin by Ulbricht's government. Macmillan was almost alone in urging the need to negotiate with Khruschev. Dulles wanted to follow a hard, anti-communist line even if that led to the need for 'brinkman-ship' and the threat of war; both de Gaulle, anxious to assert himself on the international scene, and Adenauer supported the need for a stiff negotiating position vis-à-vis Russia and East Germany. In February 1959, Macmillan went to Moscow to persuade Khruschev to withdraw his ultimatum and so provide a better climate in which preparations for the 1960 summit could go ahead.

The summit was arranged for May 1960 in Paris. Khruschev approached it with the knowledge that, at home, the Party ideologues and the leaders of the Army were united in their doubts as to the possibilities of arriving at a settlement with Dulles and Eisenhower. Khruschev feared that a rebuff by the Americans would lead to a loss of face, the end of his ability to conduct a campaign for peaceful co-existence, and that the opposition in the Politburo would gain control. Before the Conference opened, he told newspapermen that he intended to sign a separate treaty with East Germany and so force the western powers to negotiate directly with Ulbricht. As soon as the Conference opened, Khruschev announced that an American U-2 'spy plane' had been shot down over Russia and that he was no longer prepared to discuss the German problem with the untrustworthy Americans. Eisenhower refused to accept that such a plane had been shot down. Khruschev then produced the unfortunate Gary Powers, the pilot of the ill-fated U-2, as evidence not only of US spying activity but of Eisenhower's lying. Khruschev called the summit off and cancelled the invitation which had been extended to Eisenhower to visit Moscow. Back home, Khruschev could claim a 'triumph' for having shown up the Americans, while his supporters could argue that progress to co-existence had been halted only by US behaviour.

In September 1960, Khruschev gave an angry speech at the UN General Assembly. Further confirmation of the apparent end of the 'Thaw' was provided in 1961 when he met President Kennedy at Vienna. He threatened Kennedy that if the western powers did not sign a peace treaty with East Germany 'in the next six months', he would do so unilaterally. Kennedy's response was to accept the threat as a serious one, to say that 'We do not want to fight, but we have fought before.' While many Americans rushed to buy air-raid shelters strong enough to survive atomic blast and radiation, many more East Germans took note of the threat and fled to the West. It was this which led to the building of the Berlin Wall in August 1961 (pp. 96–7).

The building of the Wall was at once a sign of failure and of success. It was the sign that there would be no settlement yet of the problem of divided Germany; it was, in fact, the *de facto* boundary of East Germany, whether the western powers wanted to admit it or not. But it also reduced the possibilities of future crises in Berlin. The Wall had, in that sense, contributed to peaceful co-existence, for it removed one of the most dangerous issues in the Cold War. During the next twenty years, the superpowers would be in conflict outside Europe – in Vietnam, the Middle East, the Horn of Africa, Iran, Afghanistan and, in 1962, in Cuba.

Cuba, 1962 (Figure 12.1)

'Your rockets are in Turkey. You are worried by Cuba . . . because it is 90 miles from the American coast. But Turkey is next to us.'[5]

Khruschev to Kennedy, October 1962

'If we had invaded Cuba I am sure the Soviets would have acted. They would have had to, just as we would, too.'[6]

John F. Kennedy

Between 1952 and 1958, Cuba had been ruled by ex-army Sergeant Batista who organised a reign of terror, exiling or executing his enemies and so misusing dollar aid that Cuba became bankrupt. In 1959 he was overthrown following a guerilla war in which Fidel Castro's forces were supported by the majority of Cubans. Thousands of Batista's followers fled to the USA, their propaganda contributing to

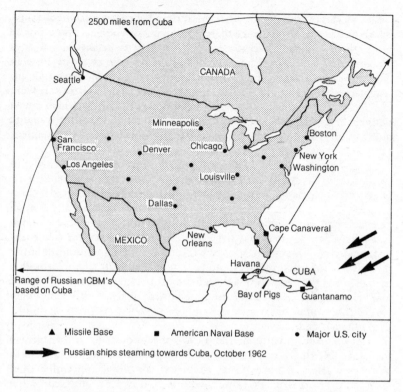

12.1 A sketch map which helps to explain US fears of Cuban-based Russian missiles.

US anti-communist feeling. Cuba's financial problems were made worse when no western power or agency would provide the aid needed to rebuild the island's economy. Castro was driven to seek aid from communist sources.

As part of the redevelopment of the island's economy, Castro nationalised some American-owned industries. This confirmed US suspicion that Castro was creating a communist state some 90 miles from the US mainland. Eisenhower allowed the CIA to undertake the training of Batista supporters who planned to invade Cuba. In 1960, the US increased the pressure by refusing to buy Cuban sugar, which was bought by the Russians instead, so increasing their leverage on Castro. He accepted Russian aid and technical assistance, another 'proof' of the creation of the Russian satellite in the Caribbean.

In April 1961, the new President, Kennedy, authorised the planned attack on Cuba. At the Bay of Pigs, the invasion was shattered and the invading force compelled to surrender (Document 13.1). Meanwhile, Khruschev took advantage of his control of the Cuban economy to create a series of missile sites on the island. In February 1962 the Warsaw Pact countries were informed that, in the event of a nuclear war with the USA, the Russians would attack US cities with rockets launched from Cuban bases. The Americans seemed to have become aware of this plan only in August 1962, when 30 Russian ships arrived in Cuban ports. US spy planes brought back photographs showing that the Russians were installing intermediate range ballistic missiles (ICBMs) which had a range of 2,500 miles. If these were armed with nuclear warheads a large number of US cities were threatened with atomic attack (Document 12.1).

On 22 October Kennedy ordered a quarantine, or naval blockade, of Cuba; 'This . . . build up of Communist missiles . . . is a deliberately provocative change in the status quo which cannot be accepted by this country. . . . To halt this offensive build up a strict quarantine on all offensive equipment under shipment to Cuba is being initiated.' Castro and Khruschev argued that the missiles were defensive in character, instancing the US-supported attack at the Bay of Pigs as evidence of the threat to Cuba. Kennedy refused to accept the argument. Khruschev then claimed that the US was threatening Russia with its missiles based in Turkey and elsewhere in Europe. Kennedy insisted that these were part of the 'containment package' and had no offensive purpose, unlike the Cuban-based missiles.

The two leaders maintained contact by means of letters and telephone messages. Neither wanted the world to be plunged into war; both were under a variety of pressures. Kennedy consulted Macmillan and received support from de Gaulle, who was, however, angered by the President's apparent willingness to consider a nuclear war without asking the advice of Europe's leaders (pp. 177–8). Left wing and 'liberal' groups in Europe held anti-US demonstrations, claiming that the US had brought the world to the brink of war – a curious interpretation of events.

Kennedy insisted that the US had to make it as easy as possible for Khruschev to climb down; there was to be no 'crusading warrior' behaviour by US forces. While ships were stopped and searched, those which had innocent cargo were allowed to enter Cuban waters. Khruschev took advantage of the week-long period of tension to order Russian ships, carrying additional missiles, to turn back. Kennedy ordered that there should be no crowing over this partial victory which, on 27 October, was followed by Khruschev's letter announcing the agreement to remove the offensive weapons from Cuba (Document 12.1).

For Europe, the crisis had been the plainest evidence that there was now a bi-polar world, in which decisions would be reached by the superpowers without Europe being taken into account. For the future of the relationship between the superpowers, the crisis was important because it caused both Khruschev and Kennedy to take steps to improve contact between Moscow and Washington. A new telephone link was established and on this 'hot line' the leaders could be in more immediate contact. The letters which passed between them during the crisis also indicated a will, on both sides, to try to ensure that their future policies would be more evidently defensive in character. There would be no more 'brinkmanship' on the one side or the other.

The US shift to co-existence, 1964–74

'In many countries it looks as if the United States is in retreat (but) we are doing what we are doing because we believe that if America is to remain related to the world it must define a relationship that we can sustain over an indefinite period.'[7]

Secretary of State Henry Kissinger

Between 1963 and 1973 the USA and Russia fought a proxy war in Vietnam (p. 250). In other parts of the world, too, they vied for power and influence, regarding each other's policies as 'interference' while claiming their own as 'furthering of peaceful interests'. The Cold War was extended by Russian policies in India, Egypt, Eritrea and the Horn of Africa, the Yemen and, with the aid of the Cubans, in Angola and Mozambique (p. 214). And almost everywhere Russia seemed to enjoy victory.

During the same period there was a deeping of the division between Russia and communist China (Fig. 6.1a, p. 120), a division of which the US took advantage to come to terms with China and, with China as a seemingly 'benevolent neutral', to undertake a revision of attitudes towards Russia. European statesmen made their contribution to this change in attitudes: Brandt's *Ostpolitik* (below) helped create an atmosphere in which the USA and Russia could begin the discussions which led to the signing of the first Strategic Arms Limitation Agreement.

China had never been the 'Russian client-state' so feared by many western observers. Both countries had memories of long-standing hostility. As far back as the seventeenth century the Chinese had resented Russian occupation of the Amur Valley; in the nineteenth century they had clashed over rival claims to Mongolia; in the early part of this century they had quarrelled over the mineral-rich area of Sinkiang, bordering on Kazakhstan. Nor had things changed when Russia came under communist rule. Stalin had provided little aid to Mao during the 1930s; he condemned Mao's concept of a peasant-based revolution. Even after the Japanese invasion of China, Stalin provided more aid to the 'bourgeois' Chiang Kai-shek than to Mao. In 1945, Stalin stripped Manchuria of its industrial wealth, refusing to allow Mao's communists to take control of the region.

There was some improvement in Sino-Soviet relations after Mao had established the People's Republic in 1949. Russia provided aid to help Mao's programme of modernisation. But, as the Chinese pointed out,

Russia gave more aid to India which was, at times, positively anti-Chinese. And the aid was limited; Stalin did not share Russia's atomic secrets with the newly established communist state.

On Stalin's death, Mao claimed the title of 'elder statesman' in the communist world, a title which Khruschev and the Russians refused to allow him. The denunciation of Stalin in 1956 angered Mao who claimed that it was impossible that Marxism could have produced such a monster. Mao denounced Khruschev's 'revisionism' (p. 246) with its claim that war with the capitalists was not inevitable. When Khruschev claimed that in a nuclear war there would be world-wide destruction, Mao claimed that, whatever happened elsewhere, there would always be millions of Chinese survivors of a nuclear holocaust. The atomic bomb he dismissed as 'a paper tiger' (Document 12.2), used by the USA to frighten reactionaries, which included, it appeared, Khruschev.

Meanwhile, Khruschev and the Russians were critical of Chinese domestic policy. While supplying technical and material aid for Mao's 'Great Leap Forward', Russian ideologues condemned the Chinese system of communes because they did not follow the Russian model. On his part, Mao condemned Russian ambitions to produce an increased quantity of consumer goods as being an apeing of the capitalist West, a search for a 'goulash Communism' in which material affluence would have a more important place than purity of doctrine (p. 119).

In 1958, Communist Chinese guns maintained a barrage of fire on the islands of Quemoy and Matsu which the nationalist Chinese regarded as part of their front-line defence of their Taiwan stronghold. The USA sent US Marines to Quemoy and transported nationalist troops from Taiwan to both islands. The Russians did nothing, other than offer verbal reassurance, to help the communist Chinese. Again, in 1962, when India and China went to war over Ladak and other disputed border areas, Russia remained neutral, which China regarded as an affront.

But by then the split between the two communist giants was wide and well-publicised. In 1960 there was a good deal of Chinese criticism of Khruschev at the Communist Party Congress in Bucharest. In retaliation, Khruschev withdrew all Russian aid from China and 1,390 technicians returned to Russia.

Mao condemned Khruschev's Cuban policy in 1962, both for its 'adventurism' and lack of planning, and for the 'cowardice' of the withdrawal in face of the US threat. Mao did not believe that the USA had the will to use its 'paper tiger'. However, as a further guarantee of China's ability to maintain an independent foreign policy in the nuclear age, he organised a series of Chinese developments which led to China's first atomic test in October 1964 (Document 12.2). The ambition to have nuclear weapons was one reason for China's refusal to sign the Partial Test Ban Treaty in 1963 (p. 118).

The fall of Khruschev did not improve the relationship between Russia and China. Brezhnev and Kosygin were as committed to peaceful co-existence as Khruschev had been, so that Chinese hostility towards Russia grew, if anything, deeper. There were border clashes which broke out in August 1969. Both Russia and China claimed lands north of the Amur and Ussuri Rivers and there were heavy fighting on Damansky Island in the middle of the Ussuri River (Figure 6.1a). There was also fighting along the Sinkiang section of the 4,000 mile long border between the two countries. So serious was the fighting that *Pravda* hinted at the possible use of nuclear weapons by the Soviet Union, while eastern European newspapers carried reports of an imminent air strike by Russia against the Chinese nuclear installations at Lop Nor to the south of Sinkiang. The Soviet military journal, *Red Star*, called Mao 'a traitor to the sacred cause of Communism' and compared him to Hitler. When Kosygin flew to North Vietnam to attend Ho Chi-minh's funeral (September 1969), his plane was routed the long way round so that it avoided Chinese territory.

This dispute affected Russia's relationships with her eastern satellites. Many of them were sympathetic to China's claims to decide her own destiny. Russia used her satellites in her struggle with China; their embassies in Peking were staffed, on Russian orders, with intelligence agents reporting to Russia;[8] as the threat of a Sino-Soviet war loomed larger, the Warsaw Pact states were advised that this would lead to a fall in the number of Russian troops in eastern Europe, so that the satellites would have to be prepared to accept a greater burden of the defence against the West. Rumania and Albania took advantage of Russia's preoccupation in the Far East to stake out claims for greater freedom of action for themselves (pp. 100–1).

But, in global terms, these developments in eastern Europe were 'little local difficulties' compared to the developments in the Far East and to the effects of those developments on international relations. Following the funeral of Ho Chi-minh, Kosygin and the Chinese Prime Minister, Chou En-lai, held a series of meetings which went on throughout 1970 but which failed to heal the breach. Marshal Grechko (p. 122) expressed the Russian view when he ranked China with Germany and the USA as a major enemy of the Soviet Union. The Chinese were, in spite of Mao's contempt for the 'paper tiger' (p. 265), aware that they did not have a strategic retaliatory force against a Soviet nuclear attack, while the superiority of the firepower of Russian ground and airforces suggested that Russia could defeat the Chinese army even if she could not conquer the whole vast country. It was the realisation of their perilous position which brought China to accept the need for a détente with the USA.

Talks between the Chinese and US Ambassadors in Warsaw had gone on throughout the 1960s without any agreement between their two countries being in sight. Communist China's claim to Taiwan was denied by the US, which also vetoed proposals to allow the Chinese seat in the UN Security Council to be taken by Red China. But, in November 1968, the Chinese announced that they were prepared to live on terms of peaceful co-existence with the USA; they might have added that 'we are all revisionists now'. However, it was not until December 1969 that the ambassadorial talks were resumed at a more serious level. Throughout 1970 the Nixon government carefully avoided the Cold War rhetoric which had been its normal way of dealing with Red China. In February 1970 Nixon's foreign policy statement noted that 'the success of our Asian policy depends not only on the strength of our partnership with our Asian friends, but also on our relations with Mainland China and the Soviet Union'.[9]

Nixon had already decided to extricate the USA from the Vietnam War. He was also busily supervising the progress of the SALT negotiations (pp. 268–70). He had to consider the possible effects of a US-Chinese rapprochement on those (to him) vital negotiations. He had also to consider the effects of a Sino-US détente on China's neighbours, who had been persuaded that the US would be their shield against the threat of Chinese expansionism.

The Chinese, also, had to consider carefully the possible effects of a détente with the USA. It would deepen the hostility with Russia and might raise doubts in the Third World about China's commitment to the world-wide revolution. There were Chinese leaders, particularly among the military, who would have preferred a rapprochement with Russia, their 'natural' ally, and the maintenance of the anti-US status quo. Would a shift of policy lead to stresses inside the Chinese leadership which might outweigh whatever benefits would be derived from the changed policy?

Such considerations help to explain the slow progress that was made. Only in March 1971 did the US government lift the restrictions on travel to China; only in June did the US end the embargo on trade with China. In April a combined US and British table-tennis team visited Peking, when Chou spoke of 'a new state in the relations between the Chinese and American peoples'. In July, Secretary of State Kissinger arrived in Peking on the day on which, in Washington, Nixon announced that he had accepted Chou's invitation to visit Peking in May 1972. While making this dramatic announcement, he carefully noted that this would not alter the US attitude towards negotiations with Russia, which he promised to visit after he had been to China.

British diplomats had been used by the US as channels of communication with the Chinese during the years of estrangement. But there was little, if any, US consultation with the outside world, including Europe, before the announcement of the major shift in policy. In the field of economics, too, Nixon equally ignored the wider world when he announced that the dollar-based international monetary system, set up at Bretton Woods, was at an end and that the dollar would no longer be tied to a fixed rate of exchange for gold (pp. 147–50). He seemed to be unaware of the effect which this would have on European economies, already suffering recession and high unemployment.

With hindsight, we can see that this attitude – the ignoring of allies – was all of a part with what had gone before and with what was yet to come in the Nixon presidency. He was, after all, in 1973, to help arrange the cease-fire in Vietnam (January 1973) and order the evacuation of the last of the US combat troops from that unhappy country a fortnight later. This may be claimed as an acceptance of the realities of the Vietnamese situation; the Americans could not win this war and he accepted this unpalatable truth. Nixon had earlier shown a similar sense of reality in November 1969 when he made a speech in Guam which included what became known as the 'Nixon Doctrine'. Unlike Truman and Eisenhower, Nixon said that while the US would honour its treaty commitments in Asia, it would expect its Asian allies to assume a larger share of the burden of local defence. Nixon called for a US partnership with, rather than a commitment to, her Asian allies. US troops were withdrawn from South Korea, Japan, Okinawa, the Philippines and Thailand. 1969 may be seen as a watershed; de Gaulle had been driven from office; the Chinese Cultural Revolution was winding down, with the pragmatic realists beginning to take hold of the reins again. And a born-again-to-détente Nixon was in the White House.

Arms and disarmament, 1953–68

'What in the name of God is strategic superiority? What is the significance of it politically, militarily, operationally at the levels of these numbers? What do you do with it?[10]

Henry Kissinger

Few subjects have received so much attention since 1945 as the arms race and the need for international agreement on disarmament. But few subjects can have been the cause of so much international disappointment: the great powers have conducted an arms race, especially in nuclear weapons, and neither Russia nor the USA has been willing to risk the sacrifice of what is seen as 'our legitimate interests'.

In 1946, the United Nations Organisation set up the Atomic Energy Commission; in 1947, it set up a Conventional Armaments Commission. Russia's withdrawal from both Commissions led the UN to merge both Commissions into a new Disarmament Commission, in the hope that this might lead to a new and more successful approach to the problem. Talks were held from 1955 to 1957 on the banning of nuclear weapons and on cutting the size of conventional forces. When the Russians walked out in anger at the lack of progress, the Commission continued to function and sponsored a Disarmament Conference at Geneva in 1966.

While these international attempts were failing to produce results, some statesmen worked through normal diplomatic channels to try to find some, if only small, ways in which disarmament could be furthered. The topic was on the agenda of each of the summit meetings which were held between 1955 and 1961. After the failure of the 1955 summit and the crises over Suez and Hungary in 1956, Bulganin and Eisenhower re-started their correspondence in March 1957. Bulganin suggested a new approach to a nuclear test ban in the form of a moratorium on tests for two or three years, under the control of an international commission. While these tentative suggestions were being discussed by policy makers in Russia and the USA, Britain exploded its first hydrogen bomb (May 1957); the problem of nuclear disarmament now became a tri-polar matter. In October 1957, the Russians launched their first Sputnik; the missile which had put this satellite into space could easily carry a warhead so that, for the first time, 'Fortress America' was itself vulnerable to attack from Europe.

Macmillan, Prime Minister of Britain, took advantage of American fears to get an agreement on the mutual exchange of nuclear information between Britain and the USA. In return, Britain became the base for medium-range Thor missiles, which gave the USA an even greater preponderance over Russia, while also providing Britain with a nuclear shield until she equipped her own V-bombers with hydrogen bombs and developed her own missile to carry the nuclear warhead. The cost of such nuclear development was high, and the 1957 White Paper on British defence made it clear that Britain was going to have to spend less on conventional forces while increasing its spending on nuclear weapons.

In February 1958, the Campaign for Nuclear Disarmament was launched in Britain; it called for the abandonment of the British nuclear weapon and a cut in defence spending. Pressure from CND and his own awareness of the danger from nuclear weapons led Macmillan to support the Disarmament Conference while, more significantly, attempting to achieve the more limited goal of a nuclear test ban. In 1958 he persuaded the Americans to accept the Russian proposal that a test ban could be negotiated separately from other disarmament proposals. His discussions with Dulles of the USA and Khruschev took place against the background provided by Khruschev's threat over Berlin (p. 247), which had led to a stiffening in the position of de Gaulle and Adenauer and to Eisenhower's becoming convinced that a Foreign Ministers' Conference would be the best means of settling outstanding issues.

In February 1959 Macmillan went to Moscow and obtained Khruschev's agreement to a test ban treaty which would include provision for on-site inspection. Tri-partite discussions were then held by officials and experts from Britain, the USA and USSR. During the five years which it took for these discussions to lead to fruition, the three nuclear powers agreed not to hold further tests. In the meantime the world lived through the Cuban crisis (pp. 248–51) which provided grim evidence of the danger of a nuclear war. In 1963, Macmillan took these discussions from the level of officials, and persuaded the Russians and the Americans that the issue ought, again, to be discussed at ministerial level. In July 1963, the three nuclear powers signed a partial Test Ban Treaty in Moscow. They agreed to cease testing nuclear weapons in the atmosphere or under water, with a view to limiting radio-active debris. The Treaty allowed the testing of nuclear weapons underground, so that its critics claimed that it was more concerned with pollution than with real control over nuclear developments.

The length of time taken to reach even this partial ban agreement is an indication of the reluctance of any power to make what may be seen as a sacrifice of its own interests. The need for such sacrifice became all the greater as scientists and technologists collaborated to produce more powerful weapons and rockets. The efficacy of the Test Ban Treaty was also challenged by the development of the multiple warhead weapons and by the anti-ballistic missiles (ABMs) which could destroy enemy missiles in mid-air. Military leaders, foreign policy makers and politicians of the nuclear powers became engaged in an arms race in spite of the Test Ban Treaty, for none of what was going on broke any of the terms of that very limited Treaty.

Politicians, especially finance ministers, in the nuclear power countries became increasingly concerned at the cost of maintaining parity with the enemy in weapons development. Taxes had to be increased, more desirable projects had to be put aside so that money and resources could be provided for these developments. And, as Kissinger asked, 'What do you do with it?' once you have obtained such a mass of weaponry? Britain couldn't have used its H-bomb against Nasser in 1956, even if it had had one at that time; the Suez War would have been lost by the nuclear power. The USA lost the Vietnamese War in spite of being one of the two leading nuclear powers.

And while weapons development proceeded apace, there was always the danger that more nations would gain the knowledge and ability to produce these weapons. After another long series of discussions, the three signatories of the Test Ban Treaty signed the Non-Proliferation Treaty (1968) which aimed at preventing the spread of nuclear weapons. The USA, Russia and Britain undertook not to transfer such weapons to other states. Unfortunately, neither France nor China signed this Treaty, just as they had refused to sign the earlier Treaty of 1963.

This 1968 Treaty did nothing to limit the development of weapons by the nuclear powers, and the USA and Russia were engaged in a grisly arms race which forced the wider public to become accustomed to new words and acronyms, as they read of 'second strike forces' made up of Minutemen ICBMs and Polaris submarine-launched missiles which could be 'knocked out' by ABMs which, however, might be overcome by MIRVs. And if the public was dazzled by such language, it was further baffled by the conflicting claims of the two sides over the numbers and efficacy of each other's weapons systems. The following table shows the relative strengths of the USA and USSR in strategic nuclear delivery vehicles from 1963 to 1976. The three classes of strategic delivery vehicles are the land-based intercontinental ballistic missile (ICBM), the submarine-launched ballistic missile (SLBM) and the long-range manned bomber aircraft which can deliver its weapons and return to its base.

Historical changes of strength 1963–76 (mid-years)

	USA			USSR		
	ICBMs	SLBMs	Long-range bombers	ICBMs	SLBMs	Long-range bombers
1963	424	224	630	90	107	190
1964	834	416	630	190	107	175
1965	854	496	630	224	107	160
1966	904	592	630	292	107	155
1967	1054	656	600	570	107	160
1968	1054	656	545	858	121	155
1969	1054	656	560	1028	196	145
1970	1054	656	550	1299	304	145
1971	1054	656	505	1513	448	145
1972	1054	656	455	1527	500	140
1973	1054	656	442	1527	628	140
1974	1054	656	437	1575	720	140
1975	1054	656	432	1618	784	135
1976	1054	656	387	1527	845	135

Source: International Institute for Strategic Studies,
The Military Balance 1977–8.

The table illustrates the arms race which took place, although it does not provide the answer to important questions. How many warheads does each of these missiles carry? And of what tonnage? And with what accuracy will they be used? How many of these systems would be 'knocked out' by an enemy's 'first strike' and how many would survive to be used as 'second strike' systems against the offensive enemy? Inability to answer these questions was a major cause of the continuing arms race, which was supported in Russia and the USA by that military-industrial-ideological complex which has such influence in both countries. Both countries had reached 'mutually assured destruction' (or MAD), which meant that both sides could survive a first strike and have sufficient second strike weapons to destroy the enemy. MAD indeed. Even madder, was the continued search for refinements to provide one side or the other with superiority, the fear of which led the other side to search for expensive and destructive retaliatory methods of its own. It is against this background of weapons pile-up that there were moves made for further treaties and agreements, moves which were helped by an easing of tensions in Central Europe.

Germany – the defusing of the critical area, 1966–73

'At the moment, nothing indicates that the fragmented German state could be restored in its old form.'

Chancellor Willy Brandt, 1973

Germany was both cause of and affected by the Cold War in the years between the end of the Second World War and Stalin's death (pp. 64ff.). Even when the 'liberal' Khruschev was in power in Russia, the German problem remained a bone of contention between the Eastern and Western blocs. In Chapter 9 we traced the political developments in West Germany where, in 1966, the rival CDU and SPD parties joined in the 'Grand Coalition' under the CDU leader Kiesinger who appointed the SPD leader, Brandt, as Foreign Minister. Following the 1969 Election, Brandt became Chancellor in an SPD-dominated coalition with the FDP.

Between 1966 and 1969 the CDU-SPD government had held discussions with the Soviet government about the basis of a new relationship. At first, (1966–68), the Kiesinger-Brandt initiative was greeted with enthusiasm in the West, but treated with suspicion by Russia and her satellites. The East Germans were afraid that any improvement in relations between West Germany and the countries of the Warsaw Pact would lead to East Germany being abandoned by her allies in the Pact. The Polish government was all too conscious of the former German territories which now formed western Poland (p. 76). Gomulka had only recently quarrelled with the leaders of the Polish Catholic Church who wanted to work for a reconciliation between the German and Polish peoples, which, the government feared, might be a 'churchy' way of advocating the handing back to Germany of the Oder-Neisse lands. The Polish government did not want to see any relaxation of the anti-West German attitudes currently held by Russia and the satellites. Any weakening of the fear of Germany would, perhaps, undermine the Polish people's need to be protected by the Russians, which, in turn, would fundamentally affect the basis of the communist rule in Poland. The Russians, too, regarded the proposed détente as a major threat to their own security. They saw that *Ostpolitik* might isolate East Germany, Russia's most faithful satellite, might split the Warsaw Pact countries and might reduce the East European fear of 'the threat from West Germany' under 'a new Hitler' which, taken together, were the strongest chains which bound the Pact together.

Indeed, there are commentators who believe that the Russian invasion of Czechoslovakia (pp. 97ff) was due, in large part, to Russian fears of *Ostpolitik*; they saw Dubcek as 'Brandt's stalking-horse' and they accused the West Germans of inspiring the Czechs. It is not surprising that, in the wake of the Czech crisis, Brandt's policy appeared to have had a short life. However, Brandt had used the Czech crisis as an opportunity for telling the West Germans that they had to get rid of illusions about the possibility of changing the politico-geographical nature of the Europe in which they lived. He insisted that the West Germans had to learn to accept the post-war status quo; they had no option but to consider the need for a new relationship with East Germany.

Perhaps the major bone of contention between the two Germanys was the eastern frontier of the GDR, that Oder-Neisse line which had been drawn by the Allies as part of the post-war settlement (pp. 24–5). In May 1969, Gomulka of Poland proposed that Poland and West Germany should undertake negotiations on this subject. Kiesinger responded favourably and Brandt, as Foreign Minister, opened the negotiations. In the autumn of 1969, Brandt became Chancellor (p. 199) and was in an even stronger position to develop his *Ostpolitik*. This required a number of inter-related moves. There was, first, the negotiation of a treaty with Poland to settle the question of the frontier and the problem of the German minorities living in the formerly disputed areas. Then, while this treaty was being negotiated, Brandt had to assure Russia that these negotiations were not aimed at undermining the Soviet position in eastern Europe; if Russia had thought that Brandt was using the 'salami technique' (p. 45) she might have taken steps to halt the Polish-German negotiations. But Brandt also had to assure West Germans, long accustomed to the rhetoric of Adenauer and Hallstein (pp. 76 and 195) that West Berlin would not be sacrificed as a pawn in the negotiations, although these negotiations would require the participation not only of Poland and the Soviet Union but also of East Germany.

In August 1970, Brandt signed a non-aggression treaty with Russia which acknowledged the existing frontiers of Europe, including the frontier between the two Germanys. In November 1970 the Polish-West German Treaty was finalised. Treaties with the other Warsaw Pact countries were to follow, the last, with Czechoslovakia (December 1973), annulling the consequences of the Munich agreement of 1938. The most difficult negotiations involved East Germany, which insisted that there was to be no 'special relationship' between the two Germanys and that normalisation of relations hinged on the recognition of each other's state sovereignty.

While Nixon and Kissinger were opening communications with China (p. 254), Brandt continued to seek new links with the East. By the autumn of 1971, Russia indicated that she was prepared to allow discussions which might lead to a new four-power multi-lateral approach to the Berlin problem. In September 1971, a new four-power agreement on Berlin was signed – the first since 1947. In October 1971,

Brezhnev visited Berlin on his way back from a visit to Paris. He had become convinced of the genuine nature of Brandt's search for solutions to the problems of Central Europe. He forced the reluctant East Germans to enter into negotiations with Brandt for an agreement on access and traffic between the two Germanys. This Berlin agreement was finally signed in June 1972 following the ratification by the Bonn legislature of the Moscow and Warsaw Treaties.

Brandt believed that his *Ostpolitik* would prove to be popular in the country in spite of the gradual erosion of the parliamentary majority of the SPD–FDP coalition in Bonn. He continued negotiations with the East Germans with a view to the signing of a Basic Treaty to regulate relations between the two Germanys, to recognise each other's membership of rival alliances (NATO and the Warsaw Pact), and to allow the admission of both Germanys to the United Nations. These negotiations were concluded in November 1972, the month in which Brandt won a parliamentary majority of 46 seats in the General Election, confirming his belief in the popularity of *Ostpolitik* (p. 200). The Basic Treaty was signed in December 1972. In May 1973, Brezhnev visited Bonn to indicate that Russia endorsed the agreement, and, in September 1973, both Germanys took their seats in the United Nations Assembly.

The various negotiations and treaties had rid Europe of almost all of the problems which had strained relations and had made easier the campaigns of the Cold War 'warriors'. The 'German problem' would not have to appear on any future agenda; it was now possible to bring forward other problems. And if the seemingly insoluble could be solved, if East and West Germany could come to agreement, there was hope that solutions might be found to other problems. In this atmosphere, Brezhnev sought a way of relaxing tensions between East and West; the road to Helsinki was opened.

Détente, a problem of definition

'The pursuit of détente means the attempt to identify and build on areas of common interest between East and West with the aim of establishing more understanding and more confidence between them. . . . Arms control agreements which enhance security, and trade which is of genuine benefit to both sides are examples. . . . The strength of détente is that neither side can do without trade. A genuine relaxation of tensions serves everybody's interests. . . . But [this] . . . depends on the Soviet Union accepting that it must behave with restraint, and accepting that détente applies to all areas of international relations, not just to Europe.'[11]

Francis Pym, British Defence Minister, 1981

By 1972 Brezhnev had obtained a degree of that 'relaxation of tensions' which, for various reasons, he wished to achieve. In the next chapter we will examine the processes by which that relaxation was formalised in trade agreements and in treaties. Détente became part of political and diplomatic rhetoric, a welcome change from the threatening language of the Cold War. But there remained, in the West, the suspicion that Russia might not be willing to go far along the road down which, for their own reasons, western politicians wished to travel. Pym voiced some of these suspicions in 1981. They had been encapsulated in 1945 in a question put to Churchill during the debate on the ill-fated Yalta Agreement. 'Did Russia hold approximately the same ideas and conceptions of the structure of Europe as we did?' asked the future Lord Home (pp. 37–8). And, we might add, did she have the same ideas and conceptions of such an intangible as human rights?

We shall see that the Russians were quite prepared to sign 'arms control agreements' and to develop trading links; they accepted that 'in the nuclear age there is no alternative to conducting mutual relations on the basis of peaceful co-existence'; they promised to 'always exercise restraint in their mutual relations'. But even while signing such agreements and while negotiating arms limitations (pp. 273–4) the Russians left no one in doubt as to their commitment to the ideological struggle, to that war between capitalism and socialism as defined by Marxist ideologues. In 1970, while SALT was being negotiated, *The War of Ideas in Contemporary International Relations* had been published by Arbatov, the leading Soviet expert on Soviet-US relations. In 1975 shortly after the signing of the Helsinki Final Agreement (p. 271) the Russians embarked on their expansionist policy in Angola (p. 251), illustrating by their actions their peculiar definitions of peace and co-existence (Document 13.2).

In the Final Agreement at Helsinki in 1975 the Russians accepted in 'the third basket' their need to recognise 'human rights'. However, there was no let up in the attack on critics of the Soviet régime; religious groups continued to be harried; the labour camps and 'psychiatric' prisons continued to be filled. For Brezhnev and his colleagues, this Agreement was merely 'a scrap of paper'. Western optimists may have hoped that détente might lead to changes in Russian policies at home and abroad. But the Russians had a narrow, if well-defined, interpretation of détente. For them it consisted entirely of a military core; they would work for a mutual lowering of spending on arms – while maintaining their lead over the USA – because this would have economic, social and political benefits for the various power groups which make up the Soviet leadership. The other parts of the détente 'package' – trade, human rights and the rest – were, in the Soviet view, peripheral only, and would be acceptable only if beneficial to the Soviet Union, as for example, a trade agreement might be if there were no 'human rights' strings attached to it. If, however, there were such 'strings', as in the case of the Jackson Amendment (Document 13.3), the Russians would be prepared to forego even the benefits of a trade agreement.

Many western observers claim that Brezhnev's 'programme for

peace' was a trap into which over-eager statesmen and politicians fell. The Russians, they argue, do not look for any real accommodation with the West; they are still, primarily, concerned with the victory over capitalism; détente is only a tactic (p. 246) which Russia may or may not employ as part of the ideological struggle. These critics claim that recent history – since the signing of the first SALT agreement – has shown the folly of trusting the Russians, who have extended their influence in Africa, invaded Afghanistan and attacked their own dissidents, in spite of their apparent promises to follow the path of 'peaceful co-existence' and 'to extend human rights'.

The arch-apostle of the more optimistic approach was Kissinger. He claimed in the early 1970s that it was possible to create 'a web of interests' which would both create a climate of better understanding and also bring about such an interdependence that stable relations would be bound to develop. For this reason, once the first SALT agreement had been signed, Kissinger arranged a series of trade deals with Russia and organised cultural and scientific exchanges between Russia and the USA. He claimed that by promoting Soviet economic development, the USA would help raise living standards, create rising expectations among the Soviet people and produce pressure for reform and democratisation. Cultural exchanges would provide more Russians with a glimpse of life abroad and so increase their desire for change in Russia itself. There would also be economic benefits to western industry which would be asked to supply the capital equipment and technical know-how; and if, for example, European firms helped build the natural gas pipeline from Siberia to the West, they would also be helping to ensure a source of cheap fuel for the industries of western Europe.

In 1980, Soviet bloc trade with West Germany amounted to 200 dollars per head of population, far more than for any other western country; it is little wonder that the Bonn government refused to react strongly to the Soviet invasion of Afghanistan. By 1990, France plans to obtain one-third of its natural gas from Russia and may then find herself dangerously dependent on Soviet supplies. Kissinger's critics, who make this overdependence a matter for attack on his policies, also claim that western aid to Soviet development strengthens the Soviet economy and its military capacity. Soviet troops in Afghanistan are fed by US grain and EEC butter. To deny the Russians this easy access to 'capitalist' food would strain the Soviet system and, it is claimed, force the leaders to make the changes which might lead to that political reform so feared by the Russians.

A balanced analysis of what has been so far achieved by détente suggests that peaceful and fruitful co-operation between East and West has to be viewed as a long-term objective, which will be difficult to achieve. There has to be, in the first instance, a closer agreement on the objectives sought and on the definitions of such terms as 'human rights'. In the shorter term, it is possible to hope for an accommodation between the two groups of nations which may lead to the recognition of each other's security interests and of the need to renounce the use of force, to settle differences peacefully by negotiations and to exercise restraint. That, it might be thought, is sufficiently long a list of demands for the foreseeable future.

A Sino-Russian rapprochement?

We have seen (pp. 251ff) that the breakdown in Sino-Russian relations was one of the features of the international scenario which encouraged, if not, indeed, allowed, the USA to undertake a revision of its international policies. The Chinese, for their part, saw a number of advantages in the pursuing of a possible détente with the USA at a time when, after 1969, there seemed to be the possibility of serious fighting between Russia and China (pp. 253–5).

Not all China's leaders saw international affairs in this pro-US and anti-USSR light (p. 254). Some of them would have preferred a resumption of friendly relations with the other communist giant andwere suspicious of the Chinese leaders who sought a rapprochement with the USA. When Andropov became the leader of Russia, he, too, sought to rebuild relations with China. In part this was forced on him by the military-economic imperative; Russia was being forced to keep 500,000 members of its forces along the Sino-Russian border. Some one-quarter of Russia's military strength is devoted to ensuring the security of this frontier; Andropov and other Russian 'realists' would prefer to have these forces stationed in the West.

Under Andropov's guidance, talks were opened between Russian and Chinese leaders with a view to bringing the two nations into closer relationship. These talks have continued – in Peking and in Moscow – throughout 1984 but they have, so far, produced no settlement of the problems confronting the two leading communist states. Indeed, they have served rather to emphasise the points which divide the two countries. China, on her part, is both angered by and fearful of Russian aggression in Afghanistan and, particularly, in Cambodia and Vietnam. In November 1978, the USSR signed a Treaty of Friendship and Co-operation with Vietnam, an act which emphasised Russia's support for the Vietnamese invasion of Kampuchea (as Cambodia has become known). Russia shipped tanks and heavy artillery to Haiphong; SAM missiles were sent to strengthen Vietnam's air defence units; 5,000 Soviet advisers and hundreds of Cubans were sent to Kampuchea to support the invading Vietnamese. In return, the Vietnamese government allows the Russian Pacific Fleet to use Danang and Camranh Bay naval bases (both built by the USA in the 1960s) for operations in the South China Sea, the Indian and Pacific Oceans.

China has already fought an unsuccessful war against Vietnam, and regards Russian aid to her southern neighbour as an anti-Chinese move. Equally, she sees the Russian invasion of Afghanistan as an attempt to gain power and influence in another country bordering on China. China already faces the Russian SS20s which are stationed along the northern border with Russia; she fears that Afghanistan may become yet another base for the stationing of Russian missiles.

In the current Sino-Russian talks, China urges a Russian withdrawal from Afghanistan, Vietnam and Kampuchea. Chernenko, on the other hand, has said that Russia 'cannot make any agreement to the prejudice of the interests of third countries' such as Afghanistan and Vietnam. While the two communist giants hold to these diametrically opposed and entrenched positions, there cannot be any rapprochement and, for the time being, the US can afford to consider China as, at least, a benevolent neutral. This may help to explain why the Reagan administration held discussions in the spring of 1984 with the Chinese government, which wanted to buy US arms, including anti-aircraft and anti-tank weaponry. These, both sides claimed, would be used for defensive purposes so that they ought not to affect US relations with Taiwan. However, the sale of such weapons to Peking would be taken by the Russians as an 'unfriendly act', one which would deepen the hostility between Russia and China while ensuring the maintenance of the frigidity of US–USSR relations.

Documentary evidence

Both Khruschev (Document 12.1) and Kennedy (pp. 249–50) claimed a victory at the end of the Cuban crisis of 1962. The Chinese government saw it as a sign of Soviet weakness in the face of 'nuclear blackmail and nuclear threats' (Document 12.2). The Chinese government had once mocked the atomic bomb as a 'a paper tiger' (Document 12.2) but China joined the 'nuclear club' when she exploded her own atomic bomb in 1964. Like the Soviet Union and the nuclear powers of the Western Alliance, China protests that possession of such weapons is one of her methods of ensuring world peace.

It is a salutary reminder of the seeming permanence of the external policies of Russian governments that a commentator sees a strong continuity in their aims 'since the foundation of the Kiev state in the ninth century . . .'. (Document 12.3).

Document 12.1

The Cuban missile crisis, 1962

'I will explain what the Caribbean crisis of October 1962, was all about. . . . After Castro's crushing victory over the counter-revolutionaries we intensified our military aid to Cuba . . . we were quite sure that the Americans would never reconcile themselves to the existence of Castro's Cuba. They feared, as much as we hoped, that a Socialist Cuba might become a magnet that would attract other Latin American countries to Socialism. . . . The fate of Cuba and the maintenance of Soviet prestige in that part of the world preoccupied me. . . . We had to establish a tangible and effective deterrent to American interference in the Caribbean. . . . The logical answer was missiles. . . . I had the idea of installing missiles with nuclear warheads in Cuba without letting the United States find out they were there until it was too late to do anything about them. . . . We had no desire to start a war. . . .

. . . We sent the Americans a note saying that we agreed to remove our missiles and bombers on the condition that the President give us his assurance that there would be no invasion of Cuba by the forces of the United States or anybody else. Finally Kennedy gave in and agreed to make a statement giving us such an assurance. . . . It had been, to say the least, an interesting and challenging situation. The two most powerful nations of the world had been squared off against each other, each with its finger on the button. . . . It was a great victory for us though . . . a triumph of Soviet foreign policy . . . a spectacular success without having to fire a single shot!'

(Khruschev Remembers, pp. 488–506)

Document 12.2

China and the bomb, 1964

'China exploded an atomic bomb at 15.00 hours on 16 October 1964, thereby carrying out its first nuclear test. This is a major achievement of the Chinese people in their struggle to strengthen their national defence and oppose the US imperialist policy of nuclear blackmail and nuclear threats. . . . The mastering of the nuclear weapon by China is a great encouragement to the revolutionary peoples of the world in their struggles, and a great contribution to the cause of defending world peace. . . . China is conducting nuclear tests and developing nuclear weapons under compulsion. The Chinese Government has consistently advocated the complete prohibition and thorough destruction of nuclear weapons . . . But our proposal has met with stubborn resistance from the US imperialists. The Chinese Government pointed out long ago that the treaty on the partial halting of nuclear tests signed in Moscow in July 1963 by the US, Britain and the Soviet Union was a big fraud to fool the people of the world. . . . "The atomic bomb is a paper tiger." This famous statement by Chairman Mao Tse-tung is known to all . . . and this is still our view. China is developing nuclear weapons . . . to break the nuclear monopoly of the nuclear powers and to eliminate nuclear weapons. . . . China will never be the first to use nuclear weapons. . . .'

(Statement of the Government of the People's Republic of China, 16 October 1964)

Document 12.3

The aggressive continuum in Russian foreign policy

'Since the foundation of the Kiev state in the ninth century, Russia has been expanding, despite temporary setbacks, until it has become the immense empire that is still expanding today . . . It has been a defensive expansion, based on the insecurity of a nation . . . invaded from one side or another for a thousand years [and] suffering massacre and devastation in almost every generation – [a] nation [which] has had no other recourse than to push the hostile and encircling foreigners ever farther back. So the empire has grown, and so the Russian state has come to regard the outside world as made up of deadly enemies who must be foiled by guile, by deceit, and ultimately by as much military force as the state can generate. It is not too much to say that the outlook of the Russian state . . . has become paranoiac. This is not something the rest of the world can change by its own behaviour except over historical time.'

(Louis Halle, *The Times*, April 1980)

FURTHER READING

BEGGS, R., *The Cuban Missile Crisis*, Longman, 1971

BRANDT, W., *A Peace Policy for Europe*, 1969

BROWN, A. and GRAY, J., *Political Culture and Political Change in Communist States*, Macmillan, 1977

BROWN, A. and KASER, M., *The Soviet Union since the fall of Khruschev*, Macmillan, 1979

BUCHAN, A., *The End of the Post-War Era*, Weidenfeld and Nicolson, 1974

CALLO, D., *The German Problem Reconsidered*, 1978

DAVISHKA, K. and HANSON, P., eds., *Soviet East European Dilemmas*, Heinemann, 1981

DE PORTE, A. W., *Europe between the Superpowers*, Yale, 1979

EDMONDS, R., *Soviet Foreign Policy, 1963–73*, OUP, 1975

GARVER, J. W., *China's Decision for Rapprochement with the USA, 1968–71*, Westview Press, 1983

GARVEY, T., *Bones of Contention: An Enquiry into East-West Relations*, Routledge and Kegan Paul, 1978

GROSSER, A., *The Western Alliance*, Macmillan, 1980

HANSON, P., *Trade and Technology in Soviet-Western Relations*, Macmillan, 1981

KAISER, R. G., *Russia*, Secker and Warburg, 1976

KHRUSCHEV, N. S., *Khruschev Remembers*, Penguin, 1974

KISSINGER, H., *The White House Years*, Weidenfeld and Nicolson, 1982

KISSINGER, H., *Years of Upheaval*, Weidenfeld and Nicolson, 1979

LAQUEUR, W. and RUBIN, B., eds., *The Human Rights Reader*, New American Library, 1979

MCCAULEY, M., ed., *The Soviet Union since Brezhnev*, Heinemann, 1983

MAYALL, J. and NAVARI, C., *The End of the Post-War Era: Documents on Great Power Relations, 1968–75*, CUP, 1980

PIPES, R., *Soviet Strategy in Europe*, Macdonald and Jane's, 1976

RIGBY, T., et al., eds., *Authority, Power and Policy in the USSR*, Macmillan, 1980

RUBINSTEIN, A. Z., *Soviet Foreign Policy since World War II: Imperial and Global*, Prentice-Hall Int., 1983

SHORT, P., *The Dragon and the Bear: Inside China and Russia Today*, Abacus, 1982

URBAN, G. R., *Détente*, Temple Smith, 1977

13

Détente: Successes and failures, 1969–84

SALT One, 1969–77

'A new "golden age" has arrived. Let the sceptics scoff; ten years hence they will be convinced. The world is moving towards generations of peace.'[1]

The Washington Post, October 1972

In the mid-1960s there were preliminary discussions between Moscow and Washington about the possibilities of negotiations on strategic arms limitations (SALT). The Russians were not enthusiastic; the superiority which the Americans then enjoyed suggested that any agreement would maintain indefinitely the US superiority in missiles. By 1968 the Russians were rapidly increasing their missile output (p. 258) and might have been willing to start negotiations, but the Johnson government's involvement in the Vietnam War and the Soviet invasion of Czechoslovakia made negotiations impossible. For Brezhnev, the unity of the Eastern bloc was more important than détente with the West. In November 1968 he justified the invasion with the 'Brezhnev Doctrine': the right of the socialist community to intervene in the territories of one of its members when internal and external forces hostile to Communism tried to restore a capitalist-style régime. The western powers could only object to this restriction on a nation's territorial, sovereign and human rights.

On 20 January 1969, as Nixon was being inaugurated as US President, the Soviet Foreign Ministry announced that Russia was prepared to negotiate on 'the mutual limitation and subsequent reduction of strategic delivery vehicles, including defensive systems'. The US replied favourably early in February. However, negotiations did not begin until November 1969; both sides had to work out their bargaining positions. The Americans, for example, considered the possibility of linking weapons negotiations to the lessening of political tensions in Europe, the Middle East and Asia. In the end they accepted that missile negotiations were, *per se*, sufficiently important a subject;

they therefore ignored the Russian re-arming of Egypt, the build-up of the Russian fleet in the Mediterranean and the continued clash with the Russian-backed forces in Vietnam. On their side, the Russians took into account the deepening division with China and the diversion of their forces to the Far East as well as the potentially crippling costs of the continued escalation of weapons development. Having achieved strategic equality with the USA, the Russians were prepared to try to come to terms with their rival. For Russia, as for the USA in 1969, the essence of détente was essentially a military concept.

The negotiations took place in Helsinki and Vienna between November 1969 and 1972. The bi-polar nature of the negotiations emphasised the true state of international affairs. The US kept its European allies informed of the progress of the talks but did not consult them; Britain, co-signatory of the 1963 Test Ban Treaty, was not involved in these SALT negotiations.

While the negotiators met at Helsinki and Vienna there were non-military pressures building up on both sides. Russia had had a poor harvest, following the severe winter of 1971–2 which, coupled with the growth in population, led to a food shortage. She had to buy 32 million tons of grain from Canada and the USA (p. 124). At the same time, Nixon's economic advisers were alarmed at the growing trade deficit and the weakening of the dollar (pp. 147–50). They saw Russia as a potentially large market for medium and high technology goods, provided that the US amended its definition of 'strategic' goods whose exports to Russia were banned. Already the US was beginning to consider trade and technology as levers which might be used to bring the Russians to terms.

While the negotiations were still in progress the two powers issued a list of twelve Basic Principles which outlined the responsibilities each had to the other and which both had to the international community as a whole. These did not make any ideological concessions on either side; they were concerned with environmental protection, an agreement about conduct in space research and a promise to avoid 'incidents at sea'. The two countries set up a US-USSR commercial commission which organised a trade agreement in October 1972. This provided for some 500 million dollars of trade, a figure which was doubled in 1973. Kissinger was creating that 'web of interests' (p. 263).

In November 1972 two agreements (usually known as SALT One) were signed. One, of unlimited duration, was the Treaty on the Limitation of Defensive Anti-Ballistic Missiles (ABMs). This Treaty restricted each power to having only two complexes of 100 ABMs, one to cover their respective capitals, the other to cover one complex of ICBM launch silos. This agreement also forbade the transfer of ABM systems to any other country – in Europe or the Far East, for example. This concession by the USA was matched by the Russians' concessions which appeared in the second agreement, the Interim Agreement on Certain Measures with Respect to the Limitation of Strategic Arms.

This 'Interim Agreement' was to last until 3 October 1977 and would ensure that the level of missile numbers would remain at the level which would be reached by 1 July 1972. After that date, there would be no construction of 'fixed land-based inter-continental ballistic missile launchers'.

The US accepted the quantitative inferiority involved, because of their qualitative superiority. Both sides connived at the ambiguity and uncertainty of parts of the agreement. There was no mention of the modernisation of weapons or the replacement of older missiles by new, more sophisticated ones, essential if the US was to maintain its qualitative superiority. The agreement specifically forbade the replacement of 'light' by 'heavy' missiles; it failed, however, to define 'heavy', while it did allow the enlargement of existing missile silos – to take, presumably, larger and 'heavier' missiles.

Almost before the ink was dry on the SALT agreement, a new generation of Soviet MIRV missiles was being built; they were deployed in 1975. These SS-17, SS-18 and SS-19 weapons fitted into the quantitative limits set by SALT One. They were, however, much longer range, more accurate and of greater megatonnage than the missiles which they replaced. Russian technology also produced the SS-20 mobile launcher (deployed in 1977), which threatened the American fixed-silo Minutemen and so threatened the US second strike capability. On its side, the US developed the 'cruise' missile which did not fit into any of the SALT One categories. This is a sonic-speed 'flying bomb' which has a pinpoint accuracy over ranges exceeding 2,000 miles. The US claimed that it was a tactical and not a strategic weapon (in SALT One terms). The Russians, however, saw it as a major threat to their existing systems. Other new developments had similar effects of blurring the significance of SALT One, while providing threats to one side or the other. The Russians produced their Backfire bomber which could fly in inter-continental strategic missions. The Americans retaliated with the B-1 inter-continental bomber, the Trident SLBM to replace Polaris, and new warheads to increase the accuracy and penetration of the Minutemen targeted on hardened Soviet silos.

These post-SALT One developments took place against a critical background. Brezhnev had agreed in May 1972 not to try 'to obtain unilateral advantage at the expense of' the USA. In spite of that Moscow agreement, the Soviets intervened in Angola in 1975 where, via their Cuban proxy, Soviet arms won more influence for the Russians. It is little wonder that, after 1975, there were calls in the US for the abandonment of the search for détente.

The Conference on Security and Co-operation in Europe (CSCE), 1973–5

'At the beginning of 1973 the ordinary citizen might pardonably feel that for the first time in forty years (that is, since the Japanese invasion of Manchuria or Hitler's re-occupation of the Rhineland) something that could be called peace had descended on the world.'[2]

Alastair Buchan, 1974

During the SALT negotiations, the Russians had asked for a European Security Conference. The USA, already involved in winding down the Vietnam War and in developing closer Sino-US relations, preferred to concentrate on SALT. Britain and France, the European members of the nuclear 'club', were also hesitant in their initial response to this Russian suggestion. When Nixon and Brezhnev met in Moscow in May 1972, the SALT negotiators had almost completed their task. The two leaders agreed that 'multilateral consultations looking towards a conference on security and co-operation in Europe' could begin after 'careful preparation' but without 'undue delay'. They were careful to emphasise that this Conference was not to concern itself with the question of the size of the forces deployed by NATO and the Warsaw Pact. These forces were to be the subject of separate negotiations (below).

The CSCE opened in Helsinki in July 1973 and went on, in Helsinki and Geneva, until the 'Final Act' was signed in Helsinki on 1 August 1975. Thirty-five heads of state or government signed that 'Final Act', negotiated by multi-national teams which worked together for 22 months (Figure 13.1). The 'Final Act' was not a legally binding document, nor did it have any force in international law, although the signatories agreed to 'adopt' its terms. There was no machinery of enforcement or for monitoring the degree to which the participants lived up to their promises to 'adopt' the agreement.

The 'Final Act' was, in part, a follow up to Brandt's *Ostpolitik* in that it recognised the existing frontiers of Europe; there was now a multilateral agreement to the terms reached by Brandt in his negotiations with the Soviet bloc. The 'Act' called for closer economic and technological collaboration, for that 'web of interests' which Kissinger and Pym believed would lead to wider political agreement. Perhaps the wider public was more interested in what became known as 'Basket Three' of the 'Act' – ten principles to be adopted as guides to relations between the signatories. These included the promise to respect 'human rights' (Document 13.1) and to provide facilities for 'Co-operation in Humanitarian and Other Fields'.

Cynics noted that this 'Third Basket' contained nothing new; its terms had been spelt out in international documents such as the UN Charter on Human Rights (Document 1.1). Given the history of the post-war world, why should the West expect the Russian leopard to change its repressive spots because of a non-binding 'agreement' signed at Helsinki? Moreover, the critics claimed, the 'Final Act' had provided the Russians with formal recognition of the gains they had made in Europe since 1944; where, now, was the promise to 'roll back' the

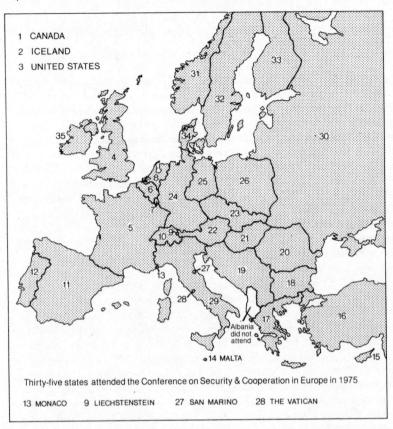

1 CANADA
2 ICELAND
3 UNITED STATES

Albania did not attend

14 MALTA

Thirty-five states attended the Conference on Security & Cooperation in Europe in 1975

13 MONACO   9 LIECHTENSTEIN   27 SAN MARINO   28 THE VATICAN

13.1 Thirty-five countries took part in the Helsinki talks which ended with the signing of the Agreement in 1975. (See Figs. 10.1 and 11.2, pp. 217 and 236, for the divisions inside the continent).

frontiers of Communism? Finally, said the cynics, the 'Act' had not reduced the size of armed forces on either side of the Iron Curtain; the Russian expansion of its conventional forces and its stockpile of sophisticated weapons went on.

On the other hand, western optimists argued that the 'Final Act' was a significant marker on the road to détente. The Russians had, again, been made to sign a document which could be used against them in future disputes over human rights. This updating of the responsibilities accepted by the signing of the UN Charter (Document 1.1) brought the issue of these rights to the attention of a new generation – on both sides of the Iron Curtain – to whom the Universal Declaration of 1948 was merely history. Furthermore, the 'linkage' of the economies of East and West Europe would not only provide economic benefits to western industry; it would also bring about the hoped for 'rising expectations' in the East which would be, said the optimists, the forerunner to the demand for democratisation (p. 263).

The years immediately following the signing of the Helsinki Agreements showed that the Russians had not changed their spots, that the cynics had been right. In Russia itself, and in the other satellite states of eastern Europe, dissidents were harassed and imprisoned as was shown by both the claims of and the treatment of the Charter 77 group in Czechoslovakia, and by the Russian treatment of such dissident leaders as Sakharov (p. 129). In 1977 Brezhnev addressed the Sixteenth Trade Union Council of the USSR. In this speech he condemned Russia's critics for trying to interfere in her internal affairs by their condemnation of Russia's record on human rights (Document 13.2). On the other side, Carter, who had placed much hope on Helsinki, was forced to become increasingly critical of Russia and its leaders' attitudes towards human rights.

In 1975 the signatories of the 'Final Act' had agreed that they would meet in Belgrade in 1977 to review the progress that had been made towards the implementation of the 'Final Act'. Carter had already affirmed 'America's commitment to human rights as a fundamental tenet of our foreign policy'. With Brezhnev condemning such attempts at 'interference with our internal affairs', it is small wonder that the Belgrade Conference consisted largely of charge and counter-charge. Subsequent conferences of the 35 nations which signed the 1975 Agreement have seemingly abandoned the futile search for agreement on the definition of human rights; western participants no longer waste much time on condemning Russian behaviour. Instead there has been a switch of attention away from human rights to the problems of disarmament. In January 1984 delegates from the 35 nations opened the Conference on Confidence and Security-building in Stockholm. Few people expected that Conference to make much progress; its first phase was expected to continue until the next Helsinki Review Conference is due to meet in Vienna at the end of 1986. There is little, now, of that earlier optimism expressed by Buchan in 1974 (pp. 270–1).

SALT Two, 1974–9

'Détente is a process of managing relations with a potentially hostile country in order to preserve the peace while maintaining our vital interests.'[3]

Kissinger, 1974

'The class struggle of the two systems in the form of economics, politics and ideology will be continued. But we shall ensure that this inevitable struggle is transferred to a channel which does not threaten wars, dangerous conflicts and an uncontrolled arms race.'[4]

Brezhnev, June 1973

In the winter of 1972–3, after Nixon's re-election, negotiations opened for SALT Two which Kissinger and Nixon hoped would take the form of a fundamental review of the needs of the world as a whole. This optimism disappeared in the wake of the Watergate scandals and Nixon's resignation in August 1974. It is likely that, even if Nixon had been unscathed by scandal, there would have been major difficulties attached to a new set of negotiations. The 'interim agreement' of 1972 had not, yet, been converted into a permanent treaty, largely because of the problems created, since 1972, by the technological advances noted on p. 270.

In particular the Russians were alarmed by the US lead in the development of MIRVs which led to a disparity in the numbers of warheads deployed by each side.

However, for a time there were hopeful signs. The atmosphere of cordiality was emphasised by Brezhnev when he visited Washington in June 1973 to sign the Agreement on the Prevention of Nuclear War. On television he announced to the American people that 'mankind has outgrown the rigid armour of the Cold War which it once had to wear'. In July 1974, Nixon visited Moscow where he and Brezhnev signed an agreement to reduce the number of ABM sites from two to one. The two leaders also signed a treaty banning the underground testing of nuclear weapons with yields above 150 kilotons. Talks were also started on further 'threshold test bans'. The Russians claimed that they used 'peaceful nuclear explosions' (PNEs) in such developments as the digging of canals, the excavation of harbours and the alteration of the course of rivers in their development of the vast Siberian wilderness. The Americans feared that these might be, in reality, evasions of the Test Ban Treaty of 1963. They insisted that PNEs had to be subject to on-site verification by outside inspection. Only in 1976 was agreement reached on this issue, the delay being due, largely, to Russian fears of 'foreign spies' coming to Russia.

Nixon and Brezhnev had agreed to meet at Vladivostock in November 1974 to review progress on SALT One and to prepare the ground for SALT Two. However, following Nixon's resignation, it was President Ford who met Brezhnev. Ford's attitude towards possible agreements with the Russians was coloured by two major factors. In the USA there was growing criticism of the behaviour of the Russians, who paid lip service to human rights in the continuing talks at Helsinki (pp. 271–3) but who violated those rights in practice (Figure 13.2). There was further criticism of the continued Russian violation of the agreement reached at the 1972 summit, when Russia had agreed not to seek unilateral advantage, which, in reality, she was doing in Angola and Mozambique. Perhaps more significantly, the US Congress had become more conscious of its powers during the Watergate crisis and was less prepared to be 'smooth talked' into accepting presidential policy.

Evidence of Congress's new attitude was provided during the debate on the US–USSR trade bill in 1974. Kissinger and Nixon had seen the bill as part of that 'web of interests', as part of that 'leverage' which they believed they would be able to exercise on the Russians. They could point to the Russian agreement to permit large-scale Jewish emigration to take place. It was left to Senator Jackson to point out that, in fact, 'the Emperor had no clothes on', that, in reality, the Russians were not fulfilling their promise. He proposed amendments to the trade bill. This would permit the extension of 'favours' to Russia only on condition that the Russians lived up to their promises (Document 13.3). Kissinger tried to halt this 'blackmailing attempt' to control US–USSR relations, but in the post-Watergate climate Congress would not be denied. The Russians, in retaliation, suspended the operation of the trade agreement; they would not be driven to live up to their promises.

'Nuts Are for Cracking.'

13.2 Brezhnev and dissent, 1980.

In spite of this, Kissinger still travelled hopefully. His critics argued that 'linkage' would work only when the USA could force the Russians to accept a quid pro quo. Kissinger could have influenced Russian policy in Angola by threatening to call off the SALT negotiations. However, on their side, the Russians knew that arms control was as important to the Americans as to themselves; the taxpayers in the USA would not approve a continued escalation of defence spending. However, in January 1976 Kissinger went, again, to Moscow, hoping to get agreement on the limitation of the numbers of the new and more sophisticated weapons which had been developed since 1972. The negotiations were still under way when Carter became President in January 1977.

Carter had made 'human rights' a central part of his electoral platform. In his first days in office he made it clear that détente could be carried no further until the Russians had shown that they were ready to comply fully with the agreements reached in 1972 and 1975. He published a letter he wrote to Sakharov, the leading Russian dissident; he received at the White House another dissident, Bukovsky; he condemned Russian violation of human rights in its Czechoslovak satellite. All this marked what appeared to be a radical shift in US attitudes.

That shift was illustrated by the proposals which the new Secretary of State, Vance, took to Moscow in March 1977. The Americans claimed that this was 'the first truly disarmament-orientated proposal introduced in SALT'. Vance wanted a lowering of strategic delivery vehicles of all sorts from the Vladivostock-agreed figure of 2,400 to somewhere between 1,800 and 2,000, while the ceiling on MIRV missiles should be reduced from the agreed 1,320 to somewhere between 1,100 and 1,200. He wanted a freeze on modification of existing ICBMs, the abandonment of the plan for deployment of mobile missiles and the prohibition of the production of 'cruise' missiles and Backfire bombers.

If the Russians would not accept such a change in scale, Vance was prepared to accept a SALT agreement which contained the Vladivostock ceilings only. This would leave the Russian Backfire bombers and the US 'cruise' missiles to be dealt with in subsequent negotiations.

Many influential Americans hoped that these disarmament proposals would be rejected. The industrial-military complex feared a reduction in arms and a loss of contracts, profits and jobs. The 'hawks' in the national security system feared that, once again, the Russians would outwit the 'naive' American negotiators. There were equally powerful influences in Russia insisting on the rejection of the US proposals. The lowering of the Vladivostock ceilings would require a cut in the Soviet ICBM strength while leaving the US force untouched, because it had already been lowered following SALT One. The proposed freeze on modification and deployment of ICBMs required a cut in the development of SS-18s and the abandonment of the SS-20 which was about to be deployed. This new weapon was at the centre of Russian defence strategy.

The Russians rejected Vance's proposals, claiming that the US was seeking a unilateral advantage and that Russia would 'never' agree to destroy half its rockets merely because the Americans thought them 'too heavy' or 'too effective'. However, behind this public rhetoric, the statesmen from both sides had, in fact, set up working groups to discuss the possibilities of reaching agreements on less substantive issues. In May 1977 Vance and the Russian Foreign Minister, Gromyko, met in Geneva to agree on a 'three-tiered framework' within which they planned the signing of a SALT Two agreement to last until 1985, a separate agreement (to run for three years) on the Backfire bomber and cruise missiles, and, thirdly 'a statement of principles' to point the way to further reduction in strategic arms.

Carter took a softer line when, in June 1977, he postponed the deployment of the Mark 12-A warhead and the production of the B-1 superbomber. He also pointed out, in a speech in July, that the US had made fresh proposals to the Russians about the cruise missiles. Gromyko also took a softer line when, in September, he indicated that a SALT Two was 'completely possible'.

He visited the USA later in September. His report back to Russia was sufficiently optimistic for Brezhnev to announce, in October, that the SALT negotiations had 'taken a turn for the better'. The Russians and Americans agreed, as a first step, to extend, informally, the life of the 1972 'Interim Agreement' which was due to expire in October 1977. This had enabled the Russians to gain and maintain not only equivalence but also invulnerability to an American first strike while the US strength had remained relatively static.

Carter was anxious to reduce nuclear armaments. In February 1979 he spoke of the danger of uncontrolled nuclear development:

'Each crisis, each confrontation, each point of friction – as serious as it may be in its own right – will take on an added measure of significance and an added measure of danger. It is precisely because we have fundamental differences with the Soviet Union that we are determined to bring this dangerous element of our military competition under control.'

Carter and Brezhnev signed SALT Two in Vienna on 18 June 1979. This new Agreement defined precisely the weaponry available to each superpower up to 1985. Carter called it 'the most detailed, far-reaching, comprehensive treaty in the history of arms control'. The weapons allowed were:

	USA	USSR
ICBMs	1054	1398
ICBMs & MIRVs	550	608
SLBMs	656	950
SLBMs & MIRVs	496	144
Heavy Bombers	573	156

This grisly list was based on the number of such weapons possessed by the superpowers on 1 November 1978. Replacement of obsolete weapons was to be permitted within these figures.

The SALT Two Treaty was presented to the US Senate in June 1979. By then there had been a major shift in US public opinion against détente; there was increasing anger at Russian violation of existing agreements and its disregard for the Helsinki promises; there was both anger and frustration at the US inability to free the hostages held by the Iranian radicals in the Embassy at Teheran while, on the other hand, the Russians seemed to succeed in gaining influence in Africa and in Asia where they supported Vietnam's invasion of Kampuchea. The Senate responded to this 'hawkish' public opinion by refusing to ratify the SALT Two agreement.

The Russians, like the Bourbons, seemed to have 'forgotten nothing and learnt nothing'. They had not forgotten their long-term aim of achieving the final victory of messianic Communism over capitalism; they had not learnt that their behaviour since 1975 had led to the emergence of anti-Soviet feeling in the free world which, earlier, had placed great store by détente. At the end of 1979 the Russians invaded Afghanistan to overthrow an existing Marxist government and to put an even more amenable puppet into power (Document 13.4). For many westerners this was the last of the many incidents which would force western governments to concede that Russia would not 'exercise restraint' but would continue to employ, in Africa and in Asia, 'the Salami technique' once so successful in Europe.

Carter's response to the invasion served to illustrate the inability of even the nuclear-strong USA to counter Russian aggression. He proposed a boycott of the Moscow Olympics due to open later in 1980, a restriction on those cultural exchanges by which Kissinger laid such store, the suspension of credits to Russia and a ban on the sale of high technology items, and a postponement of further consideration of SALT Two. But it was noticeable that he proposed only a partial ban on the sale of US grain to Russia; he feared the backlash of the anger of US farmer-voters in an election year. And, as could have been foreseen, none of this deterred the Russians, who held the Olympic Games and used western criticism of the Fatherland to call for even greater loyalty on the part of the 'besieged' Russian people, whose nationalism and traditional anti-westernism was reinforced throughout 1980.

Mutual and Balanced Force Reductions (MBFR) 1973–84

'The World is unhappy. It is unhappy because it does not know where it is going, and because it guessed that if it should know, it would be to discover that it is going towards catastrophe.'

Giscard d'Estaing, 1974

In June 1968 the NATO council had proposed that steps should be taken to bring about mutual and balanced force reductions (MBFR) in concert with the Warsaw Pact countries. By 1971, Brezhnev was working for détente in other fields and, realising that there was every chance of success in the SALT field, he agreed, in a speech in Tblisi, that Russia was prepared to consider MBFR in Europe. In the Moscow summit with Nixon in May 1972 he agreed that preparations should go ahead for negotiations on MBFR, but separately from the Conference on Security and Co-operation in Europe negotiations.

MBFR talks opened in Vienna in January 1974. The Russian team presented a less-than-flexible approach; they refused to reveal the size of the Warsaw Pact forces and they made it clear that they were seeking to retain the military superiority of that Pact's forces in Central Europe. NATO negotiators believed that their forces were outnumbered by Warsaw Pact forces by some 150,000 men, while the Pact countries' tank strength (16,000) far outnumbered that of the NATO forces (6,700) as did the number of Warsaw Pact aircraft (3,075 to 1,344). The majority of the Warsaw Pact forces were provided by the Soviet Union which claimed that they were defensive in character. The nature of that defensive posture has, however, changed since 1974 as new weapons have been developed; the new multi-role aircraft, for example, have offensive as well as defensive capabilities. This change has been matched by others, so that the qualitative superiority which the NATO forces once enjoyed (as distinct from their quantitative inferiority) has been eroded.

This erosion, this changing pattern of Soviet forces, may explain why there has been no progress in this series of negotiations. The failure may also be seen as the by-product of the West's realisation that, after Helsinki, the Russians had no real interest in détente as understood in the West. In January 1984 the diplomatic correspondent of the *Daily Telegraph* wrote: 'The Soviet Union will return to the Vienna talks on troop reductions in central Europe on March 16 but since its bored delegations have done little more in 10 years than design a club tie, that may be of mainly cosmetic significance.'[5]

A new stance by the West, 1980–4

'Where the age-old antagonism between freedom and tyranny is concerned, we are not neutral. But other imperatives impose limits on our ability to produce internal changes in foreign countries. Consciousness of our limits is recognition of the necessity of peace – not moral callousness. The preservation of human life and human society are moral values, too.'[6]

Kissinger, 1977

'Human rights may be defined as the right to live under a rule of law that protects against cruel, arbitrary and degrading treatment, to participate in government and its decisions, to voice opinion freely, to seek peaceful change.'[7]

Secretary of State Vance, 1977

In May 1979, Margaret Thatcher became Britain's first woman Prime Minister. Within a short time her critical comments on Russia's failure to live up to the terms of the recently signed agreements earned her the nickname, in Iron Curtain countries, of 'The Iron Lady'. But she was not alone in her criticism. There was a dramatic change in the American national mood. By May 1980 public opinion was running ahead of even the most hawkish members of Carter's administration. Brzezinski took note of this change when he spoke to a gathering at Los Angeles:

> 'We, as a people, must avoid swinging from euphoria about détente to hysteria about the Cold War. The problem we confront is not one of a head-on confrontation with the Soviet Union, but rather the danger that in some vital part of the world there will be a progressive disintegration of existing political structures resulting in an expansion of direct Soviet influence.'[8]

By the end of 1980, Ronald Reagan was on his hawkish way to the White House having advocated, during his electoral campaign, a more combative and unyielding policy towards the Russians that was in tune with the new assertiveness in the country as a whole.

In November 1981, Soviet-American talks opened in Geneva on the limitation of intermediate nuclear forces (INF) in Europe. The Russians made no prior commitment to 'exercise restraint' before entering these talks; there was to be no linkage of trade or human rights with these talks. Nor did the Americans call off the talks when the Russians ordered a state of emergency to be declared in Poland.

Brezhnev offered 'very substantial reductions' in Soviet intermediate range missiles if the West would renounce the deployment of Pershing-2 and cruise missiles. NATO, on the other hand, proposed that there should be a 'zero option' – that both superpowers would dismantle all their long-range theatre force systems. Neither of these were realistic proposals; but the Russian proposal did take account of Soviet superiority in weapon numbers, something which the Russians had previously denied. While these Geneva talks went through their preliminary ritualistic pavane, with claims and counter-claims being made in an effort to build up a negotiating position, Reagan ordered the reinstatement of plans to manufacture the neutron bomb which would kill or immobilise human beings while leaving buildings untouched. He also set in train, again, the manufacturing of the B-1 bomber which Carter had cancelled in his search for détente. The President also promised to increase defence spending from 27 per cent of the national budget in 1982 to 37 per cent by 1986. At the same time as he took this hard line, he also lifted the grain embargo, so that he seemed to be reverting to the Nixon stance of mixing military toughness with 'linkage'.

US refusal to halt the deployment of Pershing-2 and cruise missiles led the Russians to call off all talks for some time, only to agree later to their resumption. Thus the INF talks (on the deployment of long-range weapons in Europe) had a chequered history; they opened in Geneva in December 1981, survived Soviet walk-outs and reluctant resumptions until, in January 1984, they seemed to have collapsed, again, in the wake of a 'final' Russian walk-out. The Russians had hinted that they would put their SS-20 missiles on the territory of Warsaw Pact allies, so threatening Western Europe, unless the US agreed not to deploy Pershing-2 and cruise missiles. Reagan, addressing the UN in September 1983, offered some limited concessions which the new Soviet President, Andropov, denounced as mere 'prattling about a burning issue' by which Reagan sought to create a 'deceptive' screen to cover the reality of the deployment so feared by the Russians. They were angered by Reagan's reference to their 'evil empire'. Reagan's Vice-President, Bush, made a blistering attack on the Soviet system in a speech at Vienna made shortly after the shooting down of the Korean airliner (below). In his aggressive speech Bush referred to the 'ill-fated Yalta Conference' which had divided Europe into 'spheres of influence'. He spoke of 'the wound which runs through the heart of Europe' and, in terms reminiscent of Dulles in his 'roll back days', he called for 'a united Central Europe free from the alien influence of the Soviet Union'. The states of eastern Europe, said Bush, should choose to free themselves from Soviet domination and join the Free World. Either that, he said, or they would be forever condemned to what he called a life of ignorance, backwardness and poverty.

Behind this Cold War rhetoric, Reagan and his advisers showed that they were prepared to negotiate. In June 1982 Reagan called for a re-opening of talks on Strategic Arms Limitation. With SALT Two a bad memory in the USA, a new acronym was found and these talks were given START – in the hope that there would indeed be a fresh start to the process which had been halted in 1979. The talks resumed in October 1983, but in February 1984 there had been no progress to report, as the Soviet negotiators take soundings in a Russia which has had two successive changes of leadership in a mere two years.

Under the leadership of 'the Iron Lady' and the realistic Chancellor Schmidt of West Germany (who was in power until 1982) the powers of the European Economic Community came together to work out a new, more united policy than the derisively disjointed one which had been followed in 1979 when the Russians invaded Afghanistan. Some member-states voted to allow the US to install cruise missiles on their territory, partly to aid the US in its negotiating with Russia, partly to ensure their own safety. This has given rise to a resurgence of the Campaign for Nuclear Disarmament throughout Europe; its members seek to compel their governments to rid their countries of these missiles and, if need be, to withdraw from NATO which shelters beneath the protection of the US nuclear force.

The support for the hard-liners grew in the wake of the shooting down on 1 September 1983 of a Korean aircraft which had wandered off course and strayed into sensitive military zones in the Soviet Union's Far East region near Japan and Korea. Two hundred and sixty passengers were killed by the Soviet attack, which was justified by the accusation that the civilian passenger-carrying plane was, in fact, 'on an American spying mission over Soviet sacred territory'. Even this admission, that the plane had been shot down by a Soviet fighter, was not revealed for some days after the disappearance of the 747 jumbo. The revulsion in the West was such as almost to justify the claim that 'one startling development can help alter the course of history'. Certainly it helped the Reagan-Thatcher cause as regards the deployment of missiles. It also stripped away a few more of the remaining illusions about Soviet interest in human rights.

Reagan also reversed, at least in part, the Kissinger-Nixon process of creating that 'web of interests' through trade agreements. He used the powers given him under the Export Administration Act to impose sanctions on US and foreign companies which violate export bans imposed for foreign policy or security reasons. This Act was invoked in 1982 to try to end, or, at least, limit the participation by European firms in the construction of the gas pipelines from the Soviet Union to Western Europe. The European firms did not accept the US guidelines, pointing out also the peculiar position taken by the US administration, which, while trying to harm the Russian economy via controls over European firms, was seemingly afraid to impose sanctions on the sale of grain to Russia. This, the Europeans noted, would have hurt US farmers and the popularity of the government.

The well-publicised disagreement between the USA and its European allies provided opportunities for re-evaluating the Kissinger 'doctrine', namely that it was possible to construct a 'web of interests' between East and West. The gas pipeline from the Siberian gasfields to Western Europe is 3,600 miles long and provides supplies of natural gas for customers in Germany, France and, of course, Russia itself. Western European governments provided the money needed by the Russians to pay for the pipe, the equipment and the technicians to help lay the pipeline. Britain, for example, provided 350 million dollars. Britain, France, Germany and the other Western European governments provided this financial aid by way of long-term loans, which will be repaid from the earnings derived from the sale of gas to Western European countries. The Thatcher government provided the loan at below-market interest rates, thus making it harder for borrowers in Britain to obtain the money they needed for investment in Britain itself.

Firms in Britain, France and Germany competed with one another to gain the contracts to provide the pipe and equipment. Since they were suffering from the effects of the world-wide depression, they allowed the Russians to drive down the prices to be paid; France, for example, provided some pipe at 60 per cent below the market price and so succeeded in driving the perceptive Japanese from the bargaining table.

The Russians also persuaded western buyers to agree to take supplies of gas through the rest of this century at prices above the current market prices for natural gas provided by Holland, Norway and Britain. These contracts took into account the going rate of inflation. Since they were signed, the rate of inflation has come down throughout Europe, so that the purchasers of Russian natural gas are now trying, without much evident success, to persuade the Russians to re-negotiate the deal.

The Russians have benefited from these arrangements. They have a 3,600 mile pipeline for which they have had to provide no money from their own hard-pressed sources. They have the benefit of the gas supply which they will draw from the line as it passes across their vast country. This will enable them to develop a number of energy-based industries, including, for example, the manufacture of artificial fertilisers. It will ensure some economic growth in a country which has shown all too little ability to provide for its own growth. The government will enjoy the benefit of consumer satisfaction with the new gas supply, the greater availability of fertilisers and of jobs in gas-based industries.

It is, perhaps, not surprising that the Americans have made it clear that they believe the Europeans have provided for the growth of Russia's economy. Kissinger would have argued for such a development in the 1970s; he would have claimed that trade with Russia, even if it brought no evident advantage to the western supplier, was, *per se*, to be welcomed, since it was bound to ensure the growth of that interdependence which he saw as one aim of détente. The Reaganites see things differently.

In March 1984, the US government announced a further crackdown on the flow of data from US laboratories, seminars and research institutions. The ultimate aim of this set of sanctions is to prevent the Soviet system benefiting from US-based research. One of the immediate effects has been to limit the flow of such data to British and European institutions and scientists who have tended to work on a reciprocal basis with US institutions and scientists. It is argued that the latest ban will 'seriously restrict western scientific work', so that the US will be as much a loser as the other members of the western bloc.

The second prong in the administration's 'banning fork' is the tougher sanctions which will be imposed on companies that break US export embargoes. These include the power to impose an import ban on products from any US subsidiary or foreign company which violates US export controls. Closing the US markets to offending companies would cripple many of them. The US government is also seeking power to order US companies to break their supply contracts with foreign firms which refuse to accept the US export regulations. Senator Garn, spokesman for the administration's new and tougher line, dismissed the Europeans' complaints: 'For a mess of potage, for a few jobs, they are willing to sell almost anything to anyone.' A far cry from the days of Kissinger's 'web of interests'.

On their side, the hard-liners argue that events indicate that the

Eastern bloc has to, and will, come to terms with the new, harder line. They point to the Thatcher visit to Hungary in 1984 as a sign that 'the Iron Lady' is now more respected in the East precisely for her hard-line approach, which did not deter the Hungarians from inviting her to come to their country. Even more significant is the development of closer relations between East and West Germany. Chancellor Kohl became Chancellor in succession to Schmidt after the 1982 elections. Like Schmidt, he welcomed the siting of Pershing missiles in Germany. The East German leader, Honecker, warned that their siting would lead to a 'new Ice Age', presumably a chillier version of the old Cold War. However, the Pershings now deployed, Honecker has sent a message of 'personal regard' to Kohl, and the Economics Ministers of the two governments are negotiating new and more important trade deals. The East Germans have also relaxed their attitude towards people seeking to go to the West. In February 1984 some 2,600 East Germans were allowed to leave for the West – four times the total allowed exit permits in 1983. It is expected that in 1984 there will be over 20,000 permits issued.

This easing of relations is due, almost completely, to the economic imperative; a proof that Kissinger's 'web of interests' can lead to major changes. Honecker said, in February 1984, that the siting of the Pershing missiles in West Germany did not alter the need for dialogue. For the fact is that East Germany is dependent on trade with West Germany, a trade which totalled some £3.75 billion in 1983. It is this trade which allows the East Germans to have the highest living standard in the Eastern bloc. West Germany also needs that trade and provides large credits on easy terms to facilitate its continuation and development. In 1984 there will come to fruition the project to build Volkswagens under licence in East Germany, and the links between the two Germanies will be strengthened. Honecker's relaxed views on the siting of the Pershing missiles are at odds with those expressed by Moscow. It is a sign of the times that the leader of East Germany, once, under Ulbricht, 'the most faithful satellite', is taking a new and independent line.

Documentary evidence

The growing interest, in the 1970s, in the theme of human rights, was a reason for the inclusion of so-called 'Basket Three' in the Helsinki Agreement (Document 13.1), although that Agreement had its origins in politico-military considerations. Optimists in the West hoped that the Soviet government would honour this Agreement. They chose to forget that the Soviet leaders have a different concept of human rights. When some westerners tried to bring pressure to bear on the Soviet government and tried to show that it had not improved its record in the field of human rights, the Soviet leadership reacted angrily (Document 13.2).

Some members of the government headed by US President Nixon had hoped that closer economic ties between the USA and the Soviet Union would create a 'web of interests' that would smooth the path to détente. US Senator Henry Jackson led the campaign in the USA to try to create a link between favourable trade agreements and Soviet agreement to allow the free emigration from the Soviet Union of such Jews as wished to leave the country (Document 13.3). This, too, was seen, by the Soviet government, as an attempt to interfere in the internal affairs of the Soviet Union; rather than accept the provisions of the Amendment, the Soviet government rejected the favourable trade agreement.

The invasion of Afghanistan in the winter of 1979–80 (Document 13.4) was, for many, the proof that the Soviet government had its own interpretation of détente and of peaceful co-existence. That Russian expansionism of which Halle wrote (Document 12.3) was, it seemed, to go on in spite of SALT, Helsinki and other agreements. Other observers noted the weakness of the US response to this invasion and drew attention to the divisions which appeared in the Western Alliance.

Document 13.1

The Helsinki Agreement, 1975

'VII. *Respect for Human Rights and Fundamental Freedoms, Including the Freedom of Thought, Conscience, Religion or Belief*

The participating States will respect human rights and fundamental freedoms, including the freedom of thought, conscience, religion or belief, for all without distinction as to race, sex, language or religion.

They will promote and encourage the effective exercise of civil, political, economic, social, cultural and other rights and freedoms all of which derive from the inherent dignity of the human person and are essential for his free and full development.

Within this framework the participating States will recognise and respect the freedom of the individual to profess and practise, alone or in community with others, religion or belief acting in accordance with the dictates of his own conscience.

The participating States on whose territory national minorities exist will respect the right of persons belonging to such minorities to equality before the law, will afford them the full opportunity for the actual enjoyment of human rights and fundamental freedoms and will, in this manner, protect their legitimate interests in this sphere.

The participating States recognise the universal significance of human rights and fundamental freedoms, respect for which is an essential factor for the peace, justice and well-being necessary to ensure the development of friendly relations and co-operation among themselves as among all States.

They will constantly respect these rights and freedoms in their mutual relations and will endeavour jointly and separately, including in co-operation with the United Nations, to promote universal and effective respect for them.

They confirm the right of the individual to know and act upon his rights and duties in this field.

In the field of human rights and fundamental freedoms, the participating States will act in conformity with the purposes and principles of the Charter of the United Nations and with the Universal Declaration of Human Rights [Document 1.1]. They will also fulfill their obligations as set forth in the international declarations and agreements in this field, including inter alia the International Covenants on Human Rights, by which they may be bound.'

Document 13.2

Russia and 'interference': Leonid Brezhnev's speech to the Sixteenth Trade Union Council, 1977

'Attempts are being made to weaken and to undermine the solidarity of the socialist community. Attempts are also being made to weaken the socialist order. . . .

Our opponents would like to find the forces to oppose socialism from within our countries. Since there are no such forces, however, as there are no oppressed, exploited classes within socialist society, and no repressed nationalities, false publicity is being used to create the appearance of 'internal opposition'. It is exactly for this reason that a clamour is being raised about the so-called 'dissidents' and about 'the violation of human rights' in socialist countries. . . .

The Soviet Union does not interfere in the internal affairs of other countries, although we do have our own firm opinion about the reigning orders of imperialism in the world, and we do not conceal that opinion. Our relations with capitalist governments are in full accordance with the decisions of the Twenty-fifth C.P.S.U. Congress, which were to strive for long term mutually advantageous co-operation in various spheres in the interest of strengthening world peace. . . .

But there are circumstances directly hindering further improvement and development of Soviet-American relations. One of these is the ballooning of the scandalous campaign against the fictitious 'military threat' posed by the Soviet Union. . . . Another is constituted by the outright attempts by official American departments to interfere in the internal affairs of the Soviet Union.

The claims on the part of Washington to be able to teach others how to live cannot be accepted by a single sovereign state, especially since neither the US situation nor its actions and policies in the world give any justification for such pretensions.

I repeat, we will never tolerate interference in our internal affairs by any country under any pretext. A normal development of relations on such a basis is unthinkable. . . . At the same time we will always greet a constructive, realistic approach by the other side with understanding and willingness to come to an agreement.'

Document 13.3

The Jackson Amendment to the Trade Reform Act, 1972

'EAST-WEST TRADE AND FREEDOM OF EMIGRATION
Sec. 507. (a) To assure the continued dedication of the United States to fundamental human rights, after October 25, 1972, no nonmarket economy country shall be eligible to receive most-favoured-nation treatment or to participate in any programme of the Government of the United States which extends credits or credit guarantees or investment guarantees, directly or

indirectly, during the period beginning with the date on which the President of the United States determines that such country –
  (1) denies its citizens the right or opportunity to emigrate; or
  (2) imposes more than a nominal tax on emigration or on the visas or other documents required for emigration, for any purpose or cause whatsoever; or
  (3) imposes more than a nominal tax, levy, fine or other charge on any citizen as a consequence of the desire of such citizen to emigrate to the country of his choice and ending on the date on which the President determines that such country is no longer in violation of paragraph (1), (2) or (3).
(b) After October 15, 1972, a nonmarket economy country may participate in a programme of the Government of the United States which extends credits or credit guarantees or investment guarantees, and shall be eligible to receive most-favoured-nation treatment, only after the President of the United States has submitted to the Congress a report indicating that such country is not in violation of paragraph (1), (2) and (3) of subsection (a). Such report with respect to such country, shall include information as to the nature and implementation of emigration laws and policies and restrictions or discrimination applied to or against persons wishing to emigrate. The report required by this subsection shall be submitted initially as provided herein and semi-annually thereafter so long as any agreement entered into pursuant to the exercise of such authority is in effect.'

Document 13.4

A British view of the invasion of Afghanistan, 1979–80

'Deplorable and arrogant and dangerous as the Russian invasion of Afghanistan is, let us not forget that it has all been done before. The first major invasion of Afghanistan happened in 1839, and it was done by the British, who showed more or less exactly the same emotional anxiety of the Russian Bear as everyone is, understandably, showing now.

We went into Afghanistan to topple its ruler, Dost Mohammed, and replace him by a more amenable puppet called (as though it mattered now) Shah Shaja, following exactly the same pattern as Mr Brezhnev is using now, to swap an Amin for a Karmal and get in before the others do.

The Soviets want access to the warm-water ports, which means edging ever southwards, and which will inevitably involve Iran.

The US feels that Iran needs but one involvement at a time, namely hers. Britain, scampering eagerly at her heels, proclaims a sort of powerless devotion, and sends Lord Carrington off to Turkey and Pakistan on a wholly enigmatic errand.

America proposes to cut her grain exports to Russia, from which several million Communist cattle will mainly suffer. We threaten darkly to boycott the Olympic Games. A pettifogging gesture indeed, but if all international crises could be resolved by eliminating the world's most numbing public event then it would be only too welcome. But the Olympic Games won't save Afghanistan, because they can't, and everyone knows they can't.

Somebody wrote to the papers urging that Afghanistan must remain a buffer state 'as Nature intended her to be'. Nature had nothing to do with it, but never mind. It could be said that destiny ordained President Carter to be a buffer man, poor soul. Yet, if the situation has proved anything it is that Brezhnev can be as clumsy and cruel as Carter can be clumsy and well-intentioned. The Soviet Union has done itself the worst P.R. job since Hungary, and it will not be forgiven any more readily than will the Americans for Cambodia.

Everyone must denounce the cynical and in the end stupid Russian action in Afghanistan. Let us make our disapproval clear, even though we are disappointed parties in the power game. We are all in this for the ultimate lolly, as we always have been.

But for any sake, let us not adopt this high moral attitude of being concerned for the integrity of a single non-aligned country, that we are defending the principles of the U.N. when we are in fact concerned solely (a) with pride, (b) with oil, (c) with Presidential politics, (d) with the imminent succession in Moscow, and somewhere (down in x, y, and z) the future of Afghanistan.'

(James Cameron, *Guardian*, 8 January 1980)

FURTHER READING

See Reading for Chapter 12, p. 267.
Additionally:

BERTRAM, C., *Prospects of Soviet Power in the 1980s*, Macmillan, 1980

BYRNES, R., ed., *After Brezhnev – Sources of Soviet Conduct in the 1980s*, Frances Pinter, 1983

CARLTON, D. and SCHAEF, C., eds., *The Arms Race in the 1980s*, Macmillan, 1982

GEORGE, A. L., et al., *Managing US-Soviet Rivalry*, Westview Press, 1983

HAMMOND, P. Y., *Cold War and Détente*, Harvester Press, 1975

HOLM, H. H. and PETERSON, N., *The European Missiles Crisis*, Frances Pinter, 1983

KINCARDE, W. H. and BERTRAM, C., *Nuclear Proliferation in the 1980s*, Macmillan, 1982

KISSINGER, H., *Nuclear Weapons and Foreign Policy*, Westview Press, 1984

RUBIN, B., et al., *Human Rights and US Foreign Policy*, Westview Press, 1979

SCHIAVONE, G., ed., *East-West Relations: Prospects for the 1980s*, Macmillan, 1982

STANLEY, T., et al., *US Foreign Economic Strategy for the Eighties*, Westview Press, 1983

TOKES, R., ed., *Dissent in the USSR*, Johns Hopkins UP, 1976

SHARP, J. M. C., ed., *The Warsaw Pact: Alliance in Transition*, Macmillan, 1984

VOLTEN, P. M. C., *Brezhnev's Peace Programme*, Westview Press, 1983

Epilogue

There are a few dates which mark the onset of one or other of history's major discontinuities: 1914, for example, is now widely accepted as 'the end of the nineteenth century' or 'the end of the Edwardian twilight'. No such distinctive claim can be made for the years which mark the starting and finishing points for this introductory study.

It is clear from the early chapters that the politicians, diplomats and others who created the material of our post-war history were also victims of earlier history. While 1945 is obviously a significant date, marking as it does the end of the Second World War in Europe and Asia, it was not immaculately conceived; the peoples of post-war Europe – east as well as west – carried their historical past in their post-war 'bag and baggage'. We have seen that to understand the history of post-war Russia, we have to compare Stalin with pre-1917 Tsars, while to understand US–USSR relations we have to know something of inter-war history.

Nor is there anything distinctive about the year 1984, our finishing point. If, in the West particularly, there are few signs of Orwell's imaginary *1984*, there is no sense, either, in which the real-world 1984 may be seen as a turning point. With apologies to T. S. Eliot, 1984 ends our period 'not with a bang but a whimper'.

In the midst of the whimpering we may perceive some louder cries. In the West, for example, there is widespread despair about the economic and social outlook. During the depression of the 1930s, my parents' generation was sustained, in part at least, by the Keynes-inspired belief that there was a relatively simple cure for the then prevailing large-scale unemployment. In 1984, there are few people in western Europe who look to a Keynesian solution to the massive economic and social problems which afflict their part of the continent. People of my children's generation do not have the hopeful faith which helped their grandparents. Nor, on the other hand, can they be expected to put much trust in the modish monetarist policies which are being pursued throughout the West; one does not have to be 'a wet liberal' to believe that the social and economic costs of monetarism are too high a price to pay for the promised land of 'economic upturn' which, more and more, seems to be more a mirage than part of a realisable world. Too many people see that world as one in which the outstanding features of western Europe will be continued de-industrialisation, large scale unemployment, increasingly large pockets of poverty, further cuts in public expenditure and the run-down of public services.

However, in eastern Europe too there has occurred, as we have seen, 'a loss of faith', 'a crisis of confidence' in the ability of Marxist-Leninism to create the once-hoped for 'golden land'. If, as in Hungary, a Communist government does appear to be economically successful, a closer examination reveals that the success is due to that government's acceptance of a private enterprise system which Communism was supposed to have replaced.

In 1972, the *Washington Post* heralded the arrival of 'a new "golden age". . . .' (p. 268). In 1974, Alistair Buchan wrote of the belief that 'at the beginning of 1973 . . . peace had descended on the world.' (p. 271) The history of the years since 1972 is littered with the reasons for, and proofs of, the quick end to that 'golden age': oil-price increases, inflation, unemployment. Since 1973, too, the descent of Buchan's 'peace' has been hampered by increasingly war-like rhetoric as well as by war-like actions: the superpowers war vicariously in such regions as Angola, Mozambique and Afghanistan while they deploy, on the one side or the other, murderous weapons such as the SS-20 and cruise. It is not possible to end this study with optimistic references to a coming 'golden age' or descending 'peace'. But it is just possible that the Reagan–Gromyko talks which are due to start as this is being written (September 1984), may herald a brighter, more peaceful future. It is possible, too, that the recovery of the US economy may stimulate the recovery of the economies of western Europe, while the now-cancelled talks between Honecker and Kohl may yet take place so that the German problem, which lies at the heart of the European problem, may be solved. Let us hope so.

References

Chapter 1, Pages 13–20

1 LAQUEUR, W., *Europe Since Hitler*, Penguin, 1982, p. 16
2 SEAMAN, L. C. B., *A New History of England, 410–1975*, Harvester Press, 1981, p. 457

Chapter 2, pages 21–39

1 TAYLOR, A. J. P., *English History, 1914–45*, OUP, p. 576
2 LAQUEUR, op. cit., p. 102
3 NORTHEDGE, F. S. and GRIEVE, M. J., *A Hundred Years of International Relations*, Duckworth, 1971, p. 252
4 SPEER, A., *Inside the Third Reich*, Macmillan, 1971, Chapters 32 and 33
5 HOME, LORD, *The Way the Wind Blows*, Collins, 1976, p. 91
6 quoted in CATCHPOLE, B., *A Map History of Russia*, Heinemann, 1974, p. 77
7 BUDENZ, L., *This is My Story*, Brown and Nolan, 1946, pp. 350–1
8 NEAVE, A., *Nuremberg*, Hodder and Stoughton, 1978, pp. 7, 23–4
9 CRAWLEY, A., *De Gaulle*, Collins, 1969, p. 268
10 CHILDS, D., *Germany since 1918*, Batsford, 1980, p. 112, and ARNOLD-FORSTER, M., *The Siege of Berlin*, Collins, 1979, p. 23
11 LAQUEUR, W., *Out of the Ruins*, Alcove Press, 1972, p. 343
12 NEAVE, A., op. cit. pp. 116–7, 229, 277, and seriatim, and LAQUEUR, W., *Europe since Hitler*, Penguin, 1982, pp. 37 ff
13 CHILDS, op. cit. p. 111
14 CRAWLEY, op. cit. p. 266
15 MEDLICOTT, W. N., *Contemporary England, 1914–64*, Longman, 1978, p. 485
16 NEAVE, op. cit. p. 23
17 ibid, pp. 43 and 77
18 ibid, pp. 44–5
19 LAQUEUR, op. cit., p. 35
20 NEAVE, op. cit. p. 115

Chapter 3, pages 40–55

1 BULLOCK, A., *Ernest Bevin: Foreign Secretary*, Heinemann, 1983, p. 214
2 STRANSKY, J., *East Wind Over Prague*, Hollis and Carter, 1950, pp. 22–3
3 WEISSKOPF, K., *The Agony of Czechoslovakia, 1938–68*, Elek Books, 1968, p. 155
4 SEJNA, J., *We Will Bury You*, Sidgwick and Jackson, 1982, p. 20
5 President Truman speaking to the US Congress, 12 March 1947
6 SINGLETON, F. B., *Background to Eastern Europe*, Pergamon Press, 1961, p. 156

Chapter 4, pages 56–81

1 SHERWOOD, R. E., *Roosevelt and Hopkins: An Intimate History*, p. 870
2 SMITH, W. B., *Moscow Mission, 1946–49*, Heinemann, 1950, pp. 41–2
3 ACHESON, D., *Present at the Creation*, p. 217
4 George C. Marshall speaking at Harvard University, 5 June 1947
5 quoted in BULLOCK, op. cit. p. 485
6 Lord Attlee to Lord Francis-Williams, *A Prime Minister Remembers*, Heinemann, 1961
7 quoted in BULLOCK, op. cit. p. 644
8 ibid, p. 493
9 ibid, p. 804

Chapter 5, pages 82–105

1 SEJNA, op. cit. p. 24
2 AUTY, P., *Yugoslavia*, Thames and Hudson, 1965, p. 135
3 SEJNA, op. cit. p. 35
4 ibid, p. 35
5 quoted in LEWIS, F., *The Polish Volcano*, Secker and Warburg, 1959, pp. 131–2
6 SEJNA, op. cit., p. 37
7 quoted in MIKES, G., *The Hungarian Revolution*, Andre Deutsch, 1975, p. 152
8 SEJNA, op. cit. pp. 171–2

Chapter 6, pages 106–35

1 CARR, E. H., *The Bolshevik Revolution*, Vol. 1, Macmillan, p. 238
2 SHORT, P., *The Dragon and the Bear*, Hodder and Stoughton, 1982, pp. 371–2
3 HILTON, R., *Military Attaché in Moscow*, Hollis and Carter, 1949, p. 41
4 YEVTUSHENKO, Y., *A Precocious Autobiography*, Penguin, 1965, p. 95
5 Khruschev, speaking at the 20th Party Congress, 1956
6 Schwartz, H., in the *New York Times*, Sept. 1956, quoted in SHORT, op. cit., p. 372
7 quoted in FRANKLAND, M., *Khruschev*, Penguin, 1966, p. 194
8 SEJNA, op. cit., p. 89
9 ibid. p. 94
10 In this section, I have drawn heavily on the autobiographical memoir by Sejna, op. cit.
11 *International Herald Tribune*, 10 March 1980
12 quoted in *Time*, 27 February 1984, p. 7

Chapter 7, pages 136–63

1 quoted in ROSTOW, W. W., *Getting from Here to There*, Macmillan, 1979, p. 16
2 *Economic Progress and Problems of Western Europe*, June 1951
3 MADDISON, A., *Economic Growth in the West*, 1964

Chapter 9, pages 189–215

1 quoted in BULLOCK, op. cit., p. 636
2 *The Basic Law*, 8 May 1949
3 SMITH, D. MACK, *Italy*, University of Michigan Press, 1969, p. 489

Chapter 11, pages 222–43

1 Lord Boothby in Thompson, A., *The Day Before Yesterday*, Granada, 1971, p. 88
2 ibid.
3 BELOFF, N., *The General Says No*, Penguin, 1960
4 Statement by Walter Hallstein
5 Speaking in the House of Commons, 26 November, 1956
6 de Gaulle, General C., *Memoirs d'Espoir: Vol. 1: Le renouveau, 1958–62*, 1970, p. 200
7 *Daily Telegraph*, 19 March, 1984
8 CRAWLEY, A., *De Gaulle*, Collins, 1969, p. 443

Chapter 12, pages 244–67

1 Robert Murphy, US diplomat, quoted in THOMPSON, A., op. cit., p. 176
2 Philip de Zulueta, British diplomat, in THOMPSON, A., op. cit., p. 176
3 SEJNA, op. cit., p. 72
4 ibid.
5 Khruschev in a letter to Kennedy, 23 October 1956
6 quoted in SCHLESINGER (JR) A. M., *A Hundred Days: John F. Kennedy in the White House*, Fawcett Press, 1967, p. 759
7 STEVENSON, C. A., *The End of Nowhere: American Policy towards Laos*, Beacon Press, 1972
8 SEJNA, op. cit., p. 60
9 *United States Policy for the 1970s*, p. 44
10 BELL, C., *The Diplomacy of Détente: The Kissinger Era*, Martin Robertson, 1977, p. 60
11 Francis Pym in a speech to the Atlantic Treaty Association, 30 September 1981

Chapter 13, pages 268–88

1 quoted in LAQUEUR, W., *Europe since Hitler*, Penguin, 1982, p. 515
2 BUCHAN, A., *The End of the Postwar Era*, Weidenfeld and Nicolson, 1974
3 From an address to Congress, April 1974
4 quoted in EDMONDS, R., *Soviet Foreign Policy*, OUP, 1975, p. 122
5 *Daily Telegraph*, 24 January 1984
6 BELL, op. cit., p. 33
7 From a speech to the Asia Society, New York, 29 June 1977
8 From a speech to the World Affairs Council, 9 May 1980

Glossary

ABM Anti–ballistic–missile. A ballistic missile is first powered by some explosive or fuel, then depends only on gravity. ABMs are meant to shoot these down.

co-existence A state of international relations in which rivals (such as the USA and USSR) tolerate one another. Neither seeks to bring down the other by force (a 'hot war') although dislike remains. When the dislike becomes very strong the world may have a period of 'cold war' – see below.

Cold War Such a 'war' is fought by various 'peaceful' weapons – such as propaganda (see below), economic sanctions (see below), aid (even military) to opponents of the rival régime. The rivals (since 1945 the USA and USSR) have stopped short of military confrontation although they have supported rivals in various 'local' wars as in Vietnam.

Comecon The Council for Mutual Economic Assistance.

Cominform The Communist Information Bureau.

EEC The European Economic Community, or Common Market.

EFTA The European Free Trade Association.

enosis The proposed political union between Cyprus and Greece.

EOKA The initials of the Greek words meaning Revolutionary Organisation for Cypriot Struggle. The organisation was founded in 1955 and had a campaign of anti–British sabotage and terrorism in the hope that this would force the British to agree to enosis (see above).

FAO The Food and Agricultural Organisation (of United Nations).

GATT The General Agreement on Tariffs and Trade was signed in 1947 as an interim measure pending the foundation of an International Trading Organisation (ITO) which was to do for international trading agreements what the IMF (below) was to do for international indebtedness. Although GATT has led to some relaxation of restrictions on trade, it has not led to the founding of the ITO; in the post-war world, too many nations (including Britain) re-developed their sense of almost parochial nationalism – leading to the search for GATT-avoiding methods of trade protectionism.

GDR/DDR The German Democrat Republic (East Germany).

ICBM Intercontinental ballistic missiles (see ABM above).

IMF The International Monetary Fund was set up in 1945.
MBFR Mutual and Balanced Force Reduction.
MIRV Multiple Independently-targeted Re-entry Vehicle – a ballistic missile.
NASA National Aeronautics and Space Administration (USA).
NATO The North Atlantic Treaty Organisation.
OEEC The Organisation for European Economic Co-operation.
OPEC The Organisation of Petroleum Exporting Countries.
SALT The Strategic Arms Limitations Talks.
SAM Surface to Air Missiles.
UNICEF The United Nations International Children's Emergency Fund.
UNO The United Nations Organisation.
UNRRA United Nations Relief and Rehabilitation Administration.
WHO The World Health Organisation.

Index